G000025612

Once There Was A Boy Who Survived

ORLA
KELLY
PUBLISHING

Maurice Heffernan

978-1-915502-66-7
All rights reserved
Copyright © Maurice Heffernan 2024
Cover design: 2funkidesign.com

Maurice Heffernan has asserted his moral right to be identified as the author of this work. The material in this publication is protected by copyright law. Except as may be permitted by law, no part of the material may be reproduced (including by storage in a retrieval system) or transmitted in any form or by any means, adapted, or lent without the written permission of the copyright owner. Published in Ireland by Orla Kelly Publishing.

Orla Kelly Publishing
27 Kilbrody
Mount Oval
Rochestown
Cork
Ireland

Dedication

I dedicate these memories to the memory of the Heffernan family, some of whom I never knew during my lifetime.

My father John "Jack" Heffernan whom I only knew for six years of my life, my mother Hannah Heffernan whom I never knew as she passed away when I was six months old. My brothers, Michael and Jeremiah, both of whom I met for short periods of my life, Paddy and John, two brothers I never met. All four are now deceased.

My sisters, Mary, Joan, Ann, Lily and Kathy, all of whom I met later in my life, all of whom are now deceased.

Acknowledgments

I would like to thank my own family members, Mark Niall, Ger, Noleen, Anne Marie and Aoife for inspiring me to put my memories down in writing.

To my good friend Henry Bauress, formerly of the Leinster Leader newspaper for his assistance and guidance along the way, with the help of his good wife, Aida.

To my wife Sonya, who has put up with my many interruptions when testing something I was going to write, for her reaction.

To Roger Murray solicitor who kept me advised regarding legal implications of what I have written.

Last but not least, Orla Kelly Publishing, whose faith in me never waned, and got me published.

Contents

Introduction

In early 2020, a third world war was being fought on all fronts by every country on planet earth. There were no bombs, no jet fighters, no battleships, and no tanks involved. It was a war against the Corona virus that began to plague the world. The WHO [World Health Organization] gave it an official name, Covid- 19.

Around that time, I had started to put down my memoirs of what I thought was an eventful, and extraordinary life that I had been through from my birth to my present time. I give an account of how I was impacted by certain events as I went through my life.

I was, as were most of the people, confined to my home on the Island of Malta as a precaution against catching the deadly virus, which gave me the opportunity to concentrate more on writing my memoirs. Because of my age, "over 65", I was assessed as a person at risk. All persons over that age, as well as persons not that age, but who had underlying health problems, were asked to stay in their homes, and not go out unless they had to, for keeping a hospital appointment, going to the pharmacy, and do necessary shopping.

I could not even visit my sister Joan, who was in a nursing home here in Malta, not too far from where I lived because no visitors were allowed. This was to prevent the spreading of the virus to nursing homes where the majority of the residents were elderly, putting them most at risk because of their age, and other underlying problems. I had contact with her by telephone. It was a worrying time for everybody.

I continued to take advantage of this lockdown period to continue to pen some notes on my less than normal life that I had lived. Of course, it also gave me something to do to pass the time while confined to my "cave". I was also spurred on by my children to write my memoirs, and the fact that they had an interest kept me going. I also had the advantage of having a retired journalist friend of mine, Henry Bauress, to whom I turned for advice and guidance. Because of the lifting of some of the restrictions, he, and his wife Aida were able to visit Malta in early September 2021, when we had a good chat about my "work" in progress.

How did I end up living in Malta? Well that is a part of my story, hence the writing of my what I believed to be an extraordinary life history, in which I give an account, as best I can, of what I learned about my early years, and remember about my life throughout the following years.

Originally, when I started my writing, I kept the knowledge of my proposed work within my family group, with the only other person I had spoken with about it being retired journalist, Henry Bauress, formerly of the Leinster Leader. Later on, I let it be known among a few of my previous work colleagues what I was doing.

One of my former colleagues, John Kelly, then said to me, "Maurice, you know you were known as a mystery person by many of the people you worked with; they knew so little about you or where you came from". You became known as the mystery man among many of your colleagues". I thought when I was told this by John that it sounded something like part of my life story.

In these memoirs, I have tried to put down as true an account of the various happenings in my life as I could recall. They include my being sent to an orphanage, being fostered by a family, being institutionalised in a Residential Institution, and eventually being sent out into the big world of work before I was 16 years of age. Later, I started the job of tracing members of my family. I joined An Garda Siochana. I went on to get married, had six children, got divorced, and emigrated in my later years, for reasons as I describe, to Malta, where I remarried.

I hope this effort to tell my story will hold the interest of many as I go behind the scenes to give a picture of what my life was really like.

Maurice Heffernan

The ultimate value of life depends upon awareness and the power of contemplation rather than upon mere survival.
Aristotle

CHAPTER ONE

Beginning of my life
Killarney, Cahersiveen

Strangely, I was born at the end of another war, World War II, which ended around September 1945, the year, and the month I was born. Ireland stayed out of the war as the government of the day kept the country neutral. The government had a majority of seats of the one hundred, and thirty eight seat Parliament of the time. The government was led by Eamon De Valera, who was the then Taoiseach [Prime Minister], and leader of the Fianna Fail Party who were in power.

I was to learn much later in my life, that I was the last child in a family of ten children, five boys, and five girls. I was born at home with the help of a midwife in a small town, in the north of Kerry, called Ballylongford. I suppose you could say I nearly never was, if my mother had taken the advice of the doctor after the previous child, my youngest sister was born. My mother had, at that time, been diagnosed with a heart problem, I believe, and warned not to have any more children. That was something I learned later in life from one of my older sisters. My early association with my large family ended very abruptly with the death of my mother on the 10th of March 1946; she was not yet forty years of age; I was just six months old.

Taken

A number of months after my mother died, according to my older sisters who had looked after me, I was taken from my family home, and placed in an orphanage in Killarney, Co. Kerry. This, of course, I wouldn't have any recollection of, but I would have obtained the details in later life from members of my family, whom I had located after many years of searching. It was from here in Killarney, I believe that I was fostered out to a family in west Kerry, which my own family knew nothing about to my knowledge, as they were never kept informed of my movements or whereabouts.

I have since also discovered new information as to what occurred with regards to other members of my family following the death of our mother on the 10th of March 1946. These family members were three of my sisters, Ann, Lily, Kathy, and my brother Jerry. From information obtained by three of my nieces, Catherine, Eileen, and Jeannie, regarding their mothers from the Department of Education under The Freedom of Information act 2014, I can now update the information regarding these family members as follows.

With respect to the documents obtained regarding my sister Ann, by her daughter, Catherine, one is a form "A" headed," Particulars of a child ordered to be detained in a reformatory or industrial school".

Part 1: To be completed as far as possible by the resident manager, and returned to the Reformatory, and Industrial schools branch, Department of Education, Dublin, immediately after the admission of the child.

This form contained the following particulars in part 1.

Pembroke A. House...................................Certified. Reformatory / Industrial school. Tralee.

[1] Ann Heffernan, [2] number in register 953, [3] date of birth, 28.7.35, [?]

[4] place of birth, Lislaughtin, Ballylongford, [5] court where committed, Tarbert,

[6] date of committal, 18.4.46, [7] date of admission, 19.4.46,

[8] previous character, good, [9] religion, roman catholic,

[10] legitimate or illegitimate, Legitimate,

[11] local authority responsible for maintenance, Kerry co-council,

[12] parents' names, father, John Heffernan, mother Hannah Heffernan,

Address: Lislaughtin, Ballylongford, mother deceased,

[13] accommodation limit, 85, [14] number of committed cases, including this child, 76.

Part II- to be completed by the Superintendent, Garda Siochana, who should also, if possible, supply any information omitted from part 1. Report on parents' circumstances;

Other children dependent; [a] boys, aged, one] eight months,

[b] girls, aged, two] 13 &half years, and 12 years.

[c] schools they attend: Ballylongford National School, Particulars of children, if any in Reformatory or Industrial schools, ----------as above.

Parents [a] weekly wage, 12/6p, employer, unemployment assistance, [b] weekly rent 1/9p,

School which the child attended before committal; Ballylongford National School.

A note by the Garda at the end of the report stated; The parent is only getting 12/6p unemployment assistance & this is barely enough to keep life in him & his children.

There were a number of other points in some of the other documentation obtained;

[1] Full name of the place the three girls, including Ann as above, were committed, Nazareth House/ Pembroke Alms House, Industrial school for girls, Tralee.

[2] The NSPCC Inspector involved was Mr. William J Armstrong,

[3] The register numbers for the three girls were, Ann 953, Lily 954, and Kathy 955.

[4] A letter from the Department of Education to the Institution, with the caption Heffernan Children, [953-5] confirms the numbers in the register. This letter was dated 5-6-1946.

[5] Ann's date of release, or "Ultimate Disposal" as shown on the copy of the register, was the 27th of July 1951. This date is also shown on the report by school number, and pupil number.

With respect to part II of form "A", and the mention of the boy eight months old, that child would have been me, which indicates I was still at home at the end of May 1946, according to Garda reports. The two girls mentioned would have been my sisters, Mary, and Joan, who were both looking after me at that time before I was eventually taken away.

I also received documents obtained by Eileen regarding her mother, Lily, my sister, which she also got through the freedom of information section at the Department of Education, and Skills. These documents were similar to the documentation obtained by Catherine regarding her mother, Ann. The form "A" shows Lily as register number 954, her date of birth 27-3-36, [?], court date of committal at Tarbert district court, 18-4-46, and admission date to the institution as 19-4-46. It also shows her as the 77th child at that institution. Her date of release or "ultimate disposal" is shown as 26-3-52.

Part II of the form, which had to be completed by the local Garda, again mentions an eight month old boy at the house, which would have been myself, and mentions two girls, my older sisters Mary, and Joan.

Jeannie sent me a copy of documents, in respect of her mother, Kathy, my sister, which were similar to those I had received regarding my sisters Ann, and Lily. The form "A" was identical, showing all of Kathy's particulars, her date of birth as 14-2-42, her register number as 955, her date of committal by the court in Tarbert as 18.4.1946, and her admission to the Institution as being the following day the 19.4.1946. She was the 78th child at that institution. It also shows her date of "Ultimate Disposal" as being 13th Feb 1959, when she was sent to a job in Dublin. Again, it shows a Garda report which mentions an eight month old child, [myself], and my other two sisters, who would have been Mary, and Joan.

In an unusual twist, included in the documents obtained by my three nieces was one document relating to my brother Jeremiah [Jerry], which was a report by the Garda from Tarbert. It referred to a form "A" which had to be completed after he had been committed to St Joseph's Industrial School, Tralee. The document was dated 27/4/46. The information would indicate that my brother Jerry had been brought to Tarbert court on the same date as my three sisters, Ann, Lily, and Kathy, on the 18-4-46, where he had been committed to St Joseph's Industrial School, Tralee, more than likely on the 19-4-46. I was to meet my brother Jerry in that institution in December 1952, six years later.

Well, after my own movement from my home, the dissemination of my family was complete. Can you imagine the situation, four children from one family brought to a court on the same day, and within twenty-four hours placed into institutions?

Now, the normal situation would be, as shown on the forms that were obtained, that anybody sent to an institution would be released on the day before their 16th birthday. With respect to two of my sisters, Ann, and Lily, they were both released the day prior to the dates of birth shown on the copy of the register, and the school report forms.

It transpires that the dates of birth shown in the documentation for both of my sisters, Ann, and Lily, were incorrect, which saw Ann being released on 27-7-51 when she was just 15 years of age, and Lily being released on 26-3-52 when she was only 14 years of age.

On the 27th of July 1951, Ann was sent as a domestic to a Mrs O'Carroll in Ballylongford, Co Kerry, and was paid £3.00 a month. As it happens, Mrs. O'Carroll was the wife of Danny O'Carroll, who owned a public house next door to where they lived. It was known locally as Danny Carrolls, and it was a favourite haunt of my fathers, as I got to know later.

On the 26th of March 1952, Lily was sent to what seemed to be another convent or nursing home run by nuns somewhere in Dublin. She was being paid £4.00 a month.

On the 13th of February 1959, Kathy was sent to a job as a receptionist in a hotel in Nelson Street, Dublin. She would have been 17 years old. She was getting 30/- shillings a week.

I do not have any papers to indicate the exact dates regarding my brother Jerry's release, but in August 1956, he would have been 16 years of age, which would point to his time of release from St Joseph's Residential Institution, Tralee. I would have been in my fourth year at St Joseph's institution at that time.

The dates that appeared on the register, and forms "A" were completed by the institution to which they were sent. The correct dates should have read, Ann was born on 2-8-36, and Lily was born on 27-3-38. The incorrect dates now form part of the records held by the Department of Education, and Skills.

In the year 2012, while doing a background check on my childhood years, and looking for information about my earlier years, I called the Killarney Institution; having found it, I discovered that a number of years previous, there had been a fire, which destroyed most of the documentation records. The orphanage building had a change of use, and was now catering for social, and other public services.

With Foster Parents

I later discovered that I had been fostered out to a family called Coffey's in the west of Kerry - [Cahersiveen] of course being so young I could not recall any of this, but the documentation I got possession of in the year 2012, [over sixty years later] gave me some insight into my former years. I do have memories as I got older of being on a farm, with whom I later came to know were my foster parents, the Coffey's. I can recall a number of memories about my way of life at that time.

The farm was situated at the foot of a mountain with a stream running down one side of the farm. It was made up of a dwelling house, outhouses for the cattle, and pigs and hay barn. There were fields around the house for crops, and cattle grazing. They used to keep sheep up on the mountain behind the house, and I used to go up the mountain with my foster father to check on the sheep. I always remember a lovely lake up the mountain where the sheep were kept.

Looking out from the front of the house, there was a small front garden with a low hedge where I used to play, and further down in front was a big field where potatoes, and vegetables were planted. I used, at some stage when I was getting bigger, to help my foster father in that front field thinning the crops of vegetables. Looking further out, you could see the sea coming into the estuary. What always sticks in my mind is when working in the front field, Mrs. Coffey used to come down with milk, bread, and a large tin of mashed potatoes with butter melting on top.

I used to go to school across the fields when I got old enough, and I remember on one occasion when I was with a number of other boys on the way to school, going into an old empty house, and ended up being locked in the house. The other boys ran off, leaving me there, and in some way or another, I managed to get out, and go to school. This is a memory that has stayed with me all my life. I do not remember whether I always wore shoes to school or not.

On Sundays, I used to travel to mass at a church in the town on a pony, and trap, and of course, it was a great time for people to meet, and talk after the mass.

My thoughts go back to the time there was a pig killed at the house. This, I found out later, was the normal practice in the country areas at that time. A number of men arrived at the farm to help my foster father. The pig was brought into the kitchen, put up on the kitchen table, and tied up. The pig was then hung upside down by ropes from the rafters in the kitchen ceiling.

I was then brought outside to the farm buildings by my foster mother while the pig was being killed; when the screaming was over, I was brought back inside, and watched the rest of the process. The men drained the blood into buckets, took out the insides, and so on. The following day, my foster father made a football out of the pig's bladder. He pumped it up, and we played football with it in the front garden of the house.

The pig meat had been cut up into pieces, and put into wooden barrels, which were then filled with water, and salt. They had plenty of bacon for some time. Today, I dislike bacon.

A day or two after the pig was killed, I went with my foster mother to the river over from the house. She brought the intestines of the pig with her in pots, and we washed them in the river. They were later used for making pudding with the blood of the pig.

With the cows, we had our own milk, and Mrs Coffey used to make her own butter from the milk. She had a special churn for making the butter, and after the butter was made, she would keep what was called the buttermilk. And I used to drink the buttermilk whenever we had it. That's another thing I wouldn't do today as my tastes have changed, and I prefer fresh milk.

Looking back now, it was a very simple life. I remember one Christmas getting a drawer full of oranges. At that time, I wouldn't have known any better, and don't ever remember getting any presents as such, for either Christmas or birthdays, maybe I did. Over the following years, I would learn that because of the war, there was a big shortage of fruit, and the like. To have oranges so soon after the war would have been a big thing.

There was one incident that I have not forgotten. One day, I was out riding with a man who I think was either a friend or a relation of my foster parents. We were both on different horses, and we were riding down the old roadway leading from the house. Suddenly, the man's horse fell over into a drain full of water, trapping the rider underneath. I raced back to the house, and raised the alarm. I was not sure if the man had died as my foster parents didn't want me to know the outcome. I would have been between five, and seven years old at the time.

Leaving my Foster Parents

One day, a big black car pulled up at the house. Mrs Coffey had got me dressed up in my good clothes. I didn't know what was going on till I realised the car was for me. I was put into the car, and before it drove off, Mrs Coffey put a half-crown into my hand. I don't recall having any feelings, or if I cried or got upset. I was not sure if there was somebody else in the car with the driver. When I think back now, there must have been a social worker or somebody like that.

Later in my life, I discovered that I was taken to a Court in the town of Tralee in the County of Kerry. I have recollections of the two big cannons outside the Courthouse building, one on either side of the entrance steps. I am also now in possession of documentation which gives an account of what occurred on that date, the 12th of December 1952. I obtained this documentation in the year 2012 as a result of communications with the Redress Board, some sixty years later.

The documents show that I was brought before the District Court in Tralee, where Judge Johnson was presiding. The charges related to me "having a guardian who does not exercise proper guardianship". I was committed to St Joseph's Residential Institution, Tralee, till the 9th of September 1961. I arrived at St Joseph's Residential Institution on the 12th of December 1952. I was seven years, and three months old at that time.

Following information that came into my possession while writing these memoirs, I carried out some research, and discovered that a photographic archive existed, known as the Kennelly Archive of photographs, which dated from 1953 to 1973. I discovered while going through this archive that there was a huge collection of photographs that had been taken in St Joseph's Residential Institution, Tralee, during those years. My discoveries included the following photographs;

A photograph of the Tralee Courthouse, taken in February 1957, which was the Courthouse I had been taken to on the 12th of December 1952, and from where I was committed to St Joseph's Residential Institution until the 9/9/1961. I also discovered a photograph of Judge Johnson, taken on January 1961, who was the Judge who presided over the hearing of my case on the 12th of December 1952.

I further discovered numerous other photographs related to my time in St Joseph's Residential Institution, Tralee, which I cover further on in my story.

Now, in later years, I would dwell on the situation as to how it was known that I had been fostered out of the Killarney institution. My brother, who I later learned was already at St Joseph's institution at the time, may have mentioned something about having a younger brother.

13

More than likely, inquiries must have taken place as to my whereabouts, and I was tracked down to my foster home in Cahersiveen. My own father, who would have been in his late sixties at that time, was never informed of my movements, as I discovered during my later life.

Some years ago, I paid a visit to my old foster home after obtaining the location of the address on the documentation that came into my possession through the Redress Board in the year 2012, and also, for the first time, the names of my foster parents. They were a Mr, and Mrs Coffey, who had resided at Ballydarrig, Cahersiveen, Co Kerry, which had been my foster home all those years ago, and whom I never laid eyes on again after the day I was taken away.

It was a sad return as the farm was totally abandoned, and the buildings in ruin. I took some photos while I was there. I did meet some distant relatives of the Coffey's who pointed me in the direction of the farm, also informing me that the Coffey's had passed away many years previously. I tried to locate where they were buried, but without success. The weather on that day was very wet, which cut my visit short, and I didn't get to go up the mountain to see the lake either.

A nephew of the Coffey's now had the farm, and lived in a more modern house on the way to the farm. There were sheep, and livestock all over the lands, which more than likely belonged to the nephew. An afterthought occurred to me, on the day I was being taken away from my foster parents, I saw a boy arrive at the house of Mr, and Mrs Coffey. Could it have been their nephew?

I was just over seven years of age when I was taken from my foster parents, never to see or hear of them again. I was on my way into the unknown.

CHAPTER TWO

St Joseph's Residential Institution, Tralee 1952

In May 2009, a report was published by the Commission to Inquire into Child Abuse, [CICA] in which St Joseph's Residential Institution, Tralee, was dealt with under chapter nine of that report.

Also, in chapter one of that report, they covered the involvement of the Irish Society for the Prevention of Cruelty to Children, [ISPCC] previously known as the NSPCC, with the commitment of children to Residential Institutions. Page six of that report covers their involvement with St Joseph's Residential Institution, Tralee.

St Joseph's was opened in the year 1862, [over twenty years before my father was born,] as a boys' national school, and in the year 1871, it became a Residential School after additional buildings were added for the accommodation of pupils on a full-time basis. [9.01 to 9.04 of CICA report]

In 1944 [a year before I was born], at the behest of the Department of Education, St Joseph's Residential school, Tralee was registered as a place of detention for youthful offenders, which made it into a Residential Institution. [9.10 of the CICA report]

This was the place that I found myself in, on the 12th of December 1952, after having been committed there by order of District Justice Johnson of the District court, Tralee, the reason being "having a guardian who does not exercise proper guardianship. My sentence **of detention was 9-9-1961.**

Now one has to beg the question as to which "guardian" the court was referring to, as not "exercising proper guardianship" was it my foster

15

parents in Cahersiveen, where I spent my earlier years, or was it my father in Ballylongford, keeping in mind that I was taken from Ballylongford when I was only about nine months old, and my father had been kept in the dark as to my whereabouts from the time I was "taken".

On reflection many years later, a number of other questions come to mind;

"Was I a youthful offender at the age of seven years, and three months"?

Was I a "financial asset to St Joseph's,", as St Joseph's would be receiving a payment for each child taken into care?

Were the courts being used to enhance the numbers at St Joseph's Residential Institution, whose numbers had been declining?

Was I bounty hunted, and was there a bribe paid to the NSPCC Inspector who had me committed to that Institution?

These are questions that I may never obtain answers to, but they arise because of the publication of information in the Report of the Commission to Inquire into Child Abuse [The Ryan Report of 2009]. My treatment as a child at that time, when I was taken from my foster parents, could be closely described in today's terms as **"child trafficking".**

My father in Ballylongford, who would now have been in his late sixties, and whom I had never met, to my knowledge, was never informed of any of my movements, and was kept totally out of the picture.

I have very little memories of arriving at the institution. Sometime after arriving there, I met my "brother Jerry". That was the first time that I became aware that I had a family. I wasn't sure how I received the news that I had a brother, and even though we were both in the same institution, we didn't communicate that much with one another over our years there together. I would have thought that having a brother didn't mean that much to me at the time, as I had no understanding of family relationships. I have memories of boys asking questions of the

Brothers as to where they were born, and being told that they were" born under a head of cabbage"; that was the extent of the knowledge of family connections.

I can vividly recall an occasion, shortly after my arrival at St Joseph's, when I sat on a stool alone in the yard, and started to cry; I had even soiled my pants because of some fear that came over me. It must have been the sudden realisation that I was alone in the world. Somebody who saw me crying brought me over to the nurse, who washed me, and changed my clothes. I don't ever remember another occasion where I cried after that. One might ask where my brother Jerry was; well, he was most likely working in the tailors' shop. I think I already mentioned that even though Jerry, and I were in St Joseph's together for some time, in later years, we never discussed our time in St Joseph's; it was just something we didn't talk about.

Later information, which is covered in the Commission to Inquire into Child Abuse Report 2009, suggested that around the time of my arrival, there were problems with decreasing numbers at St Joseph's Residential Institution, Tralee. This information came as a result of visitation reports by Inspectors from the Department of Education, and covered the period between 1950s, and 1960s.

I was seven years, and three months old when I arrived at St Joseph's Institution; this was a calculation I made on the basis of the date I was brought to the court. My "brother Jerry" would have been over twelve years of age at the time, so we would have spent about three, and a half years in the institution together before Jerry was sent out to a job in Kilgarvan, Co Kerry. He went to work with the Healy Rea family tailors there, having reached sixteen years of age. I would have been about eleven years of age at this time, so I would have about another five years "detention" at this institution.

I spent over eight, and a half years in St Joseph's Residential Institution, the last four or five years without my brother Jerry there, as he had left to work with a tailoring family, who were the Healy Rae's in Kilgarvan Co Kerry. Members of the Healy Rae family have become household names over the past number of years for their political achievements. Thinking back now, while being "detained" at St Joseph's Institution, I never once wrote a letter to anyone, not even to my brother Jerry, or received one from him or any other family member.

Even though my father [when I later learned I had a father], who was now in his late sixties, only lived about twenty miles away, I never once had any contact with him through the school until just before I left St Joseph's Institution in 1961. During all of the eight, and half years that I spent there, I was never allowed to take a holiday at my home. My brother Jerry, who was working in Kilgarvan, arranged through the institution to bring me to Ballylongford to meet my father for the first time in my life before I was later "released", and brought to Dublin. I assumed that my brother Jerry used to visit our father after he went out working, so he would have had a better relationship with him than I would have had, and more than likely told him where I was "detained". That was, of course, something we never discussed, as being in the institution was a "taboo" subject.

St Joseph's was made up of a large number of buildings around a square. There was a big yard in the centre where there was a basketball court, and two handball alleys at one end. From this yard, you could access the outside toilets, and a sheltered area from the weather, which had been built on pillars with a stairway leading up to a hall, where films used to be shown on a stage, and the band used to practise, and perform on the stage.

Behind the hall, and sheltered area was the farm with farm buildings. On the same side of the yard was the shower room, the woodwork shops, the shoemakers, the tailor shop, and the technical school.

Leading out from those buildings were a number of classrooms coming around as far as an archway which led to the upstairs dormitories, and toilets. Under this archway, there was a small room, which was a nursing station, occupied by an oldish lady who was the nurse for the institution. Further down from the archway was the refectory, with kitchens, where we had our meals, and the entrance to the brothers' quarters from the yard. There was a railing with a gateway separating the yard from this part of the building.

The dormitories were on the first floor of the buildings. There were two large dormitories, one senior, and one junior, with about, as far as I can recall, fifty or sixty beds in each, and a smaller room that was used as an infirmary when there was anybody sick. This was the sleeping accommodation at the institution. From the senior dormitory, you could access the chapel, which was also on the first floor leading from the brothers' quarters. The handball alleys were simple open structures with a back wall, and two side walls. Beside the ball alleys behind a gateway was the bakery, and a graveyard.

After some time, I settled into the way of life at the institution. We rose early in the mornings. There was a time by which we had to be in bed, and then there would be time for lights out. I am unsure now, but I think that we had to go to mass every morning before breakfast. After breakfast, there was a general call under the sheltered area, and we used to line up according to classes in rows with our teachers. The superior used to stand up on the stairway, and give a short talk about something or other, and then we used to peel off in an orderly fashion to our classrooms for school.

Education

I'm not sure as to what class I started in school, but a note in documentation that came into my possession in 2012, indicated that I had been in senior infants before arriving at the institution.

Primary school had its ups, and downs for me as I went through the years. I had a number of different teachers over those years, some good, and some not so good. I still have memories of one particular brother who was one of my teachers in primary school as I got older, maybe my final year; he was Brother Bartolo, [pseudonym]; he appears with a group of Brothers in a Photograph taken in August 1957.

He was a big, tall man, well over six feet tall, who also had responsibility for the band. He was my teacher for my last year in primary school. He had two sides to him; one minute, he would be very nice, and all of a sudden, he would explode violently because of something small, like somebody giving a wrong answer to something. He would then go around the class, and if people didn't give the correct answer he was looking for, he would come down on us, hitting one of us on the head, or one of his favourite things to do was to lift one of us up by the ears.

He would clasp both hands around our head, covering our ears, and lift us off our seats. Another thing he used to do was catch our side burns, and pull them up until we would scream out. He used to do these things while tearing around the classroom in a rage. I didn't escape his tantrums.

There was a saying he used to quote during his rage around the classroom, "you blocks, you stones, you worse than senseless things".................. He never completed the saying, and never said where the words came from. It was in later years that I related them to Julius Caesar, by Shakespeare, when I saw the film. I never forgot those words as they drove fear into the whole class in the way this brother expressed them.

To be sure of the origin of what this brother used to say, I purchased a copy of William Shakespeare's Julius Caesar, which, of course, I had never studied. What he was quoting was from Act 1, Scene 1 of Julius Caesar when" Murellus, and Flavius" were telling the people to go home, and back to their workshops. The next line after what the brother used to say goes; "O you hard hearts, you cruel men of Rome"..........................., and so on. I suppose you could say I had a taste of the classics without knowing it.

During those early years at St Joseph's Tralee, there were many changes of brothers at the institution. The superior who was Brother O'Donnell, [pseudonym] left, and was replaced by a new superior, Brother Ryle, who was a much nicer man. Brother O'Donnell would have left some years before August 1957, as Brother Ryle appears in a group photograph of brothers at the institution at that time.

Again, it was a matter of getting used to the new "arrivals", and their way of doing things. The new superior was a man who tried to get things done for the boys. As I got older, I even got a job helping the superior in the general store some evenings, where clothing, and other items were stored for distribution to the boys as they were needed. For me, it was like becoming what would be described today as a "trustee".

Sometime before I finished primary school, the superior approached me, and asked me if I would like to go to the secondary school in the town. The secondary school was a day school also run by the Christian Brothers, which was based in Tralee town.

Of course, I jumped at the chance, and said I would like to go. Later, the superior came back to me, and told me he was sorry, but they weren't allowing any more boys to go to secondary school in Tralee because of the behaviour of some of the boys who had attended previously. Many years later, I would discover that was not the situation, and I was told a "a little white lie" by the superior.

When I finished primary school at about twelve or thirteen years of age, I went to the technical school attached to St Joseph's, which was situated behind the carpenters' shop. To get to the classroom, we had to pass through the woodwork room. I spent two years in the technical school, where the main subjects I took were mechanical drawing, woodwork, and Irish. At the end of my two years, I received a Manual Training Certificate, which is still in my possession. I got an honour in mechanical drawing.

My teacher in the technical school was a lay teacher from outside the school. He was an OK teacher, but very often, he would leave the class on our own after giving us some work to do while he was away. He spent a lot of his time over the two years organising the building of a house for himself somewhere out in the country.

Now, prior to going to the Technical School, when I was just 12 years of age, I made my Confirmation. I was confirmed on the 22nd of September 1957. This is supported by a photograph taken on that day in my confirmation outfit, which I discovered when checking into the Kennelly Archives. I was never aware that this photograph even existed.

The problem of decreasing numbers at the institution had a big effect on my education with the decision that was taken not to send any of us for second-level education. We would have known nothing of what was going on, and would not have realised that there was a possibility of the institution closing down because the numbers were declining. Less than ten years after I had left, the institution closed its doors in 1969.

Of course, I felt terribly let down by the system at the time, and it was very difficult to make up for lost time in education afterwards. In later years, after leaving the institution, I attended night school classes to catch up on some subjects that became important for me in later life.

CHAPTER THREE

Other activities in the school

When not in school, all of us would play games in the yard, where we would be supervised by one of the brothers. As I got older, I took to playing basketball, which I liked, and continued to play for years after. Of course, there was no such thing as holidays; the only difference was there weren't any school classes.

Sometimes, at the weekends, depending on the weather, we would all go for long walks in one large group, accompanied by a number of brothers, out on the country roads, or we might walk to the beach, which wasn't too far away. Sometimes, if the weather was bad, there would be a film shown in the hall upstairs. Again, if there was a football game on in Tralee, a number of the bigger boys would be taken to the game, and sometimes the school band might be playing at the game. Gaelic football was the main sport, of course, in Kerry, and even the mention of the word soccer would lead to being ostracised as the "ban" was strictly enforced. I would have attended some games as I got older.

Altar Boy and Irish dancing

There were a number of other things happening in the school in which I was involved. I trained as an altar boy, and used to often serve mass in the school chapel, for which there was a rota for different boys to serve on different days. I was trained with other boys by Brother Raphael, pseudonym.

As time went on, I was asked to serve mass on some Sundays for the nuns in a convent not too far from our school. Years later, I learned that it was called the Pembroke Alms House, Industrial School for girls, and that three of my sisters had been sent to that school after our mother died in March 1946. I was not aware of that at the time.

Sometimes, I would be on my own, and other times; there would be two of us. The nuns used to give us apples, and sweets after the mass, with which, of course, we were delighted. Masses at that time used to be said in Latin, so all of us mass servers had to learn all the prayers, and responses in Latin.

I was also attached to an Irish dance school, which involved us going around to different parts of Kerry some weekends for dancing competitions. We were part of a School of Dancing, which was run by a lady who used to teach us Irish Dancing, Mrs Brazil. She was from Tralee, and she had her own Dance School, the Brazil School of Dancing.

We used to train at least once a week, and coming near competition time, she would bring some of the female members of her Dance School from the town to train with us in St Joseph's. The School Dancers from St Joseph's were incorporated into her Dancing School for competition purposes. The training used to take place in one of the classrooms at the school, which had wooden floors.

We were all given dancing costumes which we wore for the competitions. I have a number of photographs of the dance troupe I was part of all those years ago. Over my years in the dancing school, I had won several Irish dancing medals, none of which I have now as they have been mislaid over the years. I expand further at the end of chapter 4 regarding a number of photographs taken of our dance troupe, including myself.

Saturday Showers

On Saturdays, all of us used to go for showers to the shower room. We used to go in groups according to age. The shower room was a large room with a row of showers in a line in a tiled section of the room. There were no cubicles, and all of us used to go under the showers completely naked. At the close of chapter four, I mention a photograph of the shower room taken in April 1955.

There was an elderly man, Brother Raphael, in charge on shower days, who at times used to strip off naked himself, and get into the shower. He used to ask one of us to scrub his back with a scrub brush, and I often had to do the scrubbing. This was a regular occurrence, and it was well-known by other brothers in the school as to what was happening. At the time, of course, we wouldn't have thought too much about it at such a young age, but it came to light during the CICA report on St Joseph's Institution. [9.262 to 9.291 refers.]

As well as being in charge of the showers, Brother Raphael was also responsible for the chapel, where he used to train the altar boys for mass serving. He was also in charge of the boys who used to attend the dancing school, so I would have had a lot of association with him during my time at St Joseph's.

There was also a school band with about twenty or thirty members, and they used to do their practice in the hall upstairs. The band gave concerts in the hall, and they used to go to the football games in Tralee to play at some of the matches. They were a brass, and reed band, and at times, they would do their marching practice in the main yard.

The band's master approached me at one time, and asked me if I was interested in music. They were always looking to keep the numbers up in the band. About two or three times, the bandmaster brought me to the hall, and started me on the piano with a couple of lessons.

Brother Raphael, who was in charge of the dancing, told me to stop going for the piano lessons as the dancing was enough for me. I had to tell the bandmaster that I was not allowed to go to any more lessons. I always regret this as maybe it was a chance lost in music.

There was also a time while I was reasonably young, and still going to school when I was sent to the Bon Secours Hospital, Tralee, which was run by the nuns, to do some cleaning one evening a week, mostly, I think, on a Saturday. My job was to wash, and clean some of the floors of the long corridors in part of the hospital. At first, it wasn't too bad as I liked the idea of getting out of the school for a break, and if my memory serves me correctly, I think I used to be paid some pocket money.

Then, I was asked to clean the floor of the mortuary, which was at the end of the long corridor I used to clean. At that young age, I didn't have any idea about death or that this was where people who had died in the hospital were put. The first few times I went to do the cleaning in the mortuary, it was just an empty room with what I thought were some hospital trolleys.

However, one day, there were a few bodies lying there, all covered with white sheets. I became very scared; it was a frightening experience for a young boy like me at that time, as I used to be on my own with nobody else around near me at the end of the long corridor. I remember I used to clean very quickly just to get out quickly. I eventually stopped going to the hospital, and I was glad that it ended. I used to have dreams of seeing the bodies covered with white sheets for some time after.

There were a number of fields around the school which were used by the farm for the animals to graze, and one of these used to be set up as a football pitch. We used to have to carry the football posts, and other equipment from the stores to the field whenever there was football training, and set them up. After the training, all the equipment, including the posts, were carried back to the school where they were stored. I didn't take to football very much, but used to go to the fields with some of the other boys who didn't play either, and played other games.

There was one day I remember at the farm; it was the day of the Threshing of the wheat. We spent nearly the full day at the farm, and were provided with drinks, and refreshments. I have a photo of myself on the top of the threshing machine. That would have been one of the better days.

After education finished - Tailors shop

When I finished technical school in around 1960, which was the year of my Manual Training Certificate that I received, I was sent to work in the tailor's shop. I must have been close to 15 years of age at the time, and would have spent just over one year at the tailor's shop.

I now look back, and have to ask the question why, after doing mechanical drawing, and woodwork, I was sent to the tailor's shop. It looks to me now that there was no plan of action as to what any of us at the school were going to do in the future.

There were, of course, a number of factors at play, unknown to us, as I would have learned in later years from reading the Ryan report in 2009. There was uncertainty about the survival of the school; time was running out as we approached the age for leaving the school, and in my case, my brother Jerry had already been through the tailor's shop, and had got a job with a tailor. Maybe the expectation was that I would join my brother, but that was not to be.

Tom was the man in charge of the tailor's shop. He was a man in his 40s or 50s. He was from Tralee town, and he was a nice man to work with. His father, who was elderly, also worked in the shop, and kept more or less to himself. He had a workbench at one end of the shop that only he worked on, and he would sit upon the bench with legs crossed doing his sewing. Tom, his son, used to prepare the work for him to do. He used to do a lot of sewing by hand, finishing garments, making the button holes, and a lot of other stuff, including orders for special customers. Tom would also prepare the work for us boys as part of our training.

A lot of work was done for people, all men, from outside, doing alterations, and making suits, and overcoats. I remember one of the shop's customers was a minister from another religion, maybe the Church of Ireland. I couldn't believe it, and I found myself very uncomfortable in his presence, especially this being a Catholic School. He turned out to be a nice person, and had been in on a couple of occasions getting work done. When I think about it now, I realise that it was part of the religious brainwashing of the time by the brothers.

A very popular thing at that time was people getting their clothing like overcoats, and jackets "turned"; this is where the garment would be totally ripped up, and remade inside out. This saved them from having to buy new ones, but there was a lot of work involved.

Now Tom used to do all the measuring of the customers that came in to have something made. They would either bring the material with them, or Tom would show them samples, and would get the material for them. Once Tom had measured up the customer, he would then take down a pattern close to his measurements, and he would cut out the garments for sewing. The customer would, sometime later, as arranged with Tom, come back for a try-on of the half-finished garment to see if any alterations were needed.

Myself, and the other boys in the shop would be helping out with the makeup of some of these garments. Of course, Tom or his father did all the important parts of the making up of these garments. Most of our job was to watch, and learn.

On one occasion during my time in the tailor's shop, there was a break-in to the shop one night. It wasn't discovered till the following morning when we all turned up at the shop. The local Gardai from Tralee were called, and local detectives from the town arrived at the shop to investigate.

There were a number of items stolen, including a jacket that I had worked on myself. I told the detectives that there was something different in the way this jacket was made up. Normally, back in those times, the inside lining of a jacket was the same colour all the way through, including the lining in the sleeves.

This particular jacket had a different colour lining in the sleeves, which was unusual for that time, and I pointed that out to the detectives, and Tom remembered that too. After they took all the necessary particulars, and they were leaving, one of the detectives turned to me, and said to me, Someday, you will make a good detective.

Little did the detective or myself realise that my life would turn out the way it did, with me joining the Garda Siochana, and eventually becoming a Detective Sergeant in Dublin City.

CHAPTER FOUR

Earlier years conditions

My earlier years at St Joseph's Residential Institution were a mixture of fear, hunger, bullying both sexual, and physical abuse, to use modern terms. There were boys there who were aged from seven years like me to nearly sixteen years, and of course, there was a lot of bullying going on by the bigger boys on the younger ones. The younger boys came in for beatings from the older boys for no reason, so much so that the younger boys used to stay in groups of our own age to avoid being picked on or walked the yard with whichever Christian Brother was on yard duty.

Some of the sexual bullying took place at the toilets in the play yard. When younger boys used to go to use the urinals, some bigger boys would come, and try to interfere with us while going to the toilet, so much so that I would not use the urinals anymore, but would go into a cubical.

After leaving St Joseph's Residential Institution, I would not use a urinal if I could avoid it, but always, even to this day, I would go into a cubical. That is the psychological impact that has stuck with me all of my life. There was also, always, the fear from the brothers who would, for no reason at all would, fly off the handle, and dig into somebody either with fists or a leather strap.

Food

When I first went to St Joseph's Institution, food was very bad, and scarce. There was always a limited amount of bread, and mostly, we were as hungry coming out after meal time as we were going in, as in some cases, you couldn't eat the food.

The hunger drove us to "steal" turnips from the farm buildings to eat. We used to get the turnips when it was dark, go to the ball alleys, break them up off the walls, and share them around with whoever wanted some. This happened a lot. It wasn't too different from conditions described in some of the Charles Dickens novels. [9.327 CICA 2009 Report refers to such incidents].

Section 9.322 of the CICA Report 2009 made reference regarding food for us, the boys at the institution, quoting comments by the new Resident Manager[superior] in the 1950s [during my time there] regarding dealings on the farm, and the disposal of produce were of particular interest.

The new Resident Manager [superior], Brother Ryle, felt that it was an understatement to say that hundreds of pounds were lost over a period of three to four years, and wondered whether it could be counted in the thousands. He noted that we, the boys, were underfed, and were denied vegetables whilst, at the same time, vegetables were on sale in the market, and shops in the town of Tralee.

The CICA Report 2009 also mentions that vegetables from the farm were being sold for private profit to vegetable dealers in the area outside the school while we, the boys, were going hungry.

According to the annals, the medical officer had noted that the vegetables were obtainable in the town, but the boys could not get any. The level of deprivation emerged in the evidence heard by the CICA Committee: two of the boys who were in the school in the 1940s spoke of taking food prepared for the pigs.

In 1953, a visitation report by an Inspector from the Department of Education recorded complaints by two Christian Brothers attached to St Joseph Residential Institution, Tralee that we, the boys, were not getting enough to eat. The Resident Manager [Superior] denied this was so. [9.323 of CICA Report 2009] Brother O'Donnell would have been the resident Manager [Superior] at this time. This would have been my first full year at St Joseph's institution.

I'm not sure how long this food situation went on; it might have been two or more years after I had arrived there, which would nearly bring it into the middle of the 1950s. Then, a new brother arrived at the institution, and took charge of the kitchen, and refectory, and he ordered the bakers to bake more bread. The institution had its own bakery, and things improved from then on.

This brother [Brother Laurence] [pseudonym] was a very strict man, and always found excuses to use his fists or his strap on somebody. I got on reasonably well with him, but without exception, I came in for the brunt of his tantrums, too. Sometimes, Brother Laurence would fly off the handle at mealtime, so imagine the fear that was there at some mealtimes. Everything had to be right for him [Brother Laurence], and even the boys who worked in the kitchen, and the refectory for him weren't safe from his outbursts. He was a law unto himself. Even the other brothers wouldn't come near the kitchen or the refectory while he was there. The brothers, of course, had their own kitchen, and dining room in their quarters. As I got older, I became a monitor in the refectory for mealtimes, and was always fearful of doing something wrong or letting the side down.

There was a boy in the institution, who was a bit older than myself, in the mid to late 1950s, called Joseph Pike, RIP. He was in the dance troupe with me, and I have a photo of that troupe of dancers with him in it. Now, Joseph was in the hospital for some reason, and died there, and I think that he was buried in the graveyard in the institution behind the ball alley.

Before Joseph died, he hadn't been well for a while, and it was known that he had a bad "boil" on the back of his neck, and he had a run-in with Brother Laurence in the refectory during one of the mealtimes. Brother Laurence gave him a beating at the table for what reason is not known, but that wasn't uncommon. Over the next while, Joseph got very sick, and had to stay in bed as he wasn't feeling too good. The next thing the doctor was called, and he was sent to the hospital, where he died within a couple of days.

At the time, there wasn't much done about Joseph's death. Things got back to normal as if nothing had happened, and Joseph's incident was forgotten about as if it never happened. I would not ever go as

31

far as saying that Brother Laurence was responsible for his death, but there was a failing in that Joseph Pike's underlying illness had not been detected earlier. It is another one of those situations that there will never be an answer to.

The School Chaplin

I remember well the Chaplin, a Fr. O'Neill who was attached to the institution during my time there. He said the masses every day heard confessions, and carried out whatever priestly duties he had to do. I'm not too sure at what age I became an altar boy, and was trained by Br. Raphael. I used to serve mass very often as myself, and the other boys were on a rota for masses.

Mass in those times was always said in Latin, and all the altar boys had to learn the prayers, and responses in Latin. There used always be at least two boys serving at each mass, and maybe on holy days, there could be more.

The Chaplin had a room, which was in the same building as the rooms of the brothers, and it was the first room at the end of the corridor nearest the chapel. The Chaplin was a nice person, and was obviously in retirement from somewhere else. I am not too sure of the period, but I was asked to look after the room belonging to the Chaplin, just making up the bed, changing the sheets, and keeping it clean, and tidy. I think that there was a housekeeper who was out sick or something, so the job lasted for a short period of time. I have some memories of the Chaplin giving me some money from time to time.

There was one occasion that I will never forget. It was at a Christmas Eve mass, and I was in a seat not too far from the front of the altar. I don't think I was an altar boy at the time. Somebody had called the school to see me, I didn't know from Adam who it was, and I got a box of chocolates from whoever it was. This, of course, was manna from heaven, and I scoffed the chocolates before the mass.

I was after receiving communion, and then the inevitable happened: I got sick all over the seat, and the floor just as mass was finishing. Now, nobody rushed in with a bucket, and mop as it was left to the poor priest to clean up my mess. Because of the fact that I had received Holy Communion, nobody could go near the mess, only the priest, because there would be traces of the blessed sacrament in my sickness. How things have changed; today, one would get the nearest bucket, and mop.

Meeting my Father

Sometime in 1961, prior to me leaving St Joseph's Residential Institution, my brother Jerry, who was out working with a family called Healy Rae, who were tailors in Kilgarvan, Co Kerry, made some arrangements with the Resident Manager [superior], to bring me home to Ballylongford to meet my father. I had no knowledge of these arrangements until my brother Jerry arrived one day, and brought me off with him.

We travelled by bus to Ballylongford; it was the Tralee to Limerick bus, and we got off the bus at a crossroads. I later became aware that it was known locally as Callaghan cross because of a family called Callaghan that lived at the crossroads. As I write this, there is still a member of the Callaghan family residing at the cross, who returned from London, where she had lived all of her life. She is a great friend of my sister Joan, and we keep in touch by phone, and cards. She reached 90 years of age in May 2021.

I always remember seeing a signpost pointing to Limerick, and showing the distance to Limerick as forty-nine, and a half miles; of course today it would be in kilometres.

We both walked in the Limerick direction for about one hundred yards or more, and arrived at a cottage. Jerry knocked at the door, which was opened by an elderly man wearing oldish clothes, and who was unshaven. Jerry said something, I'm not sure how I was introduced, but the name "Mossey" was mentioned. Of course, when meeting my father on that occasion, I didn't know the man from Adam. Unlike today's Television Programme about "long lost families", there were no big hugs or handshakes at our meeting.

I find it hard to describe the reaction of my father to me arriving, considering that I was only about nine months old the last time he laid eyes on me. He was a man of few words. The meeting was cautious, with a certain amount of trepidation on my own part that this was my father, and I was his son.

This was a whole new experience for me; here I was in a cottage that was supposed to be my home where I was actually born, and meeting with a man who was supposed to be my father. It was a lot for me to take in on that first visit, being a boy who was not yet sixteen years of age, and who had no understanding of what a family was. The fact that my "brother Jerry" was present helped to break the ice, as it were, even though I just about accepted that Jerry was my brother.

I'm not sure now how long I stayed with my father at that time; it may have been for a day or two. Life in Ballylongford was interesting at the time, and on other visits later, we would go to the village, where we would always meet somebody that my father would know. When I would be introduced, I would be introduced as "Mossey", the baby of the family. Some locals used to always, as I felt anyway, give me a second look in disbelief, "that Jack's youngest," not knowing if they were making a statement or asking a question.

As I progressed through life, I would pay several visits to my old home in Ballylongford, which way back then was a small town with a crossroads at the centre of the town. There were at one time about seven or eight public houses in the town. It had its own small sub-Garda station not too far from the centre of the town.

I think that there was a public house on each of the three corners of the crossroads at one time, and a garage on the fourth corner. When you came to the crossroads, and turned right, the road would lead to Lislaughtin Abbey, Graveyard, where I discovered my mother was buried, and my father was later buried there. The road continued on till you came to Carrig Island, where my father, and mother were both supposed to have been born, as I would have discovered in later years.

At the crossroads, going straight on, you went over a bridge, which is over a small river, which brought you to the other side of the town. Here, there was the local community hall, the parish church on the left-hand side on the bend, and the local schools on the church grounds. On the right-hand side, as you went down, you would pass a variety of shops, which included a bakery, and a large hardware store called Sullivan's.

This was my hometown, and over the years, I would make many visits, always trying to discover truths about my family. There was, as with all small towns, a divide between the town's inhabitants, who were known as" townies", and those living outside the limits of the town as we did.

Of course, my father may have been feeling guilty about what happened all those years ago, but he said very little. On calculating the age of my father, he would have been in his middle seventies at the time of our first meeting, and about six years later, in 1967, he passed away while being treated for a hernia in Tralee hospital; he was one month shy of his 83rd birthday.

I was working in Dublin at the time of my father's death, and I remember that I could not afford to go to my father's funeral. A person whom I became very friendly with saw my predicament, and offered to drive me down to the funeral. I will be forever grateful to that friend for his kind assistance to me on such an occasion.

Late discoveries

Before leaving the earlier chapters dealing with my years at St Joseph's Residential Institution, Tralee, I have to mention that I came across some more substantiated information regarding my time at St Joseph's institution, Tralee, in the form of photographs. My Niece Patrina, my late brother Jerry's daughter, brought my attention to a photographic archive put together by the Kennelly family of Castleisland, Co Kerry, which contained thousands of photographs.

I went into that photographic archive, and I was amazed at the number of photographs I discovered, which had been taken at St Joseph's Residential Institution, Tralee, between 1953, and 1973, which would have covered my time there in St Joseph's.

Going through the archive, I found quite a number of photographs that I had appeared in, as well as individual photographs of myself covering my period at St Joseph's, institution. I also found a number of other photographs of interest taken at the institution, and in Tralee.

Photograph taken on the 25th of December 1954 of Br O'Donnell, who was the Superior, [Resident Manager] at the time of my arrival. There was some controversy regarding the way the finances of the school were being managed, and also the suggestion that during his time, there may have been bribes paid to NSPCC Inspectors to have children committed to the institution.

Photograph taken in February 1957 of the Court House, Tralee, which was the Court house I was taken to, on the 12th December 1952, by a Mr O'Regan, NSPCC, Inspector, and committed to St Joseph's Residential Institution, on the same date till the 9-9-1961.

Photograph taken in January 1961 of Judge Johnson, who presided at the Tralee District Court and was responsible for my committal to St Joseph's Residential Institution.

As a member of the Brazil School of Dancing, a photograph taken in March 1955 of our troupe of dancers, I would have been just nine, and a half years of age, and it would have been just over two years after I had been committed to St Joseph's Institution.

A photograph taken in April 1955 shows the band marching in the main yard of the institution. This photograph also shows a view of the institution buildings, ground floor, and first floor where the dormitories were located.

Another one of the photographs taken in April 1955 shows part of the shower room, with three shower heads showing on the right-hand side. These photographs, taken in April 1955, were taken during a visit to the school by Mr. and Mrs Ernest Hart, from Indianapolis, the USA, who were there to promote the writing of letters to pen friends in the USA. I now have a vague recollection of that visit because of viewing these photographs. I'm not sure if indeed, I wrote any letters. The band were marching in the yard for their benefit, and there was music, and dancing upstairs, which they also attended. A photographer must have been brought in for the event for the day as there were quite a number of photographs taken on that day. I also appear as a face in the crowd in one of the photographs taken in the yard of the institution.

A photograph taken of myself on the 25th of December 1955, at a concert in the school, and an appearance by Santa Clause giving out presents. I would have been just 10 years of age at that time, and would have just completed three years in St Joseph's institution.

Photograph taken in April 1956, showing the woodwork room, through which a number of years later, I would be passing through to get to the technical school classroom, which is behind the glass panel door at the rear of the workroom.

Individual photograph taken of myself in dance costume in April 1957. I would have been eleven, and half years of age at the time. This was taken on the stage in the hall upstairs during an Easter concert in which I would have been dancing. The background of the photograph shows a painted scene at the back of the stage, which I think was painted by Brother Collins, who was a good artist.

Another photograph taken in April 1957, during the Easter concert, showing the full troupe of the Brazil School of Dancers, including the girls from Tralee, who were part of the troupe. In this photograph, I appear in the centre in the front row.

In my search, I came across a photograph of a member of the dance troupe, Joseph Pike, RIP, also taken in April 1957. Joseph died over the next year or two under circumstances which were never fully explained, which I have already touched on.

Photograph taken in August 1957 of Brother Raphael during the celebration of his Jubilee year. I have already dealt with certain issues involving Brother Raphael, and I will expand further on regarding additional issues. A further photograph taken in August 1957 at Brother Raphael's Jubilee celebrations includes a number of the Christian Brothers who were at St Joseph's at that time. Brother Raphael is in the middle of the front row, with Brother Ryle sitting on his right, who replaced Brother O'Donnell as superior [Resident Manager] some time previously.

The back row of this photograph shows, from left to right, [1] Brother Laurence, [2] Brother Collins, [4] Brother Bartolo, all of whom I have previously mentioned covering my time in St Joseph's.

Another of the photographs which I discovered was of myself, taken on the 22nd of September 1957, on the day of my confirmation, which I had never seen before. I was just 12 years of age at this time.

They say that a picture can tell a story, well during the course of my research through the Kennelly Archives, I came across a photograph of a group of boys from St Joseph's, which was taken at the train station in Tralee on the 3rd of December 1959. It was a day trip to Dublin which was organised for us by Mr Denis Guiney, of Cleary's of Dublin. I did have a vague recollection of going on a trip to Dublin at one time, but this photograph confirmed for me that the trip did take place.

We walked from the station in Dublin, and were brought to a big department store in O'Connell Street, which I later discovered was Cleary's Department Store. We were given a tour of the store, given Christmas presents, and got something to eat there. Mr Denis Guiney, of course, was a Kerry man from Brosna, in County Kerry. It was he who sponsored the whole day for us, which I later discovered. I'm not sure as to how many of us went on the trip, but I think you had to be over a certain age to travel. I would have been fourteen years of age at this time. It's amazing how one photograph can jog one's memory.

I am very much indebted to the Kennelly Archives for the amount of information I have gleaned from trawling through their Archives. As well as having the photographs available, it ties down dates, and years of numerous events during the course of my young life. What had, in some instances, been a vague memory for me has now become a clear reflection of my earlier years.

Leaving St Joseph's Residential Institution, Tralee. Released on Licence

Following my first ever meeting with my father, I was dispatched on the 5ᵗʰ of August 1961, from St Joseph's Residential Institution, and brought to Dublin City. My time of leaving the institution was always a blur to me, and still is to this day. I cannot recall all of what happened on that day; whether I was told where I was going or not, I have no recollection. When something new or exciting happens in your life, you should remember something about it. As I see it now, I must have just been brought to Dublin, and never told anything about what was going to happen until I got there. Maybe my main feeling on that day was fear of the unknown.

I was not yet 16 years of age, and my "sentence" was not yet finished, so I was released on "licence" to a" Mr. Grief, Managing Director of Weartex Clothing Factory, Kimmage Road, Dublin", which I discovered many years later from the documentation that I had obtained. I also discovered that I was discharged from my "detention" on the 9ᵗʰ of September 1961, something I was never informed about. There was also a follow-up report completed on me in December 1961, again something I was never informed about.

The Weartex advertising slogan on TV at the time was **"A Cut Above The Rest"**.

After leaving St Joseph's on the 5ᵗʰ of August 1961, I never again had any contact with anybody from the institution. I was left to find my own way in a whole new world of struggle, and survival. I also started to live my **"lie"** with regard to any connections that I had with St Joseph's Residential Institution, Tralee.

How could I ever, during my lifetime, admit that I was detained in a residential institution where young offenders were detained? Residential institutions had a bad name, as I later learned, because of their association with the court system. This stigma is forever imprinted on my mind, and will be till my dying day.

Many years later, 2009, I would read the report of the Commission to Inquire into Child Abuse in Residential Institutions [The Ryan Report 2009], which included a chapter on St Joseph's Residential Institution, Tralee. It would bring back vivid memories of the way I was treated, and abused during my time there. I would, after reading that report, seek some form of redress.

I arrived in Dublin by train, accompanied by one of the Christian Brothers; I think it may have been the superior, Brother Ryle. I was brought to a "large man's shop", which I later learned was Arnotts of Henry Street in the middle of Dublin city.

I was completely gobsmacked at the size of this store, considering where I had come from, and the age I was. There, I was introduced to Mr. Gerry Smyth, who was attached to the man's shop at Arnotts, as I later learned. Gerry Smyth was to be my mentor from that time on. Outside of his work situation, Gerry Smyth liked to use the Irish version of his name, "Gearoid Mac Gabhann," he was a very nationalistic-minded person, and had very little time for the English. Strangely enough, some years later, his eldest son Stephen, who did very well in his studies, ended up being an officer in Her Majesty's Navy.

Later, I would learn that Mr Gerry Smyth was responsible for my getting this job because of his close association with the management people in Weartex. Arnotts were very big customers of Weartex. I would over time, build up a good relationship with the Smyth family, and spend many good times with them. I used to visit them most weekends, and they had a son Stephen, who was about the same age as myself. I would accompany the family on holidays, and days out at the seaside over the next few years. The Smyths became, for me, the nearest thing to a family that I would have understood; it was akin to being fostered out again, but this time under different circumstances.

I found it hard to remember all of what happened on that day I arrived in Dublin, as I was completely in shock; I found that it was a lot to take in on my first day as a boy who was shy, introvert, alone, uneducated, and dispatched from detention in an institution, from the depths of the countryside.

I remember that I was brought out of town to my digs or lodgings that had been arranged for me at Priory Road, Kimmage, and I think it was another boy called Stephen who was also staying at Priory Road that brought me to my digs.

Before leaving Arnotts in the city, I met somebody from Weartex; I think he was one of the owners. Weartex was owned by a family whose name may have been McCullagh.

Priory Road was to be my home for about the next six years or more. My landlady's name was Mrs. Brennan, and she was a lady from Wexford who was married to a man whose first name was Ned, who worked in one of the local pubs in the area. Later on, Ned would get me a weekend job in that pub as a lounge boy for a period of time.

The accommodation was full board, and it was going to cost me two pounds, and ten shillings per week. It was a shared room with this other lad, Stephen, who also lived there.

I had no money, and would have to pay for my digs from my first week's wages. When I got my first week's wages, I only received two pounds, and ten shillings. My wages were three pounds a week, and ten shillings were deducted for tax, and social insurance stamps.

When I told my landlady what the story was, she agreed to charge me only two pounds a week until I got an increase in wages. This was a life saver for me as it gave me ten shillings a week for myself.

I started work in the Weartex clothing factory, and it was only about a fifteen-minute walk to work from where I lived. With all that was happening, I was in a complete daze for some weeks after I arrived at Weartex.

I settled into my place of work over a period of time. The floor manager showed me what my work entailed. It was a very simple task of trimming parts of the garments before going on to the next section of the assembly line beside me. My work bench was facing a wall in front of me, so I didn't have to see anybody in the factory while working except those at either side of me, and that's the way it remained for me for some time. It was a cover for me, and saved me some embarrassment; being so shy, and unprepared for this amount of exposure in the midst of so many females at so young an age, for a period of time, I was petrified of doing or saying something wrong. This, of course, would have resulted from the situation I came through in St Joseph's institution, Tralee, not being mentally prepared for the outside world.

It took me almost two years to come out of my "shell", and to begin having conversations with some workers. In the factory where I was working, over 75% of the workforce were female, and most of them worked on the assembly line. Imagine how I felt, coming from an all-male establishment, from a young male institution, from way down the country to an almost all-female one, and being just about sixteen years old. It was the most frightening situation for me.

Later, as I became more familiar with the workers, and my surroundings, I would attend the Christmas parties organised for all the staff of the factory. I still have a group photo taken at one of these Christmas functions.

All the men there worked on the cutting out of garments, making patterns, keeping the stock rooms in order, on the steam pressers, and doing checks on the garments for mistakes.

Years later, I learned that one of the men I had worked with in Weartex was Jimmy Keaveney, the father of the Dublin footballer of the same name. He was a gentleman to work with, and his son Jimmy would have been about the same age as me. Of course, there was great rivalry between the Dublin, and Kerry footballers over the years.

Attending Night classes Dublin

Part of my training with Weartex was to attend tailoring school at the night Technical School in Parnell Square, Dublin city, which I used to attend three nights a week. I'm not sure if the course was paid for by Weartex as I would not have been able to afford it on my ten shillings a week pocket money. I had to get the bus into the city centre to attend my classes, and at first, this was a trying experience for me to find my way around the city. On one occasion, on one of my earlier trips to the city, I remember getting on a bus going the wrong way; I was heading to the north of the city instead of west, and that didn't happen a second time.

This course would have lasted for a couple of years for me. I always remember one of the projects I had to do at the college was to make up something for myself. I decided to do a casual jacket for myself under the guidance of the instructor, which I completed in what would have been a very mod style at the time. I had to show it off myself at a fashion show organised by the tailoring night school. It was a blazer-type jacket without lapels or a collar. Years later, the Beatles wore something similar for some of their shows.

I would have gained a good insight into clothing manufacturing at that time, but my job in Weartex was on the production line, and very repetitive. Later, some "time, and motion" people did a study at the factory, and everybody on the production line was put on piece work. That was a system where the whole production line had to put through a set number of garments before they qualified for bonus payments, so there was always pressure to keep the assembly line moving, and of course, most of the women wanted to earn their bonus payments. Everything was alright until one of the machines had a breakdown; the rest of the line would then have nothing to do until the offending machine was fixed by our on-site machine mechanic, with, of course, panic setting in for those who might miss out on their bonus for the day because of the delay on the line.

During those first couple of years, I settled into the area where I lived, and got to know some of the neighbours. It was a very quiet residential neighbourhood. My local church was St Paul of the Cross church, Mount Argus, not five minutes' walk away from my digs. It was a seminary for the Passion of the Cross priests. Being brought up in the Institution as a good Roman Catholic, I attended my weekly Sunday mass at this church. Over time, I became settled into my way of life, and even joined the Legion of Mary group, which brought me into closer contact with the church.

With the legion of Mary, I used to do house to house visitations with another legion member, talking to people about attending church, and supporting the church festivities. It also involved doing collections outside the church on particular Sunday mornings in support of the legion of Mary, and attending meetings of the legion. For somebody who had very little money to spend, it was something for me to occupy my time, and also kept me on the straight, and narrow.

At some stage, while I was still at Weartex, I went to a local motorcycle dealer, and bought a new Honda 50cc on-hire purchase. The dealer was involved in selling bicycles, and had now moved into the motorcycle trade. Now, I was never been on a motorcycle before; I had, of course, been on a bicycle, which I had learned to ride at the Smyths, so what was the difference? I got a few short lessons from the dealer whom I had known previously because he used to fix my bicycle, and I was off. There were no driving tests at that time, and all I had to do was get a licence to ride a motorcycle. I must have been about 18 years old at the time, as that may have been around the age at which I could get my licence.

That may have been around the year 1963. The 22nd of November of that year is embedded in everyone's mind who was around at that time. President John Fitzgerald Kennedy, President of the United States of America, was assassinated in Dallas, Texas. People all around the world remember exactly where they were on that occasion. I had attended a film in the old Metropolitan Cinema on O'Connell street, and on coming out of the cinema, the paper sellers were selling the "stock press" with the headline that JFK had been assassinated. The stock press was made up of that evening's paper with a new front page with news of the assassination on it. Everybody was in shock as JFK had only visited Ireland in the summer of that year.

CHAPTER SIX

Johnston Mooney, and O'Brien, Bakers; 1965 to 1967

I remained at Weartex clothing manufacturers for about four years, and in 1965, I moved to Johnston Mooney & O'Brien, who were a well-known bakery firm in Dublin City. The money was slightly better, but not much. I started off as a helper in one of the delivery vans, delivering bread to shops, and private houses. Each van man had his own bread round, which he had built up over the years, and ran like his own business, buying stock from the bakery firm, and selling it to his customers. I would have worked on various delivery routes over time whenever help was needed by any one of the van men; if they were going on holidays, I would work the route for them while they were away, and of course, I had to balance the books for them.

Most of the vans in the city routes were electric, and very simple to drive. The biggest problem was making sure you had enough power left in the battery to get you back to the bakery that evening before you put it on charge again. I fail to see what the big problem is today in introducing electric vehicles, considering how prevalent they were back at that time, over fifty years ago.

Sometime later, I was asked by one of the managers if I could drive a van. Now, at that time, things began to change for new drivers looking for licences. They were bringing in new rules about driving licences, and people would have to do a driving test. I just missed out on getting my first driving licence before the driving tests came in, and eventually had to get driving lessons, and do my driving test. The manager at the bakery gave me a loan from one of the small petrol vans to do my test in, and I passed my test, and got my licence. Now, the fact that I was driving a van with the Johnston Mooney & O'Brien logo for my test, and this was going to be for my job must have helped me. Testers back then were quite reasonable people.

Towards the later part of my time with Johnston Mooney & O'Brien, I was driving the bigger bread trucks on the "country"runs, which covered a number of counties outside Dublin. I remember a situation that happened during a strike at the confectionery section at the bakery during one Christmas season. The bakery did a huge business in Christmas cakes, and other confectionery at that time of the year.

At the time, I was working with a van man by the name of Jimmy, who had a very big country route. We stopped at one of our customers to do a bread delivery as bread was still available, and not affected by the strike. It was somewhere in Co Kildare; the customer in question was in a barn with a friend of his, or it may have been his brother, and they were mixing Christmas cake mixture on plastic sheeting on the floor of the barn with shovels. This was to try to make up for the shortage of Christmas confectionery due to the strike. That was a sight that was hard to forget.

During this period of my life, maybe before I joined the bakery firm, I had joined a musical society which was meeting in a local hall which may have been attached to the Mount Argus grounds. Now, I never had what you would call a singing voice, but I was passable when singing in a chorus with a group. I remember one particular show I took part in, and I had a speaking part about two words, it was the musical The Desert Song, and it ran for a week. I did continue with the musical society into the next season, but because of a change of jobs, the times didn't suit me, and I had to call it a day.

Moving on to another job change; 1967

In the second half of 1967, I left Johnston Mooney & O'Brien, and got a job with a company known at the time as Stewart & Lloyds Steel Company in East Wall Road as a costing clerk. It was a change of direction, and to be honest, I didn't know the first thing about costing, but I felt that I had a flair for figures. I was brought up to speed by the people I worked with in the office, and I was very appreciative of their input in showing me the ropes. It was a small firm with a small number of employees both in the office, and the workshop. Again, it was another learning curve in my progression through life, dealing with, and meeting new people.

Before I finished my time with the Bakery, I was already doing some study, going to night school, and preparing to do the entrance exam to join the Garda Siochana. I was successful in the examination, and had put in my application to join.

When I joined Stewart & Lloyds, it was for a probationary period of six months, which was up at the end of 1967. At around that time, I had received notification of my acceptance for training for the Garda Siochana, and I was to report on the 17th of January 1968 to the Garda Training Centre at Templemore, Co Tipperary.

Around the same time as I was accepted into training for the Garda Siochana, my boss at Stewart & Lloyds had offered me a permanent position with the company as my probationary period came to a close, but I had to turn down the offer, explaining to him that I had been accepted into the Garda Siochana, and was to start my training the following January 1968.

During my time with Stewart & Lloyds, I remember the first starting gates for racing for the Curragh Race Track in Co. Kildare, Ireland were manufactured there. Well, I was a party to the making of history in Irish racing.

Part-time work

During my working years between 1961, and 1967, I took on a couple of part-time jobs, apart from doing the lounge boy work for a short while, to try, and make some extra money.

I joined an agency that was involved in selling Encyclopedia Britannica from door to door. Now, I received some training as to how to approach clients, and how to do a presentation to a prospective client. Most of the calls were contacts that were made by people interested in the package, and my job was to do a follow-up to try, and get a sale. Most of my calls were done on a Saturday or in the evening time during the week when I had to do call backs.

I did succeed in making a few sales, but at times, I felt guilty as some of the people I was selling to could barely afford to put food on the table, not to mind putting themselves into debt doing a weekly or monthly repayment for a set of books. A lot of the time, they would say they were doing it for their children or grandchildren. I didn't stay at this job for too long before handing in my presentation kit.

I also did another door to door job as a salesman selling hoovers. Again, it was on a follow-up contacts system. In this case, there were always two of us together when calling houses. Most of the sales were done on a hire-purchase agreement basis. Again, it was a job which I did on Saturdays, and some evenings.

While doing my part-time jobs, my financial situation didn't improve, and more than likely cost me more money than I made because of transport costs. Looking back now, it was a good experience meeting different people, and being in new situations; it helped me to relate more to people. It more than likely helped to keep me out of trouble; because of my background, I would have walked a fine line with so many attractions, and distractions that could have affected my young mind.

One of these attractions was an amusement arcade in O'Connell street, which I went to once. There was a roulette table there, which I started to play on with the small amount of money I would have had. Over a short period of time there, I was ten shillings up on my winnings; I put the ten shillings in my pocket, and left. I never again went back there or any other like establishment. Something in the back of my mind told me that this was not for me. Thankfully, I never became a gambler, but it didn't stop me from putting an occasional bet on a big race over the years.

Reflecting on those early years

When I look back now at this point in my life, and reflect on where I was coming from, and where it was leading me, I took a certain amount of satisfaction in the fact that I had survived my early years in the outside world, getting away from humiliation, and isolation, overcoming some of the struggles put in my path due to my institutionalization in St Joseph's Residential Institution, Tralee.

From 1961 to 1967, it was just over six years after I had left St Joseph's Residential Institution, Tralee. As well as keeping myself in work, and getting involved in my local community during those years, I did as much as I was able to get to know about my lost family. I still wasn't alive to the meaning of being part of a family. It was a slow process, which I was trying to get to grips with as a loner in a big city. At this stage in my life, in my early twenties, out of a family with nine siblings, I only had met up with three of them: my eldest sister, Mary, my sister Ann, and my brother, Jerry.

To this end, I kept in contact with my brother Jerry, who, at some time within those years, finished his job with the tailor in Kilgarvan. Jerry, around those times, used to be back, and forth from England, where he had gone, working for a few months, and back to Ballylongford to stay with our father as he was getting on in years. Jerry busied himself when at home, getting some jobs locally, mostly with farmers, which brought in much-needed money for him.

I made a few trips to Ballylongford to see my father while he was still alive. It was during one of these trips that I first met my eldest sister, Mary, who was home on holiday with her young son. During these earlier trips home, I used to go down when my brother Jerry was there because, of course, I would not yet have built up a relationship with my father to arrive down on my own unannounced. I would not yet have taken in the fact that he was my father.

While on these trips, Jerry, and I would go to the town where Jerry would point out different places, and people, some of whom would be related in some way or other to our family. I even met two of my uncles on a few occasions who were my father's brothers, and none of them were on speaking terms with each other, which wasn't unusual in small country towns. They were uncles Jerry, and uncle Maurice, and both myself, and Jerry were named after them. I also became aware of a number of cousins of mine who lived in the town. These are memories I have of those times, but in some strange way, I always had the feeling of being disconnected, as if I was looking in from the outside.

When both of my uncles died before my father, I knew nothing about their deaths; it's as if I didn't exist. I did receive a Christmas card from the wife of a neighbour of my fathers, who I had got to know on trips down, who were a very nice family. They used to take the hay from the field next to the house, and give my father some payment for it by way of money or loads of turf from the bog. On the Christmas card, she informed me that my uncle Jerry had passed away a couple of months earlier. On receipt of the card, I didn't know whether to laugh or cry. Christmas is supposed to be a time of joy, but it goes to show the innocence of people of that time.

I was, of course, an introvert, shy, quiet person, and not a bit outgoing, which was not unusual for somebody who had been an innocent detainee in an institution. My personality would evolve over time, I would change, I would become a more outspoken person, and my shyness would disappear as my life progressed. Another thought struck me later in life regarding my early visits "home"; nobody ever spoke about what had happened to me or my early years. It was as if people had a guilt complex about what happened with our family all those years ago, and didn't broach the subject.

Sometime during those early years, I received a letter from my eldest sister, Mary, asking me to go, and live with her, and her family in Liverpool, an offer which I thought long, and hard about for some time before turning her down. It may well have been a feeling of guilt on her part because of the way my life had begun, and maybe she was trying to make amends. Of course, I would never have put any blame on anyone in my family as there was never anything any of them could have done against the system that was in place at that time in 1946.

It was on some of these trips home, meeting with my sister Mary, and my brother Jerry, that I got to know the extent of my family. I discovered I had four brothers, including Jerry, and five sisters, including Mary. They were all living in England, including Jerry, who used to come, and go over periods of time. One sister lived near Mary in Liverpool, and my other three sisters lived in London. Regarding my other three brothers, one who was the eldest lived outside of London, and it wasn't known where my last two brothers lived in England.

Feelings

With respect to my family, I was void of any emotional feelings towards them; because of being institutionalised, and the way I was brought up, I would suppress any type of feelings I would have had. If I had been brought up in a normal family situation, I would have feelings for my family; how could I have feelings for people I didn't know or hadn't grown up with? As I would have tracked down my lost family over the future years, and met with them, I would have accepted with respect the fact that they were my family.

Quoting from the Ryan report of 2009, which I deal with further on, "separating siblings, and restriction of family contact were profoundly damaging for family relationships, some children lost their sense of identity, and kinship which never was, and never could be recovered."

New cottage

My father's house, where I was born, was a single-story cottage from the outside, but it had a small room built into the attic. It was situated on about an acre of land with a gateway from the main road. It was on the main Ballylongford to Limerick road in the townland of Lislaughtin. I was the only member of the family born in this house, as the other nine members of the family were born in an old thatched cottage at a place known as Saleen pier, which was beyond the far side of the town on the way to the Shannon Estuary which ran at the back of Ballylongford.

The new house had no inside toilet, and you had to go down the back garden to a kind of portaloo dry toilet, which had to be disposed of further down the garden. There was no running water to the house either; water was drawn from a well down the road called the well road, where a spring came out from a hole in the wall. It had to be brought up in buckets to the house for general use as well as making the tea, and cooking. Showers or baths, of course, were not on the menu; we all had to do the best we could, having a good wash, and shave, having got some extra water from the well road.

During some of the earlier visits, my brother Jerry used to be talking about digging a well in the field near the house. Our father would have at that time told both of us that there was water there, that there were streams running underground. To prove his point, he brought us out to the field, and got a "y" shaped small branch from a bush. He held both ends in both hands, and walked in parts of the field until the front of the "rod" began to dip towards the ground. I took a turn with the rod, and it seemed to work for me as well; maybe I had the gift. Our father pointed out a number of spots where there could be water. It would be many years later before Jerry would dig his well on one of those spots pointed out by our father.

There was an open fireplace in the cottage in which turf was burned, and a long iron bar swung over the fire on which you could hang pots, and a kettle to boil over the fire. My father, when making the tea, would boil the kettle over the fire, pour the water into the teapot with loose tea, he would then take a few cinders from the fire, and place the teapot on top of the cinders for the tea to "draw". This had to be done before the tea was poured.

Some years later, my brother Jerry brought me down to see the old family thatched cottage, which was in a very bad state of repair, and while there, I took a photo of the cottage, which I think was the only photo ever taken of it. I still have copies of that photo of the cottage. The cottage itself was near the water's edge of the Estuary, and there was a pier just down from the house where the local fishing boats used to come in. I understand that my father did some fishing over time.

The water used to come up to the rear of the old thatched cottage. One of my sisters, Joan, told me the story about my father positioning a makeshift toilet at the back of the house so that when the tide came in, it would flush the toilet. Eventually, the cottage disappeared, some of it into the Estuary, and of course, locals taking the old stone away.

Between the years of 1961, and 1967, I visited my father on a number of occasions as our relationship developed, and of course, I now had a "home"to visit. During these visits, I discovered a limited amount of information regarding my father; like I said earlier, my father was a man of few words.

At this time, my father would have been getting on in years had been living on his pensions; one was the old age pension, and the other was the old IRA pension. He would have been an active member of that organisation during the early 1900s, right up to, and during the civil war. It was something he spoke very little about up to the time he died.

One summer in the second half of the nineteen sixties before 1967, I arranged to cycle down to Ballylongford on a bicycle I borrowed from a friend of mine, which had drop handlebars, to spend some time with my father. I did the trip over a period of three to four days, staying in hostels along the route I had planned for each night on the way. When I arrived at my father's door, I was greeted with a question, "what are you doing here? You should be back looking after your job", or words to that effect.

So much for family bonding. I tried to explain to him that I was on holiday, but of course, holidays wouldn't have been in his vocabulary. I spent about a week there with him, visiting his haunts, like the pubs he used to frequent; one in particular was Danny Carroll's in main Street. Years later, I would meet one of his younger sons, John O'Carroll, for the first time in Malta on two occasions when he called to see my sister Joan. His last visit was in September 2021.

There were houses he would call into, and have tea, and cake, and nearer to home on the way back up the "well road", calling in to see Johnny, the blacksmith in the forge who was a Tarbert man. Each of the visits would take time, with conversations taking place about different things, and no hurry to get home. What a difference there is in life today.

After my visit of about a week, I took to the road again back to Dublin. A day or two before I left, I had to get a job done on the bicycle gears as they were not working correctly; this repair was carried out by Mr. McCabe, who had a bicycle shop in the town, and of course, was a friend of my father's. Thirty years later, I would meet up again with the McCabe family under tragic circumstances.

I took the same route on my return journey, and as always, it was not without incident. Travelling through some part of Co Tipperary, a dog ran from a house in front of me; I braked to avoid the dog, and went straight over the handlebars of the bike onto the road in front of me. I got a sizable cut to my chin, which was bleeding badly. In a strange coincidence, while I was lying on the roadway, an ambulance was coming up the road, but I got to my feet, and the ambulance passed.

A lady came out from a house across the road, and got me something to cover my wound. More than likely, she was the owner of the dog, but I didn't inquire at the time. I was happy to be on my feet again, and took to the road on my way. When I arrived at the next hostel, where I was going to spend the night, which was in Co Kilkenny, I had a look at my wound, and felt that it needed some stitches. I cycled to Kilkenny hospital, and had the cut stitched. I also got a tetanus injection, which hurt more than the stitching.

On the following day, I began the last stage of my journey back "home"to my lodgings, and I had run out of money to buy anything to eat on the way. It was a tough trip back for the last few hours with no refreshments, and I was glad to reach my digs to finally get something to eat.

Money, of course, was always tight at that time for me, and the fact that I had to get my bicycle fixed had not been budgeted for, leaving me short for my trip back to Dublin. I would, of course, never have asked my father for money, me being a working man in the big city of Dublin.

Well, so much for my reflections on the past; I would equate my young life, likened to a baby turtle emerging from his sandy cocoon, crossing the sandy beach of danger, to make his way to the open sea, eventually making his way through the wider oceans of life. It was time to pass into my new future, to make a new, unexpected career for myself in An Garda Siochana.

CHAPTER SEVEN

My new career

It was the year 1968 when I joined An Garda Siochana, [Irish Police force]. Prior to that, in 1966/1967, when I had made up my mind that I wanted to join the Garda Siochana, I had to bring my education up to the standard required, so I went to night school classes. I had not been educated up to the required standard, having only got the Group Certificate as it was known at that time in St Joseph's Residential Institution. I needed at least Inter Certificate standard, so I started night classes at a night school on Crumlin road in Dublin. There was also an education college which ran a correspondence course which prepared candidates for the Garda Siochana entrance examinations, which I took up in conjunction with my night classes, in around 1966/1967. This was all completed while still holding down my day jobs at the time.

I later sat, and passed the Garda entrance educational examination, and put in my application to join the Garda force. My application was processed, and I was called for an interview with the local Superintendent of the area where I lived at the time. It was a very reasonably relaxed affair; I had no criminal connections, I was a good build, my height was good, and I had passed the entrance educational examination. Application to join the Garda at that time relied a lot on what type of report would have been sent from the local Superintendent, as well as the required qualifications.

Trip to London
While waiting for the result of my application to the Garda, I also replied to an advertisement in one of the Sunday papers looking for

applicants to join the London Metropolitan Police. I made an application, and was called to London for an interview, and written test. This would have been one of my earlier trips outside of Ireland; it was just a one-day trip by boat, and train in the early hours of the morning, finding the test centre, and heading back to Ireland that evening. At that time, I had no information as to the whereabouts of any of my family who, I was aware, lived in London at that time.

Before I got the result from the London Met, I was called up to the Garda Headquarters to have a complete medical, and have my height measured. My height came to 5' 11"and three-quarters; I was disappointed that they didn't put me at 6'. My final decision was made to join An Garda Siochana.

I was still with Stewart, and Lloyd company at this stage during the course of my vetting prior to joining the force. One morning, on my way to work, I was pulled in by a Garda patrol; I think it was for speeding in a 30-mile zone. One of the officers took my particulars, and was about to put away his notebook when I mentioned that I was in the process of joining the force, and would this affect my current status if there was a prosecution. The officers let me off with caution, and wished me the best of luck for the future.

Templemore Training Centre

On the 17th of January 1968, I attended training at the Garda Training Centre, Templemore. This was sometime after the completion, and passing of my medical. I had received a communication from Garda H/Q to attend the Garda Training Centre for training for a period of 18 weeks. I left my lodgings, which had been my "home" for about six, and a half years, never again to go back as a resident.

I arrived at the training centre as instructed at the appointed time, and was met at the entrance gate by a Garda on gate duty. There were others gathering at the gate as well with their suitcases like I had, and we all had to await the arrival of the complete group. I didn't have a clue as to the size of the group that was coming. The officer at the gate had his list, so he was aware of how many to expect. Eventually, what appeared to be the full group of 15 had arrived, and we were all brought into the centre across a large square.

The training centre was previously used as an Irish Army Barracks, and was a large complex of buildings with a large square at the front. At one side of the square was an archway which led to the residential, dining areas, and classrooms. It at once brought back memories of my time in St Joseph's Institution with the similarity of the layout, although this was much larger. Part of the centre was still occupied by the Armed Forces, but they kept to themselves. Of course, the sleeping arrangements were not dormitories like the institution in Tralee, but much more up to date accommodation.

My first day was taken up with being allocated a bed, fitting for a complete uniform kit, and being shown around the centre. I was allocated a classroom, and introduced to my Police Duty [PD] instructor, Sergeant Donovan, who had good service. I was also introduced to another instructor, Sergeant John Long, who was to be my drill instructor. Both of these instructors would be with me for my 18 weeks of training. On that same evening, we were all attested, and sworn in as members of An Garda Siochana.

I had other instructors as well at various times covering physical training, [PE], first aid course, swimming, and police duties in Irish.

There were weekend passes available to the trainees to go out for the weekends, and they had to be back before a certain time on Sunday night. I did not avail of the pass too often as I didn't have any home to go to as my father had passed away at the end of the previous year, 1967. On the few occasions I did take advantage of the pass, I would have gone to visit the Smyths, and would have stayed over there for a night. Other than that, I would have had nowhere to go, and of course, very little money anyway.

Nothing in life, as I had learned, runs without incident, and my time at the training centre was no different. When I arrived at the training centre, I had a car with me, which I had purchased some time prior to being called up for training. It was a black Austin mini. I had progressed from the Honda 50.

I, and the other trainees were allowed to park our cars within the walls of the centre as long as they weren't in the way. Not too many of the trainees had cars. After a few weeks of training, I was called in by my PD instructor, and asked about my car tax. The tax on my car had expired, and I got a roasting from the instructor, and was told to get the car out of the centre straight away, and get the tax sorted. The car itself was a bit of a banger with a troublesome head gasket. I immediately moved the car outside the walls of the centre, and hid it somewhere down the town. I eventually got the car tax sorted from my first month's pay at training. Money was tight as always, but just imagine the situation of me being trained to enforce the laws of the land, and not keeping within the laws myself.

It was a wake-up call for me, and in fairness, my Police Duty instructor did not take the matter any further when I got the tax sorted. I would have been thrown out on my ear if the training Officer had heard about it.

My eighteen weeks of training didn't pass without a few more ups, and downs. On one occasion, my class was being inspected by the training Officer, who was the Superintendent in charge of the training centre, and I was told to step forward two paces. The training Officer asked me who cut my hair, and I said I had cut it myself as I missed the barber, and I didn't want to get the person who cut it in trouble. The rest of the class was dismissed, and I was to stay put, and the officer asked me again who cut my hair; I eventually said one of the other classmates cut it for me. I got a telling-off from the training Officer, and let off with a warning. The barber used to come to the Training Center at least once a week, and anybody who needed a haircut was supposed to attend.

Towards the end of the training period, we all had to sit the professional examinations which we had been studying, Police duties incorporating the criminal law, and the code of discipline, as well as being declared fit by the PE instructor, passing the first aid course, and life-saving in the pool.

Over the eighteen weeks, we had drill almost every day. When it came close to our passing out day, it was suggested by the training officer that there was no need for a drill display as we were too small a group with only 14 men. Now, we had started out with 15, but one lad pulled out halfway through for family reasons, so that left 14. Our drill Sergeant totally objected to that suggestion, and won out the day, and our class of 14 had our passing out parade with a full drill display as was the normal with other classes.

The passing out parade was an occasion where relatives, and families of the trainees were invited to the training centre to watch the drill display, and join in the celebrations. Again, it was another occasion when I was the odd one out with no family or other relatives in attendance. Mind you, I didn't make much of it at the time, as up to now, I had gotten used to being a loner, making my own way through life without family.

I later discovered the reasoning behind why there were only 14 in our class, as normally there would be 25 or 30 in each class. There had been an outbreak of foot, and mouth in England, and Northern Ireland, so they brought in restrictions on the movement of people in Ireland. They were not allowed to bring in people for training from the country areas as movement was curtailed. All the class members, including myself, had been brought in from City areas, both from Ireland, and England. It turned out well for me as I was more than likely brought in earlier than expected for my training due to the curtailment of travel from non-city areas.

Allocation to my first Station

After my "part 1 "training, as it was called, was completed, I was assigned to Chapelizod Garda Station, which was in the west of Dublin City outskirts. It was a live-in situation with sleeping accommodation upstairs in the station. Live-in accommodation was the norm in stations around the city at that time. There was a cook who used to come every day, and prepare meals for the station party, which used to be served in a fairly large kitchen come dining hall with a large table in the centre of the room. In some small way, it used to remind me of my time in the institution in Tralee, which, of course, I never discussed with anybody.

It was normal practice for trainees to be allocated to a station outside their own county of birth, and it could be anywhere in the country. There was a specific number of miles you had to be away from your hometown or any place where you might have relatives residing. Trainees would have had no control over where they were going to be sent to, but I had worked for several years in Dublin City, so I decided to make an application to be sent to a station in Dublin, knowing it was far away from my county of birth, and certainly, I had no other relatives living in any other place in Ireland at the time.

This application was done in the form of a report, [my first official communication between myself, and the Garda authorities within the Garda force]; it was met with a rebuff from the allocation department at Headquarters in Dublin, stating that the trainee in question could not have any say, as to where he would be sent, it was a matter for the Garda Commissioner as to how allocations were made. Was this the starting block of my future determination of how I would progress through my service in the force? I was eventually sent to a station in county Dublin, which was part of the Dublin Metropolitan Area.

The Station building itself was a large old building situated on a raised area off the roadway with a fairly steep driveway to the front of the Station. There was a garden area at the front with a parking area also at the front entrance for the Garda patrol cars.

The main parking area was to the rear of the building, and there was a fairly large garden which was used by some of the station party to grow vegetables. There was a high wall at the rear of the garden, and in the wall of the garden, there was a gateway that led to a large park called the Phoenix Park, which was the biggest public park in Ireland.

Members of the station party used to use this gateway to go out to the park for training, and I used to use it fairly often myself to go running when I became a member of the Garda Boat Club, which was based in Island Bridge. I had to keep myself fit.

There was a "sitting room" with a television, and a fireplace, which was used by the residential members of the station party. The members who were using the accommodation also had to look after the fire, and keep it lit as the building was very cold, especially during the cold spells. There was also a piano in the dining room. There was another benefit to having members living in the station quarters; at times, there would be a call for backup when one of the beat members who would be on duty would be coming under attack, or there was trouble brewing in our area, and anybody who was in the station at the time would go to give assistance using our own transport, even though we were off duty. This was a regular occurrence.

There were a number of members of the station party living in the official accommodation. I was the newest addition, and many of the others had been there for some time, and were a mixed bunch, some of them with a lot of service. Unlike the present day, all the members had to be unmarried when joining the force, and it was not till years later that married men, and women were allowed to join the force.

The station of Chapelizod was a District Headquarters, with a Superintendent, and an Inspector in charge. I was in the day room with my Sergeant, Gerry Harrington, waiting to be partnered with one of the other members during one of my first weeks. I was leaning on the counter while waiting when a man who looked like a country farmer walked in. I said hello to him, and was about to ask him if I could help him when my Sergeant introduced him as the Inspector in charge. I immediately jumped up to attention, and saluted the Inspector as was the normal routine in the training centre, and the Inspector said it's alright that I didn't have to do the saluting now that I was out of the training centre.

I suppose when you think of it, it was less than seven years since I was "released" from the institution in St Joseph's, Tralee, so I would still be on edge to be sure of doing the right thing, and it seemed that I had left one institution, and ended up in another, the Garda Training Centre.

This Inspector, Joseph McGovern, was a nice man. He liked to play the piano with a number of lads who used to play other musical instruments. One played the saxophone, another the violin, and now, and again, we all used to get together in the dining hall, where we had a few great musical evenings at the station. The staff Sergeant who was attached to the Superintendent's office used to compare, and of course, sing a few songs. That all changed in a couple of years when the station closed down, and we all moved into the new station up the "hill" in the middle of the housing estate.

My pay came rolled up in a plain white sheet of paper from the pay sergeant, with my name, and the amount I was receiving written on it. Of course, there were deductions made for all my meals, my live-in accommodation, and of course, my income tax, and social insurance. I didn't have much left for myself to carry me over to the next payday. There were times when we would have to ask for an advance of some of our pay.

As my particular station was a District Headquarters, it was a very busy place; although it was set in a small village, it was responsible for a large housing estate with a sizable population of more than 40,000, which was about 15 minutes' walk from the station. There were two other stations attached to the District, Lucan, and Clondalkin. I worked on a three-roster system during my first year or two there, working two months on days alternating late, and early shifts, and one month on night duty. On the day shift, I was entitled to two days off each month, and on the night shift, I would be entitled to four nights off; this was, of course, only if I could be spared. Any days not taken were put into an extra duty book, and in most cases, forgotten about. Married members, and those with some service got the first choice of days, and nights off.

There were a few internal incidents of note that happened in the unit that I worked with while at the old station in Chapelizod. Now, upstairs at the front of the building, there was a snooker room with a full-size snooker table, which was used fairly frequently by the station party. On each unit, there was a station Sergeant, and a beat Sergeant, and when the station Sergeant was off, the beat Sergeant took up the office duty.

Now, the beat Sergeant in my unit was a bit "soft ", and used to be taken in by some of the members of the unit. One of the unit members, who was a motorcyclist, with the help of another, brought the motorcycle upstairs to the snooker room, and left it running on its stand. The beat Sergeant was down in the office underneath, and heard the noise, and couldn't make out what it was until he went upstairs, and discovered the motorcycle running on its stand. He lost his cool, and for the rest of the night, he couldn't be spoken to. Nobody, of course, owned up to it, but he had his suspicions. Now that Sergeant was very committed to his work in the Garda Siochana was very proud of the force, and was the type of man who did not look forward to retirement from the force, as the Gardai was his life. After he did retire, he only survived for one year in retirement before he died.

On another occasion, there was a report about a double-deck bus being stolen in the area. A lookout was kept for it, and later that night, the bus was located, and driven by one of the members of the unit down to the station, and parked up right in front of the station. It took up the whole front of the station. The same beat Sergeant was on office duty. Under normal circumstances, the bus company would be called out to take in the bus from where it was found; this was done to get up the nose of the Sergeant. The bus company sent somebody out later, and the driver had a lot of difficulty getting the bus back out onto the road.

What I was not aware of at that time was that in June of the following year [1969], it would be the start of far-reaching changes in the working conditions of the Garda Siochana as a result of recommendations made by the Conroy Commission of inquiry, being implemented, which would bring big improvements in the Garda Siochana pay, and conditions of work.

Gone would be the months of night duty, which would be replaced with one week on night duty every four weeks, extra days off each week, and of course, extra pay. This, of course, brought its own administration problems as the three-unit system became a four-unit system, which left it that there would be less numbers on each working unit. Eventually, the new system got up, and running, and there was no going back.

I recall my first "big" case, being a chase after a young fellow who had failed to pay for his bag of chips at the chip shop near where I was on my night duty. I managed to catch him, and brought him back to the chipper. I don't recall what the outcome was, but it stuck in my memory as my first piece of action as a young Garda eager to get into my stride.

During my first months of service as a trainee Garda, I would have had a little more freedom on my own sometimes as, at that time, many of the senior Garda had been transferred to the border areas because of the foot, and mouth outbreak, which had occurred in 1967. The normal routine would have been for new recruits to be accompanied by a senior Garda at all times for at least the first six months.

My duties varied from doing beat duty, and being an observer in the patrol car to being station orderly with the Sergeant at the station. This variety of duties gave me a great early insight into the workings of the Garda. At this stage, too, I had a new station Sergeant, Michael Concannon, who was a great mentor to me. Gerry Harrington had been transferred to Lucan, which was closer to his home, as he was getting over a medical condition.

Ironically, where I had been transferred to, for my first station, I had worked with the bakery firm, and had delivered bread to some parts of the area I was now working in as a Garda.

Early in my service in my first station, I was asked to join the Garda Boat Club, and started to train with them a couple of evenings a week. This would have been in late 1968 or early 1969. It was a good way to keep fit, and pass the time as I didn't have a lot of money anyway to do anything else. I got to row in the maiden eighths, as we were called, because we were beginners. It was a great experience for me as I went around the country with the boat club, and even went across the border up north to row in Belfast, even though it was during the time of the troubles. Also, I was given time off from work to train with the boat club, so it had its added advantages too.

I was supposed to return to the training centre for my part II training sometime in April or May 1969 for two weeks with my original class. Because the rowing season was in full swing at that time, I got a dispensation through the Boat Clubs committee intervention, and my part II training was put back to July of that year. Of course, on the 20th of that month of July 1969, history was made with Apollo 11 landing the first man on the Moon, which I duly watched with everybody else at the Training Centre that evening. After that, I never again looked at the Moon with the same reverence.

My return to the Training centre was, of course, not without incident as after doing my part II examination, I became ill with a bad attack of tonsillitis, and had to be confined to bed on doctor's orders. On that particular weekend, we were supposed to return to our stations, and the Training centre was closing down completely for holidays.

I was taken from my sick bed, got dressed, was driven down to the railway station in one of the driving school cars, and put on the train. I was told that I would be met off the train in Dublin by a car, and brought to the Garda hospital at Garda Headquarters in Phoenix Park. At that time, the Garda hospital was used for Gardai who were ill, and were committed by the local Garda Doctor for treatment. That was a delightful bit of VIP treatment for a trainee Garda at the time. I spent over a week in the hospital, and was released back to my station, where I spent some time on sick leave. Mind you, for years after, I used to suffer a lot from tonsillitis.

My return to my old station didn't last long as politics had intervened as always. They had completed building a new station in the middle of the housing estate which was the main working area covered by my station. This was the first of many moves from old buildings to new buildings that happened throughout my career. My old station closed down so I had to go, and find accommodation elsewhere as there was no living accommodation at the new building. Luckily, I found a room in a house close to my area of work that one of the more senior Garda had rented out for himself. This would have been maybe around early 1971.

I can fix that date reasonably well with another event that occurred, as on the 10th of November 1970, while still at Chapelizod Station, I with other members of the force from other districts, attended the District Courts in Dublin, where we were presented with certificates by a District Justice, from the Irish Society of Prevention of Cruelty to Animals, for Meritorious Service in the protection of animals.

It was a great feather in my cap as a young Garda with just over two, and half years of service in the Garda Siochana. The case involved the death of a horse in one of the parks in the area where I worked. I had carried out the investigation as to who was responsible for the death, and found the culprit, who was dealt with in the courts. We got a bit of media exposure with our photographs appearing in one of the daily papers. I still retain copies of the photographs to this day.

Sometime before moving out of Chapelizod station, I had my first experience of meeting with death during my service. I was on station duty one night with my Sergeant, and we were out on the front lawn of the station. Now, the station was on a higher level than a road that passed in front of it, and when you looked over the wall, there was about a ten-foot drop onto the footpath below. We were taking in the fresh air when we heard a loud bang.

On looking over the wall, we saw a small car buried into the pillar of the front gate of a school down below. We both rushed down, and found that there were two people in the car, one male, the driver, and a female in the front passenger seat. The Sergeant went to the driver's side, and I went to the passenger side, where there was a young blond girl. Sadly, the girl was dead; she had died on impact. It was one of those incidents that has always stayed in my memory.

Many Garda stations over that period of time used to have callers to the stations who were "Knights of the road", and slept rough. Chapelizod was no exception, and there was one particular man who used to call fairly regularly to our station. He would be fed in the kitchen of the station, and had been "adopted" by the station party so much so that sometimes he would be given a shower or maybe some clothes to replace what he was wearing, especially during winter time for the cold weather.

The sad news arrived that this particular man had passed away, so the station party got together, and arranged his funeral in the local church not too far from the station. A big number of the station party turned out in uniform for the funeral, and gave him a guard of honour from the church, with uniform members, including myself, carrying his coffin. Independent Newspapers were on hand to record the sad occasion.

I'm not sure at what juncture I started operating from my new station up the hill, but it would have been around 1971. I would have been in that new station at the time I had been asked by my Superintendent if I was interested in joining a new crime task force that was being formed at Dublin Castle in the second half of 1971.

As well as all the movements, and changes within my job in the Garda Siochana, I had a lot going on in my private life, not least of these was trying to locate my family members whom I didn't know. There were six of my family members I had never met. I only knew of my brother Jerry, who had been in St Joseph's with me for some years, and who had brought me to see my father for the first time in my life in 1961. I also had met my oldest sister Mary, who lived in Liverpool, some years after I had reached 16 years of age while visiting my father in Ballylongford. My sister Mary, who, I later discovered, was the eldest girl in the family had wanted me to go to Liverpool to live there. That was before I joined the Garda Force. I visited my sister Mary in Liverpool at some stage, where I met up with another sister, Ann, who also lived in Liverpool, not too far from Mary.

CHAPTER EIGHT

Family Tracing

I had met my eldest sister Mary, at our home in Ballylongford some-time in the mid-sixties when I used to make trips home to meet my father, and she was home from England on holiday with one of her children. I had, at this time, with the help of my brother Jerry, and my sister Mary, tracked down some addresses in England where some of my family members lived. It was that time in the nineteen sixties that I learned I had four brothers, and five sisters, all of whom had moved to England years before.

London to meet family members, and putting my foot in it
Now, there was a practice in place at the old Chapelizod station, where some members of the station party, took a month off during the summer months for the purpose of doing work in England for the four weeks to earn a little extra money as the pay was so poor. This had gone on for a number of years. One of the lads had contact with a builder in London who was from the west of Ireland, and he agreed to take on most of the boys who travelled for the four weeks. Of course, as everybody knew at that time, Irish builders were in great demand for building in England.

In the summer of 1970, I took part in one of these ventures, and got a job on a building site in Slough, in London, which was hard work, and long hours. There were about six in the group that travelled, but when we got there, I discovered that we weren't the only group making the trip; there were others there from other districts in the city. It was like a Garda convention. There was a well-known meeting place that was used by many builders to meet up with clients called the "Rising Sun Pub", and that was also the meeting place for the payouts on a Friday night.

I was also going to take the opportunity to make contact with some of my lost family members in London. I worked for three of the four weeks on the building site, and then informed the boss that I had to go into central London. Of course, I kept all of this to myself, and didn't disclose to anybody the purpose of my visit to London central. I had an address I had got for one of my older sisters, Joan.

When first I knocked at the door of her house at Inverness Terrace, Bayswater, in London, and it was opened by a lady I didn't know, but she knew instinctively, straight away, who I was even though she hadn't seen me since I had been taken away at about nine months old nearly twenty-five years previously. I had made no contact with her before I went over; it was to be a surprise call, which it was.

We would reminisce about that first meeting during some of my visits to her at her nursing home residence in Malta. She used to tell me she remembered that from her downstairs apartment in inverness Terrace, she was looking out her window, and spotted me coming down the stairs before I had knocked at her door. She knew instinctively who I was, even though she hadn't seen me for all those years since I was a baby.

I stayed with her, and her family for the week. I also met two of my other sisters, Lily, and Cathy, and my eldest brother, Michael, who lived in Harlow in Essex on the outskirts of London. At long last, I had discovered some members of my lost family whom I had never met before in my life. I would find it difficult to describe the feelings I had at that time; it was the opening of a door to a new world of family.

Over that couple of years, I had met up with many members of my lost family who lived both in London, and Liverpool. Most of them were married, and had their own families. From time to time over the coming years, I would visit them, and they would come to Ireland on visits. The fact that many of us had passed through institutions as children was never discussed; it was a taboo subject.

But there was still a void in the family makeup, I still had to locate two of my older brothers, the second eldest, and the third eldest, Paddy, and John. Every time I met up with my older sisters, they always spoke about Paddy, and John, as nobody had a clue where they were. After I had retired at the end of 2000, I increased my efforts to carry out searches for my two brothers. In 2003, I eventually made contact with my brother John's wife, June by phone in Derby, who informed me that my brother John had died on the 9th of December 2000.

That contact was made on the 9th of January 2003, and later that year, I made a trip to their home in Darby, and met John's wife, and family. Around the same time, I had also traced my other brother Paddy, whose family lived in Nottingham, but unfortunately, he had passed away on the 31st of May 1996. I went to Nottingham as well that year, and met Paddy's two daughters, Mary, and Patricia. In September 2004, John's wife, June passed away, and I travelled to Derby to attend the funeral.

While with my sister Joan on my first visit there in 1970, my visit didn't go without incident. Now Joan was living with her partner Frans, who was Maltese by birth, and had lived in London for a number of years. [now we have hit on the Maltese connection] They had two daughters, Francesca, and Maggie, who were very young. Frans was into the property business in a small way, and was in the process of renovating a fairly large house, and converting it into flats. He had a number of people working for him, and he brought me to see the house.

The front downstairs flat was completed, and they were expecting someone to move into it in a couple of days. It was a one-room self-contained flat with an ornate ceiling. Frans brought me upstairs to a room just overhead that the men were working on. Now, they had floorboards taken up, and were in the process of laying pipes, and electric cables. I did the unthinkable, and put my big foot through the ceiling of the flat below that had been made ready for occupation. This incident was always brought up every time I met Frans for years afterwards. It was always a good laugh.

One of my sisters that I had met while with Joan was Cathy. She was living in a small flat, in a house that was owned by Frans, not far from Joan, which was provided to her by Frans, and Joan. She had a small child, about 3 or 4 years old, and she looked to be living in very poor conditions. This was a huge shock to me as, of course, I would have known nothing about it. She was embarrassed at meeting up with her long-lost younger brother under these conditions.

She was an unmarried mother living in the heart of London, being catered for, to some degree by her older sister. I had a camera with me, and took a photograph of Cathy, and the child. We spoke for a while, and of course, she couldn't work because she had to stay at home, and mind her child. The father was nowhere to be found, and Cathy herself wasn't too forthcoming with his particulars, only that he was an Irishman. After some time, I left with Joan, and couldn't get Cathy's situation out of my mind. I promised my sister Joan that I would try to do something about her situation when I got back to Ireland now that I had all the particulars of her, and her child.

That was a week that I will never forget. I returned to my station with mixed feelings, on a high at meeting with long lost family members, and of course, huge concern at the state I found my sister Cathy in. These were matters I of course, could not discuss with anybody, as I would have too much explaining to do about my past, and family situation. I had to keep my mind on my job.

Now, when I got back from London, Cathy was foremost on my mind, and I had to think up a plan of action to assist her in her situation. My sister Cathy was the youngest of my three sisters, sent to The Pembroke Alms House, Residential Institution for girls, around April 1946, after the death of our mother in March of that year. This was information that came into my possession when I had almost completed my writing of the account of my life. It was a convent school in Tralee, not too far from St Joseph's Residential Institution, where I had been detained myself. It also turned out to be the same convent that I used to go to serve mass for the nuns, which I discovered at a later time.

My mentor, Gerry Smyth, who was instrumental in having me placed in my job in Weartex, had a sister who was a nun in a convent in the south east of Dublin City. I had become very friendly with her over the years, as myself, and her nephew, Stephen Smyth, who was Gerry's son, used to go out to the convent very often to do some odd jobs like cleaning windows, some painting, and putting up the Christmas Tree, and decorations for them. The convent was an orphanage for young girls that the nuns cared for, and it seemed very well run with only about 20 girls there from young age to about sixteen years. They went outside to the local schools. There was a reverend mother with about four or five other nuns, including sister Frances, who was Stephen's Aunt.

I had kept up contact with the Smyth family, and sister Frances, even after joining the Garda. I made contact with sister Frances, and gave her the details of Cathy's situation in London, and asked her if anything could be done about it. I left it with sister Frances for a time, and when she came back to me, she told me to get Cathy to bring the child over to the convent, and they would make a place for her. I was over the moon as during these discussions, I had been in constant touch with my sister Cathy, and she was willing to have her daughter cared for.

My sister Cathy arrived with the child, and she was taken into care by sister Frances in the convent. A condition was put on Cathy that she would visit the child as often as she could once she got herself settled into a job, and was earning some money. Cathy was good to her word and, when possible, made visits three, and four times a year to see her child. In later years, when I was married, she used to stay with me on some of these visits, and sometimes would bring her daughter with her. The child stayed at the home until she was sixteen, and then joined her mother in London, who had built up steady employment over the years, and even purchased her own apartment in the heart of London.

Cathy's daughter went on to get married in Ireland, and was given away on her wedding day by myself, her uncle. She is now resident in Ireland with her own three grown-up children. Unfortunately, her husband passed away some years ago from a long-term illness, leaving her to bring up her children herself. Cathy passed away on the 3rd of April 2016, leaving a nice legacy of an Apartment in the heart of London to her daughter.

When I think back now, it was a correct decision at the time, but I had my moments of hesitation in consigning a second-generation child to institutionalised life. I always kept my own experiences in mind, and of course, my sister Cathy's, of our time in institutions.

CHAPTER NINE

New move, new building

Sometime within the next twelve months, Chapelizod station closed, and we moved up the "hill "to our new station in Ballyfermot. Now things were a bit reversed; if we were put on the beat in the old village of Chapelizod, we had to go down the "hill "to do our duty there, from the way it used to be going up the hill from the old station to the large housing estate called Ballyfermot. As I said before, it was a busy place, and there were always some incidents happening, a few of which I will go into to give a flavour of the type of things that were part of the everyday happenings for us doing our duty in the Garda force at that time. I was a reasonably active member of the force, and liked to keep busy, hence the teaming up with another active colleague in several cases.

Electrified door handle

I was involved in an investigation with another colleague regarding property being stolen from cars, including car radios, and we had arrested a suspect who lived on the north side of the city. During the course of the investigation, thousands of pounds worth of property was recovered at various locations in the north of the city near where the suspect lived. He had taken over several garages in a flat complex where he stored the stolen property. He was charged, and brought before the courts, and allowed out on bail pending the preparation of the case. He failed to appear for his trial in court, and a warrant was issued for his arrest.

My colleague, and I, accompanied by a number of other Garda for backup, went with the arrest warrant to the culprit's address in the north of the city. The address was a flat which was several floors up in a block of flats. We knocked on the door of the flat, and got a very negative response from the occupants. We heard movement inside the flat, and knocked again, and we called out that it was the Garda, and to open the door. A man's voice came from inside the flat saying not to come near the door as the door lock had been electrified, and anybody touching the door handle would be electrocuted.

We stayed outside the door on the balcony, and kept the occupant talking for a while until things got very quiet. On looking over the balcony towards where the front of the flat was, we saw the culprit drop two of his children from his balcony down to somebody on the next balcony below. Immediately, some of the officers went down to the next balcony.

There was a standoff situation for a period of time, and eventually, we put the door in with force, and gained entry. When entry was made, we did find that there was an electric cable coming from the kitchen area to the door with exposed wiring, but it hadn't been plugged into any socket. The culprit was arrested, and brought away, and the social welfare department were notified of the incident with the children. This gives an insight into the many dangers we face in such situations.

Injured during an incident; 1st of July 1971

This was an incident in the afternoon of the 1st of July 1971 involving a stolen motorcycle that had been abandoned, and a suspect was being chased on foot by a patrol unit from the neighbouring district. I was an observer in the patrol car at the time, and we went to the assistance of the other patrol unit. The chase ended with the suspect jumping into the river, and swimming towards a weir down from the Garda boat club.

There was a boat just leaving the river's edge, and I asked them to take me to the other side of the river to cut off the suspect from going over the weir. We succeeded in diverting him to the other bank, and I took off my shoes, and socks, and [foolishly] waded to the other side of the river, near a wooded bank where the suspect was making his exit from the river. When I got to the bank, I raised my foot to get onto the bank when I saw that my left foot was bleeding badly.

Luckily, there were other Garda on this river bank, and they helped me out of the water, and put something around my foot to ease the bleeding. They brought me to St James's hospital, and I got thirteen stitches on the sole of my left foot. I must have walked on a piece of broken glass. I was off duty for some time, and had to recuperate at my new lodgings for some time after. Of course, like all incidents of this nature, I had to make out a report for record purposes. I still have a copy of that report.

In early 1971 I had been sent to the Training Centre, Templemore, to do the official Garda driving course, which I completed. I was then deemed eligible to drive Official Garda Vehicles when required to do so.

There were many other incidents that I was involved with during my time at Chapelizod, and Ballyfermot stations. These would include accident investigations, attending to burglary scenes, family disputes, and investigating money lenders who were giving loans to people, mostly women with children, while holding on to their children's allowance books. They would meet them outside the post office on children's allowance day, give them their books, and meet them on the way out to take back the books, and take the cash for payment as well. It was a method of extortion used by several money lenders, and I am glad to be able to say I had some success in a number of these cases.

Crime Task Force

During the second half of 1971, it was decided by the powers that be to set up a Crime Task Force to be based at Dublin Metropolitan Area Headquarters in Dublin Castle. This was to be a uniform unit working in two shifts, afternoons, and late evenings. Each unit was made up of about a dozen Garda, with a number of patrol cars, motorcycles, a unit Sergeant, and foot patrols. We operated out of prefab buildings because of the shortage of office spaces in the Castle, as there were a lot of renovations taking place at the time.

The Task Force was to be used to saturate a particular District or sub-district that was having an increase in crime in that area. A local District Officer would send in a request to have the Task Force brought into his District to bring crime under control in a particular area. The Task Force operated in the City Centre Districts at first, but then we had to expand our operations to surrounding Districts because the criminals started to move from District to District away from where the Task Force operated.

The Task Force was made up of men from many of the Districts in the Dublin Metropolitan Area. I was asked by my District Officer if I was interested; of course, I jumped at the chance; I was going into the unknown, and it was something new. I started with the Task Force in September 1971, and the duration of duty was for a period of six months. I would have had just over three years of service in the Garda Force at that time.

When the Task Force members met for the first time at Dublin Castle, we were brought up to speed as to our duties by the Superintendent in charge of the Task Force. I discovered at this meeting that I was one of the few who were sent in straight from the uniform section.

All the others had been working with their local Detective Units, and had to go back into uniform when they were assigned to the Task Force. Many of them weren't too happy about that, but part of the reason they were chosen was because of their knowledge of criminals in their respective areas. We all eventually settled into our new tasks, and all got on well together.

It was a busy six months. We worked in several of the city centre Districts over time, and it helped me to get to know Dublin city better. As members of the Task Force, we also became well known to the various stations where we brought our prisoners for processing, and of course, got to know the desk Sergeant at these stations. The officer in charge of the Task Force was a gentleman, and he, and I were to meet up again in the not too distant future; he was Superintendent Tim Farrell.

At that time, in Dublin City, there was what was known as "no go areas". If the Garda had to go into those areas, they had to go in with plenty of manpower. One late evening, while on the late shift, my partner and I decided to have a look at one of these areas. Now, we didn't go right in, but were walking close by when suddenly there was a crash over our heads. A bottle had been thrown from one of the flats at us, which goes to show that they, the villains, never sleep; it was well after midnight when that incident occurred.

British Embassy Duty

In early February 1972, while I was still in the Crime Task Force, the unit was called on to back up Garda members doing duty at the British Embassy, which was based in Merrion Square, in the heart of Dublin city. A few years previous, the "Troubles" in Northern Ireland had flared up, and were spilling over into the Republic. Protests were happening in many areas, but the biggest was at the British Embassy, and it went on for three nights. The protesters, who were being urged on by members of the provisional IRA, were gathered in their hundreds around Merrion Square.

It was a very tense time for the Garda, including us, the Task Force members, lining up across the front of the Embassy, and the protesters throwing missiles from the crowd towards the building over the heads of the Garda, at first breaking windows, and causing damage to the building. It was a very frustrating time for us, the Garda, as we were not allowed to take action or retaliate against this behaviour. The protesters had a lorry across the road from the building, which was being used as a platform for speech makers who kept urging the crowds along. The missiles then became Molotov cocktails being thrown at the building, which set parts of it on fire. This situation went on for three nights, and eventually, on the third night, with a different Officer in overall charge, he ordered a baton charge on the protesters after first warning them to disperse before the charge. That was the end of the protests in that area for some time.

The Embassy building was completely destroyed by the fire, and one has to ask the question now: what was the policy behind the indecision on the first two nights of the terror? The Garda were put in serious danger on those nights by inadequate leadership, or did politics play a part? A number of Gardai were assaulted by the crowd withdrawing as a result of the baton charge.

On that third night before the baton charge, there was an incident when the driver of the lorry being used as the platform tried to drive it near the steps of the Embassy building, almost running down a number of the Garda in the process. I was near the steps, and almost had my foot run over as the wheel of the lorry grazed the toe of one of my boots. The driver was quickly overpowered, and dragged from the cab of the lorry, and detained.

Marriage

In the mists of all this, I had arranged to be married within two weeks of the events at Merrion Square. I had been engaged to a girl, Margaret, from Johnstown, Naas, whom I had met some time previously at a dance in the Garda club Harrington Street. The wedding took place on the 15th of February 1972 at St David's Church, Naas, Co Kildare. I didn't have a great representation at the wedding as most of my family members didn't attend I only started to trace most of them, and was only in the process of getting to know them. I think my brother Jerry was there. I do remember Joan's partner Frans turning up at the wedding from London.

I later heard the story of how Frans got to the wedding. Seemingly my sister Joan couldn't travel so Frans decided he would come, and he never informed me he was travelling, and he hadn't a clue where he was going. When he arrived in Ireland by car, he was driving a V8 Rover at the time; he made his way to Naas Garda station to ask where I lived, and was informed that there was a Garda with a similar name living in Naas, and they gave him the address. Frans called the address that was given to him, but when he met that man, he saw it wasn't me. Luckily, the man he spoke to was aware where there was a wedding taking place that might be the person he was looking for, and directed him to St David's Church.

The wedding was a small enough affair, and after the reception, we drove off on our honeymoon; I had hired a car for the week. We travelled to Limerick for the first few days, and then went up to Galway for the rest of the week. When we arrived back, we had to stay at Margaret's parent's house for a few weeks. The house I had bought at the time wasn't yet completed. I had purchased it for something in excess of £4000.00 Irish pounds at the time. We eventually moved into the house, and had a lot of cleaning, and furnishing to do over time. The normal practice during that time was that when a woman got married, she had to give up her job, and wasn't allowed to work, so we became a one-wage family.

I had purchased the house sometime in the previous year; it was a three-bedroom, end of terrace house in an estate of about two hundred houses near Leixlip village in north Kildare. Because it was an end house, there was a side entrance to the back of the house, but unfortunately, it was not wide enough for a garage space. At that time of purchasing, the house was in my name only, as was the normal situation, but in later years; the law was changed to have both husband, and wife as joint owners even though only one of the couple actually paid for the house.

I went back to work in Dublin Castle as I was not yet finished with the Task Force. When I arrived back, I was given a presentation by my unit, and Superintendent as a wedding gift. I was very taken by the thought as it was something I wasn't used to, and I never had a presentation made to me before.

We, as the first Task Force group, remained together till the end of March 1972, at which time all of us went back to our stations. Any member that wanted to could have stayed for a further six months, but we all declined the invitation, it was a voluntary duty, and most of the members who had been in plain clothes, which were nearly all of them, wanted to get back with their Detective Units, and back into plain clothes.

They still felt the discomfort of being back in uniform, and of course, were coming in for some good-natured slagging from their own station parties about being back in uniform. Overall, we had some good successes over the period of our time in the Task Force. Over the following years, the Task Force became the training ground for future members of Detective Branch Crime Ordinary.

Return to Ballyfermot

When I arrived back at my own station, Ballyfermot, back to my own unit, I became a bit unsettled as I had gotten used to plenty of activity during my time in the Task Force, the increased new experiences I got, and of course the extra daily allowance I received while doing duty away from my station. After some time back at my station, I saw that they were looking for applicants for the Traffic Department who were based at Dublin Castle. I sent an application through my Superintendent to go forward for an interview to join the Traffic Department. This would have been mid to late 1972.

My Superintendent called me a few days later after receiving my application, and asked me if I was really interested in the Traffic Department. He told me the reason he was asking me was that he was considering asking me to go work with the local Detective Unit in plain clothes if I was interested. At the time, this position would have put me as a trainee Detective. I jumped at the chance, and immediately wrote to withdraw my application to join the Traffic Department. Not long after, I started working with the local Detective Unit, and settled in, in due course. The fact that my Superintendent at the time, Eugene Clifford, was a "Kerry man" wouldn't have influenced his "decision" in any way!!!

Prison Protests

Sometime towards the end of 1972, there was another flare-up of the troubles in the republic of Ireland. A high-ranking member of the PIRA had been sentenced by the courts to prison, and was being detained in Mountjoy prison. There were protests taking place around the prison, and a large force of Gardai was sent to secure the external perimeter of the prison. I had to return to uniform duties, and was sent to the area of the prison with other uniform members as backup.

Family moments

Now, at the time, my wife was expecting our first child. I had worked over a twelve-hour shift, and got home late that night, well after midnight. When I got home, and was getting ready for bed, my wife mentioned that she might need to go to the hospital as she felt what she thought were labour pains starting. Of course, this was our first child, and neither of us had any experience of this situation before. There was a discussion as to whether we should go to the hospital or not. I remember saying to her, "make your mind up because if my head hits that pillow, I will not be getting up", I was out on my feet.

The decision was made, and I drove my wife to the maternity hospital, and left her there, saying I would see her the next day, and went home to bed. The next morning, I had to go to the courts in the city as I was dealing with a case in court. After the court, I went straight to the hospital to find that I was a dad, and the baby was a boy. This was on the 27th of November 1972.

It was a trying time around the city at that time as on the previous day, the 26th of November 1972, as well as the protests, a car bomb had gone off in the city centre, injuring about forty people, some seriously, so there were huge traffic restrictions in place. It could be said that my first child was born at a traumatic time.

But that wasn't the last traumatic situation with a child born into my family. On the 23rd of May 1974, my second child, also a son, was born six days after three bombs were detonated in different areas in Dublin city on the 17thh of May, killing at least twenty-six people. On the same day, a bomb was also detonated in Co Monaghan, killing at least another ten people. These were dangerous times on the island of Ireland.

I applied for a few days' leave after the birth of my first child, and then returned to duty with my detective unit at Ballyfermot Station in late 1972.

CHAPTER TEN

Ballyfermot Detective Unit

It would be difficult to describe all of my time with my local Detective Unit, as the work was very intensive, and it was an exceptionally busy area, and a busy time. While in plain clothes, I worked two shifts, a day shift, and an evening shift, and would have been involved in a variety of investigations, and incidents. The people working in the Detective Unit became very good colleagues, and shared their experiences, knowledge, and advice in being a detective.

Without going into too much detail about the many cases I was involved in, there are a couple of incidents that stick in my mind. Now, when there was a serious incident in another part of our division, and backup was required from other detective units in the division, whoever was on duty would respond.

Bomb on the Railway

One of these incidents happened in the early 1970s; while I was on the late shift one night, my partner, and I were called on as backup, and went to the scene of an explosion on the railway tracks running north of the division. When we arrived, we joined other units in a search of the area, and discovered a body on part of the tracks with the head missing. It was a gruesome discovery and, for a young trainee Detective like myself, not an easy scene to forget. A further search along the tracks not too far away, the head was discovered. Like many other incidents throughout my service, this was one never to be forgotten.

The local Detective Unit of the area, with the assistance of the Special Detective Unit who dealt with terror-related incidents carried out further investigations. At the conclusion of the investigation over the following weeks, it was established that the body was that of a known terrorist, and that he was carrying a bomb that exploded prematurely, killing him before he could plant it. This would have occurred at the early stages of my attachment to the Ballyfermot Detective Unit when terrorists were beginning to cause havoc in the Republic of Ireland.

Murder, and Robbery

The second incident was a robbery, and murder of a man on Friday, the 3rd of August 1973, in west Dublin. That man was on his way from the bank with the wages for his staff at the old British Leyland car manufacturing plant when he was attacked, robbed, and shot dead on the old Naas Road, Dublin. About two weeks later, a number of people had been arrested in connection with that murder, and some of them were being detained at a Garda station, which was in my division.

They had all been detained under the Offences against the State Act 1939, which was introduced under the Emergency Powers Act of 1939. The Emergency Powers Act was enacted for the purpose of the preservation of the state [Ireland], in time of war, and the maintenance of public order. Also, under the Emergency Powers Act, a Special Criminal Court was established, with three judges sitting in judgement. Several amendments have been made to this legislation over a number of years.

On the evening of the 14th of August 1973, with two Detective Sergeants, my partner, and I were asked to go there to assist in the investigation, and the interrogation of the suspects.

At the time, it was a shocking incident, but for me, it was a great experience to be involved in such a serious investigation so early in my detective career. I also had the opportunity to interview one of the suspects on the night in question. Three of those detained were later charged with murder, and robbery on the 3rd of August 1973. They were members of a breakaway terrorist group from the PIRA.

Because of the nature of the case, and the involvement of terrorists, the Director of Public Prosecutions had the case transferred to the Special Criminal Court.

The case was heard before the Special Criminal Court, which had been set up under the Offences against the State Act 1939 to deal with terrorist organisations. This was also a first for me when I was called to give evidence in this case in the Special Criminal Court. All three were convicted. They were sentenced to life imprisonment, and sent to Portlaoise maximum security prison to serve their sentences. Sometime later, these three prisoners were involved in an attempted escape from the prison, and one of them was shot during the course of the attempt by a member of the armed forces on duty at the prison, and died later in hospital.

I had been involved in the investigation of these incidents, which included my part in my first murder investigation, which led to a Special Criminal Court trial. This was just about five years after I had joined the force, and about 12 years after I had departed St Joseph's Institution.

Every now, and then, I would pause, and contemplate my satisfaction with how I was progressing in my life, considering my humble, and traumatic beginnings. Being involved in cases such as those described gave me great momentum in pursuing my future career. The comments the detective made to me in the tailor shop in St Josephs, Tralee, in 1960/1961, "That one day you will make a good detective," very often came to my mind as a true prediction of my future.

Making the headlines

Towards the end of 1973, a case I had been involved in made the headlines in the Irish Times when a solicitor made allegations against the Detective Unit in Ballyfermot. It involved the search of a house on the 7th of November 1973, in which I was involved, and the arrest of a suspect who was brought to Ballyfermot, and detained for questioning. The report didn't mention any members of the search party by name, but went on to mention the names of the Superintendent, and two Inspectors that this solicitor had been in communication with regarding the complaint he had made.

That put pressure on the named officers to have the matter investigated, which they did over time. As the investigation was ongoing, its outcome had to be awaited. The allegations included "that his client's wife, and children were frightened", "that the man was taken to a Garda station on false pretences, and questioned for hours"," he was technically assaulted by one of them[the Garda]", ", and his wife was told that her husband could be held in custody for a week".

The solicitor looked for a copy of the search warrant used on that occasion, which he got, and he continued to bombard the investigating Inspector with written requests regarding the investigation. He also stated that he was sending copies of all correspondence to the four Dail deputies for his client's constituency, and to the Dublin morning papers, hence the report in the Irish Times on the 12th of December 1973.

This date of the 12th December brought back memories to me as on that date twenty-one years previous; I had been brought to court at Tralee, where I was sentenced to St Joseph's Residential Institution, and brought there on the 12th of December 1952 at seven years, and three months old. Where were the legal eagles at that time when a real breach of human rights was being committed?

It was not uncommon for certain solicitors to make complaints against investigating Garda by way of trying in some way to frustrate the investigation of a suspect. I would learn that fact over the following years as I became the subject of numerous complaints, which, when they were investigated, were found to be baseless, and false.

The solicitor also quoted in the paper, "the disgraceful incident that occurred as a result of your officer's actions deserves to be known, and you must agree you have had a chance to settle it privately". I often wonder what he was looking for when saying that, maybe cash under the counter.

I have no problem recalling this incident as I still have a copy of the cutting from the Irish Times paper, but I don't have any recollection of what the particular case was about at the time. As stated in the newspaper article, the person was never charged with any offence.

It would be the first of many reports that would involve me to appear in the media during the course of my service in the Garda Siochana, the majority of which would be favourable.

Now, being attached to a close-knit Detective Unit, there was always a bit of banter going on between the members of the Unit, and one of the main instigators of this was Detective Garda, who was one of the more senior members of the unit. The unit was overseen by two Detective Sergeant's, and a Detective Inspector. Also starting with the unit as a trainee at the time I returned from my stint in the Crime Task Force was another Garda, who had been on the same uniform unit as myself, where we did beat duty together, and got on reasonably well with each other.

The senior Detective Garda was of the old school; he presented an air of superiority, giving the impression he was different from others. I suppose I would say that I got on reasonably well with him, except that I became a target of some of his banter, and in later years, for his deviousness.

Me being a Kerry man, and the other trainee being a Dublin man made us perfect subjects for his attention, and his deviousness. The Detective Chief Superintendent in the crime section for the DMA was a Kerry man named John Joy. The senior Detective Garda used this to play the other trainee off against myself by making up stories, and situations involving both myself, and the Detective Chief Supt. Giving the impression that I got to visit John Joy very often. He would do this by making a reference to John Joy, the Detective Chief of Crime, for the other trainees' benefit, asking me if I was going to visit the Detective Chief of Crime on my way to the city for some inquiry or other. I would, of course, play the game, and say yes, if I get time, I will call to see him.

Unfortunately, the other man was easily impressed, and the mention of something in that line would get under his skin. He was inclined to believe anything he was told. This was the type of banter that went on, which on occasions, the senior Detective would carry too far, and would have to tone it down.

I was to spend just two years with the unit, after which I was appointed to the Detective Branch, and assigned to the Fraud Squad in August 1974. Prior to this in 1973, both the other trainee, and I had gone forward for an interview for Detective Branch, and both of us were successful in the interview, and later appointed to Detective Branch.

When the list came out with the names of those appointed, I remember the other man coming up to me, and saying that he was number six on the list, and I was number nine, and saying, "I got ahead of you". I was the second most junior man on the list, with the most junior man going through the training centre some months after myself in the same year. I had just six years of service.

I was in later years to cross paths again with the other trainee Detective when we were both Detective Sergeant rank. I was also to cross paths with the senior Detective on a number of occasions as he rose through the ranks, under different circumstances, as I will be expanding on later.

CHAPTER ELEVEN

To Pastures New 1974. Appointment to Detective Branch, and Fraud Squad

On the 16th of August 1973, I attended an interview for an appointment as a trainee in Detective Branch [Crime Ordinary] D.M.A. The interview was held at the Central Detective Unit, Offices at Dublin Castle.

On the 22nd of July 1974, I was appointed as a trainee to the Detective Branch, and on the 20th of August 1974, I was transferred from Ballyfermot Garda Station to the Garda Fraud Section, which was attached to the Central Detective Unit in Dublin Castle. This assignment was to have a huge influence on my future service in An Garda Siochana, considering I had only about six, and a half years of service, which was junior at the time for appointment to the detective branch.

The offices of the Garda Fraud Squad were in one of the old Dublin Castle buildings, with the entrance from one of the old gates at Ship street. Now, I was attached to "Dublin Castle, "which was the Garda Headquarters of the Dublin Metropolitan Area, and the Headquarters of the Central Detective Unit, which the Fraud Squad was part of. During the course of our investigations, we would always introduce ourselves as being from "Dublin Castle, ", and people would know that it was something serious. We had our "Dublin Castle "like London had its "Scotland Yard".

The offices in this old building were badly in need of repair, and upgrading. Transferring from old buildings to new buildings seemed to have followed me wherever I went as I wasn't in the old buildings too long before the Fraud Unit, and other Central Detective Units were moved to a new building just outside the Ship Street gates, which was known as Osmond House. My second move to a new building in the space of three to four years.

The new offices were a big improvement on the old Castle buildings, and after some time we all settled into our new "home". I have a photograph which was taken around 1974/1975 of the Garda Fraud Unit of that time, which included Detective Inspector Con Donoghue, and Detective Superintendent Tim Farrell, who headed the Fraud Unit, taken in the new offices at Osmond House.

There were in excess of twenty detectives in the Fraud Department, including the Detective Superintendent, Detective Inspector, and a number of Detective Sergeant Ranks. I was very lucky to have been assigned to the unit I started to work with. Most of the Fraud Units worked on different aspects of fraud, including cheque fraud. The unit that I was attached to dealt mainly with company, and bank frauds.

Many of the members attached to my unit were of senior service that had spent many years investigating fraud cases, and were very eager to share their experience, and expertise with me. I built up great self-confidence during my years in the Fraud Squad, as I dealt with bank managers, company directors, politicians, and the like during the course of investigations. The late Detective Sergeant Matt Madigan RIP, as well as the rest of my unit, were all great mentors, all of whom became great colleagues during my years with the unit. It was another huge change for me, and a new learning curve, which also provided a new set of challenges.

There was a whole raft of new legislation to get to grips with, covering the investigation of Fraud, False Pretence, and obtaining cash, and goods by dubious, and devious means, other than burglaries, and larcenies, which were the main crimes that we dealt with at district stations. The investigation of fraud incidents was centralised at the Fraud Department at Dublin Castle/ Osmond House, as culprits committing these types of crimes would be crisscrossing the country, and the British Isles. No one District or Division would have the manpower or the expertise to investigate most of these incidents, which resulted in many complaints being forwarded to the Fraud Department from various Divisions in the country. The legislation relating to fraud at that time also needed updating as the current laws made investigations more difficult.

The Fraud Department worked Monday to Friday, 9 am to 5 pm, and maybe on occasions on a Saturday with most weekends free. Part of the reasoning behind this was that Banks, and Businesses worked similar hours, and were more readily available at these times during the course of fraud investigations involving their institutions. People charged with these types of crimes were described as being involved in "white collar" crimes, with even the courts, and legal profession looking at it as such.

During my time with the Fraud Department, I was involved in many fraud investigations with my colleagues, a few of which I have good memories of because of the nature of the incidents. Most of the complaints regarding suspected fraud would go through the office of the Detective Inspector in charge of the Fraud Department, who would then pass on the complaints to the Detective Sergeant of one of the units for investigation.

Printing press case, mid 70's

There was one particular case sometime after I arrived at the unit; in around 1976, Detective Sergeant Matt Madigan of my unit was handed a file by the Detective Inspector for investigation. The file related to the cashing of forged bank drafts in English banks, which were alleged to be drawn on Irish banks. At the time of receiving the complaint, a number of men had been charged in England with the cashing of these drafts, which were for varying amounts from ten thousand pounds to more than twenty-five thousand pounds sterling. There had been a bank strike in Ireland around that time.

The British Police were of the opinion that the forged drafts originated in the Irish Republic, and that one of the terrorist organisations were the one to benefit from the scam. At the time of receiving the initial complaint from the police in England, there were no leads as to who was behind this, and no information as to who might be responsible for the printing of the forged drafts. The suspects who had been charged were tried, convicted, and given prison sentences in England with respect to the cashing of the drafts. None of them gave any information or any indication of who was behind this crime.

My Detective Sergeant, with the members of our unit, kept this file open, and all the available information was reviewed on an ongoing basis. A period of time had elapsed before what appeared might be our first break in the case, and it came from an unusual source, through the Northern Ireland Police Force. This was a very disturbing, and dangerous time because of the terrorist activities which were ongoing in both Northern Ireland, and the Irish Republic. The Police in Northern Ireland had arrested a suspect in connection with terrorist offences, and he mentioned to the police there that he had information regarding the cashing of the forged drafts in England sometime in the past year or two.

The Police who were interviewing him were unsure about what he was talking about, as suspects in his situation were always inclined to give uncorroborated bits of information as a bargaining tool to ease their own situation. Contact was eventually made with my Detective Sergeant regarding this information concerning this case.

Travelling North during the troubles

Arrangements were made to meet the officers from Northern Ireland, I was asked to travel with my Detective Sergeant across the border to familiarise the arresting officers with the facts of the case, and to see if the information could be developed any further. At the time, it wasn't safe to have these types of discussions over the phone, hence the decision to travel north.

The travel date was decided on, and there were strict security arrangements put in place. My Detective Sergeant, and I travelled as far as the border in our official car, leaving it at the checkpoint on the Republic side, and then walked across the border where we were met by two Northern Ireland Police cars, one that we were to travel in, and the second was an armed security backup car that travelled with us to our destination. That was the way it was, as the terrorists did not take too kindly to the Garda, and the Northern Ireland Police force cooperating in any investigations.

We arrived at the police headquarters of the investigating officers, and had a very good meeting with them, bringing them up to speed with regards to the case of the forged drafts so they would know more about what their suspect was talking about. We were to travel twice more to Northern Ireland in respect of this case, the second time to be briefed by the investigating officers on their further interviews with their suspect, and to clarify if the Garda investigators would meet with their suspect. On the third occasion, we met up with the suspect, who was supplying the information by arrangement with the Northern Ireland Police investigating officers. He was still in custody.

For all the trips across the border, there was tight security provided for the two of us Detective Officers in the course of our investigations with the Northern Police force into this case.

My Detective Sergeant, and I were satisfied with our meeting with the suspect, who did not have the name of the man who printed the drafts, but gave a good indication of the area that he lived in. The suspect was also aware that the printer was associated with a high-profile person in Irish Politics. The suspect also informed us that this printer, as well as doing the drafts, printed forged passes for access to secure areas, and that he made false tax discs for haulage companies.

When we got back to our office, we reviewed all that had taken place, and as was always the situation with unusual cases, it was a full unit discussion as to what the next move would be. It was of great importance that this printer be identified, and if possible, his printing works found. Over time, we got a fix on an individual who lived in the north of the city, but there was no certainty that it was him.

From investigations, it was confirmed that this suspect did work as a printer, and his place of work was identified, which was a genuine printing company that he worked for. I couldn't believe it when I discovered that the printing company was right next door to the building that was my old station in Chapelizod. From confidential inquiries with the company he worked for, it would not have been possible for him to carry out the fraudulent printing at his work, so it was now down to finding his own printing press.

An operation had been set up to track this suspect's movements. Now, as it transpired, I had a friend living not too far from the suspect's house on the same road in the north city housing estate. From conversations with this friend, I discovered that this man, and his family took holidays in the sun at least three times a year, and it raised questions as to where the money came from. I also confirmed that he was very friendly with a senior politician, Charles J. Haughey, and had attended functions at this politician's house, who had in the recent past been involved in a very serious case before the court, involving the obtaining of firearms for the IRA, where he was found not guilty.

This information tied in very well with what the informant in Northern Ireland had indicated to us. At long last, after a considerable period of time since the investigation first started, we were getting somewhere. Now it was time to try, and find his printing press where the forged drafts, and other documents were printed. He was a very difficult individual to track with our limited resources.

A case conference was held with the Detective Superintendent, and the Detective Inspector of the Fraud Department. All the available evidence was placed before them as it was decided by my Detective Sergeant, and the rest of our unit, that we should bring him in for questioning, and he might divulge the whereabouts of his printing press, and workshop. Now, he was a person of habit, and it was known that he dropped his children to school each morning, so we moved in one morning after he dropped off his children, and arrested him on suspicion of fraud. He was brought to a Garda station for questioning, not too far from the fraud offices, as Osmond's house wasn't deemed to be a station for detaining prisoners.

After being interviewed for a short period, he told us where he had his own printing press, which was in a garage in a lane way off the South Circular Road Dublin 8. He seemed very confident when giving this information that nothing would be found to incriminate him. It was, after all, a considerable period of time, since this case first came to the attention of the Garda.

It was a long way from his home address on the north side of the city, hence the reason for the difficulty in finding it. My Detective Sergeant then went to the Detective Superintendent in charge of the fraud department, and obtained a search warrant under the Offences against the State Act 1939, which could be issued by a Superintendent.

As it happened, the Detective Superintendent was the same man who was in charge of the Crime Task Force, which I was part of in 1971. He was very cautious about issuing the warrant under section 30, as it was an unusual request for a fraud search, but when he was reminded about the forging of Northern Ireland documentation, and the links to terrorist involvement, he relented; he did remind us to be careful how we handled things.

During the course of the arrest of the suspect, his car was also seized for examination, and search. We went to the address to carry out the search, and gained entry with the suspect's keys, which he had in his car. We had at least four or five people in the search party, as well as the suspect, who remained in the car with two other detectives.

The search area was just the size of a normal garage, but laid out as a printing works. In the middle of the garage, nearest the back wall, was the printing press, which was a sizable machine. The whole place was cluttered with printing paper, boxes, inks, and other paraphernalia to do with printing. There was shelving on both sides of the garage, which was full of material to do with printing. We began our search of the building in a methodical fashion, going through every piece of paper, packaging, presses, and cabinets. Early on in the search, it was decided to have the suspect, who was still in a fairly confident mood, returned to where he was being detained once he had identified that this was his printing works, and he could be brought back again if needed. The search went on for most of the day.

Now, I was examining, and searching an area that included a cutting table which was used for cutting finished work to size. I was pulling at the cutting table, and got it out from the wall, and low, and behold, what did I find, but a full-sized, finished forged bank draft. There was an air of delight, and satisfaction in the camp, and everything was left as it was until we brought the suspect back to the scene to show him what was found, and get his explanation for what was found. When the suspect was brought back to the printworks, and was shown what was found, he was speechless, and his face became as white as a sheet; he knew the game was up.

As well as the completed draft other smaller cuttings of parts of other drafts, and parts of other forged documentation were found. The suspect was returned to the station, where he made a statement admitting to his involvement in the printing of the forged drafts, and other documents. He was later charged in respect of the offence of forgery resulting from the investigations.

This was a very significant find as up to then, no one could say when, or if ever before, a forger's printing press had been located. When the search was completed, and the technical bureau had completed their work, the printing press, along with all the printing material, including inks, were moved to the Garda printing works at John's Road, which was part of the Garda Technical Bureau at the time for further examination, and testing.

Later, the Garda printing department carried out a number of tests, and detailed examination of the printing press. During the course of the tests of the printing press the Garda Technical Department were able to reproduce perfect copies of the forged drafts that had been cashed in England a number of years previously, and the one found during the course of the search at the suspects printing works. It proved that the printing press that was found during the course of the search was capable of printing these drafts. The printing press, and the printing materials found at the suspects printing works were used in this reproduction. This evidence supported, and was a huge factor in the decision to prefer a number of additional charges against the accused.

When the case eventually came before the courts for a hearing, the accused pleaded guilty to a number of sample charges. The case was put back for a time for sentencing, and when it came back before the courts, the accused received a suspended sentence, which means he was able to walk out of the court without having to go to prison. At first, I was disappointed with the outcome because of the work that went into this investigation by the team.

Of course, it was not lost on the accused that his political contact was regaining his political popularity, and who, in the not too distant future, was to be the head of an Irish Government.

Over time, as I went through my service, I learned not to take cases personally. My job was to investigate, get the case before the courts for presentation by the prosecution, and leave the outcome in the hands of the court system.

CHAPTER TWELVE

Circuit Criminal Court case incident

During my service with the fraud department, I had many cases of fraud in which I was involved in investigating, and bringing the culprits before the courts, but there is one incident that sticks in my memory due to a confrontation with a judge of the Circuit Criminal Court. The case itself involved a fraudster who was a Cork man, and a very smooth operator. It involved several thousand Irish pounds obtained by means of fraud. When he was arrested, and charged, he threw himself at the mercy of the court, and made an offer to pay some compensation.

The judge relented, and remanded the case for a number of months to give him time to make good his promise of compensation. In doing so, the judge, in his wisdom, ordered that I, as the prosecuting, and investigating officer, open an account in a bank under my own name, and arrange with the accused to make the necessary payments into that account.

I complied with the Judges direction, and opened the account in my own name at a bank near the Fraud Offices through somebody in the bank that I became acquainted with, through my contacts with the banks in the course of some of my fraud investigations. I informed the bank of the circumstances of opening this account. At that particular period of time, there was no problem opening bank accounts, which, of course, the fraudsters took full advantage of. Afterwards, I met the accused, and gave him the account number to which he was to lodge his payments.

I wasn't too confident that this was going to work out. My fears were well founded, as after a number of small payments, money stopped going into the account. I tried to make contact with the defendant at his contact address, but he was no longer there. I returned to the Circuit Criminal Court, and had a warrant issued for his arrest. Under normal circumstances, the case would not come before the court again until the culprit had been arrested, but there was an unusual twist to this case.

Now, the Fraud Department was part of the Central Detective Unit of the Dublin Metropolitan Area, which also included such units as the Serious Crime Unit, Stolen Vehicle Unit, the Drug Squad, and Crime Prevention Unit. The person who headed the Central Detective Unit was the late Detective Chief Superintendent, John Joy, who happened to be a Kerry man. He was a gentleman, and it wasn't unusual for him to come into one of the units, sit down, have a general chat about how investigations were going, and get some views on matters affecting the investigations, including the need for more legislation, and any unusual happenings.

It was during the course of one of these visits one Saturday morning to the Fraud Unit while I was on duty that a conversation came up for discussion about the Gardai being responsible for the collection of money on the orders of the court. The Detective Chief Superintendent was curious as to how much of this was happening, and what it entailed. I, of course, related my involvement with my recent case in the Circuit Criminal Court with the fraudster from Cork, the opening of the bank account to facilitate the accused to pay back compensation, and eventually having to have a warrant issued for his arrest. The Detective Chief Superintendent wasn't happy with what he heard, the idea of the Gardai becoming bankers for the courts. He thanked all of us for our input to the discussion, and left.

Some weeks later, I received a phone call from John in the Chief States Solicitor's office, whom I knew well from the courts. He informed me that I was required in the Circuit Criminal Court some days later in connection with one of my cases. This was an unusual request as normally, notification would be sent out in writing from the Chief States Solicitor's Office. The case was the fraudster from Cork, and I intimated that there was a warrant out for his arrest, which, to my knowledge, had not yet been executed. John didn't give any more information, only that it was up for mention in the afternoon of the said date.

I attended the Circuit Criminal Court at the appointed time, and after some time, the case was called, and as was usual, the court papers were given up to the judge. I was called, went into the witness box as would be normal practice, and waited to be asked a question by the state representative, who was the man I knew, John.

It didn't happen, but instead, the judge opened up with a rebuke towards me, and berated me in open court. I was stunned, and didn't know where the judge was coming from. It seems he said that it was too onerous, and difficult a task for this Detective to carry out the directions of the court in this particular case. He continued his castigation of me for what seemed like forever. He ordered that the account opened for the monies to be paid into, be closed, and whatever monies that were there were to be refunded to some of the injured parties. The judge mentioned something about me having made a report to my superiors without first coming to the courts. I stepped out of the witness box without uttering a word.

It was a most embarrassing situation to have found oneself in, not knowing what the judge was on about, and to have been so humiliated before the open court. I waited outside the court to meet up with John from the chief state's office, and find out what the hell was going on. John was all apologies for what happened, but there was nothing he could do as the judge requested the case be mentioned in court, and to have the Detective present. Later, John informed me that this resulted from a letter sent to the President of the Circuit Criminal Court from the Garda Commissioner's office, Dublin Castle, mentioning the case in point.

The penny dropped; this had come out of my long-ago, Saturday morning discussion with the Detective Chief Superintendent at the Fraud Department. I had been a regular attender at the Circuit Criminal Courts, before that particular Judge with cases, but I didn't darken the door of his court again for almost twelve months after what occurred that day.

Then, the opportunity presented itself. My fraudster from Cork was arrested on the warrant that had been issued, and he was to appear before the same judge at the Circuit Criminal Court. I spoke with John from the chief state's office, and arranged for him to mention the previous matter that had come before the court in connection with this case, as I wanted to inform the judge of the circumstances surrounding the communication from the Garda Commissioner's Office, Dublin Castle.

The accused case was dealt with, and John got to his feet, and told the judge that he wanted to ask the Detective something related to the case. The judge agreed; John then asked me what the circumstances were regarding the letter from the Commissioner's office in connection with this case.

I then related the discussion that I had, at the request of my Detective Chief Superintendent, and that at no time was I aware that the discussion had gone any further until I was summoned to the court by the judge. Neither was I objecting to the carrying out of any instructions issued by the courts, and I went on to cover factors relating to the case.

The judge then turned to me, and told me he wished to apologise if he caused me any distress, as his initial reaction was a result of a misunderstanding as to where the correspondence had originated. He wished me luck for the future. At least I got my apology in open court.

Politician son in court

As I previously mentioned, I crossed paths with people from all walks of life, and as well as being an investigator, I also had to be a bit of a diplomat, depending on the circumstances. Now, there was a case of fraud involving a suspect opening up bank accounts in false names into which a forged stolen cheque would then be lodged, and money withdrawn before the cheque was cleared. This case came across the desk of my Detective Sergeant Matt Madigan, which needed to be handled with delicacy because of the suspicion as to the identity of the person who might be involved.

My Detective Sergeant, and I carried out this investigation, which occurred in the middle of the 1970s. The suspect was alleged to be the son of a very high-ranking politician who was part of the Government at the time.

In the course of the investigation, a suspect was arrested, and interviewed with respect to the case under investigation. To our surprise, he turned out to be the youngest son of the head of the Government of the day. The young man made a statement regarding his involvement in the matters under investigation; he was charged, and brought before the district courts. My Detective Sergeant, and I arranged for the case to be listed last in the afternoon court so that the press would not get to hear of it, as they usually left early to catch the evening papers with their scoops.

The case was called, and he was remanded on bail for a number of weeks to have the investigation completed. We then made contact with his father, and arranged a meeting to brief him as to what was happening regarding the court case. When we met with the father, we filled him in on all the facts of the case, including the fact that from our investigations, we believed that his son was being used by a number of known fraudsters to carry out these crimes because of who he was, and of course the promise of easy money.

The boy's father was, of course, very shocked that his son could be involved in such incidents, and found himself lost for words as to what to do in this unusual situation. We informed him that we, the investigating officers, were doing our best to keep it from the media, which included trying to keep it in the late afternoon court because of the nature of the boy's relationships.

The boy's father asked my Detective Sergeant, and myself about what he should do. We informed him that the first thing he needed to do was to have a solicitor instructed, and we provided him with our contact numbers to give to whatever solicitor would be looking after the case. Because of his high-ranking position in the government, and dealing with day to day issues involving the whole country, it was difficult for him to take in the realisation that one of his family could let him down like that. We both left the father, and told him we would keep him informed of developments.

Then, of course, all our good work trying to keep the incident from the media was in vain, as while he was out on bail on the Dublin charges, he was arrested in England on similar charges, where the police in England were less diplomatic, and gave the press the full story as who his parents were, which was copied by the Irish media.

It must be pointed out that this boy did not receive any preferential treatment from my Detective Sergeant or me with respect to the prosecution of the case; it was only out of respect for his father, and who he was that we attempted to keep it away from the media in the early stages.

The case was eventually dealt with through the courts both in Ireland, and in England, leading to a suspended sentence due to his cooperation, and his guilty plea.

CHAPTER THIRTEEN

St Paul's Garda Medical Aid society, forgotten history note

During my time training at the Training Centre, Templemore, as well as doing our police studies, we, as new recruits, were also introduced to the various societies, and organisations within the Garda Siochana, we were encouraged to join some of these societies; one being the Garda Medical Aid Society, and a second being the Garda Representative Body. As I would learn later, both of these organisations were linked as the Garda Medical Aid Society was managed by the Garda Representative Body.

The deductions for membership were made at source from our salary. At the time, health, and representation were important for members of the force. When I finished my training, I was assigned to a Garda Station in Dublin city, where there was another society called St Paul's Benefit society, which covered a number of other medical expenses. It was confined to members of the Dublin Metropolitan Area, and I was also encouraged to join, which I did.

In the 1970s, while I was attached to the Fraud Squad, at Dublin Castle, I became aware that there were discussions going on regarding the amalgamation of both St Paul's Benefit Society, and the Garda Medical Aid Society to create one society to cater to the medical cover of the whole force. These discussions had started in the early 1970s, some time prior to me joining the Fraud Squad, and had been ongoing for a number of years.

The members of the Central Detective Unit were in close contact with representatives of St Paul's Benefit Society as one of the main negotiators for that society was attached to the Crime Prevention Unit, which was attached to the Central Detective Unit. He was a man who was well-versed in all matters relating to health cover, social welfare, and pensions. He would be deemed to be an expert on these matters, and anybody seeking advice would go to him.

Sometime in the mid-1970s, while I was attached to the Fraud Squad, it became apparent that the Garda Medical Aid group, which was made up of members of the executive of the Garda Representative Body, were faltering in the negotiations regarding the amalgamation of the two societies. Information began to circulate that they were in talks with an outside medical insurance group regarding the taking over of the cover in respect of the Garda members.

This gave rise to all sorts of insinuations as to what was going on behind the scenes, who were the insurance company involved in the talks, what was in it for the negotiators for the handover of such a sizable portfolio of about 7500 clients in one swoop.

With this information circulating, St Paul's committee set in motion a call for a special EGM of the Garda Medical Aid Society to rekindle the amalgamation talks. To get this special EGM convened St Paul's had to get a sizeable majority of the members of the Garda Medical Aid Society to agree to this special EGM.

This entailed making contact with every single member of the Garda Medical Aid Society all over Ireland, giving them the facts as they knew them, and getting them to sign a declaration in support of holding an EGM to put a special motion to the floor of the meeting in support of the amalgamation of the two societies.

This was my first involvement in the internal politics of the Garda as I gave of my time voluntarily, as did many members of the Central Detective Unit, and other units around the country, after working hours in addressing envelopes to be sent to all Medical Aid Society members containing the documentation prepared by St Paul's benefit Society committee.

There was an overwhelming response from the whole country, with many more than the required quota of members supporting the call for a special EGM of the Garda Medical Aid Society. Arrangements were put in place to hold the meeting at the Garda Club in Harrington Street on a particular evening, which resulted in a packed house. The Garda Medical Aid Society committee was, of course, kept informed of all developments, including the date, and venue of the meeting.

The Garda Medical Aid Society committee representatives were given their seats at the top table as, after all, it was a Garda Medical Aid Society meeting called by the members of that society. I took a seat up near the front of the hall to have a good view of the proceedings. The meeting opened with one of the members of the Garda Medical Aid team getting up to speak, and I could not believe what I was hearing when a statement came from the top table that the meeting was illegal, should not go ahead, and that their solicitor was present to give his advice on the matter.

Well, there was uproar in the hall at this arrogant stance taken by the top table, which nearly led to a flare-up, with calls for the committee to resign. Eventually, order was restored, and the motion was put to the floor by St Paul's Benefit Society representative, and carried by the floor.

The motion to the floor had the effect of requiring the committee of the Garda Medical Aid Society to rekindle the amalgamation discussions with St Paul's Benefit Society to form one Medical Aid Society for the entire Garda force. In 1980, the new society was formed, and named St Paul's Garda Medical Aid Society, which is still going strong to this day.

It is the envy of many other organisations, including some Insurance companies, as it has gone from strength to strength, and has become one of the most beneficial medical cover organisations in the country. But for the diligent dedication of the committee members of St Paul's Benefit Society, and their foresight in pushing for this amalgamation, where would we as members of the Garda be today as regards medical insurance cover, in the hands of a private insurance company?

When one reads the history of St Paul's Garda Medical Aid Society today, there is no mention of the internal struggles that ensued, and the huge intervention by the members of the Central Detective Unit, and all the other members of the Society. Members are now reaping the benefits of having their own successful society rather than relying on a private company.

Back to studies

During my busy time with the Fraud Squad, I was being advised that I should go, and do the promotion examination for Sergeant. This advice was given to me by my Detective Sergeant, and other senior members of my Fraud Unit that I worked with. Now, to go forward for the promotional examination to either Sergeant or inspector, I first had to pass the educational examinations for those ranks passed first, which were known as class 111 A for Sergeant, and class 1A for inspector. Because of my own educational qualification limitations, I had the good sense to sit for the class 1A examination in 1971, which covered the qualification for both Sergeant, and inspector ranks. The promotion examinations were known as class 111B for Sergeant, and class 1B for Inspector.

I found time with my busy schedule to go back to do some studies for the promotions examination to the rank of Sergeant. There were members of senior rank who ran courses of study for the promotion examinations to both the ranks of Inspector, and Sergeant, which I took advantage of in my own time. In 1976, I sat the promotions examination for Sergeant, and passed it to my delight. I had just eight years of service, and was qualified for promotion to the rank of Sergeant.

Sometime around 1978, I had a meeting with one of my Detective Inspectors in fraud to see what I could do about working weekends so as to qualify for an unsocial hour's allowance. I was told that the Fraud Unit would not be going over to working weekends, certainly not in the foreseeable future. It was costing me a lot in fuel to drive from north Kildare to Dublin Castle every day, and home again, where I was residing with my wife, and a growing family of four children.

In fairness to my Detective Inspector, he came back to me, and told me that he would arrange for me to work with the Stolen Vehicle Unit as they worked weekends, and were in the same building if that would suit me. I took up the offer, and I was later transferred to work with the Stolen Vehicle Unit at Central Detective Unit, Dublin Castle, or Osmond House, where we were then.

I left many good friends, and colleagues at the Fraud Squad, but I wasn't going a hundred miles away. Not too long after I had left the Fraud Squad, there was a change of heart, and weekend work was introduced there. I still wonder to this day if my move caused the change of heart or if there were other rumblings in the camp about the weekend payments that followed my move.

Reflections on my Family, brother Jerry, house renovations

During the years between 1970 and 1979, while doing my service in Ballyfermot, the Fraud Squad, and the Stolen Vehicle section, I still had a number of my missing family siblings on my mind. By 1979, I had four children of my own, three boys, and a girl. Through those years, I was still keeping in touch with my brother Jerry, who was in the process of getting the old home renovated. I also kept in touch with my family members I had traced from the late 1960s into the 1970s in both London, and Liverpool.

Now, my brother Jerry decided he was going to put in a new septic tank, sink a well in one of the spots that our father had indicated there would be water, build on an extension consisting of a new kitchen, bathroom, bedroom to the rear of the house. Jerry wasn't too familiar with the planning system, so I got my rule, and pencil to work, and made out a plan for him, and sent in the completed application with the drawings I did myself to Kerry Council for permission to build.

The permission was granted, and Jerry got to work getting the well sunk, and the septic tank organised. I went on-site a few times to measure up the extension, and helped Jerry to start the foundations. After that, Jerry got contractors to complete the work, and I went down from time to time to see how things were going. Jerry, of course, at that time was commuting between the home, and England, where he made up the money to pay for the building.

Sometime around the time the building was completed Jerry got married to a girl from Clare whom he met in London. I attended the wedding, which happened in London. The hotel where the wedding was held was in Inverness Terrace, in Bayswater, London, not too far from where our sister Joan was living with her family. They had an events manager there, who was an Irishman from Galway in the west of Ireland. Many years later, he would return to his home in Galway on the death of his father, and take his seat in the Dail, the Irish Parliament.

It was the only wedding of one of my siblings I ever attended. Later, Jerry, and Kay, his wife, had a child, a girl, and they came back to Ballylongford to live in the old home that Jerry had renovated. In later years, their daughter finished her education in Ballylongford, and Tarbert, and then went to England to do a nursing course.

In November 1998, Jerry travelled to London to attend at his daughter's graduation ceremony, where after the ceremony, he suffered a stroke, and died some days later in hospital in London. I went to London, and accompanied his body back to Ireland, where he was brought home for burial in the family plot at Lislaughtin Abbey, Ballylongford. His daughter did return to their home sometime later with her husband to be, and stayed on, and off for a few years. Both of them then decided to return to England, and they sold the family home at Lislaughtin, Ballylongford. When I think back now, it was only my home for about nine months of my life, and even after all the trips I made to the house, I never felt any attachment to the house as a home. I suppose there is no better time than now, at this sad juncture, to give a further extended insight into my family that I eventually traced, and the current situation of my family as it is today.

My father was John "Jack" Heffernan; he was born on the 10th of December 1884 at a place called Kilelton, Ballylongford, Co Kerry, his father, and mother [my grandparents on his side,] were Michael Heffernan, and Joanna Heffernan, nee Dissett. My father died on the 9th of November 1967, and is buried at Lislaughtin Abbey Cemetery, Ballylongford in the same grave as my mother. I had met my father for the first time in 1961, before I left St Joseph's Residential Institution, Tralee. We did build a type of relationship over the six years I had known him, during the course of visits home from Dublin, before his death in 1967.

My mother was Johanna Heffernan, nee Hingey, born on the 20th of May 1906, at Coolkeeragh, Ballylongford. Her parents [my grandparents on her side,] were Richard Hingey, and Lizzie Hingey nee Kelly. My mother died on the 10th of March 1946, I was exactly six months old to the calendar date.

She is buried at Lislaughtin Abbey Cemetery, Ballylongford. Not knowing my mother, I did try to locate even a photograph of her without success. Now, there are a number of different ways my mother's maiden name is spelt. On her birth certificate, it is shown as "Hingey" as above, but on my own birth certificate it is spelt as "Henchy", and I have also seen it spelt as "Hinchy". Recently, I had to point this out to the Irish Passport Office, when I was renewing my Passport, as I had used a version of the spelling I hadn't used on a previous application, so much for official record-keeping.

My nine siblings were as follows according to age

My eldest brother Michael Heffernan, was born on the 22nd of March 1926, he left home at an early age before I was born, and ended up in London where in 1951 he met, and married Bridget McGarry, who was born on the 21th of July 1917. I met with my brother Michael, and his family in Harlow, in Essex in 1970 for the first time; after that, we met on a number of occasions over a number of years. Michael would have been the seventh, and last member of my family I met at that time. He, and his wife even came to visit us, on a number of occasions in Leixlip where I was living. He was a good man with horses, and the local bookies office were glad to see the back of him when he used to go back home to London.

Both Michael, and his wife died within two years of each other, Bridget on the 27th of December 1989, whose funeral I attended in January 1990, Michael on the 29th of September 1991, he was just 65 years, and six months old. Both are buried in Parndon Wood Cemetery, in Harlow, in Essex. They had three children, two boys, and a girl all of whom I keep in contact with by Christmas card, being the long-lost uncle.

Patrick [Paddy] Heffernan, my second eldest brother was born on the 12th of July 1927, and like my brother Michael, he left home maybe before I was born. I never met my brother Patrick as he just disappeared off the family radar. Many years later in the early 2000s, I eventually tracked down his family, and discovered that he had died on the 31st of May 1996. He had worked in the coal mines in Nottingham, England, had got married, settled down, and had a family of two daughters with his wife Ellen.

I later visited Nottingham, and met with his two daughters who related to me some aspects of his life. They told me that over the years, they tried to get him to make contact with his old home town, and he made several promises, but they never materialised. This type of situation was a common occurrence with people who left Ireland in those times, they would lose contact with family, and friends, and as the time span grew wider, contact became more difficult. I am still in contact with Patrick's daughters who are now both married, and reside with their families in Nottingham.

My third eldest brother John Heffernan was born on the 14th of August 1930. I do not have a date or time when John left home as he was the second of my brothers I had never met. Like Patrick before him John also went off the family radar, and was never seen again by any of the family or anyone from the home town. I did track down John's family in Derby, in England, but that was around the early 2000s. I went to Derby, and met his wife, June, and his family. They had four children.

John had passed away on the 9th of December 2000 only a couple of years before I had started my search for him, and his family. Around August, September 2004, his wife June died, and I managed to travel to the funeral. I did try to keep contact with the family by phone, and by writing to them, but soon after, they went off the radar, and I lost contact with them. The only explanation I can come up with is that they had to move house after their parents had both passed away. My intention is, of course, to try to track them down again.

My eldest sister Mary was the fourth eldest in my family. She was born on the 9th of September 1933. I first met my sister Mary when she was home on holidays around the same time as me, visiting Jerry, and our father at our home in Ballylongford. Mary had married in 1958/1959, and lived in Liverpool with her husband Gerald, and their family of four children. As well as my brother Jerry, Mary would have been the second member of my family I would have ever met up to that time in the 1960s. Mary, who was my eldest sister at the time of my mother's death, took on the task of looking after me as a baby for a few months, until I was eventually taken away from my family. I often joked with her that I was lucky she didn't do any damage with the safety pins when changing my nappies.

She gave me some insight into my own situation at the time of my birth. Mary was the one who wrote to me inviting me to go, and live with her, and her family in Liverpool. Sometime later, I did travel to Liverpool for a break, and stayed with Mary for a few days. On that occasion, I met a third member of my family, my sister, Ann who was also living in Liverpool, not too far from Mary, and she had a young family. Mary, and I met many times over the years both in Liverpool, and in Ireland; she even attended my retirement function in 2001 at the Lucan Spa Hotel, in west Dublin. She was a very jolly outgoing person. Mary passed away on the 10th of January 2015 at a nursing home in Liverpool not too far from where members of her own family lived. She was 81 years, and four months old. Later, her ashes were brought home to Ballylongford by her daughter, and buried in the family grave at Lislaughtin Abbey, Ballylongford, Co Kerry.

I had managed to visit her on a couple of occasions while she was being cared for in the nursing home. On one such occasion, on a trip from Malta, before she passed away, Sonia, who is now my current wife, with myself went to see her in Liverpool, and we took her out for something to eat, and a drink to a local eatery. We wheeled her out on a wheelchair, and brought her back again, and over the period of a few hours, had a great chat as well. When we got back to the nursing home we were having a cup of tea in the dining room before we left. She turned to both of us, and very quietly said to us that she was expecting her brother Mossey "[myself]", to call to see her today.

I didn't know whether to laugh or cry, it's just one of those moments one does not forget. We understood the situation as she was prone to slight memory loss at times.

My second eldest sister Joan was the fifth eldest in my family, and the fourth member of my family I was to meet. She was born on the 13th of February 1935; she is just over ten years older than me. I first met Joan in 1970 at her home in Bayswater, London where she lived with her partner Frans Dalli, who was Maltese by birth, and their two daughters. I was going on twenty five years of age at the time. Joan was the one who introduced me, and helped me to meet up with three other members of my family that I had never met.

My eldest brother Michael, and two more sisters Lily, and Cathy who were all residing in the London area at that time. I had spent a week with Joan in 1970, and discovered many things about my family. I built up a great relationship with Joan, and we kept in touch over the years. Some years after I had met my sister Joan, and her family, she moved to Malta with her husband, and her family, and took up residence there. We continued to communicate, and over time, I made several trips to Malta, and stayed with Joan, and her family. Hence, the Maltese connection.

Frans, her husband died on the 14th of February 2011, and is buried at the cemetery in Mellieha, Malta. Joan passed away on the 19th of January 2024, about four weeks before her 89th birthday. She is buried in Mellieha Cemetery, Malta, where her husband Frans was buried in 2011.

My third eldest sister Ann who was sixth eldest in my family was the third member of my family I met with when I was in Liverpool visiting my sister Mary in the mid to late 1960s. She was born on the 2nd of August 1936. Ann had a very difficult life as herself, her husband, and three children, a girl, and two boys, had her mother-in-law living with them, who controlled the purse strings in the house. That was the way then with some families. Her husband, and mother-in-law were from Achill Island, and had a house there. Eventually, a number of years after I first met my sister Ann, they all returned to live in Achill Island.

I did visit them in Achill Island a number of times over the years after, and things hadn't changed. Ann passed away on the 17th of August 1986; she was just 50 years of age, she is buried in Glencoe Cemetery on Achill Island. Her husband Michael died on the 4th of June 2005. I still keep contact with the children, who are now married themselves, and reside in the west of Ireland.

I remember attending my sister Ann's funeral in Achill after her death, and she was laid out in one of the rooms in the house. Now, these houses were very small, and as you went in the front door, there was a hallway that went to the left, and right inside the door. It was very narrow, and I wondered how they were going to get the coffin outside. When the prayers were finished, a couple of men with some tools started to take out the window in the room. When the window was removed, they proceeded to bring the coffin out through the window. This was the first time I had ever seen this done, and it brought certain wonderment to a sad occasion.

My fourth eldest sister was Lily, who was born on the 27th of March 1938. She was the 7th eldest in my family, and the fifth member of my family I was to meet during my trip to London in 1970. She lived with her husband Leo, and their three girls in London, and some years later returned to Ireland to live in Co Tipperary, where Leo was from, where they also had their fourth child, another girl. Her husband Leo passed away in 2010.

I did build up a very good relationship with my sister Lily over the years, and we often got together. I attended the weddings of some of her daughters. She even came to my wedding in Malta in 2013, and stayed with us for a week. Before I left for Malta, I would have visited Lily, and her family a few times a year. Lily passed away on the 29th of October 2019, at a nursing home not too far from where she had lived with her family. She was 81 years, and 7 months.

My fourth eldest brother Jerimiah [Jerry] was born on the 15th of August 1940, he was the 8th eldest in the family, and the first member of my family I was to meet as we both were sent to the same institution. Jerry had left the institution about five years before I did, and it was some years again before I set eyes on him. Jerry married his wife Kay in London in the early 1970s, and returned to Ballylongford to live with his wife, and young child. Jerry was I suppose, the one I had most contact with during my earlier life.

In November 1998, Jerry went to London to attend his daughter's graduation in nursing where she went to train some years previous. On the evening of the graduation, Jerry had a stroke, and a few days later, on the 29th of November, he died in hospital. He was 58 years of age, and is buried in Lislaughtin Abbey Cemetery, Ballylongford, in the family plot.

My fifth, and youngest sister Cathy, was born on the 14th of February 1942, she was three, and a half years older than myself. I had first met Cathy in 1970 when I met Joan who introduced us to each other. Cathy, like me, had been in care with nuns in a convent in Tralee, not too far from where I was detained, but we didn't get to meet. She went to London at an early age, and spent the rest of her life there. She had a daughter in the late sixties, and found things difficult for a few years until my intervention in the early 1970s which I have already covered. Cathy, and I did meet a lot over the later years with her coming over to Ireland, and I taking a few trips to London.

Cathy died in London on the 3rd of April 2016, she was 74 years of age. I attended her funeral in London with many of our nieces, and nephews, and a few of my own family. Joan, and Lily, the only other surviving family members, didn't make it as they were both in confinement in their nursing homes, Lily in Tipperary, and Joan in Malta. Later Cathy's ashes were brought back to Ballylongford, and buried in the family plot at Lislaughtin Abbey, Ballylongford, Co Kerry.

That is the current situation with the Heffernan family as things stand today, and I being the only current survivor out of our family of ten. How many people go through their early years in life not knowing they had an extended family? I didn't know I had a father until I was almost 16 years even though he was only living about twenty miles from my place of detention.

CHAPTER FIFTEEN

Promotion

Now, I was qualified to go for promotion to Sergeant rank, and the opportunity came while I was attached to the stolen vehicle section. I had the option to go for an interview for uniform Sergeant or wait till the interviews came up for Detective Sergeant in the Crime Ordinary Section. I decided to stay with the Detective Branch, and wait for the Detective Sergeant interviews to be set as I was totally committed to working in the Detective Branch. That was the promotion system that was in place at that time.

In 1979 there were interviews to fill vacancies for Detective Sergeant, in various districts. Now when people went for an interview there was no guarantee that they would be left at their current unit or district. I presented myself for an interview before a board of senior Detective Officers from the Central Detective Unit, Dublin Metropolitan Area. I was successful in the interview, and was promoted to the rank of Detective Sergeant. That was the way promotion was within the Detective Branch, it was a separate system within Detective Branch to that of the uniform section. Now, a uniform Sergeant who had previously served in the Detective Branch could also apply for an interview for Detective Sergeant rank.

I was assigned to fill the Detective Sergeant vacancy at Shankill Garda Station, but a phone call from another successful candidate on the list inquired if I was willing to change places as he wished to remain in the area of Shankill. This man had originally been assigned to Kevin Street Station in the city centre. I weighed up my options, and felt it would be more beneficial for me to take the Kevin Street assignment because of the travelling involved. That decision may have been the worst I ever made, but then I was very accommodating, and it seemed a good move at the time.

The matter was then forwarded to the Detective Chief Superintendent of crime at Dublin Castle to get his clearance for the change. Now, the fact that the Detective Chief Superintendent at Central Detective Unit, Dublin Castle, was a Kerry man would have had no bearing on the outcome of my promotion or transfer, or had it? The Kerry men's association was very well represented in the Garda Siochana at that time, and would have had a certain amount of influence within the Detective Branch. I never got around to joining that association. The change of assignment was agreed, so I was assigned to Kevin Street Garda Station as a second Detective Sergeant because of the volume of work going through that District.

I did from time to time, reflect on my progression through life, with every life bridge I crossed, I felt a great sense of achievement, and satisfaction as I stepped through my life. I could never forget where life began for me, but now, eighteen years on from the date of my "release" from St Joseph's Residential Institution Tralee, and eleven years after I had joined the Garda, I was now a Detective Sergeant with a Detective Unit in the heart of Dublin city.

I was never too pushy for myself to be climbing up the "ladder" of promotion or other heights, I just accepted things as they happened, but I was also lucky to have met some good people on my way through this part of my life. Unfortunately, over the next few years, I would come in contact with officers who would be less than understanding towards me, and here I am being more than "charitable" in my choice of words. This was going to be another whole new experience for me.

A district detective unit 1979 to 1982

Kevin Street Detective Unit members were a very seasoned crew, all of them with a good deal of service under their belts, and lots of experience built up over their years working in Detective Branch. On the other hand, I was a very young Detective Sergeant with just eleven years' service in the force, which was junior service for a Detective

Sergeant. I received a reasonably cautious welcome from all my senior staff, but of course, they would be holding their views of me until they got to see what I was made of. That would be the normal reaction when new people joined with a seasoned crew.

I would of course have met most of them over the years during the course of investigations while I was attached to the Central Detective Unit, at the Fraud Squad, and the Stolen Vehicle Squad, as I would have had reason to visit many stations in the Dublin Metropolitan Area while carrying out these investigations. My new unit members would have had a reasonably good picture of my qualities as a Detective before my arrival, but they would be testing me in my new role as their new Detective Sergeant. It wasn't long before my mettle was to be tested, not as a Detective, but as to how I dealt with the officer corp on their behalf.

Many of the crew attached to the Kevin Street Detective Unit were very industrious, and as well as being in the Garda Siochana, they had some family sideline businesses. My new Detective Inspector, who was previously well known in the building circles was greatly involved in the social aspects of the Garda. He would have been very deeply involved in the development of the Harrington Street Garda Club, which became an iconic centre for the members of the Dublin Metropolitan Area.

Kevin Street Station was in what was known as the "A" District, which also included Kilmainham Station as part of the District. I was to serve for a time in both stations between 1979, and 1982. It was going to be a rocky journey through the "A" District for a number of the following reasons as I now outline.

When I arrived at Kevin Street, it was normal practice to be introduced to, and meet with the senior officers of my new district. I first met with my Detective Inspector, whom I had previously met on a number of other occasions. He was a very approachable man, and easy to have a conversation with. He would be my immediate superior, who would in normal circumstances, be the buffer between me, and my higher officers.

Next, I met with the local Superintendent who seemed a very nice individual with very senior service. I was welcomed to the "A" District by him, and after some conversation with him, he informed me that he would not be my Superintendent for very long as he was coming up to his retirement. That was not good news for me so soon after arriving.

Within the space of a short number of months, the Superintendent retired, and his replacement arrived, and with him came an unsettling period for myself, and the crew. As happens in all these situations, when there was a new "Boss" man arriving anywhere, his previous history as an officer would precede him. He was known to have very little time for Detectives because of some previous run-ins he had with people in plain clothes. It was the beginning of total disharmony between the local Detective Branch, and the new Superintendent who had more than a dislike for detectives. It was bordering on hate, and a certain amount of jealousy.

I met with the new Superintendent, which again was normal procedure for the new officer to meet with all his staff. He had a very condescending manner, and always wanted to give the impression that he was in charge, he was the boss. This of course did not go down too well with the Detective Unit as they were used to having a good working relationship with their previous Superintendent. I had a number of disagreements, and run-ins with the new Superintendent during my short stay in the "A" District a few of them I share as follows.

Detectives Work a Roster System

The unit worked on a roster shift system with members on the day shift starting at 9 a.m., and finishing at 5 p.m. Then there would be a night crew starting at 5 p.m. or 6 p.m. till 2 a.m. in the morning. Then there would be members on rest days, so you had a situation where not everybody worked together at any one time. Any work done outside the roster times would be submitted for overtime payment. This would include time for early morning searches, court appearances, and where additional manpower was needed for carrying out serious investigations.

One morning, when I had a crew out on early morning search-es, which was a regular occurrence, I was informed by my Detective Inspector when I returned after the searches, that any of the crew, including myself, who were out on the search that morning with me were to finish early as they would not be paid for the additional hours worked. I couldn't believe what I was hearing, I said to my Detective Inspector that this was not right as I was responsible for getting these men out on this early morning, and I would not send them home or go home myself. We went, and had our breakfast which was al-ways the case after being out early, and I thought of what action I should take next in response to this outlandish direction from our new Superintendent.

I had a discussion with my crew, and my Detective Inspector about the situation. I asked my Detective Inspector to go to the Superintendent, and inform him that he was in breach of the rules re-garding the changing of the working roster, without prior notification of the changes. The Detective Inspector declined to go, and meet with the Superintendent, and I put it to him if he wouldn't mind if I went in to meet him to get the matter sorted, which he agreed to.

I went, and met with the Superintendent in his office who was there accompanied by one of his uniform Inspectors. This became common practice with him to always be flanked by this one Inspector who by the way, I had previously known as a Sergeant, from my days in the task force, and was again to meet him as my Superintendent in the not too distant future in another area.

I laid out my case regarding the instruction that was issued by the Superintendent, pointing out that the men, including myself, were entitled to be paid for our hours worked this morning as over-time. The Superintendent stuck to his guns, and wouldn't budge from his direction. After some heated exchanges, I then informed the Superintendent that as, and from tomorrow, there would be no more early morning searches carried out by the Detective Unit at Kevin Street, as they were on a roster system, and needed prior notification under the regulation to have that roster changed. I left the office.

I related back to my Detective Inspector what had taken place in the Superintendent's office regarding his directions as to the hours worked that morning, but the Detective Inspector wasn't too hopeful as to the outcome of the meeting or that the Superintendent would change his mind.

Sometime later on the same day, the Superintendent breezed into the Detective office, and directed his comments to the Detective Inspector that the men would be paid for today's hours, but that in future all searches were to be kept to a minimum. It was quite obvious that he had received clarification on the matter from some other source. That was the last we heard about efforts to try to change the Detectives roster. I had made a stand for my crew, as a result of which I gained a lot of respect from the "A" District Detective Unit.

On a later date, I had a meeting with my Divisional Detective Superintendent who was a nice guy, and I had good time for him. It was no coincidence that some of the conversation was about the Detective Units roster system. There was no need for him to go into any detail of the incident with me as it was obvious that the matter had been discussed at a reasonably high level at Headquarters. It would seem that I had been branded a bit of a rebel by my new superintendent, and this would come to the fore at a later date.

Change of Detective Superintendent

Sometime later, I was to receive another set back as the Detective Superintendent for the Division, who was near retiring age, was recalled to Headquarters for operations there, and he was replaced by a newly appointed, Detective Superintendent who was a well-known individual in Detective Branch in Dublin City north where he operated as a Detective Inspector.

I got to know him as a person who was on your side one day, and the next would be very critical of you, with respect to Garda matters, and of course, he, and my district superintendent became great buddies. They were well-matched.

This new Detective Superintendent was also the type of person who, loved to be in conversation with priests, and nuns, and was a frequent church attender, whenever he got the opportunity, even during his working day. Now, I wouldn't hold that against him, but it was a pity he didn't live up to his Christian ways when dealing with his subordinates.

I avoided when I could, any reason for meeting up with my district Superintendent, but on one occasion, he sent for me to meet him in his office. As usual, he was flanked by his uniform Inspector. I was alarmed by what I heard next coming from the Superintendent's mouth. He began by praising me, and telling me my prospects for the future were very promising as a young Detective Sergeant, and as I would put it, a whole lot of bull.

Then he came out with his reason for calling me in. He started to belittle my Detective Inspector by saying various defamatory things about him. After his berating of the Detective Inspector, he said he wanted me to keep an eye on him, and to report back to him anything I could find out. I was stunned, and informed the Superintendent that this was my Detective Inspector he was talking about, and I would not carry out these instructions as he suggested. The meeting ended at that.

At the first opportunity, I went to my Detective Inspector, and informed him about the Superintendent's request, and he was outraged at the cheek of the Superintendent to make an approach to his Detective Sergeant like that. The void between our Detective Unit, and the Superintendent became greater.

Now, the local Superintendent had the authority to use the staff within his District as he wished. Relationships between myself, and my Superintendent deteriorated so much that when we would pass each other at any point within the station complex, the Superintendent would totally ignore me as if I didn't exist, and go on his way to whatever direction he was headed for. I would pass the time of day anyway, and it didn't worry me that I wouldn't get a response, which became the norm as I was dealing with an ignorant man.

I later had a disagreement with the new Divisional Detective Superintendent regarding the charging of a suspect in relation to some local crimes. The suspect had made a statement of admission to me about the commission of a small number of crimes in the district for which he was charged, and bailed to appear in court in connection with these crimes. Now, the Detective Superintendent was at Kevin Street station, and the matter had been reported to him as a positive outcome with respect to the detection of crime in the district.

The Detective superintendent's reaction was to ask why the suspect wasn't charged with more crimes, and it would help to clear the "books", and improve the detection rate. I got into a heated argument with the Detective Superintendent regarding his suggestion that the suspect should be charged with numerous other charges that he did not admit to. I stated that I would only charge the suspect with crimes that he had admitted to.

The response of the Detective Superintendent was to turn to the other Detective Sergeant that was present, who happened to be my colleague that I did the beat with in the Ballyfermot area in earlier years. He directed him to bring in the suspect again, and charge him with a number of other crimes which the Detective Sergeant agreed to do at the time. I reiterated that this suspect would only be charged with the crimes he had admitted to. The Detective Superintendent left the office leaving an air of coolness in the office after trying to create a divide within the unit, and I suspected there would be a follow-up to this encounter.

The charging of the suspect with other crimes never materialised as nobody wanted to take the risk of a rebound, but I knew my days were numbered at Kevin Street, as the two Superintendents put their heads together, and orchestrated my transfer to Kilmainham station within the "A"District, doing a swap with the Detective Sergeant who was attached to Kilmainham station at the time.

Kilmainham till 1982

Later, while at Kilmainham station, one of my staff would recount a situation that he found himself in after charging a suspect with multiple crimes. It was a clearing of the books situation to bring up the detection rate, and the suspect was brought to the courts. As in most of these types of cases, it had been going through the courts for some time when eventually the case came to hearing. The suspect pleaded guilty to a small sample of the charges which he had admitted to in a statement, and the rest of the charges were withdrawn by the prosecution.

The Detective was in the witness box to give his evidence when an enterprising solicitor started to ask him questions on behalf of the defence. He was asked what happened to the large number of charges that had been withdrawn, were they put down as detected crimes on the books, and where was the evidence that his client had committed these crimes. The Detective was stunned by this form of questioning, and when finished, he came down from the witness box in a state.

When he came back to the office, he said never again would he get himself into that situation, no matter what the detection rate. My actions at Kevin Street at an earlier time were exonerated.

The previous Detective Superintendent, who was now attached to the Central Detective Unit at Headquarters, had a meeting with me before the transfer to tip me off as to what was going to happen, saying he understood my situation, and the pressure I was coming under. He advised me to just keep my head down, and see how things work out. This conversation took place in the front yard of Kevin Street station as the "internal walls" of the station couldn't be trusted.

Continuing Feud

Being in Kilmainham wasn't the end of my contacts with Kevin Street, as being the Detective Sergeant responsible for the Detective Unit at Kilmainham, I would make regular trips to Kevin Street, which was the District Headquarters for meetings regarding crime, bringing files for information of the Detective Inspector, assisting in carrying out searches, and investigation of serious crimes. There were times also that I would attend the weekly crime conference at the Central Detective Unit Offices, Dublin castle, on behalf of the Detective Inspector "A" District, when he wouldn't be available. We were after all the "A" district Detective Unit, which covered the whole district. Of course, I still had the two Superintendents as my senior officers.

To give an example of how the feud was ongoing, there was an incident in Kilmainham sub District on the 5th of November 1981 where a body was found on the ground beside a block of flats. I was, of course, heading the investigation, which was suspected to be a suicide case, but it had to be fully investigated to ensure there was no foul play involved before it was handed back to a uniform Sergeant for a report for the coroner. It was the normal practice for the Detective Superintendent, and the District Superintendent to visit such a scene, and to issue whatever instructions were necessary.

I met with both my District Superintendent, and my Detective Superintendent at the scene to bring them up to date with the facts regarding what inquiries were being pursued. The local Superintendent never uttered a word to me, and totally ignored me as I spoke, but before he left, he gave some instructions, speaking to the Detective Superintendent to pass on to me, even as I was standing there with the two of them. That gave me some idea as to the type of person I was dealing with. He couldn't even speak to me face to face, even at the scene of a serious incident like a suspicious death.

With regards to the Detective Superintendent, he acted as normal with respect to the investigation, and had a reasonably good discussion with me, but felt very uncomfortable in the presence of the District Superintendent. The Detective Superintendent was like that, one day, he was fighting with you, and the next, he was all over you, as we say, he had his moments.

It's not my intention to go into huge detail regarding my complete service within the "A" district which was a very busy area, with constant searching, investigations, and visiting crime scenes. This is just to point out some of the low ebbs in this part of my service, and the type of people that crossed my path during that period of time.

I would think back at some of my previous life in St Joseph's Residential Institution, Tralee, and see the similarity in the people that dealt with me then, and the mentality of the current crop of "superior officers". Bullying would be the first thing to come into my mind, belittlement, and intimidation would be other thoughts, but at this stage, I had built up my resistance to these type of characters who would try to put me back into my box.

I would put the building up of my confidence, my self-esteem, my determination, and independence of mind down to the good tutoring I received during my spell with the Fraud Squad. I was out of my box, and had become a rebel for good causes.

Visitation for Inspection of the Books

Just to dwell a little further on my time in the "A" District, while at Kilmainham Station, maybe about twelve months or so before I left, I can't put an exact time on it, I had reason the visit one of the local hospitals to visit my sister, Ann, who used to live in Liverpool, but now resided on Achill Island. She was after having a very serious operation for the removal of one of her kidneys. My sister was in good form, and I told her that she was not going to go home to Achill Island when she left the hospital, but would stay a few days with me at my house to get some of her strength back, and that I would take her from the hospital when she was released which I did.

I was working that day, so I left the hospital, went back to my office, where low, and behold I found the Superintendent, and the Detective Superintendent in my office going through my books. Before I had left for the hospital, I had left a very junior member of my staff behind to look after the office. I saw that he was in a very nervous state in the presence of these two officers, and I didn't know what they had said to him. I interjected, ignoring the two senior officers, and instructed the trainee detective to go to an observation post we had set up in the sub-district to detect people stealing from cars in the area. That relieved the situation for him, and I was now alone with my two uninvited guests.

After the trainee detective had left for his duty, I stood in the office watching what the Superintendent was doing. The Superintendent was making some comments about the keeping of the duty books, which I didn't respond to. I "bit my tongue", as they say, kept my cool, and said nothing, not even answering any of the questions which were put to me. The situation was very tense, and even the Detective Superintendent, who said nothing, was uneasy, and uncomfortable in his chair at the situation that was developing.

The confrontation lasted about fifteen to twenty minutes before the Superintendent finished what he was looking at, and then he proceeded to take up one of the books, and push it into my face, saying have these records corrected as soon as possible. Now, these records were in respect of the duties each member of my staff had worked. There were two separate books, one for extra duty, and one for night duty, and I had incorporated all duties into one book, which the Superintendent was objecting to. As this was happening the Detective Superintendent was heading for the door not knowing what was going to happen next. The Superintendent then followed, and I pushed the door hard slamming it behind him.

There was a knock at the door, which I opened, and the Superintendent was standing there saying something about the door being slammed in his face. Unless his face was stuck to his backside, then I did. I said nothing, and as soon as the Superintendent turned to go again from the door, I slammed it shut again. Now, the doors were big heavy doors as it was a very old building, and they would make a big bang when pushed shut. This is not to take away from what I did as I meant every bit of it.

I had an inkling that this would not be the last of the situation, and like Kevin Street; my days were numbered now at Kilmainham station. After this incident, I had a call from my former Detective Superintendent who was now based at Detective Headquarters at Central Detective Unit, Dublin Castle, and he wanted to meet me. Obviously, the "grape vine "was working again, and the incident had reached the ears of people at Dublin Metropolitan Headquarters. The meeting was set up, and would have taken place at either Kevin Street or Kilmainham, again in the yard or car park.

Both of us agreed that my position in the "A" district was untenable, and a move would be the best for everybody. He would later come back to me, and inform me that I was going to be transferred to the Garda Drug Squad at the Central Detective Unit at Osmond House.

It was quite obvious that my local Superintendent was making his observations regarding his dealings with me, known at Central Headquarters during whatever meetings were taking place." Oh! To have been a fly on the wall at such meetings", I thought. I could only imagine some of the reporting being made by my local Superintendent, and the picture being portrayed of this "rebellious" Detective Sergeant serving in his district.

During my service at both Kevin Street, and Kilmainham stations, I made many friends among both the detective branch, and the uniform section. I had gained a lot of respect for the way I had dealt with my authorities regarding certain matters, and a lot of sympathy for the way I was being treated. I never regretted the stance I took with respect to the running of my Detective Units or my several altercations with the man who was my Superintendent for most of my stay in the "A" district. For some reason, from the very start, my new Superintendent, and I never hit it off.

The Garda Siochana suffered many tragedies over the years, and while I was serving in the "A" district in July 1980, news came in that two members of the force had been shot dead after coming on the scene of a bank raid in Co Roscommon. They were Detective Garda John Morley, and Garda Henry Byrne. It was a black day for the force, and it affected every member when this news broke. Eventually, a number of persons were arrested, and charged, and sentenced to life imprisonment. They were members of a known terrorist organisation who carried out the killings. We were still in the middle of what became known as the "troubles". Altogether during my service in An Garda Siochana which included the time of the troubles", there were about 15 members of the Garda force murdered in the line of duty.

Back to the books again

While still at Kilmainham Station, I developed a good relationship with a Station Sergeant who was a Kerry man. I had decided to try my hand at the books again, and start back at the studies for the promotional examination for the Inspector rank. It was obvious that some people saw some leadership qualities in me, and without saying as much were pushing me to get qualified for the Inspector rank. I was being advised again, and again, by those close to me, that I should go, and do the Inspectors examination. Now, the Kerry Sergeant was of senior service, and I talked him into getting into the books as well. Both of us attended promotion classes given by a senior officer at one of the stations.

In most situations, it was deemed a two year course, and the first exam was seen as a dry run to get the experience of the questions, and layout of the exam. The Kerry man, and I did a lot of swatting together at Kilmainham, and I also did a lot of work at home, locking myself in one of the rooms in the house with all my papers during my free time. At this time, I had a growing family, four children, and another on the way. With my family, and of course, the constant intimidation from my Superintendent, I had to show my character in putting everything aside, and getting down to my studies. There were moments when the Kerry man was thinking of pulling out, but I kept him on stream, and we both sat the exam in 1981.

To our amazement both of us passed the Inspectors examination on the first go, so there was no need for a repeat. Now, I was qualified to go for promotion for the rank of Inspector. I could of course, never see myself making an application for promotion through the current management of the "A" district, as anyway my intention was to stay within the Detective Branch, and go forward for an interview for Detective Inspector when the opportunity presented itself.

At thirteen years of service, and twenty years after I was "released" from St Joseph's Residential Institution, Tralee, I was qualified to go forward for promotion to the rank of Inspector within An Garda Siochana.

What I didn't know at that time was that there were big changes to the promotion system coming down the line, which would see a huge change in the direction that my career would take, and it would have a devastating effect on promotion within the Detective Branch. I, with a number of other Detectives, were to play a key role in trying to prevent such a situation occurring, to the detriment of my own future career, in what became known as the "Detectives Case".

CHAPTER SIXTEEN

New Move to the Drugs Squad

My term of "bullying, and intimidation" at the hands of the officer corp at the "A" district ended with my transfer to the Garda Drug Squad during the second half of January 1982, which was based at Osmond House, my previous home with the Fraud Squad, and where I was promoted from. I was given my new assignment as a Detective Sergeant with one of the units in the Drug Squad. It was one of four units with a Detective Sergeant in charge of each unit, and a Detective Inspector with overall charge of the Squad.

This was another new learning curve for me in policing, with a huge change in legislation, which I had to come to grips with, and also update myself with the history of the Drug Squad. It had become commonplace over the years, as with my time in the Fraud Squad, for members from districts, both in the Dublin area, and the country at large, to make contact with the Central Detective Drugs Unit for assistance, and advice relating to all drug matters.

The Drug Squad worked on a four-shift roster system, with three weeks on days, and one week on late. When I arrived, I met, and was introduced to all the members of the Squad, including my own new unit, of course. The Detective Inspector of the unit was a very well-known man called Denis Mullins, who had a very high profile because of his involvement with, and knowledge of the drug scene in the earlier years in Dublin. He started in the drug investigations in the mid-1960s as a Detective Sergeant, later promoted to Detective Inspector, where he fought an uphill battle to convince certain people in authority of the growing problem with drugs in Ireland. He remained with the unit until his promotion to Superintendent in 1984. I served with him for his last two years there as a Detective Inspector, and we had a reasonably good working relationship.

I was well received by my new squad, and greatly assisted in getting to know the new ground I was to cover. One of the first things I noted about the drug situation was that there was never a crime until somebody who was caught in possession for either personal use or for supply to others was charged, and appeared in court.

It wasn't like crime "ordinary" in the districts, where crimes were being reported daily, and the crime problem in a given area would be supported by the figures produced whether detected or not. With the drugs scene, there was no detection rate to keep up, and no books to "clear". Of course, the squad would be judged on the number of seizures for the year, and the volume of the drugs seized by the Drugs Unit, which was a small, enough unit, and under-staffed, compared to the crime investigation units around the city of Dublin.

When you had a Minister for Justice in 1969 saying there was no drug problem, the Revenue Commissioners who were responsible for the Customs, and Excise department refusing a request to set up a special drugs investigation unit to control the importation of illegal drugs, and the hierarchy of the Garda Siochana being unconvinced that there was a drugs problem despite a growing public concern, what chance had the Drug Squad of gaining support for the fight against this new scourge on society at that time. A number of years later, these establishments would acknowledge that there was a problem, and would eventually take action to tackle the drug scourge.

When the Drug Squad had been formed a number of years previously in the late 1960s, it was made up of Detectives from the Garda Special Branch Division, as they were more experienced in dealing with foreign criminals who were deemed to be mostly involved in Ireland's deepening drug problems. Many members of the original unit were still at the Squad when I arrived there. They had a different system of investigation from ordinary crime scene, as they would have previously been keeping tabs on the movements of subversives, and gathering information for record purposes. They had many major successes over the years, and developed the drugs investigation section into a very helpful, and successful unit under the leadership, and guidance of Detective Sergeant Denis Mullins.

Of course, on my initial arrival at the Squad, there was an air of suspicion as to who this new man was, where I came from, and how I landed at the Drug Squad. The reason for this would surface later when I was approached by my Detective Inspector, Denis Mullins, sometime after my arrival there. The Detective Inspector mentioned to me that before my arrival, he was cautioned to watch out for me as I was something of a trouble maker. You know he said to me, "I haven't seen you doing anything to warrant the stories I was told".

This gave me the ideal opportunity to give an account of my term in the "A" District, as this is where the damaging information was coming from. From then on, there was never any reason for the Detective Inspector to keep an eye on me, and I settled in very well with my new squad.

I also noted an air of tension within the squad, which related to matters that occurred prior to my arrival. I was brought up to speed as to what this situation was all about. Seemingly, during the course of the previous year 1981, the Drugs Squad were involved in an ongoing operation regarding a group of international drug smugglers who were connected with Irish criminals, and who were arranging to import a shipment of drugs to Ireland.

The Detective Inspector, and a Detective Sergeant found this operation a huge drain on the normal duties of the squad so they went to Garda Headquarters to seek assistance with their operation. They got that assistance alright, with a new unit being formed at Headquarters which became known as the DIIU, Drugs Intelligence, and Investigation Unit, which took over the current operation, and kept a member of the main Drugs Squad involved for a time with them.

The operation became known as "Operation Angel", and the involvement of this new unit in what was a Drug Squad investigation initially, caused resentment within the Dublin Drugs Unit who were not now involved in the ongoing investigation, and surveillance. It also coincided with the time that the higher authorities were acknowledging that there was a drugs problem on the island of Ireland.

The operation lasted from April 1981 to middle of September of the same year. The operation ended with the seizure of nearly five million Irish pounds worth of cannabis, and afterwards the arrest of numerous suspects connected with the importation. Before anybody was charged the media got "hold" of the story with full exposure of the members of the investigating team, including photographs of the seized drugs with some of the officers. Initially, it was a huge success story, and a blow to the drug cartel.

Of the numerous people, about eight in all, who were arrested, and eventually charged in connection with the seizure, none were convicted, as all charges against them were withdrawn. The Director of Public Prosecutions had directed that the detention of the suspects was deemed to be unlawful. All evidence, and statements of admission were deemed to be inadmissible as evidence in a court of law. It was a bitter blow to the investigation team, and a loss of face for the new unit from headquarters. The old drugs unit was a bit bemused by the outcome, and their resentment lessened, as their experience in the drugs field had not been drawn on. The result showed the inexperience of the people who ran" Operation Angel" with the legislation covering drug investigations.

A short period of time after my arrival, certainly within the first twelve months, we were on the move again out of Osmond House. A brand new building had been leased as the Dublin Metropolitan Garda Headquarters at Harcourt Square. This was my third move to a new accommodation since I had joined the force. For whatever reason, maybe it was his growing trust in me, the Detective Inspector in charge of the Drug Squad asked me to take charge of the move to the new Headquarters. The Drug Squad had been assigned accommodation on the ground floor, which suited us fine. When I visited the building for the first time, it was just a large open space with no furniture. Over a period of time, we got the place up, and running.

Trip to Spain

The uneasy situation between the Dublin Drug Squad, and the Head-quarters unit was to raise its head again in early 1982, shortly after my arrival, with the arrest, and detention in Spain, of some well-known Irish criminals who were involved in illegal drugs importation to Ireland. There was a decision taken at Headquarters with the agreement with the Spanish authorities to have somebody from the Irish Garda force travel to Spain to interview those detained.

A Detective Inspector, who had been one of the leading investigators in the "Operation Angel" case, was assigned from Headquarters to travel to Spain. To avoid further bitterness with the Dublin Drugs Squad, and to try to mend the relationship between both, it was decided that a Detective Sergeant from the Dublin Drug Squad would be detailed to travel with the Detective Inspector from Headquarters to Spain. For some reason, none of the existing members of Detective Sergeant rank, either didn't take up the offer or weren't asked to travel. My arrival was at a most opportune moment, and I was asked if I would travel to Spain with the Detective Inspector from Headquarters. Looking back now, it seems that I was being used to break the deadlock between the Dublin Drug Squad, and the Headquarters Unit.

Now, my own experience in the drugs field was limited to a number of cases I had dealt with while out in the districts aided at the time by the Drugs Squad, but I then learned that the Detective Inspector from Headquarter's previous experience was limited as well prior to Operation Angel. It was to be an early baptism of fire for me starting in the Drugs Squad. Of course, I jumped at the opportunity to travel abroad, and of course, I was seen as a person who had not been tainted by the resentments expressed regarding "Operation Angel".

I had a number of things to do prior to travelling; first I had to get a passport, I had never held a passport before. Now, at that time, one could be waiting a number of weeks before a passport would be issued. I was given the VIP treatment with a letter from my Detective Superintendent at the Central Detective Unit, and my passport photos. I went to the passport office, and obtained a passport within a matter of hours. I had of course, met with the Detective Inspector from Headquarters to go over what papers, and documentation we would need, and to sort our travel arrangements.

A trip had to be made to the Department of Foreign Affairs to get papers to allow us to carry out inquiries in a foreign country, and then to the Department of Justice for legal clearance for that purpose. The persons arrested were being detained in the south of Spain, in Malaga, in the Costa Del Sol, but in making our travel arrangements, we had to travel to Madrid first to the Irish Consulate to collect further documentation being forwarded there by the department of Foreign Affairs. We stayed one night in Madrid, and then travelled to the south of Spain on the following day.

Our visit to the Irish consulate in Madrid bore no fruit as they had not received any papers relating to the case, and had no contact with the police where the suspects were being detained. Several phone calls were made from the Irish consulate while we were there, the official doing his best to get the matter sorted. The official got the name of a Detective Inspector, who was familiar with the case in the Costa Del Sol, who spoke a little English, whom we were to meet on our arrival, but there was no guarantee that we would get to interview the detained persons.

That's how things stood as we made our way to Malaga in the Costa Del Sol, the following morning. We were met by the Detective Inspector as arranged by the consulate, and were brought to the apartment where we were to stay. The local Detective Inspector promised to try to arrange a meeting with the detained persons, but said it might take a couple of days. There was of course, another situation at that time in Spain, they were preparing for the world cup which was being played in Spain in July of that year, and almost all the police attention was being diverted towards that event.

While waiting for the meetings to be set up, we busied ourselves visiting the known hotels, and establishments that the detained persons had either been staying or had been known to visit. At one particular bar we got talking to a barman who knew the people that had been detained, and he showed us a 100 Irish Punt note he had been given by one of them, which he had hung up behind the bar. Now, at that time, the biggest Irish Punt denomination note that could be presented in Spain was I think a 20 Punt note, anything bigger had to be presented at a bank to be exchanged.

Eventually, we got to meet with the detained persons in the company of the Detective Inspector from the locality. Nothing of value was gained from the interviews, as they weren't saying anything other than idle chatter.

After the interviews were completed, the Spanish Detective Inspector met with us, and brought us out for a bite to eat, and a few drinks. We returned to Dublin on a flight from Malaga, and on our arrival back the Detective Inspector from Headquarters insisted on going to Headquarters, where a report was made to senior officers that evening. The trip may have seemed a wasted trip, but it put the drug dealers on notice that no stone would be left unturned to track them down. I would remember this trip for the rest of my days as my initiation into the Drug Squad. We did of course, bring back some memorabilia with us on our return, I bought a bottle of red wine, "Rioja Siglo "1976 vintage, covered in a sack wrapping, which I still have, and is now over 40 years old. I'm not too sure if it's drinkable.

I was to serve four good years at the Drug Squad between 1982, and 1986. I was involved in a great many cases, and investigations with my unit over the period, including some cases, which would stick in my memory because of the out of the ordinary detail surrounding some of them, a few of which are worth a mention, not in any particular chronological order. During those years, I would also be involved in events that would affect my future career, and also the devastating loss of a member of my unit who was shot dead while on duty.

Revisiting some of the cases, and happenings while attached to the Drug Squad

There was the case of information which we received regarding a suspected heroin dealer, who resided in an affluent part of Dublin city in a house where he had rented rooms. The house was in a cul-de-sac, and it was difficult to get surveillance on the residence. We did manage to get a room in a house opposite to the suspect's house to keep it under observation. We found it very difficult going to, and from the observation post for fear of exposure, which could cause the operation to falter. This was partly due to the extremely good street lighting in the area at night time.

To negate this situation, I got a member of my unit to make contact with the lighting department of the local counsel, and have the lighting in that particular area extinguished for the duration of the operation, and it worked wonders as, after dark we could move in, and out as we pleased. The operation was a success, and the culprit was arrested in possession of a quantity of heroin, charged, and appeared in court. He was allowed out on his father's bail, who described himself to the court as a banker. A later check on his father's credentials showed him working as a porter in a bank.

This is just an indication of some of the measures that were taken over time in order to carry out a successful operation with the help of someone of the public bodies.

Another case I bring to mind is one regarding a person found dealing in a "white" powder in the centre of Dublin city, which was suspected to be cocaine. He was selling it in ten pound deals to drug users. He was arrested, and brought in for questioning on suspicion of drug dealing. During the course of the interview the suspect owned up to the fact that what he was selling was, in fact, "Lignocaine" which is used by dentists as an anesthetic when pulling or filling teeth. He was passing it off as cocaine to the drug users.

He then informed us that he had a bag of the powder concealed in a safe deposit box at a bank in the city. We arranged to get a warrant to carry out a search of the deposit box, and when we got it opened, we found a plastic bag, over a kilo in weight, containing a white powder. Later tests carried out at the Drugs Laboratory found he was telling the truth, and it was Lignocaine. He was of course, charged with the illegal supply of a drug. His story as to why he was doing this was that he was trying to get people to stop using cocaine. Whether that was true or not, he was making money out of his dealings, and conning the drug users into believing that they were in fact buying cocaine, which was a dangerous game he was playing.

The case of the unshaven man

Much of the information regarding drug dealing came from the drug users themselves, which was offered in the hope of a favourable outcome of their own predicament that they found themselves in, and of course had to be taken with a certain amount of caution. There was one such case again in an affluent part of Dublin city in a respectable-looking house. My team, and I were working on such information regarding an unknown person involved in drug dealing, when we carried out a search on a particular house under warrant. I had brought out my full team with me on the search, on gaining entry to the house, we split up, half going upstairs, and the rest staying downstairs to carry out the search as well as keeping an eye on whatever occupant or occupants were in the house. In this particular case, there was just one person in the house, a male in his late 20s or early 30s.

Searching for drugs was a slow process, which entailed a very systematic search of the whole house, areas being searched twice, and maybe three times by rotating the search areas between the searchers. I was in the upstairs part of this particular house with one half of my team, when after a chat with the rest of my team, we decided to change search areas, the downstairs crew swapping places with the upstairs crew. At this stage of the search after a couple of hours, a certain amount of doubt was creeping into the team with regards to the correctness of the information we were working on, and the occupant sat in wonderment as to what was going on as he pretended.

The occupant of the house was kept in sight at all times, and now, and again would be asked to clarify certain things during the course of the search. I, with my part of the team, were now downstairs doing the search, when in the kitchen area, I came across a tin of shaving foam. I was examining the tin of foam when I looked again at the occupant, and saw that he had a good growth of beard on him. He certainly was not a person who shaved, and he was asked what the shaving foam was doing in the kitchen area. This was not a flat, but a two-storey house with a bathroom upstairs. I turned to one of my team beside me, and handed him the shaving foam. My colleague took the tin, and examined it closely, he then began to twist the bottom of the tin, and it unscrewed.

The bottom half of the tin of shaving foam was filled with a quantity of drugs of differing varieties, the top half of the tin worked as a tin of shaving foam. The occupant of the house was stunned that his hiding place for his supply of drugs had been found. This was a good day's work, and worth the time taken to carry out the search, with another new hiding place for drugs discovered. The occupant of the house was processed, and was eventually brought before the courts. The method of concealment of the drugs was photographed, and was shared with other police forces through Interpol.

African Imports

I had another case sometime around August 1983, involving the importation of illegal drugs, cannabis, by a group of Africans from Ghana. It was a joint operation in conjunction with the customs authorities who had suspicions regarding several cardboard cases of goods coming through the airport. These goods were kept at a warehouse in the airport, and arrangements were made with the people to whom the goods were addressed to have the consignment collected.

Three African people, two males, and a female arrived to collect the goods, and we were waiting for them. After receipt of the goods, they were stopped, and arrested on suspicion of importing an illegal substance.

On searching the large cardboard cases, we found they contained wooden carvings of African origin in each of the cases. After a more thorough examination of the cardboard cases, we discovered that all the cases had double-sided sheeting of cardboard on the insides. We parted the cardboard sheeting from the inside of the cases, and discovered cannabis resin hidden in thin lairs on each of the four sides of each of the cardboard cases. There was quite a quantity of drugs seized that day, it would have had a street value of about 100,000 Irish pounds, and it came about as a result of the help from the customs authorities, and their sniffer dog. The suspects were later charged, and processed through the courts.

Well-known criminal family investigation
In September 1982, with members of my unit, we carried out a search of a residence in a flat complex in the south inner city area, which was well known to me from my days in the "A" district. It was the flat next door to a member of a well-known criminal family, Michael Francis Dunne, who had a very big involvement in the drug scene. It was members of his family that were detained in Spain when I accompanied the Detective Inspector from Headquarters to Spain to interview them earlier in 1982.

Because of the type of information we had received, we armed ourselves with a search warrant, for the flat next door to Michael Francis Dunne. We searched the flat next door where we found 4950 Irish punts, 500 pounds sterling in cash, a passport in the name of Michael Francis Dunne, and hanging out the window of this flat on the end of a string was a bag containing a quantity of Heroin. This flat was occupied by a young couple with a child.

The young mother was arrested, and charged in connection with the finding of the Heroin; she pleaded guilty before the district court, and was fined twenty five pounds. She had made a statement outlining the series of events that led to the items being found in her flat. She implicated Michael Francis Dunne as the person who paid her to hold the items for him.

Some weeks later, after the case of his neighbour had been heard in court; we arrested Michael Francis Dunne, and charged him with possession, and supplying the drug to his neighbour. He was eventually sent forward to the Circuit Criminal Court on this, and other serious drug charges. In October 1983, Michael Francis Dunne appeared before the Dublin Circuit Criminal Court, where he pleaded guilty to all charges before the court, and was put into custody for sentencing on a later date. On the date of his sentencing Michael Francis Dunne was sentenced to seven years imprisonment on all the drugs charges.

This case did not end with the sentencing of Michael Francis Dunne; there was the important witness in the case to be considered. After the sentencing the neighbour next door, who was prepared to give evidence for the state case, fled to England on the day of the sentencing. She was in fear for her life because she had been prepared to give evidence against Dunne before he pleaded guilty, and there was huge media coverage of the case, which outlined some details of the case.

She subsequently returned to Ireland in 1984, and got in contact with my unit members outlining her fears for herself, and her child. At this stage, her husband, and she were living apart, and she was still residing at her original flat. I was in the middle of doing my Addiction Studies Course when one of my staff discussed the circumstances of her situation with me. I instructed him to write to the social services, and see if they could facilitate her with a change of residence. In May of 1986, I was still receiving communications from the local authorities regarding her case for relocation. This was a case of officialdom dragging their feet, and not being as cooperative as they would be expected to be. I do understand that at some later date, she did move out of her original flat.

In 1985, I was approached by two journalists, Sean Flynn from the Sunday Press who has since passed away, and Padraig Yeates a freelance journalist who were writing some articles about the criminal drug racket in Ireland. They were interested in my involvement with the arrest, and charging of Michael Francis Dunne, in 1982, one of the criminal Dunne family who controlled a lot of the drug racket in Dublin City. Later, it developed into a book called "Smack" which was the slang name for heroin. I got a mention in the book a number of times in connection with the drug scene, relating to my trip to Spain, and the Michael Francis Dunne case.

The publication, and distribution of the book in Ireland was stopped when an application was made to the courts by somebody against its publication for some reason, and it was upheld by the Courts, but not before I had received a copy signed by both authors. It did circulate in a number of other countries, and there were occasions during the course of doing searches for drugs we found it was also reading material for those involved in the drug scene.

Doctors come under Scrutiny

In the early 1980s around the time I had joined the Drug Squad, legislation to deal with the drug problem was being strengthened, and included the tightening of controls over doctors who were over prescribing to drug addicts. I was nominated shortly after I had arrived at the unit to liaise with the Medical Council of Ireland with regards to the investigation of doctors who were suspected of over prescribing by issuing prescriptions to drug addicts. When a report would come to the Medical Council of a suspicion that a doctor was providing prescriptions to drug addicts, they would send a report to me, and I would open a file, and carry out an investigation of the complaint.

Now, up to this very few, if any, investigations were ever carried out involving doctors by the Garda as they would generally be the subject of inquiries carried out by the Medical Council themselves. There was no template for carrying out these investigations, so I set up my own procedures for the investigations, and reporting to the Medical Council.

This entailed getting the co-operation of certain Pharmacies where it was known the drug addicts were presenting prescriptions for obtaining their medication, and collecting all these prescriptions issued by whatever doctor I was investigating. There would, in some cases, be a number of Pharmacies involved, and hundreds of prescriptions to be collected. I then had to interview the addicts concerned, and obtain statements from them, and also get statements from the Pharmacists with respect to the handing over of the prescriptions. I then interviewed the doctor concerned with issuing the prescriptions, and obtained a statement after caution from him.

I then prepared the file with my covering report for forwarding to the Medical Council, which in the more serious cases would be in maybe two to three volumes of about one hundred pages each containing copies of all the prescriptions issued by the particular doctor under investigation. The Medical Council would then arrange a date for a hearing before the Medical Council Board, which I attended as the main witness to give evidence of my investigations.

The punishment dealt out by the Medical Council depended on the seriousness of the case, the number of prescriptions that had been issued, and the length of time it was going on. Generally, the penalty handed out by the Medical Council would be disbarment from medical practice for a period of time, maybe up to twelve months. This penalty had then to be confirmed by the High Court through an application made by the Medical Council, which I also attended in case something needed clarification.

In the course of these investigations, I came across several situations that doctors found themselves in, from being alcoholics to being blackmailed by addicts over a period of time. Addicts, as some doctors found out to their detriment, were dangerous people to get involved with, and once they got them into their grasp, they found it very difficult to break loose.

I continued to do these investigations involving doctors for a number of years while at the Drug Squad, and some of my work colleagues were concerned that if I had a health issue, I might not get a doctor to treat me. Well, that was another thought, but that situation never arose.

Judge on Drugs Search

I cannot refrain from mentioning now, many years later, the occasion on the 16th of March 1986, when myself, and my unit were discreetly accompanied by one of the District Justices of the Dublin Courts on a search for drugs. It arose as a result of a discussion with the District Justice at a Garda social function which she had attended. She mentioned quietly in passing that she would love to go on a drug search to get a first-hand experience of the drug scene as there were a rising number of drug related cases coming before her court. She was also very interested in the Drug Addictions Studies course that I had completed sometime previously, and would have great interest in doing the course if she would be allowed to do so by the authorities.

The judge in question was none other than the Honourable District Justice Gillian Hussey, who was appointed to the bench in 1984, the same year that I was doing my Addiction Studies Course at Trinity College. She was assigned to the Kilmainham District Court, which was one of the busiest courts in the country outside of the Dublin district court in the city centre.

The area covered by Kilmainham District Court was very large, and as a result, we at the Drug Squad were regular attendees at her court during the course of our work, where we became well acquainted with her, and she with us. Judge Gillian Hussey was a very outgoing person, and attended many Garda functions over the years, and indeed also attended at the golf course for many outings. When she intimated that she would like to see how drug searches were carried out, I promised her that I would arrange something at a future date for her to accompany us.

On the 16th of March 1986, the occasion presented itself, and we arranged for her to accompany us on the search of the flat of a reasonably well-known drug user, and supplier. We had arranged to carry out the search during the evening time after sunset around eight o'clock when our "guest" would be less conspicuous in our company. We travelled in two cars, one with Judge Gillian, and me, and the other car with the rest of the search crew. The plan was for the main search party to gain entrance first, and I would follow in with Judge Gillian. Everything went to plan, and as soon as entry was gained through the main door, I brought Judge Gillian with me, and entered, and went up the stairs, and were just in time to see the door opening, and we all gained entry.

I kept Judge Gillian at the open doorway for her safety until the search party got things under control as there were four occupants in the flat, three of whom were brothers, and the fourth was a known abuser. There were drugs, and other paraphernalia laid out on the table, and one of the brothers had a syringe in his hand, possibly in the act of shooting up, when a struggle ensued to retrieve the syringe, and in the struggle one of my staff, Pat, got a jab of the needle into his hand. This was of course, of great concern to us all as there was the possibility of becoming infected with HIV by the syringe jab. When things got quiet, and under control, the search was simple enough as most of what we were looking for was already on the table. I brought Judge Gillian through the flat to have a look around; she of course, had a scarf around her head to hide her identity. The occupants were strung out on heroin anyway, and would not have been too aware of who was present.

When the search was completed, we got the assistance of the local Garda force members to help with the transport of the four suspects to the local Garda station for processing. We immediately had our colleague Pat brought the Jervis Street Hospital to be treated against HIV infection. At the hospital, he received an inoculation against the HIV, and was informed that it would take at least six months to determine if he was going to be infected or not. He was to return to the hospital again in a few weeks for a booster shot. It was going to be a long six months for Pat, who later joined the rest of us at the Garda Club, at Harrington Street, where we had a prearrangement to bring Judge Gillian after the search as there was a function on, the following day being St Patrick's Day so celebrations were starting early.

Gillian was overawed by what had happened on the night, and it brought home to her the dangers associated with drug investigations. Over the following days, I received a handwritten letter from Gillian at my office at Harcourt Square dated the 18th of March 1986, in it, she wrote the following;

My dear Maurice, Tom, Pat, Con, Sean, and Paddy,
The title of a song in the charts long before your time, but certainly in my time, comes to mind, 'Oh what a night it was, it really was '. It may have been routine for all of you, but it was one I won't forget, and best of all I enjoyed it thoroughly. It certainly gave me an insight into what

you have to deal with. If anyone had told me a year ago that I'd have gone on a search I'd have laughed.

Tom, I'll return your books in due course. I've started to read them, and hopefully when I've got through them I'll be more informed.

Maurice, perhaps sometime you could tell me more about the Trinity course you mentioned. If I'd be allowed attend it I'd like to do so.

I hope Pat is not too sick after his injection. It's just one of the hazards of your job that most people wouldn't realise.

Again, many thanks to each, and every one of you.

Very Sincerely
Gillian

In September 1989, and August 1990, I received further letters from Gillian in respect of two other functions I was involved in organising, indicating her appreciation for being asked to the functions, and her respect for the Garda force. Gillian was always a very thoughtful, and sincere person in both her professional life, and socially. I was attached to Lucan Garda Station at this time, and Kilmainhan was our Court Area.

CHAPTER SEVENTEEN

A taste of college life 1984

Fate was to play another part in my progression through my service in the Garda Siochana. Around the time of my joining the Drug Squad, people in authority were beginning to take the drug problem seriously, and new legislation was being prepared by the government to strengthen the powers for the investigation of the drug problem. Included in the proposals were additional powers for the Garda, better control of prescribing by doctors, improvement of information, and education regarding the drug problem? A course in addiction studies was to be set up to be held in Trinity College Dublin for which a Diploma in Addiction Studies was to be awarded.

Sometime in late October or early November 1983, I was approached, and told that I was nominated to apply to do the Diploma Course in Addiction Studies, at the department of Social Studies, Trinity College, Dublin. I was a bit apprehensive at first due to my limited educational qualifications. College was somewhere that only persons with honours in leaving certificate attended. I sent in my application anyway for the course on the 10th of November 1983, which was the latest date for receipt of applications. The decision to send somebody on the course must have been made in haste, hence the reason for my almost late application. I was called for an interview at Trinity College to be assessed regarding my application to take part in the course. I was accepted on the course, even with my limited educational qualifications.

As part of my application for the course, I recounted a situation I had come across in my operational duties in the Drug Squad. It was a case of a search of an apartment in a flat complex in south city centre under search warrant for drugs. On gaining entry to the flat, we found five occupants in the flat, two females, and three males. There was a quantity of heroin found on the table in the apartment, and on examination of the arm of one of the boys, we found fresh needle marks on his arm, we had obviously disturbed him while injecting himself. I could also see that this boy was very jaundiced, and he had a bad rash on parts of his body.

All five occupants of the flat were arrested, and charged under the Misuse of Drugs act, and brought before the courts, where they were remanded on bail to appear again in a number of weeks' time. On the next appearance in court, only four of the persons charged appeared. The fifth, the boy who was jaundiced, had died. All those charged were of a young age, the oldest being only 22 years of age. I quoted this case as confirmation of the need for cooperation between agencies dealing with the drug problem.

The course started on the 9th of January 1984, and ran for twenty-six weeks, which comprised two eight-week blocks of college-based lectures, and ten weeks of field placement with a specialist agency in the drug addiction field. In terms of college studies, it was classed as a full year. While taking part in the course in March, and June 1984, I was receiving copies of communications regarding financial approval for the start of the next course in October 1984, relating to the Department of Justice, which goes to show how unprepared they were at Garda Headquarters for this development.

Did I ever think I would be getting inside the gates of a university college in Dublin to do a study course? It was of course, beyond all my expectations considering my limited educational qualifications. I was well educated in the hardships of life, and this stood well to me during my six months of college studies. The studies ran from Monday to Friday each week, and instead of using my car to get to the college because of the parking situation in the city centre, I got the train from my home town of Leixlip, each morning which was very relaxing, I became a rail commuter for most of my six months at the college. A big change, and rest from early morning knocking on doors in the course of searching for drugs.

The course coordinator was a man named Shane Butler, with whom I got on reasonably well. He spent a lot of time with us doing brainstorming sessions, and having group discussions about ourselves, and the addiction problems in Ireland. He spent some of these sessions attempting to draw us out, to speak about ourselves, and our lives. I'm afraid he didn't have much luck in getting me to openly discuss my life. He summed it up that I had built a wall around myself, and wasn't allowing anybody in. How right he was as I was living behind that wall, ["lie"] that I previously mentioned. My wall was not for knocking down. I was in my self-preservation mode.

He also provided us with a reading list of books which were available at the Trinity library, indicating which reading would be suitable with respect to each of the professions of the group. I'm not sure now as to the size of the group, but I think there were about twelve of us. Over the two eight-week blocks based at the college Shane had arranged several of the college lecturers from several departments to provide an input into the course.

I suppose we all at some time in our lives get a chance at "name dropping". Well, I had the pleasure of being lectured by none other than Professor Mary McAleese, who at the time was a professor of Criminal Law, Criminology, and Penology at Trinity College. I attended two lectures that she gave to our Addiction Studies group on the 29th of May 1984, and the 5th of June 1984. She was later in 1997 to become President of the Republic of Ireland. I must say she was a very charming, and sincere person, and her lectures went down well with the whole group.

My ten weeks of field placement was with the National Drug Treatment Centre at Jervis Street Hospital, in the centre of Dublin city. I was to spend ten weeks working with, and learning from, a senior Drug Counsellor, Social workers, and Doctors who were attached to the centre, how the treatment centre worked with people with addiction problems.

My mentor for the ten weeks at the Drug Treatment Centre was a lady named Barbara Law who was a senior counsellor at the centre. She had a very precise approach to her job, and would take no non-sense from the attending clients that she dealt with, this of course, suited me fine considering the agency I had arrived from, and my previous dealing with abusers.

The National Drug Advisory, and Treatment Centre at Jervis Street, Hospital, was opened in 1970 as an out-patient clinic to pro-vide treatment, and advisory services to drug abusers, and their fam-ilies. The treatment was free, and was of a confidential nature. Five years later, in 1975, an in-patient Detoxification Unit with a number of beds, was opened at Jervis Street, to assist patients "withdrawing" from their addictions.

Initially, I worked in the out-patients section, meeting people who presented with a drug problem. I joined the team, and overtime gave some counselling, and advice to the people who presented. There was also a withdrawal programme where Methadone was used to re-duce their dependence on opiates. Even though I was introduced as a member of the Garda working in the treatment centre, there were no great objections to my presence made by any of the clients who came to the centre while I was there. It was a different situation for me to change from an enforcer, to being a counsellor, and giving advice to persons involved in the drug scene.

Over my ten weeks course, I visited many other outreach centres dealing with those addicted to drugs that were in collaboration with the Jervis Center. The day Centre at Ushers Island, Dublin, Coolmine Therapeutic Community Centre, and Rutland Centre, Clondalkin to name, but a few.

I also got a good insight into the drug problem of the time, and the numbers of people who were recorded as being addicted to drugs. There was a huge increase in numbers recorded attending the treatment centre, from 1979 to 1982, according to a study that was carried out in 1983. In 1979, there were 415 people attending the treatment centre, and in 1982, this jumped to 1307. In one month alone in June of 1983, there were 260 people attending. One could go on quoting figures from different studies, but these figures only cover those who were attending for treatment in the Dublin area. Later studies would show that the numbers given as attending Jervis Street Treatment Centre were not a true account of the overall numbers who were abusing drugs in the country as they were not presenting for treatment.

I must say that my time spent at the Jervis street centre over the ten weeks was a great experience for me, and would have enlightened me to the fact that there was a much larger problem with drugs in Ireland than was realised. Drug abuse became a pandemic in Ireland in the early 1980s, which could have been brought under control earlier if the powers that be, intervened when they should have. They closed their eyes to the problem when Detective Inspector Denis Mullins warned them in the early 1970s, and then panicked in the early 1980s with rushed legislation, and other methods for dealing with the problem.

After my placement at Jervis Street Treatment Centre, I returned to the college to complete my second eight-week block of college-based training. At this time, we were informed that there would be no examination as such, but we all had to complete a project report as to what we would hope to do on our return to our own agencies. It should contain some proposals as to what aspects of the drug problem I could change my approach to.

Many hours of the last college-based block were taken up with exploring what changes I could bring to my agency's approach to the drug problem. I had a fixed time limit to have my Project Report completed, and lodged with the college. I fixed my sights on one aspect of the Garda approach to the problem, and I'm reproducing my Project Report in the following pages, a copy of which was left to the college authorities for assessment, and a copy forwarded to the Garda authorities at Garda Headquarters.

DIPLOMA IN ADDICTIONS STUDIES

PROJECT REPORT

Maurice Heffernan

Project Report   **Maurice Heffernan**

Introduction

Do I go back to doing exactly what I was doing before I came on this course? Will I be able to make any impression on my agency when I return to it? What new approaches to the drug problem can I bring about from a Police point of view? These are some of the many questions that I have asked myself prior to writing this report.

I would hope in this report to make some useful suggestions which might answer some of my questions without getting carried away with ideas. I know that when I rejoin the Drug Squad, I will be doing a lot of the same work I was doing before I started this course, but I do not doubt that I will be able to use some of the skills, and knowledge gained from the course in one way or another in my daily routine, and certainly my approach to some aspects of the problem of drug abuse will have changed.

It's not my intention to make suggestions that any of the structures within the Garda force should be altered, as those structures exist for all other aspects of law enforcement, but there may be areas within the existing structures where there may be room for improvement to deal with the problem of drug abuse. It is through the eyes of the Law Enforcer I must look to see what influences I can have on the thinking, and policies in relation to drug abuse, and control, and I ask myself the following questions, which I consider to be relevant, a] what effects can I as a person in authority have on the families, and persons who are involved in the drug scene?, b] can I assist any of our young people to stop before it's too late, by early intervention?, c] can we in the drug squad or indeed the Gardai in general develop more awareness among parents of young people, with better contact with other agencies regarding the drug problem.

I know as I write this report that foremost in my mind is the knowledge that the primary role of the Gardai is the protection of life, and property, and the prevention, and detection of crime, in that order. Certainly, anything that can be done to ease the situation created by the abuse of drugs must come under the first category in the primary role of protection. The fight against the abuse of drugs is aimed in that direction, whether it involves law enforcement, prevention, or treatment agencies. I hope to outline in this report some suggestions to cover the questions I have raised above.

Brief account of Present position

Before I go further, I feel it is necessary for me to outline briefly what the present approach to the drug problem is by the Gardai as I see it. The responsibility for enforcement of the law in relation drug abuse, and misuse rests with the entire Garda force as a whole, because of the complexity of the problem, a specialised unit commonly known as the "Drug Squad" exists to coordinate all aspects of law enforcement in respect of the misuse of drugs. This can cover anything from finding somebody on the street with a cannabis "reefer" to arresting persons with international connections in the drug trade. In the normal course of events, a person is arrested, charged, and brought before the courts, and the Gardai do not involve themselves with the question of treatment or family involvement. In most cases, families are not involved because of a request of the person charged. I am speaking here about the general rule of things as they stand, as I know that there are individuals within the Garda force who do show a certain amount of responsibility towards persons charged in respect of drugs, who they know are addicted. I also know that these individual Gardai at times, feel frustrated because of their limitations in their knowledge of the problem, and because of the lack of communication, and contact with other agencies in the field of drug abuse.

The Garda Drug Squad do have an involvement in education against drug abuse, mainly aimed towards parents, by way of talks, and slide shows, based on prevention, and detection of any type of drug abuse in the home. In the Drug Squad we do have a lot of contact with families of drug abusers, and this contact can come about, during the course of a house search, as a result of something found on a person on the street when that person is charged, parents looking for information, and parents themselves being suspicious regarding the activities of one of the younger members of the family. Generally, these parents are referred to other agencies for further advice without any direct contact being made with the agency as to whether those people even turned up there.

When you go further afield into the Garda force in general, then the drug problem becomes plainly, and simply a law enforcement one, and there is very little advice available for persons or parents presented with a drug problem apart from legal advice. That to me, seems to be the present situation, and I think there is room for improvement in the way we in the Garda Siochana approach the drug problem.

Creating more awareness within the Garda Force

I have no doubt that the Gardai can become more aware of the overall problem of drug abuse. Police, in general, are very receptive to any suggestions which might create a better understanding of a problem they are dealing with, but until this happens, we will continue to look at things through a tunnel, and just see it as a law enforcement problem only. I think we know by now that it is not just a law enforcement problem, but there seems to be reluctance, and this is not just in the police, to involve oneself other than in one's own area of intervention. The problem is usually pushed aside as being the "welfare people "job or that of the "probation service". I am not putting forward for one minute the suggestion that the police should move into other areas like counselling or treatment, but what I would like to see is the setting up of a set procedure within the force whereby other agencies involved in the drug field could be fully briefed about particular problems encountered by the Gardai. There may, of course, be a question of confidence from time to time in respect of some matters, but where it is obvious a person needs the services of other agencies, there should be full cooperation between those agencies, and the Gardai. To do this, the Gardai will have to be made more aware of the many factors involved in drug abuse, like the effects of the various drugs on particular persons, the real meaning of addiction, the various types of treatment available, and the overall effects on families.

Some doubts certainly will be expressed as to whether a police force should concern themselves with what I have outlined above, but I know that the policeman can be called on to do many things, and looking back, I feel that I have encroached on all types of professions unknowingly in the performance of my duties in the past, and I think the following **reference from Adams [1965]** is important to keep in mind in this respect in his description of a policeman's role in society.

"The police officer wears many caps, and assumes many sub-roles when playing his part. He Is a father-confessor to the youngster who has made his first mistake, a referee in a family or neighbourhood quarrel, an actor in the drama of a high speed pursuit, and capture of a wanted felon, an investigator at the scene of a crime or accident, and a director of pedestrians, and vehicles on the street? He seldom has the time or the favourable atmosphere to vie for the popular vote of the people he serves, and he settles for at least a little tolerance for himself, and the role he fills. Some people learn to respect the policeman, some learn to fear him, and others are thought to despise, and sometimes flout him, and his authority. The most significant characteristic of the unique role of the policeman in the community is that very few people actually know exactly what that role is."

Looking at what Adams [1965] says regarding the role of the policeman in the community, and the fact that "few people actually know exactly what that role is ", should we then as a police force, be determining what our role is, I don't think so, I think we have to be able to look beyond the law enforcement side of any problem, and more so the drug problem because of the human misery, and suffering it can bring on some sections of our communities, and families within those communities.

There is no reason why we, as a police force, should not be able to develop more awareness, both within the force itself, and throughout the general public about the problem of drug abuse. I would hope in this respect, with the experience, and knowledge gained from this course, to develop a more open approach to the problem of drug abuse by trying to build up a better understanding of the workings of other agencies in the drugs area within the Garda Siochana.

I feel, because of my work experience in the National Drug Advisory, and Treatment Centre, Jervis Street, that there is a total misunderstanding, and at times mistrust within both the Drug Advisory Centre, and the Gardai of each other, all because of the lack of knowledge, and co-operation. I know that this will not be put right overnight, but I would hope to set the wheels in motion to ease this situation. I would also hope to develop avenues of communication within the force, like the in-service-training areas, and the training centre to help to create this awareness I have talked about, within the Garda force, and also to develop better cooperation with other agencies.

Having got ourselves into the position of cooperation with other people in the field of drug abuse, I feel then that the Gardai would be in a much better position to assist the families of drug abusers, who are, in a sense, the "injured parties"in most cases. Some would say there is nobody "injured" in a case of drug abuse, that the abuser is the "loser", but I would think, just as in a burglary where somebody's house is broken into, the owners of the house are "injured" in some way, so too with a drug abuser in the family. I would think the structure of the family has been "injured" in some way, and that family would need advice, and guidance to deal with the crisis. I don't think we should any longer leave a family dismayed, and upset at seeing one of their children taken away for abusing drugs, and left with a sense of hopelessness, but rather, we should, as the people coming into first contact with that family inform them of their responsibility towards their child, and also the backup services available to them to assist them in dealing with the problem, and if possible to put them in immediate contact with whatever agency best suites their present needs.

Early Intervention by the Gardai

I have already outlined above in the first section of this report a brief review of the agency to which I am attached, and it would seem that I have very little room for manoeuvre from my present position of law enforcer. Very few people within the Garda force would disagree with that position, and **Becker [1963] would seem to bear this out when he wrote,**

"Although some policemen undoubtedly have a kind of crusading interest in stamping out evil, it is probably much more typical for the policeman to have a certain detached, and objective view of his job. He is not so much concerned with the content of any particular rule as he is with the fact that it is his job to enforce the rule. When the rules are changed, he punishes what was once acceptable behaviour just as he ceases to punish behaviour that has been made legitimate by a change in the rules. The enforcer then may not be interested in the content of a rule as such, but only in the fact that the existence of the rule provides him with a job, a profession,..........."

Whereas what Becker has outlined is probably true of the general policies of law enforcement over twenty years ago, changes have come about in approaches, in relation to enforcement.

This brings me to one aspect of the service of the Gardai, which I think could be expanded, and possibly modified to meet the demands, and problems of drug abuse. I am speaking of the Juvenile Liaison Scheme, which was introduced into the Irish scene in 1963, operating within the Dublin Metropolitan Area only at that time. This scheme is now operating on an almost country-wide basis, and it does deal with a very small number of persons involved in the drug scene, but in a limited way.

Juvenile Liaison Scheme

I would like to set out at this stage how the Juvenile Liaison Scheme works or is implemented. The main theme of the scheme is that juveniles may have a caution administered to them instead of being prosecuted before the courts for a breach committed against the criminal law, provided that certain conditions are met. These conditions are;

1] The offender is between the ages of 7, and 17 years;
2] That he admits the offence;
3] That he has not previously come under the notice of the Gardai;
4] That the offence is a minor offence;
5] That the parents of the offender, and the injured party agree to have the offence dealt by way of caution.

If some person is arrested, and the above conditions apply, then the offender should not be dealt with by way of charge or summons. A report containing all relevant facts is sent to the Juvenile Liaison Officer in whose area the offender resides. The local Juvenile Liaison Officer will visit the home of the juvenile, and discuss the case fully with both the offender, and his family. With the consent of the parents, the offender's school is visited, and the opinions of the teachers are sought. The Juvenile Liaison Officer then completes his reports, and makes recommendations as to how the juvenile should be dealt with.

The final decision as to the outcome rests with the local District Officer of the Garda Siochana, who decides whether or not the juvenile should be cautioned, taking into account all the circumstances of the case, including the recommendations of the Juvenile Liaison Officer. If the recommendation is for a caution, it is administered by the local Garda District Officer, and the parents of the offender are required to attend on that occasion.

The juvenile then comes under the supervision of the local Juvenile Liaison Officer for a period of two years or until he/she attains the age of 17 years, whichever comes first. The supervision includes visits on a monthly basis to the juvenile's home or more often if thought necessary.

The Juvenile Liaison Officers themselves meet, and cooperate with Teachers, Parents, Probation Officers, Social Workers, Welfare Officers, Child Guidance Clinics, Public Health Clinics, and the courts, from time to time in relation to particular cases where they may be of some assistance to the families, and the offender.

I have outlined above briefly how the Juvenile Liaison Scheme operates at present, and one would think that there should be no problem with involving persons abusing drugs into that scheme. I would certainly like to see this scheme being used to a greater extent, but I feel that there would have to be some slight modifications to the existing scheme. I would see, for instance, a greater need for closer monitoring of a drug abuser over a period of time, and this would involve the cooperation of another agency- the National Drug Advisory, and Treatment Centre, Jarvis Street, who I know from tentative approaches would be more than willing to assist in the implementation or the extension of the scheme to drug abusers. I would put forward the following, which I think would be the minimum necessary for the Gardai to become more actively involved in preventing the spread of abuse by early intervention.

Conditions

I would propose that the conditions be modified on just a number of points starting with the age of the offender, I would suggest that in respect of drug Offences where the offence is abuse only, and that the maximum age be increased from 17 years to 19 yeast or 20 years. Why I propose this change is that from experience, very few juveniles under the age of 17 years are ever charged with drug offences, hence one of the reasons why such a small number come to the notice of the Juvenile Liaison Officers. I am also taking into consideration here the age at which persons start to abuse drugs, which studies have shown to be on average 17 years of age, [Stafford-Johnston 1983]. Taking those factors into account with a further part of the [Stafford- Johnston 1983] study that, on average persons have been abusing for four years or more before they are actually discovered, then you are talking about persons first being discovered at an average age of 21 years for a first offence. This gap in age puts them outside the scope of the Juvenile Liaison Scheme, and there is nothing left only for them to be charged or summoned. I am aware that drug abusers under the age of 17 years do come to notice, but they are charged with offences other than drug offences. This suggestion to my mind, would be worthy of consideration, and further examination.

The second of these conditions is that the juvenile admits the offence. Under this condition, the offending juvenile must have committed some crime or if it is related to an offence involving drugs then he/she would have to be found in possession of the drug, and it would not include the use of the drug by the juvenile. My suggestion here would be that the condition be extended to an admission of having used the drug to be backed up by analysis, especially in cases where the parents make the approach for help, and assistance. I feel that this would be an ideal opportunity for early intervention by the Gardai with of course, full consent by both the parent, and juvenile, of course, juvenile here, meaning the person under the extended age of 19 or 20 years.

With regards to coming under previous notice of the Gardai, I would agree with this in the majority of cases, but more than likely as indeed with other crimes, there would be exceptions, and this would depend on the type of unfavourable notice.

Having commented on some of the existing conditions, and suggested some changes, again only to relate to drug of-fences, in the existing scheme, I would suggest a further con-dition which would read something like;

"That the offender, and parents would undertake to com-ply with any conditions or requests asked if they were accepted into the Juvenile Liaison Scheme".

What I have in mind here is the acceptance of a very close monitoring that would be required, to ensure that the offender or as he/she might now be the participant is remaining "clean". This brings me to the question of how to monitor a person under the supervision of the Gardai. As I said at the beginning of this section, I have already made tentative approaches to the Drug Advisory, and Treatment Centre, Jervis Street, regarding this matter, and I would think that they would be certainly willing to assist if at all possible.

My suggestion in using the Drug Advisory, and Treatment Centre would be that the person who would be accepted into the scheme would be referred to the Drug Advisory, and Treatment

Centre for screening or if that was not possible, then some arrangement could be made through the Health Boards, with the cooperation of the Drug Advisory, and Treatment Centre to utilise the clinics for the taking of urine samples for the purpose of having a monitoring system introduced as I feel it would be complete waste, having persons under supervision, and not knowing whether or not they were abusing drugs.

Initially, I would see the scheme coordinated from the Drug Squad offices to give assistance to the Juvenile Liaison Officers in building up a working relationship with the Drug Advisory, and Treatment Centre. If such a system got off the ground, then you would have a situation of weekly reports being furnished from the Drug Advisory, and Treatment Centre on referrals, and it certainly would be more satisfactory from both the Drug Advisory, and Treatment Centre, point of view, and indeed our own in the Gardai, to have one central point for receiving of reports. This of course, would also be the case where people who are being referred to the Drug Advisory, and Treatment Centre for monitoring, they would be recorded at the central point, which I have suggested would be based at the Drug Squad offices for the time being. I do not want to go too much into minor details here, but I think I have outlined in general what I would hope could be done from the Garda point of view.

I would of course, place myself at the disposal of the Juvenile Liaison Officers with regard to advising families of drug abusers, and if necessary visit these families with them. You may also have a situation where the person who has been referred to the Drug Advisory, and Treatment Centre needs a treatment programme, well, in cases such as this, it could be left in the hands of the Drug Advisory, and Treatment Centre with the Gardai keeping interest from the point of monitoring progress, and advising the family.

For the persons who are referred for monitoring under the scheme, it does not necessarily mean that they would be monitored very closely for the full two years of supervision. I would think that the monitoring would only last for as long as the supervisors, in this case, the people at the Drug Advisory, and Treatment Centre or the Juvenile Liaison Officers, would consider it necessary.

In summing up this section, I would see no great difficulty in seeing this scheme extended as outlined above, as I believe that the people in authority in the relevant agencies would be very amenable to helpful suggestions.

Making use of Authority

In the eyes of the public, the policeman or in our case in this country the Garda is seen as a person in authority. The biggest problem within Police forces, is the correct use of authority or maybe to put it more bluntly, if the persons in authority are mature enough to use it correctly.

Of the Policeman "Skolnick- [1975] says

"He may be expected to be rule enforcer, father, friend, social servant, moralist, street fighter, marksman, and officer of the law."

To be all of these persons on different occasions, you need to be a man with authority, but one has to fashion his authoritarian approach to suit the particular occasion, and this can only be gained from experience.

Writing about the Police in the community, "Skolnic- [1975] makes a number of comments which I think gives food for thought in this matter,

"What the Policeman typically fails to realise is the extent he becomes tainted by the character of the work he performs. The dangers of their work not only draws Policemen together as a group, but separates them from the rest of the population".

He goes further to say

"The element of authority also helps to account for the Policeman's social Isolation from the community, and they are apt to weight authority heavily as a causal factor."

What Skolnick is saying is true today, but I think that the fault is not only experienced within the Police force. There are persons, and organisations who do not want to have anything to do with people in authority, and I feel that is the wrong course to take. There are also individuals within the police force who would want to create the isolation that Skolnick talks of. I am speaking here of course in the drugs context.

I would suggest that the authority of the policeman could be used in various ways within the drug setting, if proper relationships were developed with other agencies, parent groups, teachers in schools, and health boards.

Taking other agencies, there is no reason why better cooperation, and a better understanding could not be created to enable a joint approach to be made towards the problem of drug abuse. I can speak here of my experience during my placement work at the Drug Advisory, and Treatment Centre, Jervis Street, where I dealt with people who had problems with drug abuse. In the beginning, I was not too sure whether I would fit into that situation or not, as it was certainly a new departure for a member of the Garda to be in. I found to my surprise that there were no problems whatsoever with regard to the clients who were attending the Drug Advisory, and Treatment Centre, Jervis Street. I do believe that my position of a person in authority played a major role in my fitting into my placement, and the fact the I used that authority in one of the "many other sub-roles"as previously described by Adams [1965], and as if to confirm what Adams also said about the role of the Policeman, nobody ever said to me that I should not have been there. The fact that I was there offering something other than an arrest or detention, was very much appreciated by many of the clients, although looked on with a certain amount of suspicion by some. I think that that experiment should also do away with the lie that contact with the police would be detrimental to any form of treatment or rehabilitation, and should go some way to changing attitudes.

Better relationships with teachers, and schools could be used to show that the authority of the Policeman is not something that should be feared, but that a Policeman can be looked on as a person who can help, and advise people, and can use his authoritarian position in doing so. Young people are so impressionable today that it is important that they have a good attitude towards persons in authority.

Many parents abdicate their position of authority today, and therein lies some of the causes of the problems of our society. Parents today are the products of the liberation movements of the sixties who rebelled against all forms of authority, including their parents, and now, when faced with their own children of the eighties producing a mirror image of themselves involved in anti-social behaviour, they are helpless to do anything about it. They do not know how to enforce their authority on their children because they do not understand it, and have never really accepted authority themselves anyway. They have a fear of not being able to cope, so permit other organisations, and agencies to take over their role as authoritarians while continuing to enable their offspring in their anti-social activities.

The activities just described would be a summary based on descriptions of families involved with the "Tough Love "groups in America, and the problems they had in trying to lay down the law for their children. I do not think there would be a lot of difference between mistakes or the problems of the families described in "Tough Love ", and families here in Ireland. Here again, the role of the Policeman in authority could be used to influence parents to exercise their own authority on their misbehaving kids, and point out to parents, especially in the early stages of contact with the drug problems, to take a stand, and take back the authority they have relinquished so misguidedly. I think that the "Tough Love "approach, which is now widespread in America, but has not yet reached our shores, has a lot going for it, and certainly in a modified form to suit Irish society, could be made use of in a drug setting. It is based on the principle of self-help groups of families affected by a particular problem, which incorporates the assistance of many other agencies, including the Police at certain stages to achieve their objectives.

The authoritative figure of the Policeman is used here as a means, and as a help for these parents in these self-help groups to show their authority. It would be important for us in the Garda to be able to assist parents' groups in these situations when called upon to do so.

This brings to mind a true incident where a man came to see me in the drug squad office. He did not seem in good health, and he was not able to put across his problem very well to me. He had a drink taken. I got the story from him to the effect that his son was on drugs, and was sent to prison for six months a couple of weeks previous. I began to sympathise with him, and tell him that at least he will dry off for six months, and he will be away from drugs. He looked up at me, and said, "that's not my problem ", what had happened was he had been released, and he wanted to know if he could he get him locked up again. I could do nothing for him. To me, this was a man going to somebody he thought could help him, somebody in authority. I hope that if a similar incident occurs again that it will not stop there.

OTHER SUGGESTIONS
Multi-Disciplinary Committee

From experience, it always seems to me that when working parties, committees, coordinating bodies, and other such groups are set up or formed for the purpose of monitoring or implementing some recommendations or whatever, the personnel who make up these bodies are usually very far removed from the real action as it were. I know that the Minister has in mind the setting up of a coordinating committee on drug abuse, and I would hope that it will be representative of all the various agencies involved in the field.

What I would like to see also would be some type of committee of representatives of the agencies involved who would if necessary discuss individual cases of drug abuse so that there would be a united approach to dealing with any particular problem arising in a case, and the assistance or advice of any particular agency can be had on the spot. It would also do away with the opportunity of the drug abuser playing one agency off against the other, trying as it were to get the best deal. I would have in mind agencies like the Probation Services, the Drug Advisory, and Treatment Centre, Jervis Street, Local drug Counsellors, Welfare Officers, Child Care Services, and treatment areas. My suggestion would be that the personnel would be people who would be carrying case-loads, and would be familiar with particular cases. I would not go any further than give just a broad outline above at this stage as I do not have any particular details in mind, but I feel it would be a point for further discussion.

Research

This is one area where we certainly have fallen down. We do not at this time have any idea as to the size of the drug problem in this country. Any research that has been done has been in small pockets which do not reflect anything like the real picture. We then wonder in amazement at the media when they produce what seem to be unrealistic figures, and we put it down to media exaggeration. What if the figures quoted by the media are right, how can we criticise the media when we do not have any idea of the exact state of affairs.

If I might be so bold as to make a suggestion that qualified researchers be assigned to the appropriate agencies, such as the Garda Drug Squad, and the Drug Advisory, and Treatment Centre, for say a period of twelve months, and that they be afforded full cooperation in every way possible to try to discover what exactly the true picture of the drug scene is like. If that is not possible then maybe some method of co-operation should be introduced on an ongoing basis between research personnel, and other agencies that may be of assistance.

I feel that there is an over-cautious approach to availability of information on important issues such as this. I see no reason at this stage why we should not follow the Swedish example where Drug Squad Officers of the Police assisted researchers in introducing them to persons involved in drug abuse, from various walks of life. If we want to know what is going on in the drug scene, then we have to talk to people who are connected with it on their home ground.

Advice and Information

We do not have what you might call a centralised advice, and information section attached to the Drug Squad. I do not mean by this the type of information whereby we enforce the law in relation to drugs, what I am talking about is general information for parents, advising them regarding the services available for treatment, and generally to coordinate information, and communicate with other agencies in the field. This would be of vital importance in respect of some of the earlier suggestions I have made in this report.

We do at the moment give whatever advice we can to parents, but usually, it is in a rather hasty manner, and as likely as not, one is probably on the way out to do something else when the phone rings, or somebody calls, and I feel that a lot can be lost because of the lack of time to give to people on a particular occasion.

Well on summing up, I would hope to see myself getting more involved in the communicating of information to other members of the force, and to the general public, the establishment of better cooperation with other agencies, and bodies involved in the drug abuse area, and hopefully more involvement of the Gardai in early intervention through areas like the Juvenile Liaison Scheme, in helping, and advising families, and young people who become involved.

I have given a brief account of the present situation that exists within the force in relation to drug abuse, and I have made a number of suggestions of possible changes which could be implemented without any great infringement on the present structures. I know that my authorities within the force will be very open, and receptive to any suggestions made regarding the approach to the drug abuse problem, but as to how much change I can bring to my style of work will depend to a large extent on the acceptance of a need for change. I also know, and fully accept that much of the responsibility for introducing any of my suggestions, and the methods, and timing of such introductions will lie chiefly on my own doorstep.

Maurice Heffernan

BIBLIOGRAPHY

1] Adams, Thomas F. Law Enforcers- an introduction to the Police role in the community [1965]

2] Becker, Howard. The Outsiders; [1963]

3] Garda Siochana Code Instructions; Chapter on; Juvenile Liaison Scheme.

4] Skolnick, Jerome H. Justice without Trial--- Law Enforcement in a Democratic Society--Second Edition---[1975]

5] Stafford Johnson, S. The Prevalence, and Prevention of Substance Abuse in

Psychologist Ireland -----[1983]
National Drug Advisory and Treatment Centre.

CHAPTER EIGHTEEN

My Addictions Studies Project
What happened

My authorities at Garda Headquarters had a variety of views on the completion of my Diploma in Addictions Studies at Trinity College Dublin, which I feel is important to comment on the progress of my suggestions, that I made in my Project Report, and some of the communication that passed between myself, and Garda Headquarters.

While still attending the course prior to its completion, I was receiving correspondence from the Assistant Commissioners office at Garda headquarters already looking for my observations regarding any suggestions I might have to make, as a result of my participation in the course. They were also looking for precise details as to the cost of the course, and noted that the cost of the course itself was £655.00Irish punts. It also mentioned the name of the next Detective Sergeant to be released to do the next course, which was to start in October 1984, who was based at Headquarters.

On the 16ᵗʰ of October 1984 I forwarded a report as follows on the completion of my Addiction Studies Course through my Detective Inspector at the Drug Squad, and my Detective Superintendent at Central Detective Unit, Harcourt Square for the information of Assistant Commissioner, Crime Branch, at Garda Headquarters.

Diploma in Addiction Studies held at Trinity College Dublin

Reference to above, and attached, I wish to report as follows:

I have completed my course on Addiction Studies held at Trinity College, Dublin between January 1984, and July 1984, in which I was successful. I felt the course was very enlightening, and it would be most useful to persons involved in the drug addiction field.

It was to a large extent geared towards rehabilitation, and treatment of drug abusers, but nonetheless I feel it was also interesting from a Police point of view in gaining a better understanding of the problem of drug abuse, and of the persons who become involved in drug abuse.

I have also gained a good insight into, and built up good relationships with many other agencies, and people involved in the drug addiction field which I know will be of great benefit to me, and other members of the Drug Squad in the course of our work.

Towards the finish of the course I was asked to prepare a Project Report which would indicate what I may be able to do in respect of the drugs problem when I returned to my employment in the Garda Siochana. I submitted my report outlining some suggestions, and it was accepted by the college. As already stated I was successful on completion of the course, and I received my Diploma in Addiction Studies, on Friday the 5th of October 1984. I have attached a copy of my project report which I hope will receive a favourable review. I would be more than willing to discuss the Report, and clarify any points made.

Forwarded please for information of Assistant Commissioner, Crime Branch.

Maurice Heffernan. D/Sgt.

Now my report with a copy of my Project Report went to the Assistant Commissioner crime branch who forwarded a copy of the same to the Chief Superintendent at Community Relations, on the 17th of December 1984. I found it interesting to note what the Chief of the **Garda Community Relations** had to say regarding my attendance at the course to the Chief Superintendent Crime at Garda Headquarters. On the 18th of December 1984 he sent back a hand written comment as follows;

"The get together" today 18th. [This related to a meeting that was to take place at Garda Headquarters] I have no observation to make except to say that the members project report has nothing to do with his job, and if that's all the addictions studies diploma can do for him it's a waste of time."

On the 5th of February 1985, the Chief Superintendent at the **Garda Community Relations** office was again asked for his views on the proposals in my Project Report with respect to the extension of the Juvenile Liaison Scheme. He replied as follows on the 13th of February 1985;

"I am not impressed by this project report".

It seems to me that Garda personnel attending Courses like these should have adequate briefing on the purpose of their attendance. Sergeant Heffernan ought to be concerned with how he can become a better investigator, not a social reformer.

To talk about extending the age of entrants to the Juvenile Liaison Scheme beyond eighteen years is a contradiction in terms. What is being proposed is a formal method of cautioning adult offenders? There is some merit in this, but only for minor traffic offences. What Sgt Heffernan said.........and there is nothing left only for them to be charged or summoned". There is nothing wrong with bringing offenders to court. If Justices are not trained or are otherwise inadequate in how to deal with cases [something I do not necessarily accept] that is another matter. But I would prefer offenders to appear before courts as such, rather than that they should appear as persons to be "treated"-the social service approach.

By, and large it seems to me that Sergeant Heffernan's views of his functions are erroneous. It is not our function to conduct social research. It is not our business to provide an advice, and information section at the Drug Squad. If the Drug Squad put more of its energies into prosecuting users, thereby reducing the market, and the suppliers, there would be less need for advice, and information.

Chief Superintendent.

Well they were unusual comments coming from the Chief Superintendent at the Community Relations Section at Garda Headquarters, which is supposed to be the source of the distribution of advice, and information to the general community at large. These were the only disparaging comments to come from anyone that saw the report.

Also in the National Youth Policy's Committee's report 1984 which was chaired by Mr Declan Costello, section 13.7.14 recommended the extension of the Juvenile Liaison Scheme to young people up to the age of 21 years. This was information that I came across after I had completed my Project Report; otherwise I would have included the reference.

Several of the other high ranking officers who read the report thought that there was "merit" in it. The following comments were included in a report dated the 5th of May 1985.

"That he made some useful points which require further exploration",

"that he had obviously given a great deal of thought to the effectiveness of his role, and that of the Drug Squad, and the force in general in combating the serious problems caused by drug abuse",

"Makes valid points regarding the need for better understanding between the various agencies involved"

"The suggestion of the Multi-Disciplinary Committee at a functional level which could perhaps prove useful"

"The suggestion regarding the extension of the caution in certain circumstances merits further consideration".

On the 11th of June 1985, Eugene Lynch who was a Sergeant in the Juvenile Liaison Office, at Central Detective Unit, at Harcourt Square wrote a three page report to his superiors, regarding his views on some of the suggestions in my report which he had read, with regards to the Juvenile Liaison Scheme involvement in my proposals. While he had some reservation regarding some aspects of the suggestions made, overall he was supportive of the general idea, and I relate some of his comments as follows;

He agreed with me that there were few juveniles under the age of 17 years charged with drug offences, and gave some figures for 1982, and 1983 as to numbers charged.

He also pointed out that very few juveniles are dealt with under the J.L.O. Scheme in relation to drug offences. He gave figures of seven juveniles all male in 1984 cautioned. In 1985 at the end of May that year there were no juveniles cautioned.

He goes on then to deal with my suggestion regarding the age increase from 17 years to 21, and the change in conditions for entry into the Scheme. He then goes on to quote a recommendation put forward in the National Youth Policy Document to have the age limit raised from 17 years to 21 years for young persons involved in criminal activities.

He completes his report with the belief that Sergeant Heffernan's suggestion should be given serious consideration, and stating that there was no reason why drug offenders should not be dealt with under the J.L.O.Scheme.

He recommended same provided that some consultation is held with members of the Drug Advisory, and Treatment Centre in relation to their input, and also all J.L.O.members would have an opportunity to be made fully aware of any new changes.

On the 13th of August 1985, which would have been twelve months after I had completed the Drug Addictions Studies course, I received a communication from Assistance Commissioners Office from Harcourt Square, in the Dublin Metropolitan Area asking for further views in respect of the Multi-Disciplinary Committee I had suggested in my Project Report. I received a number of other reminders with respect to the request from the Assistance Commissioners Office. On the 13th of February 1986, I forwarded the following report in reply to this request.

Reference to attached minute from Commissioner Crime, my report is as follows:

"In my project report of 1984, I outlined broadly at that time the composition of the Multi-Disciplinary Committee that I had in mind.

177

I gave some reasons at that time for such a committee or body. Such as a united approach to dealing with the drug problem, and also doing away with the opportunity of the drug abuser playing one agency off against the other.

Since writing that report in 1984 I am convinced more than ever now that there is need for this type of committee or body involving people working in the drug field.

As we are well aware the drug situation is an ever changing one, and the approach to the problem needs constant review. To make one point in this area we now have more doctors Prescribing for addicts, which is undermining totally the policies regarding treatment by the National Drugs Advisory, and Treatment Centre. Drug abusers are making use of both Jervice Street, and the doctors at the same time, throwing the whole treatment programme into disarray.

Initially the committee or body could be confined to representatives of agencies operating from the various State Departments of which there are quite a few, and later other agencies could be included.

You have first of all the Gardai themselves who in many cases make the first contact with drug abusers. We enforce the law in relation to drug abuse, and misuse, and in doing so we gain an insight into the background, and character of the particular individual concerned. We know from all the information to hand how deep into the drug scene that person is, whether he/she is just a user or indeed a supplier. We do see at first hand the effects that drug abuse has on some families, and on the other hand we are also aware of the people who prosper on other people's misery. Certainly the Gardai could make a contribution into how some cases could or should be approached by other agencies, and likewise the Gardai could learn from, and assist these agencies.

The Probation Services, both in the prisons, and in the courts could benefit from an input into such a committee or body. Here you have a situation where there is quite a delay before the Probation Services get into the case, so it gives the particular individual or indeed his/her family plenty of time to do a bit of window dressing, and they will no doubt project a different picture of the situation than that existed prior to the case coming before the courts. I also know that the Probation Services now have special officers assigned to deal with drug offenders who are sent to them from the courts.

Jervis Street, which houses the National Advice, and Treatment Centre in this country sets the Policy in relation to the treatment, and care of drug abusers.

I feel that greater cooperation is needed between Jervis Street, and the various other agencies Involved in the fight against drug abuse. It is in my view, most essential that an agency such as Jervis Street, should be in possession of the full facts in respect of all the people they are dealing with, and certainly in this area the Garda Drug Squad could provide necessary data to enable Jervis Street, to formulate a suitable programme of treatment for particular individuals.

We now of course have the added problem of a greater number of doctors prescribing for addicts, and in some of these cases the drug abusers put great pressure on some of the doctors to prescribe for them, and a situation develops whereby the doctor no longer has any choice in the matter. I would add that some other doctors openly challenge the system by introducing what they would term their system of treatment for drug abusers. I would think that by giving Jervis Street, the assistance, and backing it needs it would help to establish an overall policy for the treatment of drug abusers, and would make other doctors wary of getting themselves involved outside the stated national policy guidelines.

There are a number of other agencies working in various areas, like the local drug Counsellors and welfare officers who could be consulted in relation to cases in their particular areas or indeed be brought up to date on any information which would be of benefit to them in the course of their work regarding a particular client.

At the moment the agencies I have outlined above, and indeed some others work independently of each other, and in many cases cover a lot of the same ground. I would suggest that the Committee or Body as put forward in my project report would operate on an information exchange basis, regarding particular individuals who were taking advantage of the present situation. Representatives of the agencies outlined above would be the people who would make up the Committee or Body, and they would also be the people representing the agencies who would be responsible for the supervision of the individuals involved in drug abuse.

I would be hoping that a Committee or Body as suggested, would also produce a better overall picture of the drug situation in the City of Dublin, and indeed the rest of the country, from the combined input of the various agencies mentioned. It would also allow for an exchange of information between agencies regarding certain situations that would arise, which would be of benefit in the formulating of programmes of treatment or making of court reports etc.

The Committee or Body would not itself have people referred to it nor would it be responsible for the supervision of offenders. The responsibility would lie solely with the agency concerned at the outset, but the agency could draw on any information held by the Committee or Body that would relate to a particular situation.

I would think that in the long term it would be of enormous benefit in relation to the approach to the treatment of drug abusers, and if the drug abusers see that there is a more stern approach being made in relation to their addiction it may give them a little more motivation to get some treatment for their drug habit.

I would suggest that the Multi- Disciplinary Committee or Body could be responsible to the Coordinating Body on drug abuse or a section with the Department of Justice or Department of Health or even operated through the National Drugs Advisory, and Treatment Centre at Jervis Street.

I have tried in this report to put forward an idea which might help to create more cooperation and liaison between various agencies involved in the fight against drug abuse, and misuse. It is in no way intended to cast any criticism on the existing system or existing agencies that are making every effort with available facilities. I know that most of these agencies would want to see better systems of coordination at ground level in the approach to the drug problem, and a breaking down of some of the ethical barriers that exist between them.

Forwarded please for information of Commissioner Crime.

Maurice Heffernan D/Sgt.

As is common within an organisation such as the Garda, reports keep circulating between one department, and another.

In March of 1986 Assistant Commissioner for the Dublin Metropolitan Area, John Fleming wrote

In his submission to Commissioner Crime at Garda Headquarters, "The idea proposed by D/Sergeant Heffernan has merit. It's important to have a coordination body embracing all the interested agencies".

A follow up report from Chief Superintendent Crime on behalf of Assistant Commissioner made reference to my report of February 1986, and in it he states the following;

"The suggestion in relation to the establishment of a multi-Disciplinary Committee merits exploration". He goes on to say; "The formation of such a Committee would involve Government Departments professional bodies, other interested agencies, and of course the Garda Siochana. I propose therefore, subject to approval, referring the matter to the Department of Justice for consideration".

"I do not favour any change in the upper age limits laid down under J.L.O. Scheme".

In March 1986 a further report was sent from the Commissioner Crime Branch which reached me in April 1986 while I was still attached to the Drug Squad.

"Before making any submissions to the Department, would it be possible to ascertain the degree of interest if any among other agencies referred in the proposed multi-Disciplinary Committee.

You might also let me have your views on the proposed structure of such a Committee, and suggested terms of reference".

On the 8th of December 1986 I sent my final report on my Addictions Studies Course as follows through my Detective Inspector,

"L" District Ballyfermot, and the District I was now attached to, and based at Lucan Garda Station as Detective Sergeant for Lucan sub-district.

Reference to above matter, [Addictions Studies Course,], and previous correspondence from Commissioner 1/C I wish to report as follows;

"In relation to the first question raised as to the degree of interest among other agencies I wish to state that I have been in contact with representatives of various agencies, i.e. Jervis Street, Probation services, Local Drug Counsellors, and I have discussed my proposals with them, and I have received a very favourable response from them. They would be in total agreement that some such Body or Committee involving people working in the field of drug abuse should be set up.

As to the structures of such a Committee I would suggest that it would have its base in one of the participating agencies such as the National Drugs Advisory, and Treatment Centre at Jervis Street. It would have a representative of each of the agencies nominated by the agencies concerned. It would have one full time coordinator operating where ever the Committee is based, who would be experienced in the drug addiction field. The terms of reference of such a committee would be something that would have to be agreed by the participating agencies on the formation of such a Committee.

In broad terms it would have to include a coordinated effort towards the treatment of drug addiction, a pooling of information in respect of drug trends, trying to motivate people towards treatment for their addiction by closing off avenues of abuse of the system.

In my previous report I did mention that the drug situation was an ever changing one. We have recently seen a situation where as a result of the loose prescribing habits of some medical practitioners, we now have a problem where we have people addicted to Methadone, and this is causing problems in the treatment area. I do think that it is essential that we have a coordinated effort towards drug abuse, and treatment.

I respectfully ask that this report be forwarded to Commissioner Crime, and also that a copy be forwarded to the Commissioner's Office, Dublin Metropolitan Area".

Maurice Heffernan D/Sgt.

Before I go further into my time attached to the Drug Squad, I will finish the, to, and fro of correspondence relating to my Drug Addictions Studies Course.

My report of the 8ᵗʰ of December 1986 had arrived on the desk of one of the Assistant Commissioners at Headquarters, maybe in crime branch who wrote a handwritten note to the D/Superintendent crime branch, with no department stamp, and illegible signature which stated as follows, and dated the 16. 1. 1987

"Please see D/Sergt Heffernans minute of the 8ᵗʰ of December 1986, and previous correspondence, and let me have your views.

To what extent if at all do existing committees [interdepartmental etc.]Fulfill the roles envisaged".

On the 18ᵗʰ February 1987, D/Superintendent crime sent the following reply to the Assistant Commissioner Crime, which eventually found its way to me at Lucan Garda Station sometime in March 1987.

"Reference to your minute of the 16ᵗʰ of January 1986 [this should have read 1987] I am to state that having studied the recommendations put forward by D/Sergeant Heffernan I found myself sympathetic to his train of thought. However, I doubt very much if the setting up of such a process would be of any general advantage in the overall attitude in that the people concerned, as outlined would not have power in their respective fields to make decisions. I believe therefore that another lair of bureaucracy would tend to stifle progress in general. I am satisfied that the present structure which embraces all interest groups in this area is the correct approach. I speak of course of the Government Coordinating Committee on Drugs on which the Deputy Commissioner crime, and I represent the force. The terms of reference of this committee include the provision that the meetings are chaired by a junior Minister, and therefore there is direct influence on the Government, particularly the Ministers concerned, to activate the proper policies. There is ample opportunity for members to articulate problems of coordination, co-operation etc. If any problems are encountered by any group in their efforts in rehabilitation or otherwise. The people concerned are in a position on this committee to influence policy within the framework of the particular employment or responsibility, and therefore this can filter to the operational areas. There is, and will continue to be a great need for practical cooperation on the ground, but this can be achieved through the Government Committee. If any shortfall is present in the present structure I would welcome reports on the same, and undertake to have "A" the same taken at the highest level. It is therefore in my opinion not necessary to set up a further tier of administration to have matters such as these envisaged by D/Sergeant Heffernan attended to."

Detective Superintendent.

So much for my Diploma in Addictions Studies; as can be seen from my reproduction of some of the reports going up, and down from Headquarters the plot was lost, I never suggested that Government Ministers junior or otherwise or Assistant Commissioners, and Chief Superintendents of the Garda Siochana be in any way connected with my suggested make-up of the Multi-Disciplinary Committee or Body. My suggestions were for greater cooperation, and coordination between people who were dealing with addicts on the streets, and working in the field of drug addiction. People with no experience in the drugs field who would be sitting in cosy offices, and sipping tea with ministers weren't going to help people on the street.

On the 20th of February 1987, the Assistant Commissioner crime branch forwarded the above report from D/Superintendent crime, to the Deputy Commissioner Operations with a hand written note, "For information. Your minute of the 14/3/1986 refers, I agree with "A" above". ["A" referring to the last two lines of the report]. This final instalment of what had now become a rejection of my Diploma in Addictions Studies, Project Report landed on my desk at Lucan Garda Station in early March 1987, just three years after I had attended the course at Trinity College, and about nine months after my transfer had taken place out of the Drug Squad, at Central Detective Unit. What follows gives a good indication as to why the views that I had expressed in my Project Report were confined to the storage shelves never to see the light of day again.

CHAPTER NINETEEN

Back to work after college
Life changing events

When I returned to my unit at the Drug Squad in late July or early August 1984, certain events which had occurred within Detective Branch at that time, between 1984, and 1986 would definitely have had a bearing on the outcome of whether or not my reported suggestions would be taken into consideration, and would also have a huge effect my future career.

When I left to start The Addiction Studies Course, I had six to seven detectives attached to my unit. When I returned I had one less Detective on my unit. Detective Garda Frank Hand who was a member of my squad, in my absence had been assigned temporarily to the Serious Crime Unit at Harcourt Square, which was upstairs in the same building where we, the Drug Unit were based. The reason for his temporary move was to bolster that unit who were stretched for manpower, as they had to perform armed security duties for cash deliveries to Post Offices all over Dublin City, Dublin County, and surrounding Counties.

Post Office vans doing these deliveries to Post Offices used to deliver social welfare, and pensions cash once a week, and once a month they delivered children's allowance cash. These cash deliveries, some of which were sizable, were very vulnerable to attacks by criminals, and in that current situation with the "troubles" also by subversive terrorist groups to fund their activities.

Frank Hand was a great colleague, a good friend, and a very hard working dedicated member of my unit at the Drug Squad. Our friendship wasn't confined to the work situation as away from the "office" we both worked vegetable plots beside each other for a couple of years, in the Lucan area which suited us both as Frank lived in Lucan, and I was just out the road in Leixlip. Frank loved to grow the veg coming from a farming background in the west midlands, and it was at his suggestion that we went to the Dublin County Council Office, and booked our plots. He gave me some tips regarding planting crops as I didn't have any background in that field.

We had some great conversations while at the plots, and almost every time Frank would bring up the subject of marriage. He had purchased his own house in Lucan, and couldn't wait to settle down to married life. I often had him out to my house in Leixlip for tea or something to eat after a couple of hours on the plots, and he used to love playing with the kids, always saying that he couldn't wait to have children of his own.

On the 10th of August 1984, shocking news reached my office, that Frank Hand had been shot dead outside a Post Office at a place called Drumree, Co Meath while waiting outside the Post Office for the delivery to be completed. Frank died at the scene, and his colleague who was in the passenger seat was grazed in the head. It was devastating news when it filtered through to us at Frank's unit. It was unbelievable, the shock that it caused all around, as the circumstances surrounding this tragic event unfolded, and we began to take it in. The memory of it still haunts me, as it is a day I will never forget.

Later there were three persons charged with the murder of Detective Garda Frank Hand. They were known members of a subversive organisation, they were brought before the Special Criminal Court, convicted, and were sentenced to life imprisonment. In 1999 all three murderers were released as a result of the Good Friday agreement, without as much as a word to the family of Detective Frank Hand regarding the circumstances of the release. So much for Irish Justice.

In the aftermath of the shooting of Detective Garda Frank Hand, members of the Central Detective Unit became very outspoken regarding the incident, and the method that was used to escort the cash deliveries. In late 1984, as tensions within the Central Detective Unit were rising the authorities deemed it necessary to send the Assistant Commissioner Crime Branch from Headquarters to Harcourt Square to meet with the members of the Central Detective Unit involved with the post office escorts including colleagues of Detective Garda Frank Hand from the Garda Drug Squad.

There were a number of heated discussions regarding the situation, and at times some of the Detectives aired their thoughts aggressively, so much so that the Assistant Commissioner had to intervene on a number of occasions to cool the situation down.

Many of those in attendance including myself had something to say regarding this tragic incident. There was also disquiet circulating, to the effect that the Representative Associations had completed negotiations with the Garda Commissioner regarding the doing away with the system of promotions within Detective Branch. This information had come as a complete surprise in 1983, and was an outright attack on the conditions of service within Detective Branch. The first interviews had been held in 1983 under the "new" promotion system.

The Detectives Case

Unfortunately I have very little documentation relating to our meetings, and work in the Detectives case, most is from memory, except for the Supreme Court Ruling which I held a copy of, and some dates from my old diaries relating to the High Court hearing dates. I was responsible for keeping a record of all the members who had signed up to the action, keeping a copy of all the signatures for the purpose of presenting them to the High Court if required which numbered in access of 900. Before leaving Ireland in 2013, I passed these documents on to another former member of the Committee, Detective Garda Pat Bane, for safekeeping. Pat passed away on the 2nd of June 2021 at his home, RIP. Even though now it is well over thirty years since the court case, I think these documents are important from a historical point of view, and should in my view be retained in the Garda Siochana archives or in the Garda Museum.

Around the time of the meeting regarding the shooting of Detective Garda Frank Hand in late 1984, a Detectives committee had been formed of members within the Central Detective Unit, and other city centre Detective Units to look into these changes that had been made under the new promotion system. That was in the second half of 1984, when this committee was formed, and I became involved with the committee at a later stage. I was approached to join the committee as I was a member of AGSI. I have a reference in my diary for the 1st of January 1985 that I had been given the first indications of my being transferred from the Drug Squad. On the 4th of January 1985 this was verified by my Detective Inspector at the time at the drug squad.

The following was deemed to have been the origin of where the changes to the detective's promotion system emanated from.

Garda Siochana Committee of Inquiry Report 1979

On the 2nd of November 1978 a Committee of Inquiry was set up to consider, report, and make recommendations into certain conditions of An Garda Siochana including, pay, earning differentials between ranks, work undertaken by An Garda Siochana, the promotion system, and recruitment to the Gardai.

The Committee of Inquiry concluded their report, and presented it to the then Minister for Justice, Mr Gerard Collins, on the 19th of April 1979, just four, and half months later. Looking at the time scale of this Inquiry, taking into account the time of year it was, Christmas time running into the new year, which is a busy holiday period, and taking it on the basis of a five day week, they were lucky if they had one hundred days to hear submissions, and produce this Report. This was a speedy Inquiry.

At that time I was attached to the Central Detective Unit, and like all Detectives I concentrated on my work, and over the years let my Association Representatives to negotiate on my behalf. We in the

Detective Branch, like all other members of An Garda Siochana made our financial contributions to our respective Associations to look after our interests with respect to pay, and conditions of service.

As it transpired in 1979 I was promoted to Detective Sergeant, and had transferred from the Central Detective Unit to the "A" District as I have already touched on. I did not have to go back into uniform as it was a straightforward promotion within the Detective Branch from Detective Garda to Detective Sergeant. In April 1976, I had completed, and passed the professional promotion examination for the rank of Sergeant so my promotion to Detective Sergeant was not a special promotion. I was a qualified Detective Garda, and not exempt from the promotion examination. In May 1981 I also completed, and passed the professional promotion examination for the rank of Inspector, and was qualified to go forward for promotion to the rank of Inspector or Detective Inspector, without an exemption of any kind.

The Committee of Inquiry received submissions both written, and verbal from forty eight different Associations, groups, and individuals at their hearings. They had their work cut out to go through all these submissions within around one hundred days. There were no submissions made by or on behalf of members of Detectives in Crime Ordinary Branches, Central Detective Units or the Special Detective Unit. All of us in these Detective Units as I stated previously, were relying on our respective Associations to act on our behalf, and to protect our interests, and our conditions of service.

Now like all workers the most important factor in any Inquiry discussions would be what improvements we would get in our pay structure, and there were some improvements announced as a result of this Inquiry. This of course would have an effect on all members, and ranks within the Garda force, and anything else coming out of the Inquiry was only of interest to certain sections of the force. **There was nothing regarding the Detectives promotion system included in this report.**

The following is a brief summary of some of the submissions made before the Committee of Inquiry.

In Chapter 7 of the Garda Siochana Committee of Inquiry Report 1979 a lot of the concentration was on the question of accelerated promotion within the Garda force for selected, and specially trained members of the force.

The GRA spoke a lot about other police forces mainly in England, and their systems of accelerated promotion, and the difference between them, and the Garda force.

The GRA would accept a system of accelerated promotion only if;

"The GRA were involved in the selection process,"

"A small number of people were selected each year and"

"A real effort was made to expand promotion opportunities."

In addition, some arrangement would have to be made to give a Garda who is not promoted a form of career development.

Another solution put forward by the GRA was the promotion to Sergeant for senior Gardai who would not receive any further promotion.

Another proposal put forward by the GRA, was the creation of a new rank of "Senior Garda".

AGSI also concentrated on systems in other police forces with regards to accelerated promotion, and came up with the view that accelerated promotion should not be introduced. Instead the Committee of Inquiry should make recommendations regarding the improvement in the existing system.

As stated by them in 1977 at the Conciliation Council, but without the avenue of eligibility without examination.

Another suggestion by AGSI was early retirement scheme with the option to retire after 25yrs service.

The Representative Body for Chief Superintendents [RBCS] would foresee considerable difficulty in drawing up, and administering an alternative system of accelerated promotion which could be uniformly applied to all sections of the force, [including Detective Branch, the Radio Section, and Technical Bureau]. "This was the first, and only mention of Detective Branch in the section dealing with promotion".

They go on to say if it should be deemed necessary to place more emphasis on accelerated promotion, this could be easily achieved through discussions between the Commissioner, and the four Associations who now have more ready access in matters of this nature.

The Department of Justice brought up the point made by the Garda Representative Bodies, and Associations regarding a considerable amount of dissatisfaction with the existing promotion system in the force. The revised Garda Conciliation, and Arbitration Scheme provides that an extended range of items including, **"the principles governing promotion"** is appropriate for discussion at the Conciliation Council. **"A working party of the council has been set up to examine the promotion system in detail."** Representative Associations having agreed that this matter should be referred to that working party.

Now I don't intend to go into any more detail regarding this report of 1979 other than to note a few interesting points.

Neither the GRA or AGSI made any mention of Detective's promotion to the Inquiry although the GRA did come out with some outlandish suggestions.

The RBCS did mention considerable difficulty with accelerated promotion within all sections of the force including Detective Branch. They also mention that the four Associations could discuss the matter of promotion with the Garda Commissioner as they have more ready access in matters of this nature now.

The Department of Justice mentioned the Garda Conciliation, and Arbitration Scheme could be used to discuss **"the principles governing promotion"**. But then it added **"that a working party of the council had already been set up to examine the promotion system in detail"**. Was this a contradiction in terms, and a duplication of the Inquiry into promotions? Why then were the Committee of Inquiry which sat between late 1978 to early 1979, dealing with any promotional problems if there was already this **"working party sitting behind closed doors"** dealing in detail with the system of promotion within the Garda Force.

Now looking at the time scale it begs the question as to when, and where, were the changes to the Detective Branch system of promotion discussed. There was no mention of it at all in the 1979 report, and it was not included in Committees terms of reference. Whose toes did the Detective Branch trod on over the previous few years? There is only one answer to that, the Garda Representative Association, [GRA] when the Detectives assisted in the fight for the amalgamation of the Garda Medical Aid, and St Paul's Society in the mid to the late 70s which is about the time when all this wrangling about promotion came to the fore. **Was there a lot of money lost by a small number of people as a result of this amalgamation?** Of course they had a good ally in the Garda Commissioner of the time, who held that post from February 1983 till November 1987, and who was known to have no love of Detectives. It now seems from all the information to hand that discussions were taking place under the Garda Conciliation, and Arbitration Scheme," behind closed doors" prior to the setting up of the Committee of Inquiry on the 2nd of November 1978, and would have continued until the appointment of a new Commissioner in 1983.

The Garda Commissioner, sometime after his appointment, put a Chief Superintendent who had no experience in Detective work in charge of the Central Detective Unit, and also appointed a Superintendent, to oversee certain sections within the Central Detective Unit, including the Drug Squad, who was also without experience in Detective Branch. These authoritarian appointments were made in response to the High Court action by Detectives, to carry out the instruction of the then Commissioner with respect to the Detectives actions in the courts.

The Detectives Committee was initially composed of representation from the Central Detective Unit, Special Detective Unit, and members from the District Detective Units. We met at various venues, and worked out a course of action. Of course we needed to get the majority of the Detectives in all Divisions in the country, to back our action, to this end we got out a discussion paper looking for the backing of all Detectives to proceed with taking action in the courts regarding this promotion issue. We got the backing of a huge number of the Detectives from every corner of the country, and we had over 900 signatures attached to the court action.

Prior to going to the High Court, an approach had been made to the Garda Commissioners Office, and the Department of Justice regarding our disapproval of the new promotion system as it effected the Detective Branch, and also looking to form a Detectives Association. Both departments turned us down. That was when we then decided to travel the country, and held meetings with most of the Detectives, and got them to sign up to support whatever action we deemed necessary. All this travelling was done in our own time, and at our own expense.

There were a number of things going on between 1979, and the mid-1980s which I have no doubt to this day had a huge bearing on the reasoning behind the changes to the Detectives promotion system.

"You had the GRA finalising the negotiations that they had been "dragged" back into, between themselves, and St Paul's Society with regards to the amalgamation between the Garda Medical Aid, and St Paul's Society."

"The Garda Siochana Committee of Inquiry Report 1979 had been issued, and parts of it were being implemented in respect of wage improvement."

"There were ongoing detailed discussions, "behind closed doors" regarding the principles governing promotion by a working party set up before the Committee of Inquiry had started its consultations, and made its recommendations, which was composed of the Associations, and the Commissioner's Office."

It was the normal case that most of the Detective Branch members would be putting full concentration on their duties of serious crime investigations, protection of lives, and charging persons before the courts. I am not taking away from my old uniform colleagues who of course had their duties to perform. It was of course of great concern when we as Detectives later learned that the people we were paying to look after our interests with regards to our conditions of service had "knifed" us in the back with respect to promotion within Detective Branch while we kept our heads down doing our work as Detectives.

The decision was taken by the Detectives Committee, to bring the matter before the High Court, and an injunction was obtained to prevent the Commissioner from continuing with the new promotional system until the hearing of the case. I remember standing on the steps outside the High Court with my other colleagues from the Detectives Committee, when the question came up of how we were going to fund this action.

Our activities did not go unnoticed to our authorities either as they kept us all under observation to such an extent that an Assistant Commissioner was sent to the High Court each day the case was being heard. I knew that Assistant Commissioner in question well, he was a nice man, but he was just doing what he was directed to do. We all became marked men as will become obvious later.

We as Detectives considered this to be a substantial breach of our conditions of service within the Detective Branch. It must be noted that there were no changes to the promotion system other than that affecting Detectives. As a matter of fact some of the uniform section members were of the view that their promotion chances were slimmer because of the inclusion of members of Detective Branch in the uniform interviews.

Without going into too much detail, the case came before the High Court on the 13th of March 1985. Evidence was given by a number of Detective witnesses including myself with regards to my service within the Detective Branch, and being promoted within Detective Branch to the rank of Detective Sergeant. The case lasted for some nine days, and then the court adjourned to the 18th of April to consider its verdict. On the 18th of April 1985, the High Court found against us the Detectives in the case. There was huge disappointment in our Detective camp, we put it down as an establishment decision, and the court was not going to go against the Department of Justice, the Garda Commissioner or the Garda Associations.

CHAPTER TWENTY

On the move again

Our next big decision was to make an appeal to the Supreme Court, taking into account a number of factors including the cost of such a case of appeal to the Supreme Court, the grounds for an appeal, and what would be the outcome. After discussions with our Senior Counsel, and getting the continuing backing from our members we decided to appeal the decision.

While awaiting the outcome of the Supreme Court appeal which was going to take some time, the "transfer wheels" were put in motion by the Garda Commissioner. I with a number of my colleagues from Central Detective Unit, and Special Detective Unit were put on transfer lists from our existing assignments to District Stations. A point was made to have the members transferred to stations near to their residence, but in my case it didn't happen that way. I was transferred to Sundrive Road Station in the "G" district.

Now when I became aware that these transfers were about to take place, I went to see my then Chief Superintendent, on the 27th of May 1986, [noted in my notebook] who was now in charge of the Crime Section, Central Detective Unit having been appointed there by the current Commissioner sometime previously. This would have been after the High Court Judgement had been given against the Detectives. I informed him that I had heard that I was going to the Crumlin District to which he said it was only a rumour. I told him I didn't want Crumlin as it wasn't suitable, and asked him to have me sent to Lucan Station as that was closer to my home which was the criteria being used in all the transfers being done with respect to the Detectives involved with the court case. He then relented, and stated I could have Lucan when the vacancy arose.

I was aware that the Detective Sergeant at Lucan was on a promotion list from interviews held in early 1986, which were held after the High Court decision in the Detectives case. I had attended an interview for promotion myself, on the 17th of April 1986. Needless to say, I was unsuccessful. I was in the "G" District at Sundrive Road Station within the following week after my meeting with, the Chief Superintendent. The first thing I did on arrival at Sundrive Road Station on the 4th of June 1986, was to sit down, and do an application for a transfer to Lucan Station in the "L" District when the vacancy arose. I regard the communications in respect of this application to be of interest, which I reproduce as follows;

> D/Inspector
> Crumlin.
> I wish to make an application for a transfer from Sundrive Road, Garda Station to Lucan Garda Station as a Detective Sergeant. I understand that a vacancy will occur in the near future at Lucan on the promotion of the detective sergeant to the rank of Inspector. I was transferred from the Drug Squad, Central Detective Unit on the 4th of June 1986 to Sundrive Road Garda Station. I reside in Leixlip, Co Kildare in the Lucan Sub-District.
> Forwarded please for information of Chief Supt. D.M.A. South, and Chief Supt Crime, Central Detective Unit for favourable consideration.
> Maurice Heffernan D/Sgt. [sent on the 5th of June 1986]
> The D/Inspector recommended my application, and forwarded it to the Superintendent "G" District, pointing out that Sundrive Road Station had been without a D/Sergeant for the past three years.
> The Superintendent forwarded it to the Chief Superintendent D.M.A.South with a recommendation that D/Sergeant be replaced immediately as Sundrive Road has been without a D/Sergeant for the past three years.
> [That was dated the 11.6.1986]

The Chief Superintendent forwarded it to Assistant Commissioner D.M.A. for information, and consideration stating that an immediate replacement would be highly desirable. Also stating that he is more concerned to have a D/Sergeant in Sundrive Road than at Lucan.

The Assistant Commissioner forwarded the application to Chief Superintendent D.M.A.Crime stating that "your observations on this application would be appreciated".

[That was dated the 25/6/1986].

Chief Superintendent [Crime Section] Harcourt Square, gave the following observation on the 2nd July 1986 to Assistant Commissioner's Office,

I am in favour of the transfer as requested by D/Sergeant M. Heffernan. Members with long service in C.D.U. are catered for at Stations near their homes. This would have applied in D/Sergeant Heffernan's case if there was a vacancy in Lucan at the time of his transfer to Sundrive Road. It is not proposed to fill Lucan until the present list of successful Sergeant applicants is published. There will be a number of vacancies for Sergeant in the Detective Branch at the time. Sergeant Heffernan's transfer to lucan should take place at that time.

Chief Superintendent.

The Assistant Commissioner sent the following reply back to Chief Superintendent D.M.A. South.

After promulgation of the forthcoming Sergeant's list, and subsequent appointment of Detective Sergeant's you may arrange transfer of D/Sergeant Heffernan to Lucan.

I agree that for the present he should remain at Sundrive Road.

The file eventually made its way back to me for notation, and return, which I did on the 17th of July 1986. I photocopied the file for future reference which now enables me to give an exact account of my transfer.

Well from looking at dates in one of my notebooks my "transfer" from the Drug Squad, Central Detective Unit, was completed sometime in late August, and early September 1986. Now, there were a few interesting points to note regarding our [Detectives Committee] transfers.

The outcome of the Detectives case had not yet been determined at the Supreme Court; we only had the judgement of the High Court. The Garda Commissioner was taking a big risk that these transfers would not be contested.

We were never investigated for any breaches of the Garda Regulations which would normally end with members being fined, and transferred.

There were never any disciplinary proceedings taken against any of the Detectives involved with the court action as that would fly in the face of the right to take the High Court action.

The facts put forward by the Chief Superintendent, crime section, were a total fabrication; members with long service in the Central Detective Unit were never facilitated with transfers to stations close to their homes, because they never looked for those transfers anyway. These transfers were never requested by us Detectives, they were imposed on us all, and being sent to a station close to our homes was a "carrot dangled in front of us" so as not to put up any fight regarding the transfers. Of course it nearly backfired in my case as there was no vacancy at the time near my home hence my request for my transfer to Lucan from Sundrive Road, not from Central Detective Unit, and the granting of the request some months later.

This action had been taken to the High Court by more than 900 members of Detective Branch against the Minister for Justice, the Garda Commissioner, and the Representative Associations.

The object of the transfers was to break up the nucleus of the Detectives Committee which was based at Dublin Metropolitan Area Headquarters.

The Supreme Court didn't deliver its Judgement until the 13th of May 1988. I give a short abstract of parts of the opinion of our Counsel, with regards to this Judgement, as it affects the Detectives, given by our Barrister at the time, without going into a lot of detail.

He points to the provisions regulating the right of the Gardai to form Associations comes under the Garda Siochana Acts 1924, and 1977.

The provision of the Act makes it clear that there is no prohibition on members of the Garda Siochana forming or becoming members of a Trade Union or any other Association, provided the objects are not to influence or control the pay, pensions or conditions of service for themselves or other Police Forces.

It is not necessary for the court to endeavour to enumerate all the various functions or services which members might receive from such a Trade Union or Association if formed by the plaintiffs. [Detectives]

The Plaintiffs have the undoubted right to form Associations, and Trade Unions, and that Right is guaranteed by the Constitution.

Subject to related matters it follows that it is lawful for the Plaintiffs to form an Association.

Would it be worthwhile for the Plaintiffs to do so having regard to the limitations? That is a question the Plaintiffs are in a much better position to answer.

The Judgement held that the High Court Judge appears to have decided the case on a point of Public Order under the existing legislation. The Supreme Court noted that no argument was raised on this point before this Court, and there was not any suggestion that the Plaintiffs Association would in any way be subversive of Public Order or Public Morality.

The Supreme Court also has the effect of removing completely from the Commissioner, the Minister or any other body the ability to suggest that such new Association as is contemplated could be objected to on Security Grounds.

Well it looks to me that the Supreme Court cleared the way for Detectives to form an Association, however limited in its objectives, so one could say that the battle wasn't completely lost. Of course it seems to me that the initial reasoning behind the Court Action, the Detectives promotions system, got completely swamped in the legal tangles regarding the forming of Association.

The injunction on promotions, under the new system had been lifted after the failed Detectives High Court action, which opened the way for promotion interviews to take place again. I was now attached to Lucan since late 1986. I remember on one occasion being at some local Garda function sometime, when I was approached by a member of the Garda at the function. I'm not sure now whether he was of Sergeant or Inspector rank at the time, but he started to talk to me regarding the delay on promotions, and blaming the Detectives for the situation in the promotion system being held up, as it was affecting him personally. I listened to him for a few minutes then just walked away from him, and his tantrums, and smiled to myself.

Most members of the Garda force were sympathetic to our cause, but this man was complaining because his chances of promotion were being delayed. Now, I knew the man reasonably well as he spent all his current service within the "L" District. Everybody knew he was a certainty for promotion because his brother was a Senator or a TD in the Irish Parliament. I know he was "pulled" up to the rank of Superintendent before he retired. That was still part of the promotion system, which didn't change within the Garda at that time, and I'm sure it hasn't changed to this day.

My Final Days With The Drug Squad

Now my years attached to the Garda Drug Squad was a life experience all rolled into those four years between 1982, and 1986? Before I leave that part of my service there are a few more memories I have to share.

I can't put a time on it, but it was while I was in the Garda Drug Squad, I had to detain a solicitor at the courts, and was going to put him under arrest for interfering with one of my witnesses while I was prosecuting a drugs case in the courts. He was appearing on behalf of the accused person I had before the court, and outside the court I found him interviewing one of my witnesses, and asking her questions about what evidence she was going to give against his client. This was totally against all the rules of court procedures.

I brought him to the detention centre at the Bridewell Garda Station for the purpose of putting him under arrest. Now, he was well known to me, and many of the Gardai as he was a regular at the courts in defence of criminal cases. In the Bridewell I met one of the Detective Superintendents from the Central Detective Unit, whom I knew very well. I had a conversation with him about what I was about to do, and after a short discussion he advised me that it might be better not to proceed with that line. I then turned to the solicitor, and told him he was a lucky man, and I let him off with a caution. This hadn't been his first run in with the court system as he had previously been disbarred by the court from practising as a Solicitor, and could only assist another solicitor in any particular case. This gives a flavour of the types of situations we as members of the Garda Siochana came across during the course of our service.

Another situation I found myself in which had an International flavour, was doing chaperone to a Detective Inspector Ted Cox from Wellington, New Zealand, who was spending a couple of days with us at the Drug Squad getting a handle on the drug problem in Ireland, and how it corresponded to their problem in New Zealand. I am not sure of the exact date or timing of the visit, but I look back, and ask as I always did, why me, I must have been seen as a soft touch regarding such assignments or nobody else wanted to do it. Ted was a very nice guy, and over his time with us I had him out to my house to meet the family, and dine with us.

His next stop on what he had called his world tour of police forces, was New York, he was travelling west around the world. After he left we used to correspond for a while, and swap Christmas cards, but as time went on we lost touch, mind you the last letter I received from him was in 1990. I began to concentrate on my survival within the Garda Siochana after 1986. I mention this to give an insight into the variation of duties that would be undertaken by us from time to time.

Meeting up with a former A district Inspector

Now sometime in early 1986, as I mentioned earlier, the then Commissioner, had appointed a uniform Superintendent to be in charge of certain sections of the Central Detective Unit including the Drug Unit. This man had no previous experience in the Detective Branch, but part of the reasoning behind his appointment was to put a tighter control on expenditure within the Central Detective Unit.

I knew this man previously from the Task Force, where he was a Sergeant, and when he was a uniform Inspector at Kevin Street in the "A" District. He was my superintendent's sidekick who always "flanked" him whenever I had reason to go to the Superintendent's Office, which wasn't too often. He would have known my form with respect to the Detective roster system. This man was now my Superintendent at the Drug Squad.

We had a system in place where we worked a four week cycle roster, and at the end of each cycle I would sign off on extra duty sheets worked by my unit members, with each Detective Sergeant within the Drug Squad doing the same thing for their units. Our new Superintendent started to question some of the claims, looking for explanations as to why certain overtime was worked. There was no problem at the time with this, as I would, in respect of my own unit, reply to the questions raised, and sent it back up to the Superintendent's office for payment. This became the pattern for some time, with the questioning of overtime worked, which was accepted as long as there was no holdup in the payment of a claim. Then we started to have delays in payment developing on a number of occasions caused by delays in the reports coming down from the Superintendent's Office to be replied to by ourselves. Having to respond to these reports was also time consuming, and cut across investigation time.

In early 1986, things started to get so out of hand, that there was an occasion I had signed off on the overtime for my own unit, and sent it in for payment to the Superintendent office. Now, the Superintendent Office was staffed by civil service clerks who would check the documentation, and forward it to the Superintendent to sign off on it. The particular occasion I'm mentioning was around a Bank Holiday weekend, and it was on a Thursday which was heading to the end of the week, and the end of the roster, so any delay would mean that my unit members would not be paid until after the end of the following roster.

As was now a regular routine the claim for my unit was returned for explanation as to why these hours were worked. I sent the claim back with my report attached, stating that I was not satisfied with the delaying of these claims, and there was a regulation which prohibits delays of any kind with respect to payment for additional hours worked. I also mentioned other matters regarding the questioning of these claims. Now, this as I have said, was Thursday afternoon, and I, and my unit were heading off for our long weekend, and were to be working late evenings the following week. I sent the report back up to the Superintendent's Office again for payment with my observations.

Shortly before I was to finish duty I got a phone call from one of the clerks in the office tipping me off that the claim was on the way back down to me again, I told her to send it down to me straight away that I would wait back for it. Only for this girl phoning me I would have gone home, and would not have seen the latest report regarding our claim until Monday evening when we were due back for duty. I got the report back to me as I had waited, and it contained some outlandish allegations about me being bordering on insubordination in what I had said in my report, and suggesting other breaches of regulations in what I had written.

I immediately checked if the Superintendent was still in his office, he was, I went straight up to his office, and I put the report on his desk, asking what he was talking about in sending a report like this back to me. We had a disagreeing discussion regarding his reports for about twenty minutes. Eventually he said to me to give me the file, and he signed off on the claim, and as he did so he removed his reports from the file. I brought the claim back to the main office for payment. Over time we had, had, a lot of disagreements regarding payment of overtime, but this latest incident "broke the camel's back" as they would say. It was like a replay of the incident I had in the "A" District, this Superintendent came from the same stable. For the remainder of my service in the Drug Squad there was never a question again about payment for additional hours worked by my unit. Of course, like previous occasions in the "A" District, my days in the Drugs Squad were coming to an end in line with the commissioner's instructions.

Short stint in the G District

So ended my service in the Garda Drug Squad. It was an outstanding experience that stuck with me for the rest of my service, and beyond. Now, I had to do my service for a short period of time at Sundrive Road Station in the "G" District as a Detective Sergeant, and that wasn't a quiet spot either. I would have known most of the crew in the "G" District from previous meetings, and investigations, and of course my name would have been out front, because of my involvement with the Detectives Case. On my arrival I met with the local Superintendent for the "G" District, and the Chief Superintendent of the Division who I informed immediately of my intention to look for my transfer to Lucan, and both of them would have later written on my application for that transfer.

I spent from the 4th of June to the first week of September 1986 working in the "G" District, just three months, and these dates would be backed up by notes from my notebook of the time. For those three months it wasn't a doddle, I didn't sit back awaiting my transfer, which I could have done as a protest at my treatment. It was a very busy spell as I got into the swing of things in another era of my service within the Garda Siochana.

I can't allow my three months in the "G" District to pass without mentioning a particular case that happened within my sub-District while I was attached to Sundrive Road, Detective Unit. I arrived at my office one morning in the middle of July 1986, to be informed that there was a burglary at the premises of Sanyo Ireland Limited, an electrical goods company who dealt with televisions, sound systems, and a host of other entertainment items. I went to the scene with my staff to carry out an investigation.

Being very brief, we discovered that the warehouse where the goods had been stored had been entered, and a large quantity of items were stolen including televisions, and video recorders. I spoke with a Mr. Mervyn Groves company secretary, his Chief Accountant Mr. Jim Kelly, and asked them for a breakdown on the quantity, and value of the property that was stolen. I had the scene examined by members from our fingerprint, and scenes of crimes bureau.

Jim Kelly came back to me later that evening, and I went to see him. He informed me of the amount of property that was taken, and a large container which was parked in the yard, had been used to take away the property from the scene. This container had arrived about a week ago, and was "stripped" of its contents which they stocked in the warehouse. I then asked him if he could put a value on what was stolen, and when he told me the value would be in the region of a quarter of a million Irish Punts. This was a big burglary scene. There were no witnesses to this crime.

We then set up an investigation unit within the District comprising our unit at Sundrive Road, and members from District Headquarters at Crumlin Station including our Detective Inspector who I had known previously. We also kept in constant touch with Jim Kelly of Sanyo in case there was an approach to try to sell the property back to them for a cash payment. Our inquiries at the time covered the period of the arrival of the container at the docks to its delivery to the Sanyo premises, and all persons associated with the movement of this container.

It turned out from our inquiries, and certain information that came into our possession that a criminal gang based in the northern counties bordering Dublin became our chief suspects. Our most immediate job was to find the 40ft. container that was used in this job as it may still contain most of the property that was stolen. Now, we got hold of an inside man who was offering televisions for sale, and he agreed to work with us to try to locate where the 40ft container was, but we needed money.

Our Detective Inspector did his best to try to get funding, from the Superintendent's Office information fund, at Crumlin Station, to help buy some of the televisions, but with no success. I then decided that I would approach Jim Kelly at Sanyo to see if they would put up the money for the plan. The plan was that "our man" would order fifty televisions from the contact, and would collect, and pay for twenty on his first trip. We would have him under constant surveillance to try to identify where the trailer was being kept. Jim Kelly came up trumps with the cash, and the plan was a go.

Again trying to keep it brief we located the trailer at a farm yard, and put surveillance on it for a number of days. We identified the farm for the purpose of obtaining a search warrant, which we had on hand when we decided to move in. Within twenty four hours of locating the container we observed movement as a small van had approached the container, and was loading the van from the contents of the container.

We moved in, and made the arrest, seized the van, and its contents. We went on from there, carrying out a search of the farm buildings, and then moved down to the main house which was detached from the farm some distance away. We also arrested the owner of the farm who was at the house. On searching the container we estimated that a large quantity of the goods were still intact. We arranged for the container to be taken into storage for Jim Kelly of Sanyo to do an inventory of the goods recovered from the container, and to have it technically examined. It was found that a little more than half of the property had been recovered which was valued at around one hundred, and fifty thousand punts worth. Obviously they had been removing the property bit by bit in small vehicles prior to the container being discovered, and recovered.

The farm was in a place called Bal Rath, and with the information obtained from those that were arrested we carried out further searches at Donore, Duleek, Drogheda, and Beamore recovering more of the Sanyo property on the way, and also property not related to the Sanyo burglary. The total amount of Sanyo property recovered altogether was close to two hundred thousand punts which would be seen as a successful outcome to the case.

We discovered from our inquiries that the property that was recovered which wasn't part of the Sanyo job had been stolen from another premises in an Industrial Estate in another part of the city, and had not been reported stolen. Seemingly the warehouse had a computerised stock system, and according to their systems the stock was still there in the warehouse. It was only after our approach to the company, that a physical check was carried out in the area where the stock should have been, and they discovered it was missing.

From our investigation regarding this particular stock that was missing, we took the night security man who was on duty into custody, and after questioning he admitted that on a particular night he had arranged with some criminals that he would switch off the alarm system for them to gain entry into the premises, steal the property, and he had switched the alarm back on again. Hence the reason for no report of a break-in to the premises. The alarm company was able to give us details of the times when the alarm system was switched off, and on again, and we were able to pinpoint the date of the burglary. That finished my investigations in the "G" District.

Photograph of myself with troupe of dancers taken 1955.
[I'm first on the left in the back row]

On top of a threshing machine, around 1959,
[I'm standing with my left hand on my hip]

Old thatched cottage, former Heffernan family home, at Saleen Ballylongford, where all of my siblings were born.

Family home at Lislaughtin, Ballylongford, where I was born. My sister Joan and brother Jerry in photograph, maybe taken in the late 1980s or early 1990s.

*My former foster home at Balinderraig, Cahirseevin,
Co Kerry, which I left in 1952.*

*A group photograph with work colleagues from Weartex,
at my first work place Christmas function.*

Garda Siochana Class of January 1968 in Templemore, with three training Sergeants, [I'm first on the left in the second row.]

Leaving the Dublin District Court after the presentation of Animal welfare Certificates in 1971. On the right in front three as you view the photo. [Independent Newspapers]

Funeral of homeless person," Knight of the road, around 1970/ 1971.
[Independent Newspapers]

Photograph of Fraud Squad members taken in mid 1970s at Osmond House.
[I'm 6th from the left in back row.]

Presentation made to me by Assistant Commissioner Tony Hickey, on behalf of the Veronica Guerin Murder Investigation Team at my Retirement function 2001.

Headquarters of the murder investigation at Lucan Garda Station.
Top members of the team in conference. Left to right:
DG Bob O'Reilly, DS Maurice Heffernan, DG Michael Gaynor,
DG Bernard Masterson, DG Michael Murray,
Assistant Commissioner Tony Hickey

Photo: Brian Farrell, Sunday Independent

*Photograph taken during the Veronica Guerin
Murder investigation of members of the investigation team at Lucan.
[Sunday Independent]*

Receiving my Diploma in Addiction Studies at
Trinity College, Dublin, 1984.

Photograph on my Confirmation day in September 1957 at St Joseph's Institution, Tralee,
[Kennelly Archives]

In my dance costume, on stage, Easter 1957
[Kennelly Archives]

With my dance troupe on stage, Easter 1957, I'm in the front row, centre.
[Kennelly Archives]

A face in the crowd, 1955, during a visit by an American couple.
[Kennelly Archives] I think I do stand out, the "angel"
towards the back centre.

Band marching in the square, 1955, with a view of the buildings in background. [Kennelly Archives]

Photograph of the man who was the Superior [Manager] taken Christmas 1954. [Kennelly Archives]

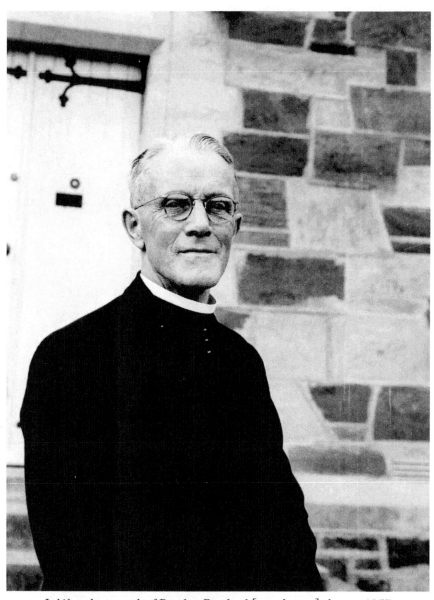

Jubilee photograph of Brother Raphael [pseudonym] August 1957.
[Kennelly Archives]

Group of brothers at Jubilee celebrations August 1957
four of whom I had close
association with during my time in the institution.
[Kennelly Archives]

Photograph of Joseph Pike, R.I.P. taken in 1957, he died a
short time later while still
at the Institution.
[Kennelly Archives]

Photograph of Judge Johnson, district court Tralee, who dealt with my case on the12th of December 1952.
[Kennelly Archives]

Photograph of the Court House, Tralee, where I was taken on the 12th
December 1952
[Kennelly Archives]
\

Photograph of myself taken in 2018 in Malta.

224

CHAPTER TWENTY ONE

Personal life outside the Gardai

Sometime in early September 1986 I arrived at Lucan Garda Station, to take up my assignment as Detective Sergeant with Lucan Detective Unit. I spent the rest of my service there until my retirement in December 2000.

Let me go back, and reflect a bit more on my personal life away from the job. Yes I did have another life, from 1972 onwards I had an increasing family, and by 1990 I had six children, three boys, and three girls. During those years between 1968, and beyond 1990, I had a lot going on in my personal life as I began to pick a pathway to my future, while I was still in my own mind, looking back at where I originated from. I had a very full life in the community that I lived in, which included a lot of involvement with my children's activities. Thinking of what had happened in my own upbringing without a family; I wanted to be as close as possible to my own children without overdoing the parenting bit.

In a quote from the 2009 Ryan report on residential institutions, "witnesses described parenting difficulties ranging from being over-protective to being harsh," the raising of my children preceded the publication of the Ryan report by many years, but I did identify with many of the findings in that report. I intend to cover in more detail further on, aspects of the Ryan report as they would have related to my own circumstances.

Boards of Management

As my children came to school going age, I was asked to become a member of the board of management of, first the primary school in

Leixlip, where all of my children attended during their primary school years, then this was followed on by being asked to be the Archbishop's Nominee on the board of management of Colaiste Chiarain, the Leixlip secondary college, where all of my children eventually attended until they had finished their second level education.

Of course it was a great honour to have been asked to serve as a member of the community on these boards, the primary school board until my children moved on to the secondary college, and Colaiste Chiarain secondary college board, until I resigned in July 2004. I had a number of reasons for my resignation from this board, firstly, because of pressure on my time being in a new work situation. Secondly I was going through a family separation, and I was in the process of making arrangements to leave my home. I felt it was the correct thing to do at that time. I did not of course mention this in my letter of resignation. My youngest girl was still attending at Colaiste Chiarain secondary college, at the time of my resignation from the board.

I have no doubt that being a member of the Garda had a huge influence in my being nominated to both boards. I would have been approached first around the late 1970s regarding the primary school board, and sometime in the early 1980s with regards to the Colaiste Chiarain secondary college board. I built up a great relationship with the principles of both schools, and often assisted in problem solving when something arose.

I had come a long way, from being an inmate in a residential institution, in Tralee, for over eight years to becoming a member of the boards of management of both the local primary school, and secondary college in my community. Of course, as was the normal practice going through my life, I never discussed my early years with anybody, even my then wife Margaret would not have been fully aware of all of the events of my upbringing. It was only in recent times, 2019/2020 that I fully informed all of my children, by giving them a written account, surrounding the earlier years of my life. I felt they deserved to know the full facts surrounding their family origins from their father's side.

It was as a result of the production of this short version of my young life that several of my children suggested that I should go on, and do a full account of my life story, so here I am.

Also of note is the fact that none of my children were ever sure of what I worked at while they were growing up, as they never had the pleasure of seeing me in a Garda uniform, because I had worked in plain clothes since 1973/1974. I never over the years discussed my work at home at any time, even as my children were growing up, I suppose it was my way of sheltering them from some of the realities of life on the other side of the fence.

My involvement with the local Athletic Club

My children over time became involved with many sporting events, starting with the local Athletic Club, which had been reformed in around 1981, I was approached to join the committee, and assist in the running of the club. This would have evolved from my children becoming participants in the local community games, following on from that they joined the local Athletic Club. Training was twice a week on Tuesdays, and Thursdays at 7.30pm. Around that time there were a large number of children of all ages training with the Club. We were members of the National Athletics, and Cycling Association of Ireland [N. A. C. A. I.] Which ran competitions all over Ireland. As a result I, with other committee members, travelled the length, and breath of Ireland in coaches with my own children, and other young members of the club, accompanied also by many of the parents.

The club was run by the parents, many of whom served on the committee. Over my years of involvement with the Athletic Club, I held many positions on the committee over time, and ended up becoming chairman of the club for a number of years. I also headed up fund raising events for the club, and was responsible for the starting up of a weekly bingo session at the local Community Centre. We had a man employed to do the calling at the bingo, we used to give him a few bob for the night, and he was reliable, but on the occasions that he couldn't make it, I had to step up myself, and do the calling. I suppose you could say that it was good training for doing public speaking in front of a crowd who were very vocal if mistakes were made with the numbers called.

The training area for the Athletic Club was in a green field area with a grass running track marked out, at the rear of the local Community Centre. This of course had to be maintained on an ongoing basis, and it was important that funds were available to carry out this maintenance.

That brings back the memory of a disastrous event at the track area which happened on the 29ᵗʰ of June 1991. I got a call from my work at Lucan station, and arrived at the Community Centre to be shown the track area full of Itinerant caravans, mobile homes, jeeps, and vans. There must have been about forty or fifty units there.

To make matters worse they were joy riding their jeeps, and vans around the grass track destroying the track area. It was likened to a ploughed field. I was fit to be tied as I watched this debacle unfold, and I was almost tempted to draw my weapon, and let off a few shots, but I held my cool. I, and my partner were in plain clothes, there was no point in us making an approach, so we called in our uniform colleagues who were able to get the matter under control, and the Itinerants agreed to vacate the area within forty eight hours which they did without repairing the damage that they caused.

It took a long time for the track area to recover from the damage, and of course there was a cost in getting the track back into some semblance of normality. I remember I took some photos of the area at the time, but I think I must have mislaid them with all my moving around. Even outside of work the "Demons" were on my back.

As I have said the committee of the Athletic Club was made up of parents, and they came from all walks of life, with one common interest, they all had children involved with the club. There were also parents who were not members of the committee, but were very good supporters of the club, and some of them joined the senior section of the club comprising different age groups up to under 50s, and into the veterans.

Some time around 1983 the committee made a decision to upgrade the running track area, and converted it into a proper grass track for athletics. I got the job of seeking out a costing for the track project. Over time I had somebody on board who gave us a quotation of around fifty thousand Irish Punts at the time, and he also provided us with a model of the new track area, which we used for display purposes during fund raising events. We even got some exposure in the local paper showing off our model of the proposed new track, and of course new methods of fundraising had to be organised to pay for the building of the track.

Now, I remember one of the parents who was involved in the building trade, put forward a suggestion that the club should run a dance night at the Community Centre to raise funds for the club. He had mentioned that he was a good friend of a well-known country, and western group "Big Tom, and the Travelers "stating he could get them at a reasonable rate for the night. He was given the go ahead by the committee to get a deal with "Big Tom", and his band. He came back with what we all thought was a reasonable price for the night. It was agreed to hold the dance on a particular night, so we as the committee had a lot of work to do.

Tickets had to be printed, arrangements had to be made to get a licence for serving drinks on the night, and the Community Centre committee had to give their blessing, and get the insurance cover organised for the occasion. Well the night arrived, and we had a fairly good crowd, and on the face of it we were going to make a few bob, but not an awful lot. I, with another committee member, were tasked to keep control of the cash for the night so I got the agreed amount of the fee ready to be given to "Big Tom", and his band. I spoke with our man who knew "Big Tom", and arranged for him to give the agreed amount of cash to the band. This man then dropped a bombshell, and said that "Big Tom" was looking for his full fee for the night which turned out to be more than twice the amount agreed on by the committee. Of course we didn't have anything in writing which turned out to be our big mistake.

So our "big" dance night turned out to be a "big" flop with "Big Tom", his band made money, the publican who ran his bar in the centre for the night made money, the Community Centre had to be paid for the hire of the hall, and the insurance company had been already paid for the insurance for the night. The Athletic Club actually lost money on the night, it was a lesson that we never forgot. That's one of the pitfalls when going to raise money for a project.

Well that didn't stop us organising other fundraising events, such as quiz nights, 10K road races, fashion shows, and monster bingo's, which were reasonably successful events, but fell far short of what was needed to get the track project off the ground. The weekly bingo was still bringing in a certain amount of funds, but keeping in mind we had to keep the club running, covering annual insurance, cost of transport to events, and entrance fees for the athletes to take part in events on behalf of the club. All club members themselves did pay an annual membership fee to the club.

Track and Field Events Memories 1985

In 1985 the all-Ireland Juvenile Track, and Field Competitions were taking place at the Antrim Forum in Northern Ireland, and the leixlip Athletic club entered a number of athletes for this event. The competitions were being held over two days so we had to arrange overnight accommodation for everyone that was travelling. I was one of fifteen adults who travelled with around twenty six Athletes by coach, leaving Leixlip at around 6am on the morning of the 29th of June 1985 heading for the Antrim Forum in Antrim Town, Northern Ireland.

It was of course as I have mentioned before the time of the troubles in Northern Ireland, and we had some parents who made the decision not to allow their children to travel because of the volatile situation that existed in Northern Ireland. Both on the way up to Antrim, and on the way home our coach was boarded twice each way, once each way by the security forces in the Republic, and once each way by the Northern Ireland security forces across the border which gives an indication of the tensions that were in the border areas. I had of course to keep a low profile due to my being a member of the Garda.

Notwithstanding the security situation that existed the trip was successful with the club bringing home eleven All-Ireland medals from the event, five bronze, five silver, and one gold. One of my own boys, Ger, was one of the five bronze medal winners. When we had arrived at the Forum before the start of the events we were met with a nice surprise, when a lady from the Northern Bottling Company presented us with several cases of 7-Up. For me this was the forerunner to a second trip with athletes, I was to make across the border over the following few weeks.

Some time after the Juveniles Competitions, five of the club veterans entered the, All-Ireland Track, and Field Competitions for veterans, which were also being held in Northern Ireland on Saturday the 13th of July 1985. The problem was to get them there, so I was approached as I possessed what could be described as "a people carrier", and I agreed to do the trip with them. Now, I think the best way to describe what happened next is to reproduce part of the report from the Leinster Leader paper following this event.

Vet's Gold

Leixlip A.C. veterans travelled to Belfast accompanied by their chairman who acted as manager, driver, coach, etc. For the Leixlip group, it was a day to remember. The secret of their success can now be revealed-- before going to Belfast they by-passed the Mary Peters Track, and went on to the Antrim Forum, where they had a special "workout". This "workout" was arranged by their "manager" who lured them to the Forum Track by telling them that the championships were in fact being held there. So great was their faith in him that they chose to ignore the correct location which was published in the daily papers that morning. Well the "workout" paid off as the "steam" began to build up on the journey from the Forum to Belfast, and it showed on the track with the Leixlip group taking 10 gold medals, and two bronze medals.

Yes I can vouch for the description given in the report; it was a day to remember in a lot of ways. The "Manager, Driver, and Coach" for that day was yours truly, I did make the mistake of thinking that the event was taking place at the Forum, where the Juvenile events had taken place. Of course when we arrived at the Forum, we found we were the "first" to arrive, and the team stripped off, and had a warm up around the Track. Then the penny began to drop. Why were we the only ones there?. We sought information from somebody who looked puzzled to see us there, who informed us that the event was actually taking place in the Mary Peters Track in Belfast.

So you can imagine the panic, with the boys still doing their warm up, they had to stop, and get into the wagon fast, as we had to travel to Belfast. We hit the road in spots as best as my four wheels could travel, and luckily we made it with time to spare for the boys to get their breath back. The events went very smoothly, with great successes being achieved by our five veterans who carried home the awards as described in the Leinster Leader report.

Now you would think that all we had to do after the presentations was to drive back towards home, and we had made plans to stop to eat at a Roadhouse on the Republican side of the border. We were travelling on our way when one of the veterans produced an Irish National Flag, and started to hang it out of the window of my vehicle while we were still travelling through the Northern Part of Ireland. This was like a red rag to a bull if the wrong people spotted it. I got into a cold sweat as I could see the situation, a serving member of the Garda driving this vehicle, we were passing through troubled areas, and if we were stopped there was a likelihood of us all being detained, and brought in for questioning.

I had to stop the vehicle, and I, with the rest of the group, pleaded with this man to put away the flag. Now, he was from the west of Ireland, and was very nationally minded, after some persuading he folded up his flag again, and put it into his bag. Like the trip with the juveniles we were stopped, and boarded both ways on both sides of the border so you could speculate on what would have happened if we still had the flag flying out the window of my vehicle when we were stopped at the northern side of the border. Yes it was a day I will never forget.

Once on the republican side again we pulled into the Roadhouse as arranged, and I was treated by the boys for the wearing of the many hats on the day. As we arrived home without incident, I reflected on my visits across the border about ten years previously in connection with our Fraud Investigation when I was with my Detective Sergeant from the Fraud Department, and we had an armed escort to, and from our locations. I would not of course have enlightened any of the boys regarding these trips.

Recently during the course of searching through my personal papers, I came across an off white sheet of paper, which has faded over the years. It was a list showing the Leixlip Athletic Club panels, for the club relays to be held at Belfield Athletics Track on the 27th, and 28 of July 1985. It contains the names, and age groups of eight teams that were to take part in these events from the Leixlip Athletic Club. Three of my own boys took part in this event, Ger, under 9 team, Niall, under 11 team, and Mark, under 13 team. I'm afraid Leixlip clubs only success on the day was in the boys under 13s, with Mark Heffernan, A. Naughton, N. McDonald, and B. Fahy. Who took the silver medal in that event? Memories!! Memories!! Memories!

During my years of involvement with the Leixlip Athletic I saw my own children both boys, and girls arrive home with medals, and trophies from event after event so much so that in later years I had to make up a special board to pin the medals to, otherwise they would be left in drawers out of sight. I took a special photo of all the medals, and trophies displayed a copy of which I have to this day, and I often wonder from time to time what has happened to them all.

As well of course as track, and field events we also had the cross country events during the second half of the year, and into the springtime. All of the boys, and the girls for a short time, took part in these events, and it was tough going running in the muddy fields, and my eldest boy Mark, in 1985, took time to put his cross- country thoughts into poetry as follows;

Amid the fields
It's back to cross-country running again
We know where to go, and we know when
We have shoes with six spikes
Running through mountains hills, and dikes

We run under bridges, and trees
Through hail, sleet or snow, and a little breeze
When we finish we are covered in muck
As for the rest we don't bother to look

On our way home in the back on the bus
Eating sweets without a fuss
Got our feet caught in a bunch of briers
Our clothes end up in our Ma's tumble driers

We hope you will come, and join us this year
If you don't you will be without any gear
Tracksuits, spikes, and singlets too
Everyone has them so why don't you.

So as you can see there is poetry in running; 1985 gives a good indication of a typical year for the Athletic Club, and its members with competitions going on throughout each year, which kept me busy during any free time I had, and kept my children busy.

Representing Ireland at Olympic Games; 1996 and 2000
Something that only happens once in a lifetime happened at Leixlip Athletic Club, when one of our club boys who had been with our club from very young, had succeeded in winning his races in all of his age groups, and in all competitions national, and otherwise throughout his

234

years with the Athletic Club. After he finished his secondary school education he received an offer to travel to America on an Athletic Scholarship, and also received an invite to a Scholarship at University College Dublin. He opted to take the one nearest home, and took the University College Dublin offer.

This was David Matthews whose family resided on the same road as my family in Leixlip Park, and would have been friendly with my own boys. His father Joe Matthews who passed away on the 23 December 2023 RIP was a great supporter of the club, and like me stuck with it for a good number of years. I mention this with a certain amount of pride for the club, and its committees, as later on David represented Ireland at the Olympic Games on two occasions, in 1996, and 2000.

By the time of his second appearance for Ireland, I would have moved on as I was preparing for my own departure from the Garda Siochana on retirement. Now, I again reflect on my situation with my job during those years before my transfer to Lucan Station in 1986. My involvement with my children in their sporting, and other activities, plus my involvement with my local community, had the effect of helping me to keep my sanity during my confrontations with some of my supervising officers, especially during my time in the "A" district, and the repercussions resulting from my involvement in the Detectives Court Action in the years prior to 1986.

CHAPTER TWENTY TWO

Family Moments

The Athletic club was a great training ground for children taking part in other sports, and my own children took great advantage of this as the Athletics kept them at a good level of fitness. Without going into too much detail I give a brief summary of their involvement with other sports. My three boys went on to play with the local GAA club, the local soccer club, and further afield.

My oldest boy **Mark** went on to play soccer for the local soccer club in Leixlip, where he took part in the Leinster Senior League. They were the winning team in the Dublin Leinster Senior League, Mars FAI, and all Ireland Youth Cup. He also played minor hurling for Kildare.

My second boy **Niall's** involvement with the Athletic club included cross country, and relay events in his age group. At some stage he took up walking racing, which he did for a number of years, and was the N.A.C.A.I. All Ireland champion for three years. He then joined the Leixlip GAA club, but had to cease training for a period, due to problems with his feet, which was later diagnosed as childhood arthritis. In 1990 he returned to the GAA, where he played both hurling, and football. In 1992 he captained the Leixlip minor team that won the Kildare minor championship, for which he received player of the year award.

In 1992 he joined the senior team where he played for two years till he received a serious neck injury which disabled him for a long period of time from involvement in any sport. Luckily I was at that particular game, and was able to take him to our local doctor straight away. He had to receive rehab for some time for his neck injury, but by 1996 he started to play a bit of football again in, of all places, Australia, where he had gone to work for a year. While in Australia he became interested in triathlons, and competed in his first triathlon in 2002 back home. Niall went on to compete in many triathlons at home, and abroad, and followed that up by competing in Ironman competitions as well as a number of marathon events.

He is now a coach with his local athletics club in Clane, in County Kildare, where his own children are also members. As he says it's a great club, and coaching the kids helps him with his own fitness. It looks like he's following a bit in his father's footsteps in his community. Nice that he is passing on some of his own experiences to a new generation of children.

My third boy **Ger** went on to play both GAA, and soccer for a number of years. He Captained Leixlip GAA u10, and u13 to Kildare titles, and in 1990 he was part of the winning team to win the Kildare u14 title. He was also part of the winning team in the DDSL League in 1990.

After being "spotted" while playing for Leixlip soccer club at under 10s, in 1987/1988 he joined Cherry Orchard Football club which was based in Ballyfermot. They went on to play in a tournament in Malta in 1990. In 1993, while with Cherry Orchard, his team won the Prestigious Milk Cup Competition, by beating Glasgow Rangers on penalties, which is held every year in Northern Ireland. Unfortunately Ger did not play in the final as he had a dislocated foot. He played in the Kennedy Cup team, which was his first time to play in Lansdown Road, now the Aviva Stadium.

In February 1991 he made his Irish debut with the underage Irish International Soccer Squad when he played against Northern Ireland, and in the same year he took part in an International Tournament in Montague in France, which I attended myself.

In October 1990 when Ger's Cherry Orchard team travelled to Malta to take part in the tournament, I got the job as driver of one of the team minibuses with another parent while we were in Malta. Towards the end of the tournament it was Ger's birthday, and his aunt

Joan held a surprise party at her house for him. The whole squad of about twenty players with their managers, and trainers attended. We had a wonderful evening, and a great finish to the tournament. Mind you that is now over 30 years ago, and it is still a great memory.

Ger. went on to play 23 times for Ireland at u15, u16, and u18 with the Irish International underage teams, which included home, and away games. One of his away games was in 1993 in the u16 Euro Championships in Turkey, where he scored against RCS, which was historically the last time a combined team from the Czech Republic, and Slovakia ever played together.

Between 1990, and 1993 he was sent by the football scouts for trials to Manchester United, Everton, and Coventry football clubs. After the trials he informed the scouts that he had made his decision to continue with his studies, and sit his Leaving Certificate Examination.

In 1994 he joined the University College Dublin football team, after he had received a Football Scholarship, and began to play in the Irish National Soccer League, which he did for three seasons. In his first season with UCD, they won the League, the League Cup, and the Division 1 shield. While at college he continued to be involved in the Irish International Underage Soccer Squad. After his three seasons with UCD, he joined St Francis Football Club.

Family Education

Touching on their education, **Mark** finished his second level education after completing his leaving certificate at Colaiste Chiarain, Leixlip. He then went onto Athlone IT, where he completed both his Certificate, and his Diploma in Civil Engineering. During those years in Athlone, both his education, and accommodation was aided by the Government of the day.

Over the following years between 2003, and 2015, he continued to study through the Open University, culminating in obtaining his MSc in Environmental Protection, through Sligo IT. He currently holds the position of European Regional Environmental Manager, for Covanta Europe Operations Limited. He is married to Yvonne, and they have two children, a boy, Oscar, and a girl, Ella, and Mark has an older boy Lewis from a previous relationship.

Government changes

Now **Niall,** my second son, in 1992, sent in his application for a place in third level college in Carlow, and was accepted for his three year course in Mechanical Engineering, again fully grant aided by the Department of Education as we thought. There were a number of other boys who were known to him also going to Carlow so they arranged accommodation between them, and were aware that there was a grant available for the accommodation, seven of them were to share a house. Then around the month of July, 1992, the Department of Education through the Government of the day brought in a means test for the accommodation part of the Educational grant.

It looked like, Niall, would not be getting the accommodation grant because my earnings at the time were just a few punts over the qualifying earnings. I was absolutely disgusted, because of this I had to budget for the payment of the accommodation. My son even suggested that he look for a change of college, and get one of the colleges in Dublin which would have allowed him to commute each day while staying at home. The difficulty with that was that all the places in colleges had been allocated at this time, and there was no guarantee of getting a place in a Dublin college. He had been accepted at Carlow, and it was Carlow he was going.

As I had said he was going to share a house with six others, none of whom were affected by the means test that had been announced by the Government who after this announcement went on their holidays. The parents of the other boys who Niall shared the house with, some of whom were known to me, were able to provide plausible certificates of earnings as they were self-employed, business people, and farmers. I was aware that their earnings were much greater than mine, with both parents working in some cases.

Because I was a Government employee every penny I earned was accounted for so there was no way I could produce an earnings certificate for a lesser amount than I was receiving. As I was the sole earner in our household it made budgeting very difficult, and I had my three girls coming after the boys. Yes the following years were going to be very tough indeed financially.

Now Niall was still playing football for his local GAA club, and there were times when I had to drive to the college, pick him up, and bring him home for the particular game, and drive him back to the college again. That was additional to having to pick him up on weekends, and bring him home as he couldn't afford to stay there as he wasn't getting the accommodation grant.

He went on to get Engineering jobs in Limerick, and Donegal, before settling into his current situation in Intel Ireland, in Leixlip, in 2013 where he has been since. In 2005 he got married to Barbara, and they now have two children a boy Dylan, and a girl Sophie.

Now my third boy **Ger** as I already stated was awarded a Football Scholarship to University College Dublin in the early 1994, where he obtained a Degree in Marketing. He went on in 1998/1999, and studied at the Smurfit Business School at UCD, where he obtained his M. Sc. In Marketing.

Ger went abroad to work with a company in Canada between 1999, and 2005. When he came home from Canada he had a number of Marketing jobs, and he is currently working in Marketing in the Cyber Security Business. He is married to Tracy, and they have three children, a girl, Hannah, and two boys-twins, Sam, and Jack.

The fact that he obtained a Scholarship was a great relief to my financial situation. I didn't have to fund his third level education, except of course for pocket money, food, and of course "football boots" as he was now going to be playing with the University College Dublin football team in the Irish National League.

There was an occasion when Ger was at University College, I received a call late one evening from him to say he wasn't feeling too good, and had a shocking pain in his tummy. I went to the college, and brought him home, and got the doctor for him. I suspected myself at the time that it was an appendix problem, the doctor agreed with me, and we got him to hospital where it was confirmed, and he was oper-ated on. Over the years we had three appendix cases in the family so I became a bit of an expert on appendicitis problems.

I have to mention the girls who for a short time were also involved with the Athletic Club. They became every bit as successful as the boys over their short time with the club. That brings me to an occa-sion that I brought the two older girls, Noeleen, and Ann Marie to an International "friendly"soccer match between Ireland, and England at Landsdowne Road Stadium now renamed The Aviva Stadium. It was on Wednesday the 15th of February 1995, the tickets were for the South Terrace, and had cost 7Irish Punts each. I got the tickets through my son Ger, who got them from his football coach, Tony O'Neill, "The Doc", in University College, Dublin. Ger did not attend with us as he had something else on that day; I still have the four tickets in my possession.

The two girls were looking forward to the game as they were never at an International match before. What happened next was some-thing that will be in the minds of all true soccer followers for many years to come. About fifteen minutes into the game Ireland scored a goal to the huge delight of the Irish spectators. The next thing there was a disturbance in one of the upper stands over to our left where the English supporters had been seated. It got worse, when they started to pull up the seating, and threw it onto the stands below, on top of the spectators in the lower stands. They then started to throw missiles on the pitch disrupting the game, causing the referee to halt the game. Things seemed to be getting worse so the referee decided to abandon the game for fear of players getting hurt.

Even though we were in the terrace area, it was still very frighten-ing for the girls as we stayed in our places until we were asked to leave. Garda reinforcements eventually got to the stand, and got the situa-tion under control, not before several people had been injured by the broken seating being thrown down on them. They kept the rioters, as that's what they had become, in the stand until the rest of the stadium was cleared. They were put on to their coaches, and driven to the exit ports, and put on board their ships.

A huge investigation followed, both within the Garda as to the security arrangements that were put in place for the game, and with the help of the British Police Forces, several of the troublemakers were brought back to Ireland during the following months, and appeared before the Irish courts. I'm afraid the girls never again asked to go to an International soccer game.

My eldest girl **Noeleen**, after finishing secondary school in 1996, decided she wanted to do nursing. Now, the entrance to the nursing profession changed in Ireland around that time, and students for nursing had to register with a college which of course involved a sizable fee. She decided to do some work with an elderly people's home, in Bloomfield Hospital, in Donnybrook, Dublin, to gain some experience dealing with the care of people.

In the meantime she checked out the system in England, and she was successful in obtaining a place as a student nurse in the Middlesex University in 1998, where she completed her Diploma of Higher Education in Adult Nursing in 2001. Her fees were paid for through a grant scheme. She's now a qualified senior nurse, and also qualified in ICU Care, with a London Hospital. She is now happily married to Andrew, and they have two children, both girls, Zoe, and Ciara.

My second girl **Ann Marie**, after finishing secondary school in 1999, went on to pursue a science degree in Chemistry, at Maynooth College. After being successful in obtaining her Degree in Chemistry, in 2003. She went on to do a Pharmaceutical Degree in a Sussex College in England where she graduated with a M. Sc. in Pharmacy in 2007, and qualified as a Pharmacist in 2008. Subsequently, Post graduate diploma in pharmacy practice, and independent prescribing qualification. She is currently working at University Hospitals in Sussex, as a senior Surgical Pharmacist: lead Pharmacist for head, and neck directorate, and specialist Uvenitis Pharmacist.

She is now married to Michael, and they have one child, a girl, Eloise.

My third girl Aoife, during the course of her attendance at secondary school got seriously ill, and spent some time in hospital causing her to lose some education time in her school. She went on to do two years at college following a science qualification. She went on to a job in a local business, later joined her older sister in London, in 2013, and some years after, went onto Australia where she is at the moment. Again while in Australia her old illness came back, and she had to be treated in a hospital there. She is now residing in Australia with her partner Piet, and they have a boy, Kai, who was two years old in December 2021.

All of my family of six children are now married or in partnerships, with their own families, which keeps me busy keeping up contact from afar. Over the years of course they didn't arrive at their life destinations without a sizable cost to both their mother, and me. I made a vow to myself that I would never leave them in want with regards to whatever support they needed, as I knew what it was like "not to have", which of course necessitated the obtaining of numerous bank loans over the years. I must of course give credit to St Rapheal's Garda Credit Union, for their outstanding assistance over the years, at times of most need. This of course put a huge strain on the family finances, and relationship at home.

My children's Educational, and Career achievements make me extremely happy, as I celebrate their successes, and achievements, and the fact that I have kept so close to them over the years. When you consider the start in life I had myself, to have my children come through their young lives as they have, with continuing successes, gives me plenty of reasons to be overjoyed, and proud of them, with very little help from the Government establishments.

Additional Community Involvement and Unable to Say No

Sometime in 1998 / 1999, I was approached by the local Parish Priest, Fr. Des O'Sullivan, and asked would I like to become involved in a committee for the purpose of building a new Parish Centre. How could I refuse the Parish Priest, knowing that I was already the Archbishops Nominee on the Board of Manage of the Leixlip secondary school collage, Colaiste Chiarain? The plan was to build the new Parish Centre beside the Church on an existing parish site. After several committee meetings, and visits to other parishes that had Parish Centers, a decision was taken to start the ball rolling.

Two sub-committees were formed from the main committee, one who would look after all planning, and building matters, and the second would look after raising the finances to pay for the project. I picked the short straw, and found myself chairman of the finance committee.

For most of 1999, the time was taken up with the design, plans, and getting planning permission for the new build. The finance committee could not go ahead with planning finance until the permission was granted to build the New Centre.

On the 30th of May 2000 a public meeting was arranged for any parishioners who wished to attend, to outline the plans for the new building, and to start the collections of money to finance the project. The outline for the proposal for the new centre, and the cost was given by the Parish Priest, Fr Des O'Sullivan. The cost of the project would be in the region of 600,000 Irish Punts, and the parish would have to raise the initial 300,000 before a sod was turned to comply with the current Diocesan Regulations.

I had been asked to outline the plans as to how the finances were going to be raised. I put forward that the most effective way to raise the funds needed was by way of direct cash donations, in the form of cash, cheque or standing order from bank accounts. I also added as a lighthearted note that "I didn't mind what the colour of the envelope was". We had already, prior to the meeting, raised 25,000 punts in cash.

We as the finance committee had our work cut out for us, as we brought together teams of volunteers to do a house by house call to every house in the parish. The reception was very mixed but we got a favourable response to our first series of house calls. It was a time consuming, and slow process; eventually we got a sizable number of people to sign up for the project.

To update people, and to put out a further appeal for support for financing the new parish centre, I had to go into the pulpit of the church at all the masses on Sunday the 22nd of April 2001. For me it was an experience to remember.

Later on during 2001, we turned to another method of raising funds by starting to organise, Golf Classics, the first of which was run on Monday the 8th of October 2001. I again was the main organiser for these events, I had of course got plenty of experience with the Lucan Spa Hotel Charity Classics, where I had assisted Frank Colgan proprietor of the Lucan Spa Hotel, for the past number of years.

As with all good voluntary charity events, there has to be hidden snags, and complaints. Some years previously the Parish sold some of its land around the church to the committee of the GaelScoil to build their school, which they succeeded in doing. There was still a part of the land which was adjacent to the GaelScoil, which was not being used, and was not too close to the church.

The Parish decided to put this piece of ground up for sale, using a well-known local estate agent. To make a long story short the GaelScoil, were interested as it would extend their green area for playing fields. The local estate agent was very anxious to have the site sold to the GaelScoil, so he put in an offer on their behalf, in the region of 70,000 to 80,000 Punts; it was under 100,000 if I remember correctly. The offer was not attractive to the committee so it was decided to seek a second opinion from an independent agent from outside the Leixlip area.

I was tasked with this assignment, and I went to a person I knew in the Lucan area who was a well-respected estate agent. I met with him at the site, and he had a good look around. I also gave him a map of the area showing the site, which was prepared by my own son, Mark, who was doing surveying at the time. Some days later my Lucan estate agent came back to me with a recommendation that the site should not be sold for anything less than 250,000 punts. I was dumbfounded at the recommendation.

The matter was referred to the Archbishop's House, who decided that an estate agent nominated by them would look after the sale of the site. Later the site was sold to an unknown buyer for a sum far in excess of even the quote given by my man from Lucan. It helped to put a big dent in the outstanding loans for the New Parish Centre.

The local estate agent felt his nose had been put out of joint. He wrote a scathing letter to the Parish Priest, with a copy to the Archbishops House, and me as Chairman of the finance committee. He tried to make a great play with the fact that the sale of the site had been withdrawn from him. Of course it was a matter of money, and his initial valuation fell very far short of what the site was eventually sold for. We had the interests of the Parish in mind when dealing with this matter.

Well I don't have all the dates of the happenings regarding the building of the new Parish Centre, but the sod was turned, the centre was built, and almost fully paid for even though it did go over the initial project cost. The existing committees had done their jobs, and a new committee, mostly of the old committees, formed a new Management Committee, which I became part of for a short period. In the summer of 2004 I resigned from the Management Committee.

In my resignation letter to the Chairman of the new Management Committee, of Our Lady's Parish Centre, Leixlip, I intimated that I was calling it a day due to ongoing commitments, and demands on my time. I stated that I did indicate earlier, my reluctance to join the Management Committee. I stated it was an honour to be asked to serve on the first Management Committee of the new Parish Centre.

I also stated that I enjoyed working with such a great band of volunteers over the past number of years. I found it a wonderful experience in facing the challenges that came our way. I wished the Management Committee continued success with the new centre.

CHAPTER TWENTY THREE

Lucan Leixlip Lions Club

Some short period of time, maybe a year or two, after my arrival at Lucan Station as a Detective Sergeant, I was approached by one of the local business people to know if I would be interested in joining a committee to form a new branch of the Lions Club, for the Lucan, and Leixlip areas. Not one for saying no I became a member of the first Lions Club covering the two areas.

I spent about five or six years with the Lions Club, and I eventually resigned due to work pressure. It was a great experience as we were involved in raising funds for charitable causes. I remember going out with other committee members with plastic buckets, standing at the traffic lights at Lucan village, which was the main road to the west. When the lights went red, then we would approach the car drivers for a donation into the bucket. It was a novel idea at the time. Thinking back now I must have had some neck. Of course it was left to me to sort out the collection permit, which I did by making an application to my superintendent as was the normal procedure.

We also had other means of collecting funds, through raffle tickets, and donations from the local businesses in both Lucan, and Leixlip. The funds were used for taking needy elderly people from Lucan, and Leixlip away for a week's holiday to Mosney Holiday Centre. Funds were also used to give Hampers to needy families over the Christmas period. It was very rewarding to be able to help people in need which also gave me a great sense of satisfaction.

Lucan Spa Hotel Golf Society and Charity Golf Classics

Sometime in the early to mid-1990s I got to know the proprietor of the Lucan Spa Hotel through contacts with him relating to some problems he was having. We developed a very good friendly relationship over time, which led to me being invited out on a few of the Lucan Spa Hotel Golf Society outings. As things developed I was invited to join the Golfing Society, became a member, and eventually ended up being on the committee of the Society for many years.

Over the years I enjoyed playing a bit of golf, I was a full member of the Garda Golf Club at Westmanstown, and played in several other societies both as a guest, and a member. Being a member of the Garda Club I had my GUI handicap, which I used when out with societies. I wasn't what you would call a very competitive type of player, I was out for the enjoyment, and I suppose the fresh air. There were many players who took golf very seriously, who were a pain to play with as they were tied up so much with their own game, that it was as if you didn't exist on the course with them, and if you were a poor player as I would have been they had no time for you.

My handicap would never have improved below eighteen, but at times it would have been a good asset to be asked to be on a team of four in a four ball competition with the likelihood of me coming in with a good score on some holes to the benefit of the team. Over my time playing golf I did win a number of prizes over the years, one being the honour of winning the Lucan Spa Hotel Societies Captains Prize in 2002. Because my prizes are so few I treasure them.

Like any organisation, no matter how big or small there will always be the ego trippers who are only out to satisfy their own ambitions. One such situation arose regarding the election of a Vice Captain for a particular year, which normally follows a procedure, with the incoming Captain nominating his Vice Captain for the coming year. At one of our AGM meetings one particular year, during the course of the nomination for Vice Captain a second proposal came from the floor nominating a second person as vice-Captain. The meeting was adjourned for a week to give the committee time to assess the situation.

Before the next meeting I found myself making out a few words as regards to my thoughts on the situation we found ourselves in. The following is what I outlined at this second meeting.

"I would like to say a few words in respect of this situation we find ourselves in.

There seems to have developed, a "them and us" attitude by a certain few of the members of the Society. We have a few of what might be termed prima-donna's in the Society who think they can ride roughshod over the rest of the Society, and look down their noses at the less proficient golfers. I believe a Society is there to nurture beginners, and create a level playing field, and not to criticise, and snigger.

Let us look briefly at where we are, we have a situation where we have two contenders for the post of Vice Captain of the Society.

Just because something like this hasn't happened before doesn't make it wrong.

The committee have accepted the proposal of --------------------
---------- for Vice Captain, but in doing so did not block the [second nominee] ---------------------- from the floor.

I think it's time for members of the Society to say where they stand,-------------- the second nominee is a controversial nomination.

We have a situation where our Patron ---------------------- of the Lucan Spa Hotel, and the [second nominee] do not see eye to eye for a number of reasons. Indeed -------------- the [second nominee] has no time for most of the committee up here including myself.

A number of things happened over the past few years in the Society where the Society took a compassionate, and soft approach. This view was unfortunately taken to mean a weakness when it comes to making harsh decisions, and may be part of the reason we find ourselves where we are today.

I personally have always tried to mediate in situations on behalf of the Society for the sake of the Society.

Like some of you I have been involved with the Society for some years now, and it was enjoyable. I am very disappointed with the stance taken by certain individuals who would be long time standing members of the Society. I'm not sure whether its blindness or did they just lose the plot, and don't have the best interests of the Society at heart.

I do not want the Golf Society to lose the Patronage of ---------
------------, and The Lucan Spa Hotel, because if that happens then we also lose a number of sponsors that we have obtained because of our close links with The Lucan Spa Hotel.

------------------------[second nominee] I don't know if you're getting the message, but I'm saying loud, and clear that I don't want to see you Captain of The Lucan Spa Hotel Golf Society now or in the future. I don't think I can put it on any plainer.

We need people who can carry the name of the Society with respect, show respect to our Sponsors, and especially to our Patron ----
------------------------, and The Lucan Spa Hotel whose backing, and support allows the Society to exist."

As on previous occasions I felt the urge to protect something we had, and not to allow it to be taken over by individuals to satisfy their own egos. The second nominee in this instance resigned from the Society, eventually getting the message.

This leads me to another role the Society played in fund raising over a good many years through the running of a Charity Golf Classic, which was suggested by Frank himself, who roped me in to do the organising with him. Again another time I couldn't say no. We set up a charity Golf committee, and we started small with not too many teams on our first outing in 1997. Eventually over time we grew our number of teams topping forty teams for some outings.

Two of our main beneficiaries were St Joseph's, Clonsilla, not too far from the Lucan Spa Hotel, and Peamount Hospital, Co Dublin, who both looked after disabled people from the communities they operated in. We didn't just want to give out a cheque or cash to anybody, so we put a proviso in place that whoever the beneficiary was for the particular Charity Classic outing, would have to nominate a project they wanted done, and we would put the funds raised towards that project. Of course we had numerous other beneficiaries that we supported over the years.

Of course our main support for teams for the Classics came from people associated with the Lucan Spa Hotel either through business or otherwise. Frank was a man you couldn't say no to. We used to start meeting around December each year to set the coming years event, organising the Golf course, setting the cost per team, and getting our sponsors for the prizes organised, the main sponsor being Matt Lee with Musgrave, Robinhood.

I remember on one occasion while organising one of the events Frank tasked me with the job of getting a particular team to get involved. Frank used to run Christmas shows at the Lucan Spa Hotel every Christmas, and this particular year he was featuring Joe Dolan, and his Band. I was to meet Joe after his show was finished in the bar at the Hotel where he always went for a drink. Now, the show wouldn't be over until around midnight, so I left my home, and went to the Lucan Spa Hotel to meet up with Joe. I arrived at the Hotel when normally I should have been leaving.

I met Joe at the bar, introduced myself as being on the Golf Classic Committee. We had a long night's conversation about golf, and other matters, and of course several drinks. Eventually Joe committed to putting in a team for the classic, and I called Frank over to confirm that Joe was entering his team for the upcoming Classic. I left the hotel at about 3am in the morning having completed my task.

There is a follow-up to this story, on the day of the classic Joe had his team there, which included his brother Ben, and they teed off, and played their round of golf. I had the job of doing the score cards which can be difficult at times. We all met back at The Lucan Spa Hotel for the prize giving, and something to eat. While the meal was going on, it was a good time for me to finish the score cards, do whatever checks needed to be done, and do the list of winners. People generally knew where they stood with their scores, and would have a good idea of who might be on the winners list.

On checking Joe Dolan, and his team's card I noticed there was something amiss, I went over to Joe, and asked about the card. He realized then that they, the team, had handed in the wrong card. The card they handed in was the card they were using for a side bet between them. I apologised to Joe, and told him that the card that was handed in, and signed would have to stay there. If his team had put in the correct card they would have won the first prize for the day. The team did go away with a prize somewhere down the winners list. It didn't stop Joe putting in teams for a number of years after, continuing to support the Charity Classic.

Now I'm living in Malta, there is hardly a day goes by that I don't hear Joe Dolan being played on one of the local Radio Stations, he became a great favourite with the people of Malta over the years. Joe unfortunately passed away on the 26th December 2007, R.I.P.

Some of the projects we helped to support included computer systems, a number of mini buses, lifting systems for moving patients in, and out of beds, and in, and out of pools. There were lots more which I can't recall now, but I was involved for up to about fifteen years with Frank, and The Lucan Spa Hotel in organising these Fund Raising Charity Classics during the course of which we raised hundreds of thousands of Pounds/Euros over that time. We used to donate sums of between €20,000, and €30,000 for the projects we were associated with from each outing. I left Ireland in the second half of 2013, and I know Frank was still carrying on the good work. Of course due to the Covid-19 restrictions all charity events were put on hold from 2020.

CHAPTER TWENTY FOUR

Arrival at Final Transfer Destination 1986

Well my arrival in Lucan Garda Station as a Detective Sergeant finally materialised in early September 1986. The Commissioner's bidding was accomplished, with I have no doubt, the backing of the Garda Associations of the time. Even though all of us who were impacted by these transfers, were still members of our respective associations, paying our contributions. The Associations were very mute during the course of all the transfers that took place, never once making representation on anybody's behalf. Of course we didn't look for help, how could we, considering they [the associations] were partly responsible for what happened initially.

There were times when I thought about making an appeal against my original transfer from the Drug Squad, as it could have been seen as a case of retribution, for my being involved in a legitimate legal battle in the High Court in the detective's case. Also there was my qualification in the Addiction Studies Course, where I spent a year in college in 1984, which of course was never taken into the equation. It would have involved going back to the courts, and I have no doubt it would have been an uphill battle as well as costly, with the establishment winning out in the end. Maybe today it would be a different story, considering the improvements with respect to individual rights.

For the next fourteen years I remained at Lucan Garda Station as a Detective Sergeant, it was a reasonably quiet place at first, when I arrived, but as the years rolled on, it became a very busy spot, with Lucan Station being made into a District Headquarters Station, for the new "Q" District that was formed in the Division, sometime in the late 1980s early 1990s.

Lucan Station Detective Unit

Lucan Station, which was a sub-district station in the "L" District, when I had arrived first, was a very old building, built in the Georgian style, but was in very bad state of repair, so much so that almost half of the building wasn't being used due its condition. The Detective offices were upstairs in the front portion of the building with windows looking out on to what was then the main road, to the west of Ireland. The Detective office was a reasonably good size office, except like the rest of the building needed a lot of repair. I did learn when I arrived that there were plans afoot for a new station to be built which I didn't pay much heed to as there were always promises being made about upgrading Garda buildings.

My doubts regarding the new building were short lived when in June 1987 we all moved into prefabricated buildings situated in the front court of the station, with parts of the prefab buildings within five feet of the main west road. One can only imagine the cramped working conditions, which created its own difficulties, with us in the Detective Unit having to bring any suspects arrested to one of the other District stations for processing, and charging. Some of the members on station duty at those stations weren't too happy with this situation as it made more work for them especially if the suspects were going to be detained for a period of time.

To all of our surprise the new building was ready for occupation within twelve months, in July 1988, with the official opening taking place the following year in March 1989 performed by the then Minister for Justice, Gerry Collins. The new Detective's office was in the same location on the new plans as the old office, as I had checked out, with the addition of a Detective Sergeants office, and a Detective Inspectors office, on the upstairs floor. These were going to be the new Detective Offices, and we were looking forward to the moving in date which had been set to allow for a smooth transfer out of the prefabs.

Another Attempted Anti-Detective Move 1988

On the day prior to the move into the new building, I was approached by one of the uniform Inspectors whom I knew well from working together for the previous two years since I had moved to Lucan. He informed me that the Chief Superintendent had issued a direction that none of the upstairs offices were to be occupied, which included the new Detectives office, and that the Detectives were to take up residence in offices downstairs which had been designated on the plans, as interview rooms near the new cells.

I informed the Inspector, with respect, that I wasn't going to move my unit into the interview rooms downstairs, that I would be occupying our designated offices upstairs as shown on the plans. I was aware that the Inspector was only carrying out the instructions as issued by the Chief Superintendent which I wouldn't hold against him as we had developed a good relationship. I felt that this was another attempt to try to belittle the Lucan Detective Unit, by not giving us our proper accommodation in the new building, or maybe an attempt to settle old scores with regards to myself, from our previous encounters.

The evening prior to the day of the move into the new building, I called as many of my crew together as I could muster, and we, under the cover of darkness moved all of our equipment, files, and papers into our new upstairs offices, and locked them. On the following day as the rest of the station party were moving into the new building, we started operating from our new Detective offices. There was never a whimper out of the Chief Superintendent, and I smiled to myself with a certain amount of satisfaction at winning that battle. My crew, and others would have been aware of the differences between me, and the Chief, but not the gritty details. As we didn't have a Detective Inspector assigned to us yet I did mention to the uniform Inspectors that they could make use of that office until there was a Detective Inspector appointed.

I had a great team of detectives, trainee detectives, and civilian staff at Lucan Station during my service there, with whom I built up a good working, and social relationship. I also developed a good rapport with our uniform colleagues over the years, and was always available to give advice when sought. After all, I had gained huge experience during my service in the various sections of the Detective Branch around the city including Fraud, Drugs, and Serious Crime Investigation, and was always willing to share my knowledge, and experiences. Of course the one thing I did not share with anyone, were my experiences in my young life prior to joining the Garda Siochana. Those matters remained buried in the back of my mind for many more years to come.

Holiday Abroad 1987, Malta

Staying with my early years at Lucan, as I got settled in, and around the same time as we moved into the prefabs at Lucan Station, I decided to take up an offer from my sister, Joan, who I hadn't seen in over fifteen years, and who had been inviting us to Malta for a holiday over a number of years. It was an ideal opportunity for me to get away with my family for one of our few holidays abroad together. We had started planning this trip some time prior to June 1987, and we were going to be away for a full month. My first port of call was to organise the passports for my wife Margaret, and our five children. I was the only member of the family to hold a passport which I had obtained in 1982 for my trip to Spain on the Drugs inquiry. At that time you could have the younger children named on their parents passports so I'm not sure how many passports I had to get.

The next thing was to get an idea of the fares, and where we were going to fly from. I think Air Malta did flights from Dublin at least once a week, but the fares were expensive, so I did a bit of shopping around, and discovered that by flying from Dublin to London, and from London to Malta it would be cheaper than getting a direct flight from Dublin, so I booked those flights for all seven of us. Taking the two flights also broke the journey up, and made it more interesting for the children.

I was in touch with Joan by phone, and I remember her telling me to make sure I brought light clothes for us, and the children. Putting my tailoring skills, and experience to good use I produced some nice bright clothes out of some old material for both the boys, and the girls. Today of course they would have been looking for branded clothing, and homemade stuff wouldn't even be looked at. When going through the boarding gates at all the airports I could feel the gaze of people taking in the size of our family group as we went through on our holiday.

When we arrived in Malta, we went to passport control where there was a long queue waiting to go through which seemed to be manned by army personnel. The place was like an oven as it had a corrugated tin roof. While we were waiting I noticed Gerard going very pale, and he almost collapsed with the heat so we had to get him somewhere where there was air. We eventually got through passport control, and I'm not sure who actually collected us, but we arrived at Joan's house in Mellieha where we met her two girls, Fran, and Maggie, and her husband Frans.

Joan's house was a fairly large house, but still not big enough for an invasion like ours. Our next big surprise was when we were brought to where we were going to stay; it was an old tower, built around the 1600/ 1700's by the Knights as a watch tower looking out over the Mediterranean. It was known locally as the "White Tower". They had it all laid out for us, with beds, wash rooms with the comforts of home, and all to ourselves. There was a stone spiral staircase up to the upper rooms where the bedrooms were. Frans had the use of this building from the Government for which he paid a small rent each year, and used it as a holiday home for family use.

We of course were already beginning to feel the heat. Also Frans put his Rover V8 at my disposal for use while we were in Malta for the month. It was a lovely car, and I remembered, it was the same car he had when I went to see them in London in 1970, which he also turned up for my wedding in. It went very well with one drawback, the exhaust was faulty, and the roars of the car as we drove around was deafening, especially going up the hills, but we managed it for the month we were there.

On our first night in the tower there was a huge storm with winds, rain, thunder, and lightning, which was very frightening for the children at the time. I was a bit scared myself thinking the roof might blow off as we were right out on the coast beside the sea. I was glad when morning came, and the sun started to shine. We didn't have another drop of rain or any more storms for the rest of our time there, the weather was just beautiful. I think that first introduction to Malta had a lasting effect on me, causing me to develop a great affection for the country.

It was a wonderful break, and we made the most of it, meeting Joan most days in Mellieha, at her favourite restaurant, "The Bellevue", which included a bakery where we often purchased our fresh bread. We also spent a lot of time on Mellieha beach which wasn't too far from where we were staying. We also had BBQ's at the White Tower, and we spent a lot of time there as it was so quiet, and out on its own beside the sea.

Frans had a small boat, a cruiser, and he took us on several trips to the other two Islands, Gozo, and Comino. On one of these particular trips when there were about 10 to 12 of us on the boat, it was a tight fit. I was taking some photos, and when passing the camera to my son Niall, the camera slipped off the boat into the water never to be seen again. The sea that day was a little rough causing the boat to rock a bit, leaving my camera slip to the bottom of the Mediterranean. Maggie, Joan's daughter, dived into the sea to try to retrieve it, but it sank too fast.

When we arrived at the Island of Comino, which is the smallest of the three Islands, Frans beached the boat up onto the sandy beach, and we all got out of the boat. I think Joan had brought a packed lunch for everybody so we had our picnic on the beach. After spending a couple of hours there it was time to get back into the boat for the journey home, but first we had to push the boat off the sandy beach into the water. The boat was about 15 to 17 feet in length, and had an on board engine which made it heavy. We managed to get it back into the water, and headed back to the White Tower.

Today that boat is still in the water with a different owner, Victor, who was a good friend of Frans, and lives in Mellieha. He runs his own garage so it was no problem for him to make the changes he wanted to. He made some alterations to it, by taking out the onboard engine, and now uses an outboard on it. We still use Victor to do work on our cars when needed. Sonia, and I pass it by now, and again when we are on our own boat, when we are in Mellieha Bay. Yes it brings back memories.

Of course time always flies when you are enjoying something, and our trip to Malta was no different. We did a bit of tourist shopping before we started our packing. I think we bought about twenty bottles of Maltese wine which we purchased at a farmers wine outlet, and lots of other bits, and pieces. Luckily we were able to spread the bottles into the large number of suitcases we had brought with us. One of the items we purchased was a small kitchen knife with a wooden handle with a fold in blade. We had no problem going through the airport at Malta with the knife in my hand luggage, but when we got to London all luggage was searched, and the knife found, and taken out of my luggage, but in fairness the checker said he would put it through on its own as I couldn't carry it on the plane. You can imagine the looks I got at Dublin Airport when this knife came down on the luggage carousel on its own with a label, I retrieved it.

The trip was a memory that stuck with the family for a long time after that, which gave us an appetite for travel, so as the years went by, smaller groups of us made it back to Malta from time to time, with myself travelling on my own on occasions to visit Joan. She had been through a tough few years, fighting cancer, making many trips to London for a series of serious operations, and treatment. It was also great to see at least one of my family doing well for herself, having like myself come from such humble beginnings

I suppose when one gets the chance to "name drop" why not take it. Frans was a member of the labour party [Partit Laburista in Malta], and was very close to the leadership of the party. He even put himself forward as a candidate for election to the Parliament on a few occasions but unfortunately had no success. Now, the leader of the party at that time was none other than Dom Mintoff who was Prime Minister of Malta a number of times, who became well known worldwide, as a result of his success in getting the British to leave Malta, having won Independence for Malta in 1964, and which became a Republic, on the 13th of December in 1976.

Frans, and Joan became very good friends with Dom Mintoff, and His wife Moira, with a great friendship being established between Joan, and Moira, as Joan spoke English, and Moira couldn't speak Maltese. Moira Mintoff was English herself, and she had met Dom Mintoff, while he was studying in England during the war years. Joan ended up going on many trips abroad accompanying Moira, to keep her company while Dom Mintoff, was going about his political duties.

While I was there with the family in 1987, Joan mentioned a few times that she would love me to meet with Moira, and Dom, but they were away for a few weeks with their family. In December 1987 I received a letter to my home in Leixlip from none other than Moira Mintoff, Dom Mintoff's wife, giving her apologies for not being able to meet up with me when I was over. She sent her best wishes for the new year 1988, and hoped that I would be over again. I did meet with her a few years later, and had afternoon tea at her house with Joan, unfortunately Dom was otherwise engaged, and I didn't get to meet the Great man. Malta is such a small Island you just never know who you might bump into.

Later, I was to meet the Lady President of Malta, Marie Louise Coleiro, whom Sonia knew personally, also we both met with Prime Minister Joseph Muscat, during his time as head of the Maltese government, and other dignitaries along the way.

CHAPTER TWENTY FIVE

Cases, and Occurrences during my time at Lucan

During the course of my service as Detective Sergeant at Lucan Garda Station from 1986 until my retirement in December 2000, there were a number of incidents, and cases which are worthy of a mention. I give her a synopsis of some of these cases as they give a good insight to the various types of investigations that, I myself, was involved in, with my unit, including some of the behind the scenes working of the Garda Detective force. It also gives one a good indication of the volume of cases, and the workload that can arise in a short space of time. Also I expand on some aspects of my planning for my future, including my further involvement outside the force within the community.

Christmas Day Call Out

One incident comes to mind regarding the "calls on a Policeman's time", showing that no day on the calendar is sacred. I cannot put a date on it, I think it was during my first couple of years at Lucan, it was on a Christmas day of whatever year, and I was on duty as happened a lot during the course of my service in the Garda, I think there were only about three Christmas days that I was not scheduled for duty during my service.

Normally within the Detective Unit we would try to facilitate each other regarding a time to go for Christmas lunch or dinner. On this particular Christmas morning I was on duty at the office when I received a phone call from my Divisional Headquarters, that the Detective Superintendent required all Detective Inspectors, and

Detective Sergeants to report to Divisional Headquarters for a crime conference at around 11am. Now, I didn't think much of it as I knew the Detective Superintendent well from my days in the Central Detective Unit at the Castle. In my own mind I was thinking that he was inviting us over for a Christmas drink.

It was not the case, at the conference we were informed that certain information had come to light, that a criminal gang was in the process of tunnelling into the vault of a bank within the Division. There was no information as to which bank it was or the location or area. We were instructed to make contact with all the bank managers in our Districts, bring them out, and have all the banks inspected, and searched for any signs of tunneling.

I returned to my office, and passed on the bad news to my crew that Christmas was cancelled, and we had to meet up in my office, and organise the calling out of the key holders for the banks in our District which included Lucan, and Leixlip. We made contact with the managers of all the banks, and made arrangements for a time to meet them at their banks as we didn't want them all out at the same time. Many of them were not happy with the call outs, but complied nonetheless. Because of the nature of the searches to be carried out we spread them out over the two days, Christmas day, and St Stephen's day. We also had the backup of our uniform colleagues.

The searches proved negative over those two days with no sign of tunnelling to any bank. Some days later, an attempt at trying to tunnel into one of the banks within the Division was discovered, but the attempted tunnelling had been abandoned before reaching the bank premises. Maybe all the police activity over the two days at the banks may have disturbed them, we will never know. It just goes to show the things that can be happening while everybody is enjoying themselves over the festive season.

July 1987, Murder by fire

Not too long after my return from my Malta holidays, I got a call to a house fire in the "L" district, which had occurred at around 3.30am on the morning of the 8th Of July 1987. When I arrived at the scene later that morning I was informed by the uniform Inspector at the scene that a woman, and her four children had perished in the fire, one other child, a boy had survived, and had been taken to hospital for treatment. The members who had arrived at the scene earlier were of the opinion that this may have been a tragic accident, and it was being treated as such at first.

I had a conversation with the Inspector at the scene, and made the suggestion that we inform our Superintendent, John Courtney who happened to be away on holidays in his home county of Kerry at the time, and had left instructions that he could be contacted with respect to anything of a serious nature that may occur. John Courtney had of course been head of the Murder Squad at Garda Headquarters for a number of years, and always wanted to be kept informed of serious incidents that might happen.

Inquiries over the first number of hours changed the direction of the investigation as more information came to light. I made contact with the Superintendent, and filled him in on the information I had to hand. He asked me for my opinion on the cause of the fire, and I told him that I think it requires a full investigation. With that he instructed me to arrange a full team from the Bureau, and a conference for the following morning, and he was returning immediately.

It was established that this was not the first fire that had occurred at this house, in a matter of days the husband, and father of the children became a person of interest. He was arrested a number of days after the fire, and during the course of being interviewed he broke down, and admitted to setting fire to the house with his wife, and family inside. He was later charged with five counts of murder. He pleaded guilty, and was sentenced to life imprisonment.

It was a sad situation with the loss of so many lives on that occasion, which goes to show one can't take things at face value. In fairness to the Inspector at the scene he had some sense of something not being right, hence his decision to call in the Detectives to assist. It could just as easy have gone down as a tragic accident with nobody being made culpable.

As to the reasoning behind the fire, it was never really established as the accused would not elaborate as to his reasons behind the setting of the house on fire. During the course of the investigation information did come to hand that one of the children, a girl who had perished in the fire had an appointment to meet with a social worker regarding some matter or other which was never divulged.

What Scott Medal November 1987

1987 was a busy year in our District, and indeed for the Gardai in general. On the 13th of October 1987 a Dr. John O'Grady, who was a Dental Surgeon was kidnapped from his home in South County Dublin. He was held captive for 23 days, and was finally rescued by armed Gardai on the 5th of November 1987 after a shootout in the north of Dublin city, between the Gardai, and the kidnap gang who fled leaving their captive behind them.

The Gardai had mounted a huge manhunt country wide, and now knew the identity of the culprits responsible for this kidnapping. During the course of these searches that were taking place, information came into the possession of members of the "L" District Detective Unit through Detective Garda Tom Costello of the Special Detective Unit, that there was a possibility that some of the culprits for this kidnapping were in a house within our District. This information came to Detective Garda Costello's attention during the course of the search of another suspect safe house where he found some written documentation referring to the target address. It was decided that on the 11th of November, the date the information was obtained, that a search would be carried out on this particular house in the Ballyfermot area.

At this time I was the Detective Sergeant at Lucan Station which was part of the "L" District. Detective Inspector John McLoughlin who was head of the "L" District Detective Unit, got a large search party of Detectives together from the District, as a result of this information coming to hand, which included myself, and one of my

Detectives from Lucan, Michael Conneely. Other members of the search party included the Detective Sergeant [not named] with two of his Detective Gardai [not named] with Detective Garda Tom Costello who was attached to the Special Detective Unit with responsibility for tracking subversive activity within the "L" District, as well as a number of other District Detectives.

A large force of uniform Gardai were also brought in to assist during the course of the search, with the responsibility of closing off all the streets, and roads surrounding the search area, and to keep people in their house for the period of the search, because there was a possibility of gun fire exchanges as happened in the north of the city six days previously.

Detective Sergeant [not named], got a search warrant from Superintendent John Courtney, issued under the Offences against the State Act 1939. The search party arrived at the target house, Detective Sergeant [not named], with one of his Detectives [not named] put in the front door, went in, and upstairs to the bedrooms, other Detectives went to the front room downstairs, Detective Garda Tom Costello went into the kitchen area at the back of the building followed by myself with Detective Inspector McLoughlin, and Detective Garda Michael Conneely, not far behind. Detective Garda Tom Costello then started to call out at somebody lying on a settee in the corner of the kitchen. Tom was armed with a submachine gun, and I had my revolver drawn, and pointed at the person in the corner. I holstered my revolver as the person began to move on the settee, and sat up with his hands spread along the length of the settee. While Tom covered him I moved towards him, and hanging on a chair close to where his head lay was a jacket which I removed, and took possession of. Detective Inspector McLoughlin went over to the individual, and got him to stand up, and began to search him all the time, covered by Detective Garda Tom Costello. In the meantime I started to examine the jacket I had retrieved which I found to be heavier than it should have been. In one of the pockets of the jacket I found a loaded .45, five chamber revolver with four loaded chambers, and some spare ammunition also in the same pocket.

I instructed Detective Garda Tom Costello to take this man into custody for the possession of a loaded firearm, and also instructed Detective Garda Michael Conneely to put handcuffs on the suspect. Just then the Detective Sergeant [not named] arrived from upstairs with Detective Gardai [not named] the suspect was then asked who he was, but he refused to confirm his identity. He was then taken to Ballyfermot Garda Station where he was detained.

While being processed at the station he made an attempt to escape, and it took several members of the force present to restrain him.

Outside the house I met with Detective Garda Seamus Quinn from the Garda Technical Bureau, and handed him the .45 revolver, and Jacket for examination by our Ballistics Section. It was a great achievement on the day to have one of the chief suspects involved in the kidnapping of Dr. John O'Grady, in custody, and without any shot being fired or other serious incident.

Later McNeil appeared at the Special Criminal Court on charges relating to the finding of the firearm, and other charges relating to the kidnapping, where Detective Garda Tom Costello gave evidence of arresting him. On a later date McNeil was sentenced to fifteen years in prison.

Now there were a few anomalies in this case with respect to my own involvement in the case, as I was never called as a witness, having been the person who actually discovered the firearm in the suspect's jacket. Afterwards I thought about this as it was most unusual that an important witness like me was excluded from the investigation file. I wasn't even asked to make a statement in the case even though I had played an important role in the initial search.

Case Anomalies

"I have an entry in my notebook for 11/11/87 which states". "went to 16 Le Fanu Drive, between 10am-11am, went to back room of house where D/Gda Tom Costello had a person under cover, who was lying down on a sofa, he got up, and was searched by D/I McLoughlin, I pulled out the settee, and found a blue jacket near where the man's head was, he gave his name as Anthony Connolly, on searching the jacket I found a revolver type gun in the right hand pocket, I took possession of the jacket, and the gun. I produced the jacket, and I asked the man who gave his name as Anthony Connolly if this was the only jacket he had, he replied "yes", I then asked what was in the pocket, and I showed him the revolver, he then said "no it's not my jacket," I then called D/Garda Mick Conneely, and asked him to place handcuffs on the man who had given his name as Anthony Connolly, before I showed the jacket to McNeil I cautioned him. Also I noted in my notebook, "4 rounds of Amo in the chambers, 5 chamber gun with the chamber under the hammer empty, .45 calibre revolver, make the British Bulldog." "Also two rounds of .45 ammo found in a plastic wallet containing a free travel pass. Jacket, and revolver, and ammo handed to D/Garda Seamus Quinn from the Ballistics Section Garda Technical Bureau."

I was aware that there was a certain amount of tension between Detective Sergeant [not named], and Detective Inspector John McLoughlin; this was an ongoing situation that could be described as a personality clash, which became more apparent at the outcome of this case. I sensed that Detective Sergeant [not named] felt a bit upstaged in not being the first person with his two sidekicks [not named], to encounter McNeil in the house. This would have reverberated on me, and other members of the search party over time, resulting in being excluded from the continuing investigation, and not being included as a witness in the case. The sentencing of McNeil in the Special Criminal Court was not the end of the case for Detective Sergeant [not named], and his two sidekicks [not named].

Now when I look back at that situation on that particular day many of the members of the search party put themselves on the front line of danger, starting with the forcing of the front door by Detective Sergeant [not named], and one of his Detective sidekicks [not named], then the discovery by Detective Garda Tom Costello with me behind him, joined moments later by Detective Inspector John McLoughlin, and Detective Garda Michael Conneely, of a person feigning sleep on a settee in the kitchen/dining room, where a loaded .45 revolver firearm was discovered in a pocket of a jacket hanging on a chair close to his head. At any time between the putting in of the front door, and the discovery of the suspect on the settee, that firearm could have been used with devastating consequences against any of us Detective Branch members that day.

The case of Anthony McNeil which started in November 1987 with his arrest went on to some time early to mid-1988. After the hearing of the case at the Special Criminal Court, [which of course I hadn't attended], and his sentencing, I would have classed the case as closed with respect to Garda involvement.

Sometime into late 1988, and maybe very early 1989, I received a phone call from my Detective Inspector John McLoughlin about the McNeil case. He asked me if I was aware of any reports with respect to an application to the Garda Reward Board for the awarding of a Scott Medal in respect of the Anthony McNeil case. He took me totally by surprise with the question, and I told him I would come into District Headquarters to meet with him. He said that out of "caution" he would drive out to Lucan, and meet me there which he did.

When we met he informed me that he had become aware of an application to the Reward Board for the presentation of the Scott Medal to certain members of the Anthony McNeil search party. There was no mention of Detective Garda Tom Costello, Detective Inspector John McLoughlin, Detective Garda Michael Conneely or myself in the application report. That was the first I heard of this application to the Reward Board, and I stated to the Detective Inspector, that something of this nature never crossed my mind.

Detective Inspector McLoughlin was incensed about this application as it didn't include a true account of what occurred that day, also the application had by- passed his office which it shouldn't have, he being the Detective Inspector of the "L" District Detective Unit. I remember him saying to me "over my dead body will this go through", so he immediately, from my office phoned Superintendent John Courtney to arrange a meeting with him. In the meantime the Detective Inspector asked Detective Garda Tom Costello, Detective Garda Michael Conneely, and I to make out reports about our involvement, and the actions we had taken during the course of the McNeil search on the 11th of November 1987, which we sent to him.

I accompanied Detective Inspector John McLoughlin during his meeting with Superintendent John Courtney which was held at Lucan Garda Station, in the conference room there. The Detective Inspector passed on all the reports regarding the incident to the Superintendent which we discussed at this meeting. Superintendent Courtney was aware of the application which had gone to the Reward Board, as it had gone through his office, but he was not aware that there was conflicting information with regards to what happened that day on the 11th of November 1987.

During the course of this meeting Superintendent Courtney asked me to arrange a meeting with all the parties involved which I undertook to do.

At this meeting after some discussion there was some agreement as to how this application to the Reward Board should proceed, with the initial application being withdrawn. A new application was to be made to the Reward Board, which would include the members who were excluded from the original application to the Reward Board.

In writing about this event I do not have all the papers from the original file nor did I ever get a glance at the original application to the Reward Board. I only received the later report, giving the "Concise details of case", and a copy of a report from Detective Garda Thomas Costello which thankfully ties down a date for me which was over twelve months after the arrest of McNeil.

Following on from the meetings with Superintendent John Courtney, and the submitting of new reports through Detective Inspector John McLoughlin, things were quiet for some time, until I later received a communication from Garda Headquarters that I had received a **second class commendation** from the Rewards Board. All the members whose names were on the new application received the same second class commendation.

The original report to the Reward Board, gave an incomplete, and incorrect account of the incident. But for the actions of Detective Inspector McLoughlin that report would have resulted in some members being acknowledged, but not all fairly.

Yes it was a dangerous mission on that morning, and I would not take away from the initial actions of others in putting in the front door of the house, but they were not the first people to eyeball this dangerous suspect, and retrieve a loaded .45 revolver from his possession. What a pity the initial application, and report wasn't a fully accurate account of the events as they occurred on the day. Some people might say that I make this assertion of events because of "sour grapes", or for other reasons, but I reaffirm what I stated to Detective Inspector John McLoughlin when he first told me about the original application to the Reward Board, "something like that never crossed my mind". To me it was just another Garda operation I was involved in, like many others throughout my service in the Garda Siochana.

If there was anybody deserving of a Scott Medal for that morning's raid Detective Garda Thomas Costello would be high on my list as he was the first person into that room, to face down the dangerous suspect.

I have to wonder what Colonel Walter Scott, who this award is named after, would have to say about the initial application. Colonel Scott was a Canadian who developed a great interest in Police Forces, and during a Police conference in New York in 1923, met with the first Garda Commissioner Eoin O'Duffy. He introduced the awarding of a gold medal for Gardai who performed heroic acts of bravery each year. Colonel Scott himself presented the first Gold Scott Medal to a member of the Garda Siochana, at the Garda Headquarters Phoenix Park, Dublin in 1924.

The Fraudster Who Got Away With It 1986/1987

In late 1986, and into early 1987, I took on the investigation of a suspected fraud case with one of my Detectives, Detective Garda Michael Conneely. I had decided to oversee this investigation myself, putting my previous experience of fraud investigation to good use. On the face of it, it seemed a straightforward enough case, of a woman defrauding people out of sums of money, in cash transactions. This woman was running a currency exchange scheme where she was offering to exchange Irish Punts for Sterling at even rates. For example she would give client one hundred Sterling for one hundred Irish Punts with no exchange rate.

She started off introducing the scheme to people known to her for small amounts of a couple of hundred to a couple of thousand Sterling for Irish Punts. Of course the word spread like wildfire, and in no time people were queuing up to take advantage of her wonderful "offer". The clients had first to hand over their Irish Punts, and she would come back to them in a few days with the Sterling, in this way she built up a trust with her clients.

This woman resided in the Captains Hill area of Leixlip, and had a daughter training as a hairdresser with a local salon which also raised peoples trust in her as they lived in the area. Her daughter also helped in her recruiting of clients through her contacts in the hairdressing salon. People did wonder how she was able to do this exchange, but she passed it off by saying it was because of her contacts that she had.

Then on the last occasion she indicated to her clients that she was going in for a "big killing", but she needed to get an investment of at least 250,000 Irish Punts. Some of her clients obliged by investing larger amounts of Irish Punts with her for this investment. There was one client who was from Northern Ireland, and was associated with a Republic of Ireland League football team. He handed over something in the region of 90,000 Irish Punts in cash, which he handed over to her in a plastic bag. I suspected at the time that this cash came from the account of the League of Ireland football club.

Another man who owned a shop in the Leixlip area gave her in excess of 40,000 in cash in Irish Punts. He had just upgraded his shop, and was hoping this would help to pay off some of his outgoings on the shop. Other clients came up with amounts varying from 5,000 to 10,000 Irish Punts in cash. She had now informed her investors that on this occasion it would take a bit longer because of the large amount of cash involved, and to bear with her. They, as before, took her at her word, and weren't unduly concerned at this stage.

It was only when a number of weeks had passed that they realised that something wasn't right. So some people went looking for her at the address she had in Captains Hill, Leixlip, to find that she was no longer residing there, and they also found out that her daughter was no longer at the hairdressing salon, which was on the main street in Leixlip. She, with her husband, and a number of children had vanished with something in the region of 250,000 Irish Punts.

Reports started to come into the Lucan Detective Unit from people who had invested money with her. Detective Garda Conneely, and myself, opened an investigation into the alleged money scam, obtained statements from the injured parties, some of whom didn't make a complaint as they were too embarrassed, but we had tracked them down through friends of theirs who had also invested in the scam.

From our investigations we succeeded in identifying the culprit, and set about trying to locate her. Information came to hand that this woman, and her family were making arrangements to travel to Australia. We made inquiries at our Garda Headquarters section who dealt with police certificates for people travelling abroad in order to obtain a visa to enter certain countries. Also because she had an address in our sub District her application would have had to come through Lucan Station, but there was no record of such an application being made. On further investigation we discovered she had made an application through another station in the Division, and a Police Certificate had been issued to her.

What we also discovered was that the Garda who processed her application for a certificate through his station was in some way, related to her family. When interviewed the Garda stated he was only doing her a favour, and hadn't a clue about what she had been involved in until we had approached him. There was very little we could do at this stage, she had gone on her way. Things didn't end there, we carried out inquiries with the help of the Australian authorities, and she was located at an address in Melbourne, Australia.

We then sent the file to the office of The Director of Public Prosecutions seeking instructions as to the course of action to be taken, and inquired as to whether we could obtain an international warrant for her arrest or arrange to have her interviewed first. We received instructions from the office of The Director of Public Prosecutions to have the suspect interviewed first regarding the alleged crimes, before getting a warrant for her arrest. This would entail somebody going to Melbourne, Australia to interview her.

I of course made out an application to travel to Melbourne to interview the suspect in the case, attaching a copy of the file, outlining the crimes committed, attaching a copy of the direction from the Director of Public Prosecutions, including a breakdown of the amount of about 250,000 Irish Punts which had been obtained by false pretences.

I received a report back from Headquarters refusing my application to travel to interview the suspect. There was a handwritten note by the then Commissioner, refusing the application to travel. I would now, on reflection of events at that time, describe the Commissioners refusal to have this crime fully investigated, as puzzling, and inexplicable.

Later we learned that the man who had handed over the 90,000 in cash flew to Melbourne himself to confront the suspect, but she had gone from the address we had tracked her down to.

Death in a Nursing Home

I did say that 1987 was a busy year; I was just over a year at Lucan Station as a Detective Sergeant. Now, by some coincidence, on the 18th of December 1987, I was with a full team of Detectives, including members from the Technical Bureau, and our Superintendent. We had just completed an investigation, which must have been a serious case, maybe a suspicious death; I can't for some reason recall what the case was. The "L" District was a busy place; there was a period between 1987, and 1990 where we were involved in the investigation of five murders in our district during the course of one year.

We had all retired to a local public house for something to eat, and have a few drinks as was often the case at the close of an investigation. It would have been early evening, sometime between 6pm, and 8pm, and everybody was relaxing. A short time after we had arrived, one of the staff informed us that there was a phone call from someone asking for a Detective to come to the phone. I took the call, and spoke with somebody from Ballyfermot Garda Station who informed me that there was a body of a woman found at a local nursing home, and things looked suspicious at the scene, and she hadn't been seen for the past three days.

I went to the Superintendent, and informed him of the situation. What luck if you call it that under the circumstances, we had a full murder team in our mists. We abandoned our leisure time, and all headed for the scene of this incident.

The location was a Nursing Home, which was made up of a main large building with a number of self-contained units on the grounds. It was in one of these self-contained units that the body was, and we were shown to the scene by one of the nuns that discovered the body. It was a one bedroom unit, and all of us held back to allow the Technical Bureau members that were with us to check the scene first so as not to walk all over the scene. The Bureau people cordoned off the area they wanted kept free to do their job around the location of the body.

The rest of us then carried out some local inquiries, interviewing nuns at the convent which was in the main building, and taking statements. An examination of the scene was carried out inside, and outside, to check if there was any forced entry into the unit where this lady lay. There didn't seem to be any forced entry to the building. The position of the body on the floor was near a table where she seemed to have been writing her Christmas cards, and what made the whole situation more suspicious was the fact that the lady's tights, and underwear were down around her ankles. Our first thoughts were that we might be dealing with a sexual pervert, who had gained entry in some way, and sexually assaulted this lady.

The big question at the time was how the body lay undiscovered for three days before being found. It was a phone call from someone who was trying to call this lady over some period of time, who eventually called the main house to tell them that there was no reply from this lady's phone. Two of the nuns then went to the unit, and found the body of the lady. The nuns were of the opinion that she had been taken out for a few days by some of her relatives, and hadn't yet returned. Seemingly what had occurred was that her relatives brought her back after one day, but hadn't informed the staff that she had returned; otherwise the unit would have been visited as was normal procedure.

After the initial examination of the scene, and external examination of the body by the Technical Bureau members, and a doctor who had been called to the scene the body was removed to the morgue for a postmortem examination to be carried out the following day. After the removal of the body a meeting took place at the scene, regarding the circumstances of this lady's death. We went through the information we had collected in our statements, and a discussion took place as to the cause of death. During the course of these discussions there were several theories put forward as to what may have occurred. Superintendent Courtney put forward a suggestion that the lady more than likely had a brain hemorrhage, which caused her to try to undress herself as she tried to control her bodily functions, reacting to her condition, and may have been trying to get to the toilet.

Experience won out as Superintendent Courtney's theory was correct, as the postmortem examination discovered the next day, cause of death resulted from a brain hemorrhage.

Also arriving at the scene later that night was our Chief Superintendent, who had been informed of the finding of the body as was normal routine in these circumstances. His only input was to inquire if it was necessary to have that number of personnel at this scene. I unusually had a conversation with him, and informed him that all was under control, and we were going to await the outcome of the Postmortem examination. He then left the scene without entering the ladies residence or speaking to anyone else.

There was certain sadness to this incident; here was an 81year old lady, supposedly under the care of a Nursing Home who lay dead for up to three days in her self-contained unit. Maybe there was a misunderstanding between the family, and the staff at the nursing home, but it showed up a deficiency in the system of care at that Nursing Home. Hopefully lessons were learned from this tragic event.

Additional Studies, back to the books 1986, 1989, 1995 ------ Forward Planning

For some reason, I decided to get back to doing a bit of study, I'm not sure what drove me to go back, maybe it was a spin off from my Addiction Studies days in 1984, and I had gotten the bug or maybe it was to have the additional attachments to my application for my promotional prospects. Of course I had failed to get promoted from my Interview of 1986, it would be another ten years before I would try again. The first of these courses was just two years after I had completed my Addictions Studies Course at Trinity College, and of course I had been transferred to Lucan the same year, 1986.

The first was an Extra Mural Diploma in Social Studies Course in 1986, which was being organised through the University College at Maynooth. It involved attending at Colaiste Chiarain, secondary college at Leixlip, which was literally at my back door, a number of evenings a week for a set period of time, where lecturers from Maynooth University gave the course. I suppose thinking about it now Social Studies would be a kind of extension to the Addiction Studies Course, both courses being closely related.

In 1989 I decided to do a Diploma Course in Business Studies, which was also an Extra Mural Diploma course being organised through University College Maynooth, and also being given at Colaiste Chiarain, secondary college at Leixlip with lectures from Maynooth University College again in attendance. Again I'm not sure what led me to do such a course, maybe my thoughts were into the future, taking into consideration that I had less than ten years before I reached my 30yrs service in the force. The prospects of any further move up the promotional ladder had gotten a lot slimmer as I felt that I had been branded "a trouble maker" by certain members of the hierarchy within the Garda Force.

In 1995 I again allowed myself to be persuaded to continue further studies, this time trying my hand at a Diploma Course in Management, and Industrial Relations, through the National College of Industrial Relations. I had two things on my mind at the time of doing this course; I could use my qualification in furtherance of my promotional prospects or make use of it at a future date back in civilian life. I was successful in all three Diploma courses for which I was presented with a Diploma on the completion of each course.

In 1996 on the 12th of September, after a ten year gap I again forwarded an application for an interview for the rank of Inspector. I presented myself for this interview for the rank of Inspector in late 1996 or early 1997. The interview was for the uniform section of the force, as there was no other route left to me. It was also in the middle of the Veronica Guerin Murder investigation. Now, my additional certificates didn't enhance my prospects or didn't seem to have any effect as once again I was passed over.

Now that promotion had been eliminated from my future plans I began in earnest from that time in 1996/1997, to start seriously considering what my future plans would be after my retirement, and even at this stage to start planning a date for my retirement from the force. To this end I started looking at my previous work history prior to joining the force. I found that I had worked in the private sector for about six, and a half years, after leaving St Joseph's Residential Institution, Tralee, in 1961. I had made social welfare contributions at that time towards a contributory pension, and what a pity to have them wasted.

During my service in the Garda Siochana I did not pay the full welfare contribution towards a state pension as I was paying a % of my salary towards a Garda Pension Scheme, and therefore would not qualify for a contributory state pension with those contributions. I carried out a lot of inquiries regarding the social welfare pension, and what I could do with my previous six, and a half years of contributions I had made. Now, I discovered to my benefit that new social welfare regulations had been enacted which allowed for old contributions made by workers in the private sector, to be brought forward, and included for the purpose of qualifying for a contributory state pension.

There were a couple of important factors to be considered, you had to have a specific number of contributions made before pension age, and you had to start making contributions again before your 56th birthday. With this information in hand I set my sights on retiring in the year 2000 or before, which would enable me to start making social welfare contributions again either by working or being available for work through the social welfare office therefore qualifying me for a state pension. I would have gone 55 years of age. I still had a good four years of service to complete, and they were going to be busy, even so over that time I kept my concentration on looking for something in the outside world of the private sector. This was of course something I kept to myself, not to have any word spreading about my future intentions.

Over a number of years prior to my retirement in 2000, I laid the groundwork for my leaving the force. I did out my Curriculum Vitae, with a number of named referees for reference, and sent them to a number of business establishments. Even while I was still serving I went for a number of interviews to test the waters. Then sometime before the end of 2000 I saw that they were looking for staff at the National Statistics Office to assist in carrying out an Irish national census in the spring of 2001, I applied for, and was successful in obtaining a position with the National Statistics Office.

Suspected Suicide Case 11th September 1989

When a suspected suicide, was not a suicide

Well that's a situation that arose on several occasions during the course of my service having attended many scenes of suspected suicide. A few years after arriving at Lucan, I attended at one such scene of suspected suicide at a house in an estate, in north Kildare. A family member returned home sometime after four o'clock, gained entry with a key which was the usual routine.

The family member looked up the stairway, and was shocked to find the deceased hanging from the opening in the attic. Immediately help was sought from a neighbour who phoned the Gardai. When the Gardai arrived they cut the straps holding the body from the attic opening. The man was completely naked at the time, they left the body down on the landing, and covered it with a sheet, and waited for a doctor to arrive to view the body.

For some reason the senior Garda at the scene asked for back-up from the detectives. I was called to the scene as the officers at the scene thought there was something unusual about the situation. When I arrived at the house I saw that the body was on the landing on top of the stairs, covered with a sheet or blanket. I was informed that the first officers at the scene had cut the ligature holding the body, and lowered it to the floor of the landing. I had a look at the body, and was struck by a number of things I saw. First the body was completely naked when found, there was a black string, later identified as shoe laces, tied around his waist, and extending to his penis which it was also tied around. On the floor right under the attic opening from where the body was hanging there were a number of towels spread on the floor of the landing.

The Garda who had arrived at the scene hadn't touched anything other than lowering the body of the man to the floor of the landing, and covering him with a sheet. On the floor of the bathroom which is off the same landing I saw that the man's clothing was neatly piled on the bathroom floor, with his shoes, watch, rings, and a hairpiece. I also noticed that there were no laces in the shoes, and I later discovered that his shoe laces were what was tied around his waist, and tied on to his penis.

I had the body removed to Blanchard town Hospital for a later Post Mortem examination. After the body was removed I carried out a further examination of the scene. A beam had been placed across the opening in the attic which had a ligature hanging from it which was made up of a number of leather straps buckled together which then went around the neck of the deceased. In that area of the landing, as well as the door into the bathroom there is what is generally called the hot press or airing cupboard, containing the hot water tank, and shelving made with wooden spaced slats for use for airing clothes. The doors of this hot press were in the open position.

On closer examination of the hot press I found that there were a number of other leather belts tied around the wooden slats, and the slats that the belts were tied to were broken. Later after further examination I came to the conclusion that these belts tied to the wooden slats were being used as a kind of stirrups for putting one's feet into. As my investigations continued, I was coming around to the view that this may not have been a suicide.

As was normal practice I interviewed, and took statements from a number of family members, and other persons who would have known him, to try to establish any reasoning behind what happened, and if they noted any changes in his mental state recently. I also made contact with his place of work to see if they noted anything unusual in the recent past with his work situation. There were three children in the family, the boy who found the body being the youngest. I also established that some time around 11am that morning, somebody had spoken with this man on the phone. That to me was confirmation, that he was still alive around that time, and whatever happened, occurred over the following five hours.

On the following day I attended the Post Mortem examination at the hospital morgue at Blanchard town Hospital where the body had been moved. With the pathologist that was present we again looked at the body, and the pathologist stated that the only marks on the body were those around the neck, where the ligature had been fixed around the neck, causing asphyxiation resulting in his death. There was no need for further internal examination of the body. The pathologist then removed the black laces which were tied around his waist, and his penis. When he released the lace from around his penis seamen spurted out onto the table which gave us some indication of what had happened.

From all my inquiries, and the results of the postmortem examination the indications were leading to the possibility that this man did not die by suicide, but that he had been involved in the act of some form of sexual self-gratification. While carrying out this act which included putting a certain amount of pressure on his neck area, and using the leathers found attached to the slats in the hot press as stirrups for his feet so he could control what he was doing, it went wrong when the slats in the hot press broke from his weight causing him to hang himself by accident.

I did my report to the coroner of my findings. Now, a journalist friend of mine, Henry Bauress, of the Leinster Leader, who was reporting on the case in his paper made contact with me, and offered me the loan of a book by some French author, the name of which escapes me now. The book was based on the bygone years somewhere in the 18th or early 19th century, and covered the lives of some of the upper classes of society, and how they behaved. It gave an account of how people of that time experimented with various sexual fantasies trying to get a higher sexual experience. I found an exact replica account in this book of people who did exactly as our deceased man was doing at the time of his death. It also pointed out that several people had died resulting from them being careless during the course of their experiment. These people were regarded as having died from "Auto Erotic Asphyxiation".

I was satisfied that this summed up the case I was reporting on, and I brought it to the attention of the coroner, prior to the inquest, outlining the facts to him, and he agreed with me. The coroner's court brought in a verdict of accidental death on the advice of the coroner without going into the finer details of the case to save embarrassment to the family.

When my investigation had been completed, and I had forwarded the file to the coroner, while awaiting the date of the hearing in the coroner's court, I called to see the wife, and family of the deceased. I asked his wife if I could speak with her alone as I didn't want the younger member of the family to hear what I had to say. Up to this time the deceased's wife, and family were still of the opinion that her husband had committed suicide.

I informed his wife that her husband had not committed suicide that his death was accidental. For a moment she couldn't take in what I was saying to her. I then explained to her the full circumstances of her husband's death, and informed her that that would be the verdict coming out of the coroner's inquest. I also informed her that the full facts surrounding her husband's death would not be revealed at the inquest because of the nature, and the circumstances of his death. I also added for her information that because her husband's death was accidental she should be able to benefit from whatever insurance cover existed.

Yes this was a strange case, and anybody within the force that I mentioned it to were of the same opinion. It did however beg the question as to how many other similar cases were deemed suicide, and all because maybe a member of the family who would have found the body in a naked condition would have redressed the body somewhat before anyone in authority would have seen it, in its original condition. That's a question that will never be answered, but it begged a whole new approach to suicide investigations.

Grooming in sexual assault case

Sometime around early 1993 I received a phone call from the principal of one of the schools in the vicinity, indicating that he wished to have a confidential talk with me about one of his pupils attending his school, regarding a very delicate matter.

I called to see this principal, and he relayed to me his concerns regarding one of his pupils, and suspicions regarding the boy. He stated that he became concerned as the boy who over the previous number of years had outstanding grades in all his subjects, was now slipping very much below what his standard should have been.

Now he couldn't put his finger on it, but there seemed to be something else going on in his life which needed to be looked at. He also stated that he had spoken to the parents who seemed to be nice people, and they did agree with him that there was something wrong, that he had changed over a short period of time.

I told the school principal to leave it with me, and I would look into it. My first port of call was to go, and see the parents, and to get a bit of background on the boy, who his friends were, what he did in his spare time, and when his behaviour began to change. During the course of having the conversation with the parents, it came to light that he used to go fishing with a man, who was a near neighbour living not too far away. There were also times that he would babysit for this man who had two children himself, and he would sometimes stay overnight at this man's house.

I then made arrangements to meet with the boy in the presence of his parents, and having spoken with him for a while in the presence of his parents I got the impression that he was not too forthcoming with his parents there. I then called the parents aside, and asked them would they mind if I had a word with him on my own for a short while, which they agreed to.

I then spoke with the boy alone for some time, and cautiously approached the problem with his school grades, who his friends were, and if there was something on his mind. He then opened up to me, and told me that the man he used to go fishing with had interfered with him sexually. I then stopped him there, and told him that I would have to have at least one of his parents present so that I could get a statement from him, and which of his parents would he agree to be present with. He said he would like his dad to be there, and I took a detailed statement from him.

Basically what had happened was that this boy started to babysit for this man, looking after his two young children. A relationship developed between the man, and the boy so much so the boy became a frequent visitor to this man's house, and they used to go fishing together in the local river, with the boy at times staying overnight in the man's house. Then a situation developed where the man started to watch blue movies in the boy's presence which developed into sexual contact between the boy, and this man. There were also times when this man would ask the boy to rub cream on his genital area.

We were also informed that a bicycle belonging to the boy had gone missing, and the parents suspected that the man who their son used to babysit for had something to do with it. This is also an added factor, and is typical in cases where someone wants to take control of somebody by the curtailment of the boy's movements when not in his company. With this information it enabled us to obtain a warrant to search this suspect's house on the 2nd of April 1993, when we took him into custody.

This was a classic case of "Grooming" being carried out by this man, and lucky for the boy it hadn't gone beyond touching each other before he was discovered. Later while in custody, we interviewed him regarding his association with the boy. After sometime he made a statement of admission regarding his sexual activities with the boy. I charged him with crimes relating to sexual assault on the boy over a period of a number of years.

I prepared a file, and forwarded it to the Director of Public Prosecutions for direction as to what court this man should be tried in. The instructions I received back were to have him sent forward for trial to Circuit Criminal Court. In March 1994 he appeared before the Circuit Criminal Court where he pleaded guilty to all charges, and was sentenced by the Judge to three, and a half years in prison with the final fifteen months being suspended because of his guilty plea. The maximum prison sentence he could have received was a total of five years in prison.

The defendant had started to receive counselling, prior to the court case, and the judge also made it a condition that he continues to receive counselling. The judge also stated that, "no court could look at the offence other than, with a considerable degree of revulsion, the activities were not of a penetrative nature, but consisting of touching". "But the defendant had abused the trust, and friendship of the victim, and his family. He had allowed the offence to continue over a long period of time."

The defendant's wife also attended the court on that day, and through his court counsel she intimated to the court that she would be staying with her husband. A report of the court proceedings appeared in the Irish Press newspaper the following day giving an account of the case without naming the victim or the defendant.

Great appreciation must be given to the school principal who took action in this case when noting in one of his pupils a change of character relating to his studies. But for his action in informing the Gardai, there may have been a far more damaging outcome.

Even when one retires from the Garda Siochana the ghosts of the past keep popping up as with this case. On two occasions after his release from prison this man made complaints to my authorities regarding some press reporting of his conviction for his crimes. One of the incidents, the second one, related to the new area he had moved to, and his getting involved with the local community.

People in his new community became concerned regarding his volunteering to become involved in the local youth organisation. One of the community had a vague suspicion, that he was somebody that she had read something about, regarding a court case. Members of this committee sought me out to verify their suspicions as to who he was. I met these concerned parents at my then office in a cash, and carry, where I was now employed. I found that the person they were talking about was, one, and the same person, that I had charged in 1993, and the case did appear in the paper in March 1994.

Following this, a letter was received at the Garda Commissioners Office which was dated the 8th of November 2005 containing a threat of civil action against myself, and the Garda Commissioner. I was retired nearly five years at this stage. A Garda file was opened to have me investigated. Following on from an "internal" investigation it was found that I had no case to answer, and no further actions would be taken on the matter. I received that in writing dated the 4th of April 2006 from a Garda Inspector.

Interestingly, all of this occurred over ten years after the court case. It begs the question do you ever retire from the Garda Siochana.

1993 Cigarette Haul, Three year case

I'm not sure of the exact date, but it was sometime in 1993, Detective Garda Michael Conneely, one of my detective colleagues at Lucan received certain information. It related to the activities at a garage attached to a house in the north Kildare area, involving a van at a particular house. Our first task was to do a reconnaissance of the area to locate the house, and get an exact location to enable us to obtain a warrant to have the place searched. We obtained our search warrant to search the house, garage, and all vehicles in the vicinity.

I brought a strong team of detectives with me, we gained entry to the house, and proceeded to carry out our search. The house was occupied by a man, and his wife, and grown up children. In the garage, which had an extension at the rear of it, we discovered a huge quantity of cigarettes of all brands stacked up against the walls of the garage. The cigarettes were in bales, with the brands clearly visible, as most of them were wrapped with a clear plastic wrapping. There were others in cardboard cartons which bore the brand of the cigarettes they contained. As we didn't receive a proper explanation as to why the cigarettes were there we told the house holder, who now became our suspect, that we were seizing everything including his van. He was claiming that he had a shop somewhere in the city centre where he sold cigarettes.

We did a detailed search of the garage, and found that some of the labelling on the cartons had been removed with a blade or knife, and left around the garage area. We found that some of the cartons, and bales still had labels attached. It took us a number of hours to carry out the search, and to load all of what we had seized into the suspects, white van, which I think, was a ford transit if my memory serves me right. The haul of cigarettes, and the van were brought to Lucan Garda Station, and driven into a secure garage store at the rear of the station. This was a separate building which was not attached to the main station building.

At the station over the next number of days, with the assistance of the Technical Bureau we carried out a detailed examination of the cartons, and bales including examination for fingerprints. I cannot recall the exact value of what we found, but it was a figure in the region of about one quarter of a million Irish pounds.

We also carried out further investigations regarding the labelling that we found both on the cartons, and in different areas including on the floor of the garage. The investigation entailed going to the cigarette companies of the brands of cigarettes we had seized. They included, Gallagher's, Carroll's, and Player Wills as well as some other smaller suppliers. We discovered that these labels held a code number for the customer that these cigarettes were supplied to originally. From the information we received from the cigarette companies, we were able to locate two customers that were supplied with these cigarettes.

One was Musgrave Cash, and Carry at Robinhood Industrial Estate, where a burglary had taken place in the recent past. They had lost a large quantity of cigarettes in the burglary when their cigarette store was cleaned out, and most of what we had recovered belonged to them. The second customer was a small wholesale store in the west of Ireland where a burglary had also taken place in the recent past, and a small quantity of what we recovered was from their burglary. I got people from both Musgrave, and from the west of Ireland to come, and look at what we had recovered, and to do an inventory for me as they would be more expert at this than me.

In a statement in his defence the suspect stated he had an account at Musgrave Cash, and Carry where he shopped for items for his shop including cigarettes. On checking his shopping invoices at Musgrave we found out that he wasn't that regular of a shopper, and his purchase of cigarettes from Musgrave were in very small quantities, never buying a bale or carton at any time. After the seizure of the cigarettes he never visited Musgrave Cash, and Carry again.

Shortly after seizing the cigarettes I had them transferred to my upstairs office for safe keeping, I must have had a sixth sense about something that might happen to the evidence. Again I'm not sure how long after the seizure, but it wouldn't have been too long as it had become obvious what had happened. I laid charges against the suspect, who was in the house during the course of the search. He appeared at Kilmainham District Court, and was remanded on bail to await the directions of the Director of Public Prosecutions. A file was prepared, and forwarded to the Office of The Director of Public Prosecutions who directed the accused in this case be sent forward to the Circuit Crimint Court for trial.

I spoke about my sixth sense, well some time after the suspect was charged, and the case was going through the courts, the unthinkable happened. The secure drive in store at the rear of the station which contained the white ford transit van connected with the case was set alight causing an enormous amount of damage, completely gutting the white van, and another black car, a Honda Civic which was also in the store, and had been seized in another case. Luckily very early on in the case, I had the good sense to have the cigarettes removed out of the van, and put into my own office upstairs in the detective's quarters.

I had to do most of my work from the main detective office as a result of the concentration of nicotine in the air in my own office.

Whoever set the store on fire had got onto the tiled roof of the one story building, removed some tiles, and poured some inflammable liquid into the store, and set it alight. The fire had to be put out by the fire brigade. Members of the Garda Technical Bureau were also called to the scene the following morning to carry out a full examination. The fire did not affect the evidence in the case in any way other than giving me the opportunity to mention it in the courts on a number of occasions when pointing out the attempts that were being made to frustrate the prosecution of the case. We had our suspect who we were sure caused the fire, but lacked any evidence to prefer charges. He was one of the regular attendees at the courts during the appearances of the accused.

Now I don't have possession of the full account of the case of the fire at this time, but I am of the opinion that it happened sometime after the 18th of January 1994 which is a date that I have in my diary for that time, when there was a Police Property Application in court number 5 made by the accused for the return of his van. He failed in his attempt to have his van returned as it was deemed to be evidence in the case against him.

This case came before the Circuit Criminal Court on numerous occasions, due to the number of adjournments, mostly as a result of applications made by the accused. One of the requests for adjournment was because his wife was pregnant, and was expecting a child. It turned out afterwards that she had twin girls. From our perspective we could see these adjournments as an attempt to frustrate the prosecution's case as it was a disruption with regards to witnesses who would have been making tentative arrangements for different dates for the case to go ahead.

To give an example, a date was set for his trial to take place on the 26th of April 1995, I would have made contact with all of my witnesses, had the exhibits made available, and made arrangements with our prosecuting counsel to prepare for the hearing. Two days prior to the date of hearing, the 24th of April 1995 his defence counsel put in an application to the court for an adjournment which was granted. All preparations had to be undone.

The case was again rescheduled for the 23rd of October 1995, and again on the 19th of October 1995 his defence counsel made an application for the case to be further adjourned, but on this occasion the Judge in the court refused the application, and stated the trial will go ahead on the 23rd of October as scheduled. The Judge took into account the length of time this case had been before the courts, and the number of previous adjournments that had been granted.

The trial took place on the 23rd, and 24th of October, and he was convicted on all counts before the court. He was sentenced to a number of years in prison. On the 19th of December 1995 he was granted leave to appeal his sentence in the High Court, and also made an application for bail until his appeal was heard. The High Court Judge put back the bail hearing to the following day the 20th of December 1995.

Now I have to point out here that during all his appearances, at the District Court, Circuit Court, and later at the High Court, there were always a number of his cohorts, who were well known to the Gardai, in attendance in each of the courts with one known individual sticking out in an intimidating manor at each of the appearances. This was all part of the process to try to intimidate any witnesses to the case.

On the 19th of December 1995 after the High Court Judge granted him leave to appeal his sentence, the Judge requested me to meet him in his chambers. I went into the Judge's chambers, and he intimated to me that he was very concerned for his own safety as a result of seeing some of the appellants "friends" in court as he knew some of them from previous court cases.

He stated to me that he feared some retaliation, and requested me to arrange for some protection for his residence with his local Gardai while this case was going through the High Court. I made the arrangements as requested through the local Superintendent of the area where he resided.

On the following day the 20th of December 1995 the bail application was heard by the same Judge in the High Court. I outlined to the court the several attempts that were made to frustrate the prosecution case including the high number of adjournments of the trail. I also informed the court regarding the fire that was caused at Lucan Garda Station during the course of this case. It was an attempt to destroy the evidence in the case which luckily enough had been moved to another area within the Station complex. I also intimated to the court that while the appellant did not set the fire I felt he had responsibility for it through one of his accomplices who we suspected had caused the fire, but because of the lack of evidence at this time we were not able to prefer charges. Bail was refused.

Again the Judge called me into his chambers to ask if I had taken any action regarding the safety of his home, I informed him that I spoke with the local Superintendent, and he had the matter in hand. He stated to me that his concern was raised further due to the evidence I had given in court. Sometime in early 1996 his appeal to the High Court was dismissed, and he returned to prison to serve out his sentence.

CHAPTER TWENTY EIGHT

Murder of Mormon Boy 1990

On the 28th of May 1990 at around 1am in the morning I got a call to go to an area in Clondalkin to assist in the investigation of a suspected murder. The victim was a young American Mormon student who had been stabbed through the heart. It happened not too far from where he was staying, he had made his way to the front door of where he, and another Mormon companion was staying, and dropped dead at the feet of his friend. He was just 20 years of age, was a member of the wider Mormon Community from Pason, Utah, USA, and had only been at that address for two weeks.

The area where this tragic incident occurred was in the area of Ronanstown, and it wasn't too far from the local pub called "Finches", which was a well-known haunt of the local criminal fraternity from the area. When we arrived at the area we discovered Finches pub was still open, and serving customers, so with the help of a sizable number of uniformed Gardai, we closed the pub down, and set up an investigation centre at the pub. All the people in the pub at the time were interviewed, names, and addresses taken, and their whereabouts noted in relation to the time of the murder.

We had a witness who thought the culprit headed in the Finches direction, and of course one of our concerns was to look for, and retrieve the weapon that was used in the killing of this innocent boy. We continued to direct our investigation from the Finches pub for a period of time, keeping the pub closed for business, while the investigation continued, to the annoyance of the proprietor.

During the first 48hrs of the investigation, we had identified our suspect, and had him picked up over the next few days, we had by then moved our investigation centre to Ronanstown Garda Station. The suspect made a statement of admission to the murder, stating it was an accident. He didn't mean to stab the boy that it happened during a struggle.

During the course of the investigation I had a number of inquiries to carry out including calling to, and making contact with the Headquarters of the Mormon Church, which was situated in the north of the city of Dublin. I gave them some particulars of the tragic events that had occurred which involved one of their young students. I also got some particulars of the area this boy was from, and his home address so as to have his family made aware of what had happened. I had already been in communication with the Police in Utah, to inform them of the situation, and to get some background information from them.

I remember receiving a return call from the police in Utah, and when I picked up the phone to answer the Police Officer at the other end of the line; he wanted to know if that was "Rodents Town". Well I smiled to myself, without comment, and gave him the correct pronunciation of the name of the area, which had gotten a bad name, but there were some good people living there.

It was a sad ending for a young man who had his whole life ahead of him, and of course heartbreaking for his family. He was doing a stint of voluntary work which is the practice in the Mormon Community, prior to his starting out in his future career.

It was the great team work by the "L" district detectives that helped to solve this murder in a reasonably short time, with the assistance of the members of the Garda Technical Bureau. This is just a short account of another of those incidents that remains in one's memory, and the sadness that goes with it.

1992, Aircraft Accident at Weston Airdrome Lucan

During one's service in a Force like the Garda Siochana you come across many sad incidents. There was another such incident on the 12th of July 1992, at around 3.15pm on the afternoon of that date, I am not certain, but I have the feeling it was on a Sunday afternoon. A small light aircraft was flying around the skies over the Lucan area, having taken off from the local Weston Airdrome in Lucan. It was flying with a trailing banner doing some promotion or other. There would have been nothing unusual about a flight like this as that would have been a regular occurrence in the locality.

The aircraft for some reason lost height, and crashed into a field near the Weston Airdrome. The aircraft was engulfed in flames, there was very little hope for the survival of the pilot. My colleague, and I were out on patrol at the time, and were directed to the scene which was part of our sub District. The local fire service was still tackling the fire from the aircraft when we arrived. They got the fire under control, and out, and then proceeded to recover the body of the pilot. On arrival at the scene we made some inquiries from one of our uniform Inspectors, as to who was in the aircraft, and were told that the pilot was flying on his own in the aircraft.

When the fire service personnel were in the process of removing the body of the pilot, they discovered that there was a second body in the aircraft. It was the body of a much younger person who had been in the aircraft. It was a devastating surprise to everybody as it was thought, and recorded by the ground staff that there was only one person, the pilot, on board the light aircraft.

The plane was a Citabria C11-10 a two seater craft, and was the property of some other person other than the pilot. It was later established that the second body was that of a 14 year old boy who was an air scout, and was a regular visitor to the Airdrome. He had developed a great interest in aircraft. Seemingly what more than likely occurred on that day was that the pilot before take off spotted the boy whom he knew to be an air scout, and invited him for the spin on the aircraft with him. There was no clearance for the boy to be on the aircraft, and no record of him going on to the craft. Hence the surprise at finding the second body in the wreckage of the aircraft.

I had, at the request of the Inspector at the scene, the unenviable task of calling on the parents of the boy to inform them of the tragic circumstances surrounding the death of their young 14 year old son. I also had to ask for some one of the family to go to the Morgue at Blanchardstown Hospital to assist in the identification of the body.

What started out as a gesture of good will towards this boy by the pilot of the plane on that day ended in a terrible tragedy, with the death of both of them?

Serious Aggravated Burglary, Lucan Area, 26th June 1992

Some weeks before the accident at Weston Airdrome, Lucan, Detective Garda Pat Bane, and I were called to investigate the armed entry to a private house in Weston Estate, Lucan on the 26th of June 1992 which had occurred at 2.30 am that morning. The occupants of the house heard loud banging at the front door of their house, and then heard someone downstairs shouting up the stairs at them. There were at least two, maybe three people downstairs demanding that the occupants come downstairs to them.

Now the owner of the house, Mr. James Kennedy, a businessman, was upstairs with his wife, and their two children. The culprits who were in the house could not get past the top of the stairs as there was a steel security gate at the top of the landing of the stairway which they couldn't get past. The culprits went back down stairs, and fired several gunshots into the ceiling of the hallway of the house, and fled the scene. Mr. Kennedy looked out of the top window, and saw the culprits getting into a car, he shouted at them, the car which was being driven by another man then drove off.

Detective Garda Pat Bane, and myself went to the scene of the shooting that morning, and spoke with the occupants of the house. The husband, wife, who were both in their 40s, and their two young children were in the house at the time of the raid on the house. The front door of the house had been forced open by the culprits, but they could not get upstairs to where the family was because of the steel security gate on the top of the stairway. From the examination of the scene it was established that the firearm used in the attack was a shotgun, as pellets were recovered from the ceiling of the hallway, by our Technical Bureau team.

Luckily for the owner of the house he had taken strong security measures to protect his property, and his family, part of his reason being that he was involved in the amusement arcade business where he had slot machines, and had been threatened on a few previous occasions. After we had finished our examination of the scene, and got all the information we could get at that time, we made arrangements with the injured parties to take statements from them.

Because of this attack they moved out of their house, and into an apartment which they had in the basement of their business in Westmoreland Street in the city centre. My colleague, and I went to meet them at their city centre apartment in the basement of the business premises which was secured like a bank vault. We took written statements from both the husband, and wife regarding the incident at their house, also trying to establish who might be responsible for this recent attack on their family home.

This was a shocking, and vicious attack at the time, with a father, mother, and young children being the targets. During the course of our investigation we discovered that Mr James Kennedy was well known in certain business circles, and had come to the notice of the Gardai on a number of occasions due to some complaints against him. Arising out of this we found a certain amount of disinterest in what had happened, and came up against a stone wall from certain quarters with regards to assistance in the overall investigation.

Notwithstanding this we continued our investigations into this serious attack on the Kennedy family, and it looked like we were on our own. We kept in constant touch with the injured parties, keeping in mind that these culprits failed on their first attempt, and may try again. We instructed them to get in touch with us as soon as they suspected something was happening. Some days later James Kennedy made contact with us, and told us he had been contacted by one of the men who had raided his house. He was to phone him back again at his Amusement Arcade.

This was our opportunity to put something in place to try, and trap our culprit. We called to see James Kennedy, and instructed him to tell his caller to phone him at a phone box on the street adjacent to the Arcade as his own phone wasn't safe to talk on. There were two phone boxes outside the Arcade so we gave him the number of one of them to pass on to his caller with a particular time so we could monitor the situation. In the meantime we got the assistance of our Technical Support team to set up a monitoring system on that particular phone box when we knew the time the call was coming in.

Our injured party got his next call, and gave the culprit the number of the phone box he was to call, and what time to make the call. With that information in hand we set up our equipment in the phone box to record the conversation between the culprit, and the injured party. When the injured party received the call at the telephone box we were in our position with our Technical Bureau Support Team in the vicinity of the phone box. It was a lengthy phone call by the culprit who was demanding a payment of forty thousand pounds in cash from the injured party. He stated that he was acting on behalf of a building contractor that Mr Kennedy owed money to. He made multiple threats during the course of the conversation, which lasted about forty minutes.

We now had a full recording of the conversation between the culprit, and the injured party. An arrangement was made between the injured party, and the culprit, on our instructions to set up a meet to pay over the cash as demanded, the meeting place to be in the vicinity of the Amusement Arcade. Of course it was never the intention that any cash would ever be paid over.

A time, and date had been set so we went to look for some assistance from the members of the Central Detective Unit. My colleague, and I went to see the Detective Inspector [not named] who was on the late shift to see what back up we could get for this operation. We had at this stage identified our culprit so we knew who we were looking for. He was a known dangerous terrorist who was acting in his own interests.

We discussed the case particulars, and shared all the information we had in our possession. The Detective Inspector was aware of who the injured party was, and was a bit hesitant about committing personnel to the operation. A number of phone calls were made by both the Detective Inspector, and ourselves, and eventually arrangements were made for us to have back up for the operation. We were given a team of Detectives from the Central Detective Unit with surveillance vehicles, and equipment whom my colleague, and I met to update them about the operation, and to stake out the area around the Amusement Arcade where the meet was supposed to take place.

The stake out started early in the evening, so we had everybody in place, and it was expected to go on for some hours into the late night. What we would have described as being half way through our operation, one of our backup detectives from the Central Detective Unit informed us that they were being recalled to their base, as the Detective Inspector did not want them to work additional hours. Here we were in the middle of an operation, and our support was being withdrawn, we were left to our own devices. I think it puts into perspective the priorities of this Detective Inspector, save money, and not hunt down a dangerous criminal on the loose.

With our back up being withdrawn, that brought an end to the surveillance operation that we had set up, but we stayed around ourselves just in case there were any further developments, and of course to make sure our man was going to be safe. As it happened the culprit never turned up, he had phoned our injured party to say he couldn't make it, and they would set another date for the pick-up. The injured party told the culprit that he wasn't going to pay him any money, and not to call him again. It looked like things had gotten out of control.

The culprit in this case, as I have said, was a known terrorist belonging to a breakaway group from the provisional I.R.A., and he was known to be a dangerous individual. After the operation ended that evening my colleague, and I made contact with someone we knew in the Special Detective Unit who kept a record on the movement of terrorists, and their groups, and we had a meeting with him.

We outlined the circumstances of this particular case to him, and informed him that we wanted this culprit detained, and brought to Lucan Garda Station. Within the space of 24 to 48 hours he was arrested under Section 30 of the Offences against the State Act, and brought to Lucan Garda Station for interrogation where we were waiting for him.

After a short period in detention the culprit admitted to the attempted armed robbery on the 26th of June 1992 at the Kennedy home in Weston in Lucan. We had also discovered that there was a warrant out for his arrest for failing to appear in court on a charge of possession of a firearm on a previous occasion. During the course of the interrogation we produced the tape recording we had of his conversation with our injured party. Our intention was to have him charged, and put up into custody for his court appearance.

We learned that this individual had been raised in Belfast by his mother who had divorced his father many years previously. His father, who was a prominent Journalist in the Irish media, now lived in the Republic of Ireland, and had done so for many years. We also discovered that recently while he was on the run he had gone to his father's house in Co Meath, and had violently assaulted him, in the course of trying to get money from him. His father did not want to press charges.

While we were still dealing with our suspect in custody we had a visit from our local Superintendent [not named], who wanted to go in, and talk to the detained man. We had no problem with that as our interrogation of him was complete, and we were in the process of preparing the charges against him. He would have been aware of the facts of the case we had been investigating, but we filled him in on the information regarding the warrant for his arrest, and also the incident of the serious assault on his father.

When the Superintendent [not named] finished speaking with the suspect he came out, and told us he had a good chat with him, and he asked us if there was any possibility of giving him station bail. We nearly dropped from our standing at such a request from a man in his position considering that we had filled him in on the full facts of the case. We informed the Superintendent [not named],that there was no way he was getting station bail, that this man was a dangerous terrorist who armed with a shotgun carried out an attack on a family, and fired shots in the house in his attempt. It seemed like there was a continuing attempt to interfere with our investigation, in our view anyway.

We had him brought before Kilmainham District Court where he was remanded in custody. On a later date he appeared before the Dublin Circuit Court where he entered a plea of guilty to all charges, and was given a prison term for his crimes.

The Kennedy family in their gratitude for the successful outcome of the investigation came to visit us at Lucan Garda Station, and made a presentation of flowers, and chocolates to the two of us. For several Christmases after that, they left a gift for us at the Station. It was a show of appreciation for the way we had handled all aspects of this serious assault on their family home. Some years after the event they left Ireland to settle elsewhere.

The culprit in the case was released after serving his sentence some years later, and was the victim of a feud within his own group who shot him dead.

During the course of my many investigations, I learned a lot about the characters of certain members of the force, and where their responsibilities lay. In most cases you get a good response from most members of all ranks, but a few of them had one thing in common, self-projection.

My colleague, and partner in the investigation of this serious crime was Detective Garda Pat Bane, who passed away suddenly on the 2nd of June 2021. R.I.P. It had been my intention to make contact with him regarding some matters I have mentioned involving both of us.

Arrest for Church crime, 8ᵗʰ June 1993

Some time around the end of May or beginning of June 1993, I had a call from the Parish Priest of Confey Church in Leixlip, he wanted to see me about a delicate matter, if I could call to see him. When I met with the Parish Priest he informed me that he was concerned about some money that might be going missing from the Church collections that were taken up at all masses in the Church at the weekends. He told me that the amounts of money from the collections seemed to be reducing even though the Church attendance had not reduced.

The procedure with respect to the collections was that all the money collected at the masses was put into the Church safe which was in a room off the sacristy, and early in the following week the Parish Committee with himself would meet, count the money, and get it ready for lodging to the local bank. It was a member of the Parish Committee who brought the discrepancy to the notice of the Parish Priest when he noticed the drop in the amount collected was going on for some time.

It seemed that somebody was taking money from the safe before it was counted or it was being taken before the cash was put into the safe. This of course put all the people connected with the Parish Committee under suspicion, and everybody was looking at everybody else with a certain amount of suspicion which made the situation unbearable.

The Parish Priest showed me the room where the safe was kept, which was a small enough room, and was used a general store for records, and boxes with papers etc. The Parish Priest was the only one with a key to the safe. Apart from the Parish Committee, and the sacristan nobody else had access to the area where the safe was located. I inquired from the Parish Priest if there was anybody else employed by the Parish, and he told me there wasn't, but they had a man who was on a work scheme from the Labour office who came a couple of days a week to do cleaning work around the outside grounds of the church, but had nothing to do in the church itself.

I told the Parish Priest that I would be back to him within the next few days when I had worked something out. I met the Parish Priest a short time after, and put a plan of action to him if he was agreeable. I told him that with the assistance of my Technical Team from our Technical Bureau I would install a camera to keep the safe in view, and record the happenings near the safe over time. He agreed to this solution, but I cautioned him not to reveal the details of what we were about to do to anybody else.

With the assistance of our Technical Team I had the camera installed to record all movements around the safe. We hid the equipment in some of the cardboard boxes that were already in this room. After a short period of time we had success as we caught our thief on camera, going to the safe, opening it with a key, and removing some cash from it, closing the safe again after he finished the theft. It turned out to be our grounds man from the Labour office, who was resident in the city centre.

On the 8th of June I took this man into custody in the grounds of Confey Church on suspicion of larceny from the church safe. I also arranged, and carried out a search of his flat in the city centre, where we found a duplicate key to the safe, and also recovered some cash. During the course of being interviewed he made a statement of admission after caution. He stated he had been taking some money every week for about two months.

With respect to the duplicate key, he got into the house of the Parish Priest, stole the keys, and made a copy of the safe key which he used to open the safe on each occasion, and left the keys back to the house. This was one of those cases that put many innocent people under suspicion, who were giving voluntary services to their parish. It was a good outcome to the situation with the help of our Technical Bureau personnel, and their equipment, with sighs of relief all around.

M.K. 1. Case 1994

Well this was a case that I named the M.K.1.case because these were the initials of the person involved, and also that he used for the purpose of registering a stolen Mercedes Benz that he had used during the course of his criminal activities. It was also a case that stretched beyond an investigation involving the general public, because it was one of our own members of the Garda Force that was the subject of my investigation.

Very briefly, in June of 1994 I was on duty at a function in a well-known hotel in the Lucan area. There were a number of my Detective Unit with me as well as a number of private security personnel from an outside security company. There were some Government Ministers attending this function which was the reason behind these expanded security arrangements.

Everything passed off peacefully without any incidents as we thought. When the main function involving the Government guests was at an end the proprietor of the hotel invited all the gardai present to partake of some light refreshment in the hotel. I knew the proprietor very well from previous meetings, and functions which I had attended.

It was while I was having some refreshments, that I was approached by the proprietor who asked me to accompany him to one of the sitting rooms downstairs. He pointed out to me that there was a mantle clock missing from over the fireplace of this particular room. The clock was in a dark "Ormolu" casing, and was a reasonable weight. It would also be classed as an antique, and was of good value. I was, as we all were taken aback with this report of a theft on an occasion such as this.

To cut a long story short I initiated an immediate investigation into this theft, which caused a certain amount of embarrassment, as it happened under our very noses. I followed up by getting a complete listing of all guests, staff, security personnel, and our own team of gardai who were present.

During the course of my investigation the name of a person kept cropping up that I didn't know, but I discovered that he was a member of the Gardai who was not on Garda duty on this occasion, but was working in a private capacity for a security company who had supplied security personnel for the function that day. I further discovered that this man had returned from a leave of absence he had spent in Australia, and had just returned to work in the force. I had noted that this man drove a black Mercedes-Benz with the registration number M.K.1.

The registration number raised a red flag, I carried out some inquiries regarding the car, and discovered that such a registration didn't exist, it wasn't taxed, and there was no insurance on this car. I had to treat this investigation with a certain amount of caution, he being a member of the force, with only a small group of personnel being aware of what was going on, including my Detective Inspector. I was also concerned that one of his colleagues that he worked with might innocently pass some remark about our investigation.

On the 21st of June 1994, armed with a search warrant, my colleague, Detective Garda Michael Conneely, and I, went to this man's house to carry out a search regarding the car, and the missing clock. His mother opened the door to us, she called her son to the door, we spoke to him, showed him the warrant, and he brought us into the house. In the house he showed us the mantle clock he had taken from the hotel, it was in a bag, in a damaged state, it got broken on his way home.

We asked him to accompany us to Lucan Garda Station, bringing the Mercedes Benz, and broken clock with us to Lucan Garda Station. When we got to Lucan Station, we had to go through the procedure of informing one of our senior officers to have him suspended from duty before detaining him for questioning, having got this done we then began to interview him, and took a written statement from him after caution in which he admitted the crime.

He also admitted to us that he had stolen the Mercedes Benz from London on his return from Australia. After inquiries we discovered that the Mercedes was the property of a taxi driver in London, and had been missing for some time. Our suspect put his own registration number on the car using the first letters of his Christian name, and his surname, which he drove around from the time of his return to Ireland.

His trip to Australia had not been a success story, he started to use drugs while there, and he was also short of cash coming home. His intention was to sell the clock, and the Mercedes to try, and make some money. We also had the task of informing his mother of the circumstances surrounding the case which of course was a huge let down for her as she had great respect for the Garda Force.

The case came before the courts on him being charged, I don't have a record of the results of the court case, but he was dismissed from the Garda Siochana.

Again it is another indication of the types of cases that one can become involved with, especially when it turns out to be one of your own. In the beginning there would be a certain amount of disbelief, and uncertainty in believing one of our own, could be so involved. At least we had one less bad apple in the force; god only knows what he might have done next if he hadn't been apprehended when he was.

Forged Dollar Printing Plates 1997

On the 6th of November 1997 a colleague, and I stopped, and searched a van at Lucan village. During the course of the search we discovered a quantity of computer components, so we detained the driver on suspicion of theft of the computer components, and brought himself, and his van to Lucan Garda Station. He was from the Dublin 24 area, and on a follow-up check I discovered that he was a well-known individual for being involved in the movement of stolen property.

At Lucan Station I carried out a further detailed search of his van, and I discovered a plastic bag which contained what seemed to be photographic negatives. On closer examination in the station I saw that they seemed to be printing plates for 5 Dollar, and 10 Dollar bills. This was a most unusual find, and of course I interviewed the suspect about these printing plates. He did not give me a reasonable account of why he was in possession of these plates other than he was holding them for a friend.

I charged the suspect with possessions of the computer components believing them to be stolen. The printing negatives or plates of the Dollar Bills were a different matter as we had to get the evidence that they were forgeries. To this end I got in touch with the American Embassy in Dublin who put me in touch with somebody at their Embassy in London who dealt with currency fraud.

I spoke with two Special Agents at the American Embassy who specialised in American currency fraud, outlining, and describing to them what I had in my possession. I made arrangements to meet them in London with these plates of the Dollar Bills to help identify them as to whether they were forgeries or not. I had of course to get through a lot of red tape at my end with my Headquarters, but eventually I got permission to travel to London in April 1998.

On the 20th of April 1998 I went to London where I met with one of the two agents I had spoken with, at their Embassy that evening. There were a number of things I wanted to get clarified, one that these printing plates were forgeries, two if there were any of these forged Dollar notes in circulation, and three their opinion of the quality of the forgeries. On the following day the 21st of April 1998 I returned to the embassy where I met both agents, and I obtained a statement from one of them regarding the forged printing plates.

They confirmed that these printing plates were forgeries, they would be checking on the circulation, and yes they were good forgeries. They also took copies of the plates, and would send on a further report in time. I did inform them that I had a person arrested for possession of the plates, but had not yet preferred charges. I'm not sure at this time how the case panned out, but I think one of the agents did come over, and gave evidence in the case regarding the forgeries. This was a case with a bit of an international flavour.

Case of video Piracy

I remember receiving a call, and a visit from a company known as IN-FACT, [Irish National Federation Against Copy-right Theft] sometime in late 1989. They complained to me that there was a suspect in our area carrying out video piracy by copying, and selling pirated videos from his video shop. Video piracy was something we knew very little about, with very little legislation covering this practice other than outdated material.

The representatives from INFACT had themselves carried out some surveillance, and inquiries in the area, and identified a suspect, who was known to us in the Lucan area as he was the holder of a Firearms Dealers License. We were aware that he had a firearms shop with a video shop attached from which he hired, and sold videos. The INFACT representatives gave us a good idea of the type of equipment that would be required to pirate videos.

With this information in hand I began to look up the legislation which would cover this breach of copy-right, and to see what powers I had to carry out a search of the premises. I found legislation which would cover us to carry out a search of the premises.

Now in the normal circumstances of getting search warrants under other legislation we would have access to already printed documentation forms, with respect to whatever legislation we were operating under. With respect to breaches of the copy-right Act no such documentation forms were in existence, nor could I track any such printed documentation forms down. I had to do a drafting job myself from the available legislation in my possession, and draft information, and search warrant document forms, and have them sworn before the courts.

The courts were happy with the drafted documents, and I obtained a warrant to search the video premises at Lucan under the copy-right

Act. We carried out our search accompanied by one of the representatives from INFACT to assist us in what we were looking for. When we entered the video shop, it was just what you would expect in a normal video for hire, and sale shop. We produced our search warrant to the proprietor of the shop which is normal procedure, and went about our search. Our search warrant gave us the power to search the whole building including outhouses, and vehicles.

In the shop there was a doorway into the back of the premises through which we entered into a small room. We found about a dozen video recorders all running at the same time copying videos. We also found a very sophisticated printer on which we discovered printed video case jackets showing the names of the particular videos being copied. Well it looks like we had found our local video pirate to the delight of the INFACT representatives. We seized all of the copying equipment, the video recorders, printer, and all the pirated videos we could find. We also discovered that he was dealing in "Adult" videos under the counter of the shop, which we also seized.

When the case came for hearing before the courts the proprietor of the shop pleaded guilty to the charges, and was dealt with by way of fine. As well as that, all the equipment, video recorders, videos, and the printing press were confiscated by court order, and directed to be handed over to INFACT representatives as part compensation for the breach of copy-right, and to partly make up for the loss of royalties.

This was again another interesting type of investigation giving another angle to the work of the Garda, and the necessity for the use of one's initiative to solve a problem that may arise. I later received a very complimentary letter from the INFACT personnel for the assistance given by the Gardai in this case, through my Superintendent, which I reproduce as follows.

17th November 1989

Dear Superintendent,

On behalf of the entire legitimate Irish Cinema, and Video Industry, we wish to express our appreciation for assistance recently afforded this office by members of An Garda Siochana, Lucan Station, in our Anti-Video-Piracy activities.

Our investigations had indicated to us that a major Video Counterfeiting Operation was being carried out within that jurisdiction, and was causing untold damage to the legitimate Video Dealers not only in the Lucan area, but in many parts of the country as well. We estimate that profits approaching millions of pounds are being made by Counterfeiters in this country, thereby depriving many in the community of their honest livelihoods, defrauding the Revenue in the form of Income Tax, and V.A.T. evasion, and infringing the Copyrights of the legitimate Copyright Holders.

Assistance was provided to us by Det. Sgt. Maurice Heffernan, and Det. Gda. Frank Timoney, of Lucan Garda Station, and this assistance proved to be invaluable to our activities. They were extremely resourceful, and always eager to cooperate. They were at all times courteous, helpful, and generally a credit to the Force.

We look forward to continuing our excellent relationship with An Garda Siochana.

Yours sincerely,
Sean Murtagh,
Director General.

The Forgotten Fingerprint

On a date which I don't have a record of, but again in my early years of service at Lucan Station, maybe late 1980s, I went to the scene of a burglary in the Lucan area. Again I'm not sure of the method of entry to the house, but more than likely it was the back door or window. I examined the scene myself which I was qualified to do as I had some years previously attended several Technical Bureau courses during my Detective Training, which included examination of scenes for fingerprints.

At this crime scene I met with the owner who showed me around the house, and gave me a listing of what was missing. I then proceeded to examine the scene for fingerprints. During the course of my examination I saw that the fridge freezer had been pulled out a bit from the wall where it stood. I asked the injured party if anybody in the house had moved the fridge, and he said no, that it should be closer to the wall. I examined this fridge much closer, and I lifted what I thought at the time was a fairly fresh print from the fridge. After my examination of the scene I left the house, and returned to my office.

Over the years I had a very good relationship with all members of the Technical Bureau, having met most of them at various scenes of crime during my time in Detective Branch. The fingerprint department was in the process of updating their system, and computerising the fingerprints held on record. There was a man in the fingerprint department that I knew well as we both served together in the "L" District some years previously. I phoned my friend, told him I wanted a print looked at, that he might be able to give the new system a test, and I could have a look at how the system worked. He set a time for me, and we met at his office in the Bureau one evening, where I handed over the suspect print to him for processing.

I sat back, and waited for this "Quick" result, knowing of course that he had to go through a certain procedure to upload the suspect print onto the system. In the meantime I more than likely helped myself to a cup of tea, and had a good chat while we awaited the outcome. Well after not too long a wait my friend came up with a match for me on the computer, I was very impressed. The unfortunate thing about this match was it was the fingerprint of the injured party in the house. Seemingly he had been printed many years ago as a young person for some reason or other, and his record had been loaded into the new computer system.

Well it did show me that the new system worked, but it left me without a suspect for my burglary. It was something I never forgot, and of course I never mentioned to the injured party in this burglary case that it was his own print, which we had matched from a set of his we had on file from a previous record he had, that were taken many years previously. Now, there were always circumstances in which we would take the prints of injured parties for elimination purposes, but not in this case.

Aggravated Burglary at the Psychiatrist's Home

Many of the serious cases that I have been involved in investigating, always had a certain degree of sadness attached to them with the case I am about to describe being high up in that category. Again I don't have a date or time of this particular incident, but it would have been in the first couple of years of my service as a Detective Sergeant at Lucan Garda Station, and a case that I have never forgotten.

I went to the scene of an aggravated burglary at the home of a doctor of psychiatry, which had occurred on the grounds of a private psychiatric hospital located in the Lucan area. The grounds of the hospital were expansive, and the house, which was a large house, was a good distance from the hospital with its own entrance from the main road. I spoke with the lady of the house who was the psychiatrist's wife, and another lady who worked for her in the house, who described what had happened.

Late the previous evening they were in the house when they were confronted by a man in the house. They hadn't heard him come into the house, and didn't know how he got there. He seemed a bit surprised at seeing them also, so he ordered them downstairs where he pushed them into a small closet which he secured from the outside, warning them not to make any noise or move from where he had put them. The two ladies were scared out of their wits, and complied with what he had told them. After some length of time had passed, and the two ladies thought the coast was clear they forced their way out of the closet, and called the Gardai. From memory I think the husband who was the psychiatrist was away at some conference or other, he wasn't around at the time of the incident.

After interviewing the two ladies I went looking to see how this culprit had gained entry to the house as the ladies didn't know. I discovered during the course of my search, that he had gained entry through the window of one of the upstairs bathrooms, which had a low roof building just outside the window, which he had climbed up onto to get to the outside of the bathroom window. He had forced the bathroom window open, and got into the bathroom. I got my scenes of crime case, and started searching for fingerprints. I found a number of marks which I lifted for further examination by the Fingerprint Section at the Technical Bureau.

Before I had left the house the lady of the house called me aside out of the hearing of the second lady, and informed me that this other lady was very disturbed over what had happened. She told me that this lady had a mental health problem which her psychiatrist husband was treating her for, that being the reason that she did some work in the house so that her husband could monitor her. She stated that the incident in the closet didn't help her situation. I told the doctor's wife that I would keep in touch, and let her know of any developments. This doctor was also a well-known personality as he was often on the national radio giving medical advice to the general public.

I felt that this case needed to be treated as urgent because of the circumstances of what had happened with the two ladies. I brought the fingerprint lifts I had taken to the Technical Bureau to have them checked against our records at the Fingerprint Section, also informing them of the nature of the crime that had taken place, and who the injured parties were. Within a short period of time I had a result back from the Fingerprint Section, identifying a culprit for this crime.

The person who was identified was well-known for committing burglaries in various areas. What followed was the normal procedure, search warrant obtained; culprit arrested, and brought to Lucan

Garda station where he made a statement admitting the crime. He was charged, and brought before the courts for this, and a number of other crimes where he pleaded guilty. He was sentenced to a term of imprisonment. Now, there was a sad follow up to this case some time later.

Around this time they were in the process of completing a bridge over the Liffey Valley between Lucan, and Palmerston which was just opening to bring traffic to the north of the city. It was also to be the first Toll bridge to come into operation. It had not been long opened when I heard that a person had jumped off the bridge, and committed suicide. I later learned that it was a woman who had jumped off the bridge. On further inquiries I discovered that it was the same lady who had been locked into the closet with the doctor's wife during the course of a burglary at the house on the private psychiatric hospital grounds some time previously, which I had investigated, and later had charged a culprit for. There is no doubt in my mind to this day that the incident of her being locked into the closet must have had a huge impact on her mental state.

Case of Fraud, Lucan Spa Hotel, 1997

From June of 1996 things got extremely busy at Lucan Garda Station, for the next number of years, as it became the headquarters for the investigation of one of the most outrageous serious crimes to happen outside of the murder of a Garda, the murder of a well-known journalist, which I will give a short account of later.

Over my years at Lucan Garda Station I built up a very good relationship with many people from all walks of life, including many business people within the District. By this time in 1996, Lucan was operating as a District Headquarters for the recently formed new "Q" District. One such relationship I developed was with the proprietor of the Lucan Spa Hotel, Frank Colgan, and we became good friends. Over time I got involved with the Lucan Spa Hotel golfing society, and became a member of the committee for organising outings, and so forth. All of our meetings were held at the Spa Hotel, which were a regular occurrence. I also got to know many of the hotel staff, and was on general friendly terms with most of them.

I suppose being who I was, the local Detective Sergeant had a big influence during my many visits there, and of course being on friendly terms with the owner Frank Colgan helped. If, and when Frank had any problems which needed some Garda intervention, he would make contact with me to see what could be done depending on the problem.

On one of these occasions, sometime in early 1997, I got a call from Frank that he would like to meet up with me regarding a problem he thought he was having with one of his staff. This meeting was arranged to be held in his brother's house, who was also a director of the company. It was important to meet away from the hotel to allay suspicions that there was anything going on. When I met with Frank, he was accompanied by his brother, and two accountants from the company that looked after the hotel accounts.

Frank, with input from his accountants, and his brother, outlined to me their suspicions regarding one of their managers who was known to me, who they suspected of stealing cash from the business. He was responsible for dealing with all the cash coming into the business, entering the cash receipts into the cash books, and putting the cash into the hotel safe for lodging to the bank. We had a long discussion about the problem during which I tried to get as much information as I could from everybody so I could form an opinion as to what crimes were being committed, and how the investigation should proceed.

I told them to leave it with me, that I would instigate an investigation into the complaint, but I would require all the books, documentation, till rolls, relating to the incidents, and also the help of one of the accountants at the meeting to bring me through the books. Larry was assigned this responsibility to assist me. Once again my Fraud investigation experience was being tested. We kept this investigation under wraps, with only a few of us knowing about it so as not to put the suspect on his guard as to what was happening.

Even though I was one of the team involved in the serious investigation that was ongoing in Lucan at the time, [the murder of

Journalist Veronica Guerin], I gave as much time to this investigation as I could, even outside working hours. As the local Detective Sergeant I still, with members of my unit, had to keep an eye on what was happening locally, with respect to crime in our District. I met with Larry on numerous occasions going through the books as I wanted to discover how these crimes were being committed so as to be able to put it to our suspect when the time came. Frank of course was anxious for a speedy result as he could not let the suspect go without having the evidence to back up any thoughts of dismissal.

Over the next few weeks with the help of Larry the accountant, we discovered the system the suspect had used for covering his tracks in the books. He was producing false documentation with respect to the amounts of cash he was taking from the business. Without going into too much detail, we also discovered that this had been going on for a number of years, and that the amount of money taken could be well in the region of 200,000 punts.

I took possession of the books, and papers relating to the investigation which I studied very carefully. On the 1st of June 1997 by arrangement with Frank, I took the suspect into custody at the Lucan Spa Hotel as he was going off duty, and brought him to Lucan Garda Station where he was processed. I interviewed him at the station which was an embarrassing situation for him to be in, as he often served me with the coffee when I would visit the hotel. At first he denied any involvement in the taking of the cash from the hotel.

While he was in custody I had his house searched where a number of things were found including cash in several different denominations. We took possession of this currency in different denominations as we were aware that many of the guests staying at the hotel would be from a variety of countries across Europe. We also invited his wife to visit him at the station. I remember when I first entered his house I made a comment to one of my colleagues, "this is where the money went". It had all the trimmings, and furnishings of somebody in a senior executive position.

Some hours into his arrest he eventually admitted to taking the cash, and falsifying the accounts to cover his tracks when the documentation, and books were shown to him. I later charged him with a number of crimes relating to the missing cash from the Lucan Spa Hotel. I also informed the injured parties at the Spa Hotel, who prepared the papers for his immediate dismissal. I prepared a file on the case for the information of the Director of Public Prosecutions office, who recommended that the accused as he was at this stage, be sent forward for trial to the Dublin Circuit Criminal Court.

The book of evidence was served on him around the 6th of January 1998, after which he was sent forward for trial. The case came up before the courts on several occasions over the next two years, finally finishing in November 1999, with him getting a suspended sentence, and paying a small amount of compensation to the injured parties, the Lucan Spa Hotel. In the intervening period before the case finished he had sold his house, and had made arrangements to go to England, frustrating any attempt at recovering any further compensation through the sale of his house.

CHAPTER THIRTY

Busy time for my closing years in the force

The Murder of Detective Garda Jerry McCabe, and Veronica Guerin, Journalist. 1996

1996 is a year that is well embedded in my memory, especially the month of June of that year. On Friday the 7th of June 1996 at the village of Adare, Co Limerick, Detective Garda Jerry McCabe was shot dead outside the Post Office while on escort duty, during the course of the delivery of cash to that Post Office in what turned out to be a botched attempted armed robbery at the Post Office by a gang of terrorist. When the news of the shooting had filtered through there was an air of disbelief as to what had happened throughout the force. Another colleague had been killed in the line of duty. For me, it brought back memories of a good friend, and colleague of mine, Detective Garda Frank Hand, who was shot dead, in much the same circumstances, outside a Post Office at Drumree Co Meath on the 10th of August 1984.

Detective Garda Jerry McCabe was attached to the Special Detective unit in Limerick, with responsibility for keeping tabs on known members of terrorist groups around Limerick, and surrounding areas. There was a suspicion, which was never rebutted, that Jerry's shooting was a reprisal shooting because of his diligent efforts to control terrorist activities within his area, and he became a marked man for the terrorists. He was a dedicated member of An Garda Siochana.

A huge investigation took place into Jerry's killing, which eventually led to the arrest of the four of the men responsible, who purported to be members of the P I R A. At their trial in 1999 the charge of murder was withdrawn, and they were found guilty of a manslaughter charge. It is believed the Northern Ireland Peace Agreement had an influence on the outcome of the case; all were given prison sentences ranging from 10 years to 12 yrs. It is believed that there are still one or two suspects on the run who are wanted for this crime.

One might ask why I bring up Detective Garda Jerry McCabe's death. Well Jerry was from my own hometown of Ballylongford, Co Kerry. I'm not sure if I ever met Jerry during the course of my younger days because of the circumstances of my upbringing. My father, and Jerry's father would have known each other very well over the years, Ballylongford being a small enough town. On one of my trips from Dublin to Ballylongford, in the 1960s when I had cycled down from Dublin, I remember having to go to Jerry's father to have my cycle repaired for my trip back to Dublin as I had developed a problem with the gears on the bike. I remember seeing Jerry's father at the funeral in June of 1996, it was a heartbreaking moment.

Even as the killers of Jerry McCabe were being hunted down, within three weeks of his shooting a further outrageous event occurred in Dublin city.

On the 26th of June 1996 I was on duty at my Station at Lucan, it was near lunchtime as I passed through the public office of the station downstairs. A message was coming through on the computerised messaging service from the Central Control room in the city that there had been a shooting on the Naas Road near Clondalkin, which was in our Division. I went over to the screen, and watched as the updated information kept coming in from Central Control. It was stating the person that had been shot was a female, and she was dead in her car.

Eventually the message came through that the lady who had been shot dead was the well-known journalist, Veronica Guerin who worked with the Sunday Independent. We were all pretty stunned at the news of a journalist being shot. She was well known for her writing about criminals, their gangs, their activities in the Dublin area, and their involvement in the drugs trade.

I knew instinctively that this was going to be a big investigation, as the shooting had occurred in our Division. My first port of call was to phone Detective Garda Pat Bane at his home, one of my squad, who was off duty at the time. I informed Pat of the news, who it was that was shot, and to come in, and meet me at the office. Now, Pat was one of the longer serving members of my crew, but he was a man who had vast experience in serious crime investigations as he was previously a member of the old national Murder Squad, and I knew he was a good man with the incident room "job" books.

Strangely enough Pat, like myself, was planning his time of departure from the Garda Force, to expand a little business he was operating on a part time basis. When Pat called into the office I remember saying to him that he would have to put his retirement plans on hold as "we need you on this one". Our next move was to go to visit the scene of the shooting which was at the traffic lights at the junction of Booth Road, and Naas Road, in Clondalkin. We were aware of course that we would not be able to get too close, because it was a crime scene, but we got close enough to see Veronica's car completely covered over with her body still inside. I was aware that Pat had on numerous occasions met with Veronica over the years during his service, and knew her reasonably well.

At the scene we also met with our District Superintendent, Len Ahern, who had spent most of his service in the Special Detective Unit at Dublin Castle, and Harcourt Square, and whom we knew well from investigations over the years. We had a discussion at the scene as to where the murder investigation incident room should be set up. Now, Clondalkin Station was the local Station in whose area the shooting took place, but it was a very old building with not too much room for a big investigation such as this would be. I made the suggestion to Len that the investigation could be run from Lucan as it was a fairly new premises, and there was plenty of room there.

Len went off, had a chat with some of the more senior officers who had arrived at the scene, when he came back to us he said, yes, the investigation will be run from Lucan Station. I was to return to Lucan immediately to make preparations to have the conference room ready for the investigation. Pat returned with me, and we set about getting things ready for the investigation team to move in.

Chief Superintendent Tony Hickey, later to be appointed Assistant Commissioner, was designated to head this investigation on his return from his holidays which he cut short as he started the ball rolling even while still at his holiday hotel. Tony Hickey put together a team of about forty very experienced detectives of all ranks, to form the main investigation team to investigate this brutal murder of journalist Veronica Guerin. From time to time this team was supplemented by additional detectives, Technical Staff, and uniform personnel when needed. This was to be one of the most extensive criminal investigations in the history of the state.

This murder investigation was to bring Lucan Station into the international limelight, and for a number of the early weeks of the investigation we had a constant stream of journalists both local, and international coming, and going from Lucan, looking for constant updates from the investigation team with some of them literally camping in their cars for long periods in the vicinity of the station so as to not miss any developments that might occur.

It is not my intention to attempt to go into all the details of this huge investigation, as there have been many books, and articles written about the case, including Paul Williams "Evil Empire", and Michael Sheridan's "A Letter To Veronica" to name, but a few. My intention is to put together some of my thoughts, which are not exhaustive, regarding some parts I played myself as part of the murder investigation team.

This was as I have intimated, a very high profile case which involved the brutal murder of a very well-known journalist. The investigation team took a very methodical approach to the case as the number of suspects that could have been responsible grew. Eventually it came down to one particular criminal, and his gang. The public, and the media began to get a bit impatient for results as the first number of weeks passed, with seemingly no advancement in the investigation.

Behind the scenes there was a lot of hard work going on in trying to establish the motive behind the murder, who organised it, and who carried it out. There was constant understandable pressure from the media for an early outcome to this tragic event. The investigation was continuing at a reasonable pace, considering the enormity of the case.

With respect to myself, as part of the investigation team, I was carrying out inquiries from job sheets I was receiving from the incident room, as was the normal procedure with the results of the inquiries being reported back to the incident room with whatever information was obtained. To give an example, one of my earlier inquiries was to one of the local banks in Lucan on the 1st of July 1996, to take possession of some video tapes that might help us regarding the movements of the main suspect in the case that used to visit a bookies office next door to the bank premises. Of course I knew the bank manager well, he being a Kerry man like Tony Hickey, and myself, I had in my possession the necessary documents to cover the seizure of these tapes.

On the 9th of July 1996, about two weeks after the murder, with a colleague, Detective Garda John Kelly, I went to a location on the Lower Road, Lucan which runs along by the River Liffey. We had received information in the incident room that a man had discovered parts of a motorcycle in the river. There was what appeared to be a motorcycle in the river so we called out one of our tow wagons from Headquarters to assist in retrieving this motorcycle. We did inform them that it was in the river so one of the members from the sub aqua squad accompanied the tow wagon, and also carried out a search of the river surrounding the area where the motorcycle was located. We recovered the motor cycle with other parts, which had been partly dismantled, from the location, and had it transported to the Garda Technical Bureau for examination, and reassembly.

On a later date we went back to the Technical Bureau to get identification on the motorcycle, which we obtained. We made contact with the registered owner of the motorcycle, and discovered that it had been stolen from his lockup garage from where he lived in Dun Laoghaire, County Dublin. The theft had taken place on the night of 7th of June 1996, the same date that Detective Garda Jerry McCabe was shot dead in Limerick. We met up with the owner, who we obtained a statement from, and invited him to view his motorcycle at the Technical Bureau for positive identification purposes. Even though the theft had taken place a number of weeks previous we still had his garage examined by our Technical Bureau personnel.

This motorcycle was a Kawasaki 500cc GPZ, with an English registration number plate on it. During the course of our interview with the injured party, whose motorcycle it was, we asked him if he had any idea who might have stolen his motorcycle. He nominated a former employee whom he had let go from his job for a number of reasons, sometime previously.

We reported back to the incident room with this information, and the name of our suspect for stealing the motorcycle. Further investigations revealed that our suspect who was involved in the taking of the motorcycle was a very good friend of an associate of our main suspect for the murder of Veronica Guerin. This associate was party to the stealing of the motorcycle, and was actually with our suspect when they stole the motorcycle from the injured party's garage using the associates van to take the motorcycle away. It was now suspected that this was the motorcycle that was used in the murder of Veronica Guerin on the 26th of June 1996. On the 30th of September 1996 with Detective Garda John Kelly, we had the motorcycle transported from the Garda Technical Bureau to Lucan Garda Station, where it was handed over to the exhibits officer in the case, and put into a secure store.

As the investigation began to gather momentum, search teams were put together, each led by a Detective Sergeant to carry out searches of suspect's houses, and places of residence, arrest whoever was in each location at the time, seize anything suspicious, and have those arrested, brought to a previously designated Garda Station for interrogation.

I had my team allocated to me, and we, over the next few months carried out numerous searches, arrests, and seizures of cash, and property in Dublin, and the surrounding areas. Many of the suspects who were being arrested were in some way connected to our main suspect in the case, or his associates. During the course of the searches we recovered a huge amount of cash, drugs, and other items. Some of the suspects were afraid for their lives as they had been asked to hold onto some cash on behalf of our main suspect. He was spreading the cash around for various people to hold for him until the heat died down, but it never did. I remember going to one particular house which was set in flats, we knocked on the door, and the next thing we saw money raining down around our heads, it had been thrown out from an upstairs window of the flat we were about to search.

During the searches we continued to find large amounts of cash being held for our main suspect, in one case we found a stash of cash in a plastic bag just on top of a kitchen press which had been given to this occupant to hold only a short time previously, seemingly he didn't have the time to hide it properly. During the course of some of the searches we didn't find anything of any significance, but we still arrested the occupants for interrogation because of their close criminal association with our main suspect in the case.

Of course many of the known hardened criminals I came across during the course of my searches, and who had been brought in for questioning took advantage of our complaints procedures, and made a number of spurious complaints of misconduct against many gardai including myself. I had several complaints made against me by a variety of known criminals, which had to be investigated by an Inspector not involved in the main investigation, which was part of a ploy by the complainants, to try to frustrate the investigation. These complaints would have ended up in the office of the Garda Siochana Complaints Board as was the normal procedure. In all the complaints brought against me it was found that I had not committed any offence or any breach of discipline during the course of my investigations.

To give one example, I reproduce here one of the letters I received from the Garda Siochana Complaints Board on their headed note paper on the completion of one such investigation on myself.

D/Sergeant Maurice Heffernan,

Garda Station,
Lucan,
Co Dublin,
15th January 1997   Name of Complainant;
Dear D/Sergeant Heffernan,

As you are aware, a complaint was made by the above named in which you were one of the members complained of, under the Garda Siochana [Complaints] Act 1986.

The report of the investigating officer appointed to investigate the complaint, and the relevant comments, and recommendations of the Chief Executive have been considered carefully by the Board. The Board is satisfied that a thorough investigation was carried out into the allegations made by the complainant, and is of the opinion that neither an offence nor a breach of discipline on your part had been disclosed. Accordingly, the Board will take no further action in the matter.

Yours Sincerely;
Chief Executive.

Out of respect on each occasion, I acknowledged receipt of the correspondence from the Complaints Board, thanking them for their time, and courtesy, addressing it to the Chief Executive of the time.

I mention this because it was a situation we consistently came up against during the course of our investigations into the murder of journalist Veronica Guerin. With such a huge investigation going on there was always room for error. One such incident involved a search that my team, and I undertook in an apartment complex in the centre of Dublin city. I had my warrant for the address I was to search; we knocked at the door of the apartment, got no answer, and proceeded to put the door in to gain entry.

When we got in we looked around the apartment, there was nobody there, and we began our search. Not long into the search we discovered that there was a possibility we were in the wrong apartment, from documentation we found which didn't add up to the identity of the person we were seeking. I found a contact number for the occupants of the apartment, and phoned one of them from the apartment. I explained the circumstances to the person I spoke with, explaining that we had burst in the door of the apartment, and could one of them come around to meet us at the apartment.

One of the occupants did come around within a short time as he worked close by. I informed him as to what occurred explaining to him that I had a warrant to search this apartment. After speaking with him, it confirmed to us that we had the wrong information. I immediately got in touch with the incident room, to find out where this information had come from. I was informed that a certain suspect who was associated with our main suspect was seen to park his car in the parking spot allocated to the apartment we were in. It looks like we were wrong footed on this one, as none of the occupants of this flat had a car so the parking spot was not being used by them.

Now the occupants of the apartment were very understanding as to what occurred, and were aware of the serious investigation we were involved with. I told them we would get their door, and door frame repaired at no cost to them which I arranged for. The incident room had an arrangement made with our Office of Public Works to carry out any repairs we requested resulting from our searches. It shows the difference in people when the occupants of this apartment made no complaint regarding the search of their apartment in error. There weren't many errors like that during the course of the investigation.

This investigation went on for over five years with numerous trials, and court appearances being attended to by members of the investigation team. It also involved many trips being made abroad by part of the team to confer with other Police Forces regarding suspects who had been detained by them on our behalf.

Quite a number of the main suspects gang were put away over those years, two of them for the murder of Veronica Guerin, the rest all related to importation, and dealing in drugs. In the year 2000, the main suspect in the case was eventually brought back from England to face charges relating to the murder of Veronica Guerin, and drug dealing. In early 2001 he was found not guilty of the murder, but guilty of several counts of drug dealing. He was sentenced to 28 years in prison.

I felt privileged to have been part of the investigation team in this case. There were some tense moments during the investigation, like the time that the man suspected of pulling the trigger of the weapon that killed Veronica Guerin, was brought to Lucan Station for questioning which was the nerve centre of the investigation. It was discovered shortly after he was brought to an interview room that he had hidden microphones under the rubber heels of both shoes. A room was also discovered in a building adjacent to the Station in which were found more listening devices arranged by the same suspect.

It was suspected that the incident room itself might be the target of a bugging attempt. Arrangements were made to have the investigation rooms swept for devices, and that was carried out at regular intervals, to protect the information going through the offices, and also the team members operating from the incident room. Armed protection was also put into operation around Lucan Station for fear of a criminal attack, which was kept on for the duration of the investigation.

That tension was even evident during a Christmas function, which I was involved in organising, to be held at the Lucan Spa Hotel on a particular evening, close to Christmas 1996, for all the personnel involved in the investigation. There would have been well over fifty people of all ranks attending, which was to bring a bit of relaxation after a busy first six months. As we were all seated down, and about to be served our meal there was a loud explosion, which came from the vicinity of the kitchens close to our dining room where we were.

There was an air of panic for a few moments as we felt we were under attack by explosives.

On investigation it was discovered that it was a gas explosion in the kitchen next to the room we were in. A man who was one of the hotel staff was injured as a result of something he did wrong while connecting a gas bottle. The fire was put out quickly, and we all went to an alternative venue to wait to be seated again in a different dining room in the hotel, where we were served our meal a little later than expected, but had an enjoyable evening.

I stayed with the investigation on, and off until my retirement in December 2000. All through the investigation I had also to keep an eye on my own district crime, and get involved when necessary to assist my unit who were keeping up to date as to what was occurring. Even after my retirement I had in early January 2001, to appear as a witness at the trial of our main suspect in the Special Criminal Court to give evidence.

During my retirement function which was held in early 2001 at the Lucan Spa Hotel, and was attended by a large number of my colleagues, friends, and family, I was presented with a specially designed, and inscribed plaque, made of Pewter, by Assistant Commissioner Tony Hickey on behalf of The Veronica Guerin Murder Investigation Team, dated the 31st December 2000. I cherish this plaque which hangs in a prominent place in my current residence in Malta.

Over the period of the investigation my thoughts were never far away from my family. In November 1998 I lost my brother Jerry, who died in England. He had gone over to attend his daughters nursing graduation, and had a serious stroke, and died three days later. He was just 58 years old.

My past was also never far from my mind, and I still had my protective memory barriers up. I remember on one occasion a number of us, including Assistant Commissioner Tony Hickey retired to a local pub not far from the Station for some light refreshments as we were finishing for the day. After some time, the others moved off, and I was left on my own with Tony. Of course Tony being a Kerry man, wanted to know what part of Kerry I was from, where I went to school, and such general information. He said to me jokingly, he always had doubts about me being a Kerry man as I didn't sound like a Kerry man. I passed it off that maybe the CBS Tralee, school teachers knocked the Kerry accent out of me as they were from various parts of Ireland.

In the end I had to change the conversation to something else, as he was getting too close to the bone with this conversation. I could not in all seriousness divulge the early years of my past, maybe I was afraid of what people would say or think, so I kept to my little white lie. Tony was a gentleman, and we got to know each other well during the course of the investigation, and of course he was residing in my District as were many other high ranking officers of the Garda Siochana.

As I said earlier on, the media were never far away, on several occasions while I was in the incident room, photographers were allowed in to take a quick picture of part of the investigation team, and one such picture appeared in the Sunday Independent on the 13th of April 1997. On another occasion a news crew for RTE were allowed in to take some shots which later appeared on the RTE news, again I happened to be in the incident room at that time. We were making the news.

On the 26th of June 2002 I attended with many of the Murder Investigation Team from Lucan, at an unveiling of a Plaque at the site of the shooting of Veronica Guerin, at the junction of the Booth Road, Naas Road, Clondalkin, Dublin. I was retired two, and a half years at this stage. It was the sixth anniversary of this tragic event. As I write this, the coming June 26th 2021, will be the 25th anniversary of the shooting of journalist Veronica Guerin, and prior to that on the 7th of June 2021 will be the 25th anniversary of the shooting dead of Detective Garda Jerry McCabe.

CHAPTER THIRTY ONE

Four Bodies Found in House
12th July 2000

The following is a short outline of one the most extraordinary cases I have come across in my career in which there was no criminality deemed to be involved. I had just about six months before my retirement from the Force. On the 12th of July 2000, I was on a rest day, I was in Dublin city centre with my former wife Margaret shopping for wallpaper. I was in a wallpaper shop in Capel Street, when I got a call on my mobile from one of my unit crew, Geraldine Ennis, telling me that four bodies had been discovered in a house in the Leixlip area. At first I thought she was having me on, but something in her voice indicated to me that there was something in what she was telling me. I informed her I would be returning immediately to the office, thus bringing a premature end to the wallpaper search, and maybe saving myself some extra house decorating.

When I arrived at my office I was brought up to date on the situation, and I was also in communication with one of the Garda Inspectors at the scene. Before going to the scene I made contact with Dr Denis Cusack, the Kildare county coroner, I also arranged for the removal of the bodies from the scene, by making contact with Cunninghams Undertakers, of Clonsilla to have them taken to Tallaght Hospital Morgue, when the examinations of the bodies at the house were complete.

I arrived at the scene at the house in Leixlip, in which the bodies were discovered, where I met with the members from the Technical Bureau, other members of my unit, and my Detective Inspector

Thomas O'Loughlin. The scene was being preserved, and the State Pathologist, Dr Marie Cassidy was at the scene doing her initial examinations before the bodies were removed, and escorted to the Morgue for Postmortem Examinations. At the scene the bodies were labelled "A" "B" "C" "D", which would be normal procedure where multiple bodies are involved, for later identification, and location as to where each body was found.

Discovery

At about 12.15pm on the 12th of July 2000, the owner of the property where the bodies were found in Leixlip, called to the house which he had leased out, through an agency, Douglas Newman Good, to four ladies by the name of Mulrooney. His reason for calling was that no payments had been made for a number of months to his account, with respect to the property. He had never met with the tenants as they had dealt with the agency.

He rang the doorbell of the house, but got no answer, so he then went around the back of the house to try the back door which he found locked. There didn't seem to be anyone home so he went back to the front door, and tried a key in the door which he had with him. The key fitted the lock which opened the door, but he could not push the door open due to the fact that there was a heavy object behind the door which he later discovered was a tall fridge. He forced his way in pushing the fridge as he pushed the door. As he opened the door he got a foul smell, and a blast of heat hit him. He was now in the house, and he saw that the door to the living room to the right was open, and he got a shock when he saw what looked like a dead body of a woman on the floor, dressed in what looked like a night dress, he withdrew immediately out to his car, and phoned the gardai who asked him to wait there, and somebody would be with him.

When the Gardai arrived he informed them as to the situation. One of the Garda went into the house, and discovered that there were four bodies in the house, three in the front room, and the fourth in the kitchen area. The owner of the house was in a state of shock. The scene was sealed off, and preserved for Technical Examination by members from the Garda Technical Bureau, and also for the visit of the State Pathologist, and the County Coroner.

Investigation

With my Detective Inspector Thomas O'Loughlin who was at the scene when I arrived, after the removal of the bodies we immediately set about the investigation of the circumstances of the deaths of these four ladies. Very early on in this investigation foul play was ruled out, so we set about trying to find the reasons behind the deaths. To this end we sought the assistance of several experts to carry out examinations, and tests on our behalf.

> These test included, full examination by members from the Garda Technical Bureau,
> A quality control test carried out by a technician from the Gas Board,
> Examination of the house structure by an Engineer from Kildare County Council,

A painstaking search of every room in the house, and contents was carried out over a period of a number of weeks to beyond the end of July 2000 by Detective Garda John Kelly, who was, exhibits officer in the case with assistance from myself on some occasions. The house was kept under our control for over one month while these searches, examinations, and tests took place.

On the evening of the 12th of July 2000, Detective Inspector O'Loughlin, and myself met with a sister of three of the deceased ladies the fourth being her aunt, and brought her to the mortuary at the Hospital for the purpose of trying to identify the bodies found in the house. We showed her two of the bodies "C", and "D" whom she identified, "C" being a Miss Josephine Mulrooney, a youngest sister, born on the 28th September 1953, and "D" being a Miss Catherine Mulrooney, another younger sister, and a twin sister of Ruth Bridget Mulrooney, both born on the 12th October 1948.

We did not show her bodies "A", and "B" as they were in an advanced state of decomposition. On the following day we met again with the sister of the deceased at the mortuary at Tallaght Hospital, where she confirmed again the identity of bodies "C", and "D" as being her two sisters. She also provided Detective Inspector O'Loughlin, and me with photographs which she identified to us, as one being her third sister, Ruth Bridget, born on the 12th of October 1948, and the second photograph as her Aunt Frances Mulrooney born on the 11th of May 1917.

Later on the same day the 13th of July 2000, Detective Inspector O'Loughlin, and myself viewed bodies "A" and "B" again at the mortuary, with the photographs in our possession, and we were satisfied that body "A" was that of Frances Mulrooney, Aunt of the lady we met, and body "B" was that of Ruth Bridget Mulrooney one of the twins, and one of her sisters.

On Friday the 14th of July 2000, I again went to the mortuary at Tallaght Hospital accompanied by Detective Inspector O'Loughlin, and Detective Garda John Kelly. There we met with a Dental Surgeon from the Dublin Dental Hospital, who was a consultant in Oral Surgery. From the dental records I had previously obtained from a dental practice in the north city area, the Dental Surgeon was able to support the evidence that body "B" was that of Ruth Bridget Mulrooney from his examination, and the dental records I had obtained.

He was not able to get a result with respect to body "A" as during an attempt, in my presence, at getting teeth impressions, all the upper gum, and teeth came away because of the advanced decomposition of the body.

Cause of Death

The state Pathologist Dr Cassidy, from her Autopsy examinations, came to the conclusion that all four females had died as a result of starvation, and food deprivation. There were a number of factors which she outlined in her reports to support death from starvation. She went on to state that starvation in adults is unusual unless it was a deliberate withholding of food. As to when the deaths occurred it was difficult to put an exact date due to the state of the decomposition of the bodies. She made a reference to a Northern Ireland report regarding persons on hunger strike, when water was consumed, the maximum limit of total fasting was approximately 60 days, and that was with respect to young healthy persons in their 20s. The individuals in this case were much older; one would expect that their deaths would have occurred much less than 60 days after commencing the fast.

During the course of carrying out these postmortems Dr Cassidy received a letter in the post from a lady who believed that she knew one of the deceased as Bridget Feeney, about 25 years ago.

She stated that she had attended classes with her, and they were members of a well-known Yoga group. This lady stated that she was told by Bridget Feeney that she suffered from a condition because of lack of vitamins, which caused her to switch lights on, and off on a continuous basis. She also stated that Bridget was one of a group of members who were interested in fasting. The Yoga group taught people about fasting, and some of the people did from 10 to 40 days of fasts, for what they believed would bring them perfect health.

Part of the contents of this letter can be verified with information obtained that identifies Bridget Feeney, and Ruth Bridget Mulrooney as one, and the same person. Twenty five years previously Ruth Bridget Feeney changed her name to Ruth Bridget Mulrooney, that being her mother's maiden name, and her aunt's name being her mother's sister. Her twin sister Catherine, and her other younger sister Josephine also changed their name to Mulrooney.

Brief Family History

The family name was "Feeney", there were five children in the family, all girls. The lady whom we had the most dealings with was the second eldest, with the eldest being another sister Frances. The three youngest were Catherine, Ruth Bridget, who were twins, and Josephine, all of whom were found dead, with their Aunt Frances, on the 12th of July 2000.

The family lived on the South Circular Road area of Dublin, over a hardware store which was run by their father, and mother. In 1945 their mother's sister Frances Mulrooney came up from Sligo to stay with the family to help out their mother Mrs. Feeney. In October 1948 the twins Catherine, and Ruth Bridget were born. Frances Mulrooney never went back to Sligo, but continued to live with the family, and in 1953 the youngest girl Josephine was born.

Around 1980 the three youngest girls, Catherine, her twin sister Ruth Bridget, and their youngest sister Josephine left home, and went to live in a rented house in the Sandymount area. A few years later they invited their Aunt Frances, who was not in good health, to live with them in this house. Sometime in the late 1990s a problem developed with their landlord who wanted them to leave the house as he required it back. Legal proceedings followed, and eventually in 1998 they moved out of the house, and moved in with their sister for a short period of time. Prior to Christmas 1998 they left their sister's house without her knowing, and she never saw them again.

It was at this time in December 1998 that they rented, and moved into the house at Leixlip, in Co Kildare.

Results of Examination of the House by the Technical Experts

The Garda Technical Bureau made the following report of their examinations.

A large fridge had been placed inside the front door, restricting the opening of the front door.

A heavy towel had been placed along the bottom of the door leading to the central heating unit.

The thermostat governing the central heating system was set at a maximum of 30 degrees.

A blue plastic bag filled with papers was blocking the chimney flue of the fireplace in the sitting room where three of the bodies were found.

All the windows, and the rear patio doors were locked, and secured.

There was a full test carried out by the Gas Company on the 13th of July 2000. At 2am on that morning the Gas Company engineers entered the house, turned on the central heating system, set the thermostat at 30 degrees, and had the house locked up. On the afternoon of the 13th of July 2000 they re-entered the house, and carried out certain tests for defects in the central heating system. They found that the central heating system was working correctly. There were no traces of Carbon Dioxide or Carbon Monoxide found in the house. The engineers from Kildare County Council found no defects in the structure of the building.

With great difficulty, efforts were made to try to pinpoint when, and where any of these ladies were last seen outside of their house in Leixlip. Results from the extensive search of the house, and follow-up inquiries would give a reasonable indication that the last date that any one of these ladies were outside their house was on Friday the 31st of March 2000. The following would bear this out.

Taxi Driver

A Taxi driver, who came forward about ten days after the finding of the bodies, after hearing about the tragic events, remembered bringing two ladies to this house at Leixlip, from the city centre. They had a very large amount of shopping so he reversed into the driveway. He then brought one of the ladies, and her "mother" who came out of the house back down to Leixlip village, to go to the Post Office, and the bank. He parked in the village, and waited for them, and drove them back to their house in Leixlip. He couldn't give an exact date, but stated it would have been two to three months previous. He brought one of the Detectives with him, and pointed out the house where he had dropped these ladies. There was something about these ladies that caused him to remember them.

Information from Documentation found during search of House

The last electricity bill to be paid was paid at the Electricity Boards, Head Office in Fleet Street in Dublin city centre, on the 31st of March 2000, by way of a Money Order obtained from a Post Office at Ormond Quay in the city on the 31st March 2000.

The last Gas bill was paid on Friday the 31st of March 2000, again by way of a Money Order obtained from the same Post Office on the 31st of March 2000.

The last transactions at Leixlip Post Office were on the 31st of March 2000, when Josephine received her carers allowance, and Frances, her Aunt, received her old age pension. This would seem to confirm the Taxi driver's account of events.

Bus tickets found in the house were dated the 31st of March 2000, there were no later dated tickets found.

The last dated shopping till receipts found, were dated the 31st of March 2000.

From all the information in our possession, it would seem, that none of these ladies left their house again after the 31st March 2000.

Other information

During the course of the search of the house an electricity bill dated the 12th of June 2000 was found in the drawer of a bedside locker. We found from inquiries with the Electricity Company, that this particular bill would have been posted on the 12th of June 2000, and by a normal post would have been delivered on the 13th or 14th of June 2000. The indication here is that one of the occupants of the house took this letter from the letter box, opened it, brought it upstairs to the bedroom, and put it into the bedside locker drawer.

We also found two letters written by Ruth Bridget dated the 11th of June 2000. The indications here would suggest that there was still life in the house between the 11th of June 2000, and the 13th or 14th of June 2000, and the upstairs bedroom was being used by at least one of the occupants.

One other interesting factor came to light, during the course of the searches at the house. We found a set of keys in a tin box in one of the kitchen presses under the sink unit. These keys fitted all the external doors. This was also the area where there were a lot of black plastic bags filled mostly with papers, and it was the location where the body of one of the twins, Catherine was found. Did she know that the keys were there, and was she trying to get to the keys when she collapsed onto the bags of rubbish, and died there?

This was a most distressing case to investigate, which caught the attention of the public at large, and the local, and international media. On the 20th of November 2000 I received the following letter, part of which I produce below, from a cousin of three of the deceased ladies, whom I had cause to meet during the course of the investigations.

Dear Maurice

I am writing a very belated THANK YOU letter for all the help you, and your fellow colleagues gave to us all during the very sad times of the deaths of Frances, Brid, Kate, and Josephine. R.I.P. The shock has been very great, and not an everyday encounter. It is tragic in so many ways that it leaves one completely baffled.

The professionalism, and humanity shown by you all has been remarkable. I was particularly struck by the strong faith which you all had in enabling you all to cope with life's mysteries. As life indeed is - a mystery.

With renewed deep thanks, and God's blessings be with you all always.

Your sincerely

The case went on into 2001, after my retirement, when like in many other cases I was summoned to attend the inquest in the Coroners Court, at which evidence was given as to the tragic circumstances of the deaths of the four ladies. The jury at the inquest brought in a verdict of suicide by starvation in all four cases.

Film Documentary 2002

That of course wasn't the end of it for me. Sometime in January 2002 I received a phone call from England from Elizabeth Dobson, who was a film director with October Films, and she wanted to meet up with me, as they were producing a documentary about the deaths of the four ladies found dead in Leixlip on the 12th of July 2000.

I met with Ms Dobson on a number of occasions between the 24th of January, and the 30th of January 2002. Arrangements were made that she would come to my house on a date in late February to do a filmed interview with me regarding the case. She had informed me that she had already carried out a number of interviews with people involved in the case, which included my colleague Detective Garda John Kelly, who had been promoted, and was now a uniform Sergeant.

The documentary was called, "The Pact", and it was completed on the 25th of April 2002, to be shown on Channel Four TV sometime later that year. In September 2002 I received a letter from Ms Dobson that the documentary was to be aired on Channel Four on Saturday the 21st of September 2002 at 8.20pm, much sooner than was expected. She also gave me a copy of the tape of the documentary which I have now converted to CD as video tapes are out of fashion.

The documentary, "The Pact" was shown in three parts, in which I featured in about a dozen different slots. I think at the time I was happy with how the interview went, as I just stuck to the facts of the case. On a later date I met again with Ms Dobson in London, where she treated me to a long promised meal. I was in London at the time visiting one of my sisters.

CHAPTER THIRTY TWO

Life after Service in An Garda Siochana

I retired from the Garda Siochana on the 31st of December 2000 after almost 33 years of service. To be precise I had served 32 years, and 350 days, somebody had updated me on that figure. I was just gone 55 years of age which was the time I had planned for leaving the force. I had secured employment with the Central Statistics Office, where I was to start in January 2001. My plan was to benefit from the State Pension, as I was going to start paying social welfare contributions again, which I had to commence prior to my 56th birthday.

The National Census for the Republic of Ireland was set to take place in the Spring of 2001. They had sought applications in late 2000, looking for people to fill various positions, to assist in carrying out the Census, and I made my application for one of the positions. Training was given over a period of a number of weeks from the middle of January 2001, for Area Coordinators, which was the position I had been assigned to.

On the completion of our training, our job was then to recruit, and train between ten, and twenty people, depending on the size of the area, to carry out the work in each of the Areas as Census Personnel. These were to be the people whose job it would be to call to each of the households, delivering the Census documentation, and collecting the forms again on completion.

All seemed to progress as planned even to the point of having a large number of boxes containing Census forms, and other documentation delivered to my own home in Leixlip. My home was now the distribution headquarters for my area of operations. This did not go down too well with my then wife Margaret as the front room was completely taken over with boxes of census material. This of course added to the personal tensions which already existed which I didn't need at that time.

As planned I had started to distribute the boxes of forms to the Census workers in my area when there was a stop put on the operation. The taking of the Census was cancelled due to an outbreak of Foot, and Mouth disease in both England, and Northern Ireland. Within a matter of days all the boxes of census material were collected again from my home, which left the front room back as it was.

Now they say that lightning never strikes twice, but the Foot, and Mouth disease played a part in my life on two occasions, the first being in 1967 just before I joined the Garda, it may have been responsible for me being called up early to training in January 1968, as at the time they would only take in people for training if you worked in the cities. The second time in 2001, I wasn't so lucky, as I was made redundant some months after starting with the Census Office due to the Foot, and mouth.

For the first time in my life I had to sign on at my local social welfare office which was at Maynooth, Co Kildare. I didn't of course receive any unemployment assistance, but I did get the benefit of my welfare contributions each time I signed on which would go towards qualifying for my State Pension some years later. In October 2001 I again became employed in another capacity, and continued to make my welfare contributions.

In March of 2001 there was a retirement function organised for me at the Lucan Spa Hotel, by my colleagues at Lucan District Detective Unit. There was a large attendance at the function, including former colleagues from the various branches I had served in, members of the public with whom I had been involved in various projects within the district, and a number of high ranking officers including Assistant Commissioner Tony Hickey who I mentioned previously made a presentation of a plaque to me on behalf of the Veronica Guerin Murder

Investigation Team. I also received several other presentations from a number of other groups, including my old unit at Lucan, and the Lucan Spa Hotel Golfing Society, and members of the public.

Several members of my own family, including, my wife Margaret, my three girls, Noeleen, Ann Marie, Aoife, and Niall, being the only one of the three boys here, as both Mark, and Ger were away in other parts of the world. Members of the original Heffernan brigade including my sisters Mary, Lily, and Kathy attended the function with my niece Jenny. I was totally taken by surprise at the huge turnout which made it a wonderful evening. I had put a few words together to say after the presentations being made to me. I give a brief summary of what I covered as follows;

> I was absolutely overwhelmed by the turnout.
> I thanked everybody for their presence on the night.
> I also mentioned several of my former colleagues that phoned me at the hotel earlier, who were unable to attend
> I thanked the previous speakers, Assistant Commissioner Tony Hickey, Superintendent Liam Maycock, and my colleague Tony Sourke, for their heartening words.

I mentioned a special thank you, to the organisers of this function, and to the L & Q social club for the wonderful presentation.

I also mentioned my friends, and colleagues in the Detective Unit at Lucan, and thanked them for their gift on the night of the 5th of January. They included Toddie O'Loughlin, John Kelly, Pat Bane, Pat Walsh, Michael Conneely, John Hart, Noel Maher, Geraldine Ennis and Mary Caine.

I also mentioned another evening that was sprung on myself, and my wife by members of the Colgan Group, Frank, Gerry, both their wives, and Larry, and his wife,

I made a reference to my dear colleague, a very good friend of mine, and my family, who was shot dead on the 10th of August 1984, Detective Garda Frank Hand, he had served on my unit in the Drug

Squad at that time, it was certainly one of the lowest periods of my service. I mentioned, "that he will always be in my memory, and will never be forgotten".

I covered my arrival at Lucan without going into any detail. At the time Lucan was a quiet place, but because of it becoming the centre of the Veronica Guerin Murder investigation in 1996, it became a place of international interest. Being associated with the Veronica Guerin Murder investigation was a gratifying experience for me. Everybody involved in this investigation has to be congratulated.

I also thanked all the female staff at Lucan station attached to the various departments, and the uniform personnel attached to all four units in Lucan, Ronanstown, Ballyfermot, and Clondalkin.

In conclusion I intimated that I had enjoyed my time in the force, certainly there were some challenging times, but I got through them in the end. I had no regrets whatsoever, and I looked forward to the future, and whatever that would bring.

I finished with a saying by a lady I had gotten to know well.

"I pass this way, but once, any good that I may do, I do it now as I may not pass this way again. Rev. Fathers, Ladies, and Gentlemen, I will not be passing this way again. Good night and God bless, and thank you."

My wife at the time Margaret attended that evening, even though there was a certain amount of tension, as things weren't good between us for the past number of years. I was of course very good at covering up things in my private life, I had plenty of practice since leaving St Joseph's all those years ago. From a public point of view things looked normal.

It is of course very hard to put a finger on it but, over time things got more, and more difficult between both of us. It's not my intention to lay blame, as to a degree I may well have been partly responsible for some of our differences. Throughout some of those years, we did go abroad on holidays with some of the girls, including some trips to Malta, where my sister Joan suspected there was something not right between both my wife, and myself. I suppose it was a woman's intuition.

After my retirement things got more difficult between us in our relationship. During the course of those early years of retirement I made several trips to Malta on my own to see Joan who was one of my older sisters, and with whom I had built up a reasonably good relationship. It was during the course of some of those visits I met with Sonia who was working with Frans, Joan's husband. She would have been aware of my predicament at home as Joan would have filled her in. Over those years in early 2000 we had built up a close relationship culminating in Sonia coming to live in Ireland in 2004 with me.

The situation at home had become unbearable, which was suffocating me, and giving me a feeling of being smothered with tension. During all those years I would have been involved with the Local Parish Centre Project, Lucan Spa Hotel Charity Classics, and other events. I was also holding down a new job since October 2001 as a Security Manager with a well-known grocery company, which was almost a 24/7 operation. I would also have been trying to locate the last two of my brothers who nobody had seen since they left Ireland many years ago. I was successful in locating their families, but unfortunately both of them had passed away a number of years earlier.

Quoting from the CICA Report of 2009, many witnesses reported that their adult lives had been blighted by childhood memories of fear, and abuse;

Accounts were given of troubled relationships due to loss of contact with siblings, and extended family;

Witnesses described parenting difficulties ranging from being over-protective to being harsh;

Many witnesses stated that their childhood experience of abuse, and emotional deprivation inhibited their capacity for stable, secure, and nurturing relationships in adult life, they described a continuing sense of isolation, and inability to trust others.

I left my home in August 2004. At that time I took it on myself to inform all of my family personally as to what was taking place, which of course came as a shock initially to them, but as time went on they accepted the outcome. It was not until eight years later in 2012, that my divorce came through. I kept up contact with all of my family, and succeeded in keeping up good relationships with all of them.

In early September 2013 I left Ireland to live in Malta with my new companion Sonia, where we were married in late September that year. I will expand further on, with respect to one of the main reasons, as to why I made the decision to leave Ireland at that time.

When I reflect back now again to my humble beginnings, and how I got to where I was, I had to give myself a pinch in case I had been dreaming as these were moments, and happenings not to ever be forgotten. Maybe I never gave myself enough credit for my accomplishments, but then that was the way I was, grateful to have the chance for such as were my achievements.

CHAPTER THIRTY THREE

The Ryan Commission to Inquire into Child Abuse 2009 [CICA]

In 2009, The Ryan Commission to Inquire into Child Abuse Report, was released into the public domain, and I purchased a copy of this report which was on CD-Rom. For a number of years prior to the release of this report there had been a huge amount of publicity in both the written media, and on the televised media regarding the treatment of boys who had for one reason or another been detained in Residential Institutions, run by the Christian Brothers. They gave accounts of serious physical, and sexual abuse during the time of their detention at various residential Institutions.

I listened with interest, and disgust, to some of the accounts given, which were horrendous, and it brought back memories of my own incarceration in St Joseph's Residential Institution, Tralee. During the course of these exposures there was no mention of St Joseph's Residential Institution, Tralee. Resulting from these exposures, and accounts given by a number of people who had been committed to Residential Institutions, the Government of the day, in 2002 put in place a Redress Scheme under the Residential Institutions Redress Act of 2002. It was set up to compensate former residents of Residential Institutions who were in some way abused during their incarceration, allowing them to make an application to the Redress Board set up under the Act. Later I will expand on, and address the treatment I received from the Redress Board, and how my application to that Board was dealt with.

It was not until The Ryan Commission to Inquire into Child Abuse 2009 Report was being released [four years after the closing date for applications to the Redress Board], that I learned that it covered all residential institutions in Ireland, hence my reason for obtaining a copy of the Report to check if St Joseph's Residential Institution, Tralee, was inquired into by the Ryan Commission, which it was.

Of interest to me was Chapter 9 of this report, which dealt with St Joseph's Residential Institution, Tralee, from 1862 to 1970. I printed out that chapter which came to a considerable number of pages. At a later date I also printed out the contents of Chapter 1, of the report, of The Ryan Commission to Inquire into Child Abuse 2009, which dealt with the involvement of The Irish Society for the Prevention of Cruelty to Children, [ISPCC] previously known as the NSPCC. I discovered that it was of interest to me, when I was looking at my earlier childhood years. The following is a small summary, first, of some of their findings with regards to the ISPCC/NSPCC, as they may have impacted those earlier years of my childhood.

ISPCC/NSPCC, Notes of Interest from the CICA Report

Back when the Society was first formed it was known as the **NSPCC**, which had originated in Britain in 1884, [the same year my father was born] with an Irish branch opening up in 1889. It was still known as the NSPCC at the time of my incarceration in St Joseph's Institution, Tralee in 1952. It was not till 1956 that it became known as the Irish Society for the Prevention of Cruelty to Children. I was well established in my detention in St Joseph's Institution by that time. The society employed Inspectors to carry out its functions, who in the Dublin area became known as "The Cruelty Men". It was not till 1968 that Social Welfare workers were appointed to take over the work of the Inspectors.

One might ask why I bring attention to the ISPCC/NSPCC, well in the account of my earlier years when I was "Taken" from my Foster Parents I wasn't sure if there was a Social Worker present, now I can definitely say there wasn't, as Social Workers had not been appointed at that time, the only conclusion being, that it was an Inspector from the NSPCC, who was responsible for my "Taking" from my Foster

Parents. The Ryan commission bears this out in its Inquiry Report, showing the history, and activities of the NSPCC Inspectors up to 1968. The following are a number of points from that Report which I suggest would have affected my own situation.

The Chief Executive Officer of the ISPCC in evidence before the CICA, stated that "there are significant limitations in the amount of material available to us. Unfortunately, we don't have an explanation as to where the material has gone, there was a fire in our head office in 1961, perhaps material was destroyed in that." [The same year that I left St Joseph's Institution, Tralee].

The Chief Executive Officer also stated that "there was no evidence that there was any structured supervision or monitoring of their role" [relating to the NSPCC Inspectors]. Maybe documents relating to myself with regards to the NSPCC were destroyed in that fire in 1961 as happened to other documents at the Orphanage in Killarney, where there was also a fire, which prevented me from discovering my movements in my early years as a child. Were all these fires coincidental?

The Chief Executive Officer also stated that "I think if we were the only child protection organisation, then I think it is reasonable to suspect that we certainly would have committed a significant number [of children] to residential institutions. But I really have no idea about the overall percentage".

Now at some stage around 1956, [I would have been over three years at St Joseph's Institution at this stage], the Archbishop of Dublin became a patron of the ISPCC. He became concerned, and had reservations about the role of the Society in committing children to Residential Institutions. The Archbishop wrote to the head of the Legion Of Mary of the time, Mr Frank Duff, and asked him to look into a number of sample cases that had been mentioned in the NSPCC report of 1939-1940 with respect to the Dublin area.

Mr Duff wrote back to the Archbishop with a scathing report regarding the activities of certain NSPCC Inspectors, stating he "profoundly distrust every word, and action of one of the Society's

Inspectors, a Mrs. XX, he goes further to say that he regards her as a danger." "She exercised an ascendancy over ex-Justice YY, and between them they simply **"shovelled"** children into Residential Institutions." It was also suggested to Mr Duff by another source, that the Charter of the Society for the PCC should be withdrawn, that the Society constituted a public menace.

The report also mentions that in 1952, [the year I was committed to St Joseph's Residential Institution, Tralee], there was an allegation that NSPCC Inspectors were taking bribes, as an inducement to send children to residential institutions. This was revealed in a Visitation Report of 1952 in respect of St Joseph's Residential Institution, Tralee. The Congregational Visitor had expressed concern about the payment of expenses to two NSPCC Inspectors, but he was informed by the Resident Manager [Superior] of the institution, [who would have been Br O'Donnell at the time], that the payment was a subscription to the Society's funds. While fundraising was the main source of income for the society, Inspectors were prohibited from collecting money. [The Inspectors Directory Stated.]

The congregational Visitor's report on his visit to St Joseph's Residential Institution, Tralee, in 1952 shows that a payment of £9.00 [nine pounds] was sought by one of the NSPCC Inspectors in respect of expenses. The normal fee of £1.00 [one pound] was all that was supposed to be paid to Inspectors for expenses incurred. There was also a reference made regarding another NSPCC Inspector, also seeking expenses, and he was considered by the Visitor, as a "well known sponger". There was also the question of boys being committed by a certain local NSPCC Inspector, under false documentation regarding the ages of the boys.

These were the type of people who were responsible for sending me to St Joseph's Residential Institution, Tralee, where I had been incarcerated in 1952.

The Society itself, down through the years reiterated that "home rather than residential institutions, was the best place for children to be brought up in". They also intimated that children to a large extent are "deprived of home influence, and it would be much better to avoid sending them to Institutions". If their own homes were impossible, "good foster homes" would give them a healthier, and happier intro- duction to life. It would seem that the Society Inspectors were not on the same wavelength as their officers at their headquarters, with regards to the treatment I received at their hands.

It would seem that some of the NSPCC Inspectors totally ignored their own regulations, did what they liked with regards to sending children to residential institutions, for their own monetary gain. From the notes of the Visitor's Report of 1952 it could be suggested that I was more than likely a £9.00 [nine pounds] bribery committal. As I have already covered with respect to my court appearance on the 12th of December 1952, there was no record of my father, my guardian or other person other than myself, and I presume the NSPCC Inspector in the court. I had been taken from my Foster Parents, committed to St Joseph's Residential Institution, totally at variance with the views held by the NSPCC management, who preferred Foster Homes to committal to institutions.

I have made an effort to put together some of the findings from the original CICA Report with regards to the involvement of the NSPCC/ISPCC, with residential institutions in Ireland, and how I became a victim of the system that pertained at the time of my incarceration in St Joseph's Residential Institution, Tralee on the 12th of December 1952. What happened to me while at St Joseph's Institution, Tralee, has to be put down to the irresponsible behaviour of the Inspectors from the then NSPCC.

In documentation that I obtained in 2012, which is a copy of a printout from the skills database at the Department of Education, the person named as being responsible for my "referral" was a Mr. M O'Regan of the NSPCC. This is a report about me by school number, and pupil number. Copy is reproduced in a further chapter.

Chapter 9 [nine] of the Ryan Commission to Inquire into Child Abuse 2009 [CICA]

St Joseph's Residential Institution, Tralee, 1862 - 1970

I have already covered most of my history, including my period of detention in St Joseph's Residential Institution, Tralee, at the beginning of my memoirs, where at times I made some references to the CICA Report 2009. In that year as already stated, I obtained a copy of the CICA Report in which there were certain findings by the Commission, which I found, made reference to, and covered the period of my detention at St Joseph's Institution, Tralee. I wish to expand on some of these sections regarding certain testimonies, and findings, with which I can relate to, as they would have impacted on me, without of course reproducing the considerable number of pages covering St Joseph's Institution, Tralee.

In 1955,[two to three years after my committal], a Visitors report suggested, there was a problem with falling numbers at St Joseph's Institution, Tralee, which created an uncertain future for this residential institution. In a 1961 visitors report, one of the reasons given for this was that there was a decline in the number of children being sent by District Justices from the courts.

District Justices from both Limerick, and Kerry were said to be antagonistic towards residential institutional education. Fostering, boarding out, and adoption are now considered preferable as children are not segregated from society. **What a pity that thinking wasn't in vogue years previously, then I might not have ended up at St Joseph's Residential Institution, Tralee.**

The Resident Manager [Brother Ryle Superior] of St Joseph's Residential Institution, expressed his concern to the Department of Education Inspector, who noted the matter in her Reports for 1960, 1961, and 1962, [which would have included the last two years I spent at St Joseph's]. In her reports she records the number of boys at the school in February 1960 as totaling 119, and in May of 1961 the number at the school was a total of 130. **Between 1969, and 1970 St Joseph's Residential Institution, closed its doors.**

According to statements made by the Congregation, between 1948, and 1969 the courts committed 700 boys to St Joseph's Residential Institution, Tralee. These 700 were committed because of destitution, homelessness, receiving alms, and wandering. They were also committed because of **improper guardianship**, and non-attendance at school. Because Tralee was a registered place of detention, a small number of boys were also sent there for criminal offences, such as larceny, house breaking, and malicious damage. Now, one can see the reason I could not divulge particulars of my "previous" life. Visitor's reports in the 1950s, and 1960 described St Joseph's Institution, Tralee, as a "most depressing establishment".

Complaints of physical abuse at St Joseph's Residential Institution, Tralee

The Ryan Report dealt with numerous complaints made against a number of the staff [Christian Brothers] at St Joseph's Institution, Tralee, covering a period of many years before, during, and after my incarceration in St Joseph's Institution, Tralee. The names of the brothers complained of have been changed to pseudonyms in the report, but I can identify a number of them, because of my close association with them while I was there.

Some time during the mid-1950s, the man who took over the running of the kitchens, and refectory for the boys was a Brother Laurence. I have already covered his dealings with me previously, he was a very tough man, but his saving grace was that he improved the food that we got. Of course like most of the boys I had several run ins with him. During the course of giving evidence to the Commission, one of the former ex-residents stated that "he would have been a great Nazis. He was the coldest cold-hearted person he ever came across..... he was cruel beyond belief".

The Report also covered the death of one of the boys, "Joseph Pike, RIP" whom I knew as we were both in the Irish Dance troupe together, which I have dealt with earlier. The Commission's Report stated that the case became controversial, and subject to speculation because the circumstances of the boy's death was never properly investigated. A three day Visitation Report conducted one month after Joseph's death, never mentioned his death, and described the boys as "exceedingly happy".

Brothers carried their "straps" at all times, with at least one brother known to have got washers put into his strap in the shoe shop so that the whole front of the strap was loaded down with washers. This information came from a witness who gave evidence to the Commission regarding a visit to the "cobblers" shop one day when one of the boys working there, pointed out a strap belonging to a particular brother, which was being reinforced with washers.

Professor Tom Dunne, who was a former Christian Brother, describing the climate of fear, referred to an article he wrote on such an atmosphere;

"It was a secret, enclosed world, run on fear; the boys were wholly at the mercy of the staff, which seemed to have entirely negative views of them"

Professor Tom Dunne who wrote several articles about his time in the Christian Brothers spent a short period of time in Tralee in 1963 doing holiday relief work. He said he had been shocked, while watching "States of Fear" by the testimony of one man who claimed to have suffered appalling abuse whilst in Tralee. Professor Dunne stated that he had spent several weeks there on relief duty in 1963, but had subsequently suppressed all memory of that time. He told the Commission that he had psychologically wiped the memories of his time there from his mind because it was such a distressing experience.

Some further comments made by Professor Dunne about the boys in Tralee, included, "they were pathetically grateful, and almost tried to form some kind of.....bond with you". The boys were very "surprised to be talked to in a way that wasn't authoritarian, and they were almost pathetic in their response". He went on to comment on the "harsh demeanour of staff, and the cowed servility of the boys, so overwhelmingly grateful for any hint of kindness".

Another witness who was in the St Joseph's Residential Institution, from the late 1950s to the mid-1960s described the environment as one "of constant fear which overrode everything else for him". It was a "frightening place", and he was "terrified of the place". [This would have covered some part of the period of my time at St Joseph's Institution].

The commission came to the conclusion that bullying was part of life in Tralee, and contributed to a climate of fear that pervaded the Institution.

When you speak of abuse, and fear, it was something all of us boys experienced. On one occasion, I'm not sure what age I was, but I was still sleeping in the Junior Dorm so I was still relatively young at the time. I was being called one morning with all the rest of the boys by a Brother Collins who was in charge that morning.

I'm not sure what actually happened, but I ended up being chased by Brother Collins [pseudonym] through the dorm. I headed for the infirmary, and ran up a few steps, and just inside the door, I hit my head on the corner of a piece of furniture cutting myself over my left eye. I was bleeding, and whatever the reason for the running was forgotten, and I was looked after by Brother Collins A few days later I met with Brother Collins at the stairs in the brothers quarters, he stopped to ask me was I alright, and said he was sorry for the incident. Brother Collins was one of the more decent brothers in the place, and he was also a good teacher. Like Professor Dunne suggested, I was so overcome by the gesture of kindness from Brother Collins that was what stuck in my memory more than the cause of the incident on that particular morning.

Sexual Abuse at St Joseph's

I have covered some of my involvement with Brother Raphael, who is mentioned under a pseudonym in the CICA, Ryan Report 2009, who looked after the Irish Dance School, the Altar Servers, and the Saturday showers. Brother Raphael was a peculiar type of man; he was elderly, well elderly to me at the time, who I think did some service in China on the missions. Looking back now I would suspect that he was sent to Tralee on semi-retirement. He seemed to be very deaf, and used to wear a hearing aid.

Apart from the unusual things he used to get up to during the Saturday showers, there were days that he used to pick out some young boys from the yard, including myself, and used to bring us one at a time to the bathroom in the brothers quarters, where I would strip off, and get into a bath full of water, and he would give me a complete bath, washing me down completely himself. After the bath he would dry me off, and I would get dressed again, and go back down to the yard.

This went on for some time. I was still very young, as I was seven years, and three months when I arrived, so it started not too long after that. I didn't think much about it at the time. Now, nothing untoward occurred during these baths. When I thought about it years later, I came to the view that he must have had a "fetish" for bathing young boys as would be described in today's terms. I wouldn't have thought at the time that there was any badness in him. Of course what he was doing was completely against normal practices, which was widely known by other brothers, but nobody interfered. Today it would be deemed some form of sexual behaviour, and could be prosecuted as such.

Strangely enough I have a memento from Brother Raphael, which he gave to me for my birthday, a small religious picture wishing me "many happy birthdays" which he signed, and is not dated. I don't remember any other time when somebody told me I had a birthday.

There were two other incidents which were definitely of a sexual nature that I suffered, the first being, not too long after I had arrived at the institution. I was just over seven years of age, and a new boy in the institution, when I was approached by a much older boy in the yard. He was on two crutches as there was something wrong with his legs. He told me he wanted me to go upstairs to the toilets attached to the dorms as he wanted to take my measurements for new underpants that were being given out.

I went upstairs with him, and he asked me to go into one of the cubicles, where he sat on the toilet seat, and took down my pants. He then took out a measuring tape [like a tailor's tape], and started to measure me around my privates. He began to feel my privates, and then he had some soap, and started to rub the soap on to my privates. On a couple of occasions he used the tape measure on me, and then stopped, I got dressed, and we went back down to the yard. I'm not sure, but I think he may have worked in the tailors shop. This happened on a number of occasions with this older boy, the last time somebody saw him with me at the toilets, and it never happened again.

The second incident happened while I was in my class room. There was a visiting priest who had come to review our religious education. He arrived, and took up the teacher's desk at the top of the class. Our teacher at the time left the class room so the priest was in charge. I was in one of the lower classes at the time, and I was still wearing short pants. The priest started to ask questions about our religious instruction, then he called a number of boys including myself, up to the teacher's desk, and we had to read something from our religion book standing beside the priest facing the class.

I went up when it was my turn, and started to read from the book. The priest put his arm around me, and pulled me closer towards him. Then he put his hand up the leg of my shorts, and started to feel my privates, and he continued to do this until I had finished reading. I then went back down to my seat. I wasn't the only boy he did that to that day. I didn't know who the priest was, never saw him before, and never saw him again.

These were incidents that have stuck in my mind all these years. I could not relate to anybody what had happened to me until I sent a report to the section in the Department of Education, who dealt with the Residential Institutions Redress Unit in which I outlined the events as I described. Copy of that report appears further on in my final chapter.

I had big reservations about going to the Redress Board, which I eventually did in 2011. When I did go before them, they refused to hear my case because of my late application. [I will cover further on the events surrounding my Redress Board attendance]. When writing to the Department of Education during 2019, and 2020, before the covid-19 took its toll, I had a certain amount of trepidation because of the stigma which is forever attached, due to such happenings.

Other Observations, Comments, Witness Testimonies, and Conclusions from the CICA /Ryan Report 2009, with respect to St Joseph's Institution, Tralee, covering the period of my detention.

The negative impact of bad Resident Managers was clearly seen in Tralee, not only in terms of the physical care of the boys, but in every aspect of life there.

Boys should not have gone hungry whilst produce from the farm was sold for private profit. This situation continued for a number of years before being stopped by a newly appointed Resident Manager.

Only two Department of Education reports were made available to the Committee of Inquiry. In 1942 the level of education in most subjects was stated to be pitched at a lower standard than the official standard. In 1952 [the year I was incarcerated there] the education was reported to be "satisfactory".

A witness, who was in Tralee from the late 1950s to the mid-1960s stated to the Inquiry, "I can't remember any education. It was terrible because of the climate of fear; I was so frightened all the time." He was able to read, and write when he left Tralee, but not too well. He did learn how to read music while at Tralee. Apart from that he came out without any education.

Another complainant who was in the institution in the 1950s, [During my time there], said that the education he received there was both "good, and poor". He noted that "education in Ireland at that time actually was nonexistent".

The Inquiry concluded that the standard of education in Tralee was better than in some other residential institutions. The small-er numbers, the two genuinely interested Resident Managers in the

1950s, led to improved standards, a fact borne out by some of the complainants.

The inquiry on its conclusion regarding training for future employment outside the institution stated, only trades of the direct benefit to the institution were offered, and those that were provided, with the exception of farming, offered very limited employment opportunities. As the years went by, the trades became more, and more irrelevant, and outdated, but no changes were made to reflect this fact. Boys were prepared for a lifetime of labouring, and menial tasks.

On emotional abuse the Inquiry found that, throughout the relevant period, Tralee had brothers who were unduly severe, and harsh with the boys. Where physical punishment is perpetrated arbitrarily, and excessively, a climate of fear builds up, which can impact on every aspect of life in the institution. The boys lived in fear, and many complainants spoke of this undercurrent of fear in their everyday life in Tralee.

Tralee also had one acknowledged sexual abuser on the staff for a period of 20 years. Fear of speaking out, lack of confidence in the willingness of Brothers to listen to them; protect them, left the children particularly vulnerable to sexual predators. The fact that this brother could operate a bizarre ritual of bathing boys, and being bathed personally by them leaves no doubt that the boys in Tralee were not adequately protected by the system, and complaints were not properly dealt with.

In 1953 [my first full year in St Joseph's] the Visitation Report stressed contact rather than a relationship. It wrote that the Resident Manager's; "main contacts with the boys are.....Inspection every morning, the store, and distribution of clothing etc. when necessary and giving boys a Religious Instruction on Sundays."

In 1957 the Report remarked on the quality of emotional support. It noted the Brothers were generally "sympathetic, and considerate in their dealings with the boys, and hence the institution does as far as possible, resemble a home", and **there was no attempt to run away.**

The 1959 visitation Report commented that the discipline was satisfactory, the boys are at their ease, and a spirit of cooperation, and good will prevails.

The School annals record in various years boys went home to their families for holidays. There are no records to show this happening after 1952.

The fact that boys were separated from their families created major problems, and had an emotional effect on the boys. They felt alienated from their roots, their family, friends, and had suffered a loss of personal identity. For example one witness told the Committee;

"The biggest abuse really is being denied any information about my family. Outside, the abuse I suffered, that has gone. You have your abuse, you have your beatings, and you take it and go. But the abuse that stays with me, and it stays with me to this day, I am now 76 years of age, is that I can never prove...I don't suppose there is one here in this room who doesn't know who their mother was, right? I never knew who my mother was, and why take me away from my mother, take me away from my brother, or my sister, and my friends, and take me and put me away? I had done nothing wrong to anybody, and I have been put away, sentenced to all those years for nothing."

I can relate to this account given by this witness, I am now going on 76 years of age myself as I write this. I was taken from my Foster Parents, and put away for many years, to satisfy the greed of some NSPCC Inspector.

Children in Tralee were susceptible to harsher treatment because they did not have parents to protect them. Troublesome Brothers, some known to be a danger to children, were posted to Tralee.

Boys recalled acts of kindness very vividly, because they stood out in a world where they were not the norm. Brothers were expected to keep their distance, and boys learned to hide their distress, loneliness, fear, and unhappiness.

I have given a brief account of the description of the situations that existed during the course of my detention in St Joseph's, Tralee. Unfortunately I wasn't called to give evidence before the Commission of Inquiry regarding my detention, had I been called to give evidence I would have replicated most of the evidence that was given as it related to me. It was a most distressing time of my

life when I think back now, and further stress was imposed on me when the "gates" were opened, and I was sent out to the wider world very much unprepared. I survived, and I think I did make a reasonable success of my life, considering the poor start I had.

Residential Institutions Redress Board

What I'm going to write about now could be classed as having one of the most profound effects on the later years of my life. It relates to what became commonly known as the Redress Board, which was set up under the Residential Institutions Redress Act of 2002. I had over time become aware of the existence of this Board, but never related its existence to my circumstances or my detention at St Joseph's Residential Institution, Tralee, and of course I was giving most of my concentration on my new life in retirement, and my family difficulties.

It was only on reading the, Ryan Commission to Inquire into Child Abuse, Report of 2009, after obtaining a copy of that Report, that I discovered that St Joseph's Residential Institution, Tralee was included in chapter [9] nine of the Report. Having obtained a copy of the Report, and reading through the portion relating to St Joseph's Residential Institution, Tralee, a number of times, I found that I could identify with most of what was contained in the Report. I found I could also identify some of the Christian Brothers mentioned even though pseudonyms were being used.

It of course brought back a flood of memories to me regarding my time in St Joseph's Residential Institution, Tralee, where I spent more than eight years of my young life. How I ended up in that Institution without any knowledge of whom I was, who my family were, and the total loss of my family. It also brought to mind the harsh regime that was at the Institution, including the physical, and sexual abuse I had suffered which I had tried to blot from my memory, and hide all my life.

I thought long, and hard as to what I should do as I had never discussed my years of detention with anyone not even my family. I opened up to my new partner, Sonia, as to my situation, making up my mind that I would put in an application to the Residential Institutions Redress Board. Not knowing who I could turn to, I approached my solicitor whom I has used on previous occasions in other matters. My solicitor made a number of inquiries for me, and came back to me with the bad news that the date for applications to the Redress Board had expired on the 15th of December 2005. That was four years before the Ryan Commission to Inquire into Child Abuse, Report of 2009, had been released.

I did of course get a copy of the Residential Institutions Redress Act 2002, and saw that it was only open for applications from December 2002 to December 2005. Now, thinking back it was a most unusual piece of legislation, putting a time factor of three years for applications to be received, during a period of time when people like myself were not sure if the legislation related to us. One has to ask why then the new piece of legislation in 2011, extending the time for applications for a further period, to the 17th of September 2011.

My solicitor did suggest another path through the courts that he was aware of, as there were a number of other similar cases before the courts at that time. Well I informed my solicitor that my current financial situation, as well as my personal situation which he was also handling for me with respect to my divorce, would not allow me to take that direction. I left things be, and put it to the back of my mind. I had at that time opened up to my solicitor with respect to my former years at St Joseph's Residential Institution, Tralee, but at the time I did not go into the full details of my abuse.

2011, A year to remember or to forget

Now 2011 was a most unusual year for both Sonia, and me with a lot of happenings taking place. It was also the year that I became aware that the Residential Institutions Redress Board gave notice in the Irish Times of an extension of time for applications to the Redress

Board. The incidents all started in February of that year. On the 14th, Valentine's day, I received word that Frans, my sister Joan's husband had passed away in Malta on that day. We did not make the funeral as Malta being a warm country; burials take place within 24 to 48 hours after a person dies. I was aware that Frans hadn't been well for some time. The previous year Sonia, and I had been to Malta, and had called to see him at the nursing home where he had been cared for. We did manage to get to Malta in April of 2011 for Easter, and of course met up with Joan, and her family to pay our respects for their loss. We also attended some of the Easter functions, as Malta is big into putting on the big religious spectacles for all occasions.

On the 21st of June 2011, Sonia's sister Doreen, and her husband Joey arrived in Ireland, for a week's holidays, staying with Sonia, and myself. We had plans to bring them to see some of the sites around Ireland, either by bus tours or driving to various places. Our first stop on their first day here was to pay a visit to Dublin Zoo on the 22nd of June. Half way around our Zoo visit I began to feel unwell, so we cancelled the rest of the day, and went home, and I went to bed. The following day I went to see the doctor, and told him I had a problem doing my pee, and he put me on antibiotics, and I went back to my bed. Sonia had to look after her holiday makers on her own. At least she could communicate in her own language, Maltese, as Joey, Doreen's husband, didn't speak a word of English.

The following day the 24th of June there was no change so Sonia brought me to the hospital in Mullingar, where I was immediately admitted, and had a Catheter inserted, and what a relief. It turned out I had a very bad kidney infection. I remained in the hospital for a number of days, and got home on the 29th of June, just in time to see Doreen, and Joey off at the airport. I still had my Catheter, and my bag attached. Sonia did her best to accommodate Doreen, and Joey, even bringing them to visit me in the hospital. I was to see a specialist over the next few weeks about my infection problem.

The day after I had been released from the hospital while at home I began to feel a strange tingling as I would call it, in my hands, and feet. Over the next few days I saw the doctor, and he couldn't understand it. Each day it began to get worse, so much so that, when my son Ger called on the Saturday the 2nd of July with his daughter Hannah, I was afraid to hold her for fear I might drop her as my hands, and feet were growing weaker. We tried to do a bit of a BQ in the back garden, but I had to let Ger do it himself. Ger went home with Hannah, and I went up to bed. Sonia was at work.

After Sonia came home from work the following day, on July 3rd, she brought me back to Mullingar hospital where I was admitted, and brought straight to an ICU ward for observation. At that time I couldn't walk or use my arms. At the hospital they carried out numerous tests which included taking fluid from my spine with a syringe. On the 5th of July I was taken to Tullamore hospital to have an MRI scan done. The Mullingar hospital Consultant came to see me, and she told me that she suspected I had "Guillain Barre Syndrome", which was a disorder of the nervous system, which was a very rare occurrence, and she was putting me on a special drip fluid to begin my treatment. I had previously met her over the past week when I had been in contact with my kidney infection.

The consultant informed me that she was going to have me taken to the Neurology Department at Tallaght hospital where I would be under Dr McCabe, who was the consultant Neurologist at the hospital. On the 6th of July I was transferred to Tallaght Hospital by ambulance, I was in a wheelchair with my tubes for my medication attached. I must have been some sight.

I will always remember when I was being wheeled into the hospital along the main corridor I met with James Flynn, whom I worked with in Musgrave Cash, and Carry. He was going the other way heading out pushing a wheelchair also, with his sick daughter on it. James stopped, and looked at me in total surprise at my predicament; we passed greetings to each other, and went on our way.

I was aware that James's daughter was suffering from a rare form of cancer, the thought crossed my mind, "there's always somebody worse off than you". While I was still being treated over the next few weeks James's daughter passed away. I was allowed out of the hospital to attend her funeral, with strict instructions that I had a limited amount of time to stay out, and I couldn't be more than ten miles from the hospital in case of a relapse. It was a very sad situation for anyone to lose a daughter so young, and here was a man in my 60s going to pull through, such is life.

All together I spent over three weeks in hospital recovering from my ordeal, which consisted of many days of severe pain early on, until they settled on a pain medication that was suitable for me. I stayed on that medication until early 2014, after my arrival in Malta, when I began to wean myself off the strong medication after spending almost three years on it. That experience I went through in June to July 2011 was something I would not want to go through again, and I wouldn't wish it on anybody.

I remember one day during the course of my treatment I was wheeled down to the physio department, for some type of workout. When I got there I was sitting on a seat waiting for the physio to appear. When she did come in she told me to stand up, which I was just about able to do, she then said to take a few steps, but I couldn't move my feet. She said to me wait a minute, and came back with a zimmer frame which I held onto, and moved a few steps with some effort. I remember thinking to myself "is this it for the future". I was told to sit down again, and she informed me she would send a zimmer frame for my size to my ward, and I was wheeled back to my room. Thankfully the zimmer frame never arrived as I began to regain my strength, and move around myself.

When I was released from the hospital I had to receive physio for some time after to get my hands, and legs working as near normal as possible. Even trying to pick something up with my fingers was difficult for a time. I had of course several consultations with my Neurologist over a period, until I departed Ireland in 2013.

To continue with our 2011 happenings, Sonia, and I made plans to travel to Malta for Christmas as I had never been there over Christmas time. We were booked to fly out on the 16th of December 2011, and return in early January 2012. Sometime in early December Sonia got word that her mother wasn't well, and may have to go into hospital. On the 5th of December 2011 I left Sonia to the airport to catch her flight to Malta, flying with Ryanair.

To add to our complications, after I left Sonia at the airport, I headed straight to see my doctor as I had a pain in my right leg, and it was swollen. I didn't mention it to Sonia at the time as she had enough on her plate with her mother being ill. My doctor told me to go to the hospital immediately as I possibly had a DVT on my right leg. I went to Mullingar again, and I was taken back into hospital for treatment for my DVT. Now, Sonia was in Malta so when she phoned I filled her in as to what was happening from my hospital bed. Her mother was also moved to hospital in Malta, and Sonia was spending most of her time with her, with other members of the family.

On the 12th of December 2011 Sonia phoned me, and told me that her mother passed away that morning early. I remember having to take the phone call in the toilet in the hospital because we weren't supposed to use mobile phones in the unit I was in. I had been released from the hospital after about a week, but I was attending daily at the warfarin clinic, at Mullingar hospital after that. Sonia arrived back on the 16th of December 2011, and I collected her at the airport. It was the same date that we were supposed to fly out to Malta for Christmas. That was a year.

Now we had our Ryanair tickets for flying out to Malta which we were not going to use. In January 2012 after the date we were supposed to return, I wrote a report for Sonia, outlining the circumstances for not using our flight tickets. Without going too deep into it, we got a full refund on our unused tickets from Ryanair, as well as a message of sympathy for Sonia's loss of her mother.

Redress Board Application 2011

During the time I was recuperating at home after my several weeks in hospital with the "Guillain Barre Syndrome", I got into the habit of buying a paper each day while on my way home from my daily recommended exercise walk. On one particular day I spotted an advertisement in the Irish Times, indicating that the Residential Institutions Redress Board had extended the time for applications to it, to the 17th of September 2011. This would have been in late July or early August of that year. I immediately made contact with my solicitor on the 9th of August 2011.

Now, an application form was downloaded by my solicitor on the instruction of a person from the office of the Redress Board, who stated that, that particular form was the one to use, even though there was a diagonal line stamped across each of the nine pages of the form showing "closing date for applications was 15 December 2005". This was the same original form that was used between 2002, and 2005 for applications to the Redress Board.

My solicitor forwarded the application by registered post to the Redress Board on the 17th of August 2011, which they acknowledged they received on the 18th of August 2011. For some unknown reason I did not retain a copy of my completed application, and I don't think my solicitor gave me a copy either. At the time I did hand a copy of notes of my memories in respect of happenings between 1946, and 1961 to my solicitor to enable him to fill out the application form which I did keep a copy of.

Maybe it was a mental thing, as here I was documenting something about incidents in my "previous" life, which I had never before discussed with anybody, with respect to my detention in St Joseph's Residential Institution, Tralee, and outlining the abuse I had suffered all those years ago.

The following is an outline of the fourteen [14] sections of the nine [9] page application form, with questions which had to be completed.

1. Details of the injured person.
2. Evidence of identity,
3. Details of person applying on behalf of an injured person,
4. Details of your Solicitor [if any],

5. Institution[s] in which the injured person was resident,
6. Description of abuse suffered by injured person,
7. Description of injuries resulting from abuse,
8. Other evidence in support of this application,
9. Civil or criminal proceedings arising from abuse,
10. Expenses,
11. Settlement of application by agreement,
12. Interim Award,
13. If you wish to add anything to the information............,
14. Declaration, plus documents enclosed with this application, and passport photo.

On the 30th of August 2011 the Residential Institutions Redress Board wrote to my solicitor with a series of ten [10] questions with respect to my "late application". I reproduce the letter from the Redress Board, including the questions, with "huge emphasis" on the words "Late Application" which by the way had been received well before the 17th of September 2011, deadline.

Residential Institutions Redress Board

My Solicitors;
Lucan,
Co Dublin.
Our Reference Code; 2713L
Your Reference code; JOD/bb
Your Client;   **Maurice Heffernan**
                            Late Application
30/08/2011

Dear Sirs,

We write in respect of the above, and refer to your letter of 17/08/2011 which was received here on the 18/08/2011 enclosing a Late Application on behalf of Mr Heffernan.

Please be advised that in order to enable the Board deal with the Late Application filed by you on behalf of Mr Maurice Heffernan, it will be necessary for you to take your clients instructions in respect of the following matters;-

1. When did your client first learn of the existence of the Residential Institutions Redress Board?
2. Who advised him of the existence of the Residential Institutions Redress Board?
3. When did he become aware that he was entitled to file an Application with the Residential Institutions Redress Board?
4. Has your client or any 3rd party on your client's behalf requested an Application Form at any time from the Redress Board?
5. Has your client or any 3rd party on your clients behalf, filed an Application with the Redress Board before the Late Application which was filed with the Board on 18/08/2011.
6. Has your client or any 3rd party on your clients behalf applied to the Redress Board before the Late Application which was filed with the Board 18/08/2011.
7. The Board also requires you to furnish it with an Affidavit of ID confirming that your client is one, and the same person as is referred to in the Long Form State Birth Certificate, and Photo ID.
8. The Board carried out an extensive advertising campaign in Ireland during the period December 2002 to December 2005.

Advertisements were placed in all National Broadsheets, and Tabloid Newspapers as well as provincial Newspapers.

Advertisements were placed on RTE 1 Television, Network 2, Sky 1, Sky News, TV 3, and TG 4.

The Redress Board also placed advertisements on all National, and Major Local Radio Stations.

The Redress Board placed advertisements in all Irish Daily Newspapers highlighting each Ministerial Order which added to the Institutions listed in the Schedule of Residential Institutions Redress Act 2002.

It also placed advertisements in the main Irish Newspapers advising Applicants of the closing date for receipt of Applications being the 15th December 2005.

Please take your clients instructions as to whether or not he saw and/or heard any of the extensive advertising campaign carried out by the Board referred to above.

9. The Board would welcome some explanation from your client as to why he was not in a position to file an Application with the Board on or before the closing date being the 15th December 2005, and whether there were any "exceptional circumstances" which prevented your client from doing so.

The Board would also welcome a further explanation from your client as to why he was not in a position to file a Late Application with the Board since December 2005 until recently, and what if any are the "exceptional circumstances" which prevented your client filing a Late Application until now.

10. Please let us have a copy of your clients Medical Records to include GP Records, Hospital Records, and any other Records and/or notes, which are in existence, and relate to the treatment of your client as an in-patient and/or out-patient in any General and/or psychiatric Hospital for the years from the 1st December 2000 to January 2006.

Please be advised the Board will not be in a position to give further consideration to this Late Application until they have heard from you with a response to the matters set out above.

Your faithfully,

Registrar to the Late Applications Sub Division of the Board.

Through my solicitor I responded to the ten queries raised by the Redress Board with replies as follows.

1. Our client first became aware of the existence of the Residential Institutions Redress Board with the media publicity surrounding high profile incidents of abuse in Institutions in Dublin. It was not until the publication of the Ryan Report in 2009

that our client related his set of circumstances with a potential application to the Redress Board. It was at this stage that he learned that the deadline for applications had passed in December 2005.

2. Our client became aware of the Redress Board himself after reading a section of the Ryan Report relating to the residential institution, which he attended namely St Joseph's Residential Institution, Tralee. He then studied the Residential Institutions Act 2002 to gain as much information as he could about the Redress Board.

3. The Ryan Report contained a section relating to St Joseph's Residential Institution, Tralee, where our client attended. He was able to identify with the accounts of abuse perpetrated there, and recognized persons named in the Report. It was after this that our client felt that as a former resident who had suffered similar abuses, he was entitled to make an application to the Redress Board. Subsequently on making inquiries it transpired that the closing date for filing applications had passed as of December 2005.

In around August 2011 our client became aware of an advertisement published in The Irish Times which extended the date for applications to the 17th September 2011 it was then that we were contacted, and instructed to file an application with the Redress Board on his behalf.

4. We contacted the Redress Board to enquire as to the application process; we were directed to use the online application form.

5. No.

6. No

7. Affidavit of Identity duly sworn enclosed.

8. Our client instructed us that although he was aware of the Redress Board he was of the opinion that it was set up to deal with the controversy surrounding a number of high profile matters that were being constantly reported on by the media.

It wasn't until our client had read the Ryan Report that he related his set of circumstances to the Redress Board.

9. As outlined above our client was aware of the existence of a Redress Board from media, and news reports. He was somewhat uncertain whether his own set of circumstances would allow him to forward an application. The reporting on high profile cases affected our client's decision as to whether to come forward or not.

Our client had never discussed what happened to him with anyone, and felt a sense of shame, and embarrassment in coming forward. When he read the section of the Ryan Report dealing with St Joseph's Residential Institution, Tralee, he realised that other people had suffered similar abuses, and had given their accounts of what had happened. This gave our client the courage to take action. Subsequently he learned that he had missed the deadline for application to the Redress Board that passed in 2005. It was when he saw the advertisement in the Irish Times extending the deadline for applications that he sought our advice on.

Our client has had to live with the stigma, and trauma of what happened to him in St Joseph's Residential Institution, which, as outlined in his statement, has effected every area of his life, the reason for his late application has been outlined above, and we hope this is sufficient.

10. Our client suffered only minor health concerns between 1st December 2000, and January 2006 as such we will not be providing you with his medical records.

We look forward to hearing from you,;

Further communications with the Board

Further correspondence between the Redress Board, and my Solicitor ensued after the lodging of my application, the contents of which, I give a brief summary of.

There was a copy of a letter sent to my solicitor, which the Redress Board forwarded to the Christian Brothers Province Centre, at Marino, in Dublin, on the 02/09/2011, outlining my name, my reference code, my date of birth, and indicating my address prior to my "admission" to the institution, as Cahersiveen, Co Kerry. They indicated in the letter that the above applicant [myself] "alleges that he was resident in St Josephs, Tralee, Scheduled Institution from 1952 to 1956".

The letter was a request in writing, under the Residential Institutions Redress Act, for any information or documentation with respect to my residence, [detention] in the said Institution.

A note of interest with respect to this information that was sought, which I will comment on later, was not received at the offices of the Redress Board until the 28th of November 2011. Also they got the years wrong, stating I was in that Institution from 1952 to 1956, when it should have been 1952 to 1961. It gave me some indication of how serious an interest was taken to my application.

My solicitor received further correspondence dated the 24th of October 2011 from the Redress Board, headed Late Application to the Board, sent by the Registrar to the Late Applications Subdivision of the Board. It made references to my Late Application to the Board, as follows;

That my application was for an extension of time,
That it was being considered by the Late Applications Subdivision of the Board,
Making reference to Section 8[1] of the Redress Act 2002,
Showing the expiry date as the 15th December 2005,

Indicating that they were prepared to hold an oral hearing regarding my application.

That they will revert back in due course to arrange a date for the hearing.

My solicitor received a communication dated the 09/11/2011, headed "Notice of Hearing". It outlined a date for the hearing of my application as, 21/11/2011, at 10am, at the Boards office, at Clonskeagh.

Well the date for my "hearing" had arrived, but it wasn't the hearing I had expected.

CHAPTER THIRTY FIVE

The Hearing

My Residential Institutions Redress Board hearing was on the 21st November 2011 at 10am. I arrived early, and I was one of a number of people sitting in the waiting room. My solicitor arrived accompanied by another lady from his office. We had a discussion about what was going to happen, and he indicated that they may not want to hear my evidence about my time in St Josephs, Tralee. I became concerned as I had my complete notes covering what I knew of my life from 1946 to 1961.

I, and my representatives were called into the meeting room where the members of the Redress Board were in their chairs. Now, the best way to describe what took place is to reproduce some of the notes of the hearing as taken down by the stenographer for the hearing.

The Proceedings Commenced On The 21 November 2011 As Follows:
Chairman; Good morning Mr Heffernan, thank you for coming to see us. We do our best to be as informal as possible, but we do ask that you give your evidence on oath. Do you wish to do so by swearing on the bible?
A.   Yes.
[WITNESS IS SWORN IN]
Q.   Registrar: State your name please?
A.   Maurice Heffernan.
Chairman; Now, Mr. Heffernan, I'll just introduce you to the people sitting at the table. The lady on your right is the stenographer who keeps a note of the evidence. The lady you just

met is the registrar who organizes the meetings of the board. The gentleman on my right is a medical doctor, and Board member. The person on his right is a counsel to the Board, that person may have some questions for you in the course of the hearing. I am by occupation, a solicitor and I'm Chairman of this division of the Board.

And just to say to you, Mr Heffernan, we're not concerned today primarily about any abuse that you might have suffered whilst you were in care in Tralee, instead we want to hear from you about the circumstances in your own life between December 2002 until December 2005, because it was during those three years that the Board was open to receive applications, and your application wasn't received until the 18th of August of this year. Now, there is provision in the Act that sets up the Redress Board at section 8 that allows us to accept late applications such as this in what the Act calls exceptional circumstances. So that's what we want to focus upon today, and why we have asked you to come here. Now, Mr O'Donoghue.

MR. O'DONOGHUE: Now, just to commence, there is not really an awful lot we are going to be able to expand upon apart from what was stated in our letter of response at the beginning of September., and I must confess I'm not overly familiar with this actual procedure, I don't know if you want me to take?

Chairman; Well would you like to have a word with Counsel before we go any further?
MR O'DONOGHUE: Yes.
Chairman; Okay, we'll rise to allow you to have a word with Counsel.
After A Short Pause The Board Resumed As Follows:

Mr. Donoghue, my solicitor then thanked the chairman for the time, and went on to ask me to give an account of problems I was having in my personal life starting from the late 1990s. I said this was something very personal covering the fact that I was having problems with my marriage for some time. The chairman interjected saying anything said in this room will remain in this room.

I went on to cover the period of leaving my house in 2004, and over the following few years had a number of different addresses up to 2006. I also covered my retirement from the police force, and the efforts I had been making to try to trace some of my missing family.

I also spoke about my new employment with the census office in 2001, and how I was affected by the foot, and mouth scare, which caused the national census to be cancelled. I had some awareness of the existence of the Redress Board, but unfortunately at the time other matters in my life took precedence, I was trying to sort my life out.

I spoke about my getting to know about the Ryan Report 2009, when it was released. When I read it I discovered it covered St Joseph's Tralee. That was when I went to find out more about the Redress Board, and looked to make an application in 2009, but discovered that the applications were closed. That was the first time I discovered that there was an application time limit to December 2005. I didn't realise that, and I was terribly disappointed.

I then covered the period of my serious illness in July of 2011, and read the advertisement from the Redress Board, about the extension of time for applications. I made contact with my solicitor straight away, and put in an application.

I finished up with my direct evidence covering my current status with respect to family law proceedings going on at that time.

Q Chairman; Are they separation or divorce proceedings?

A They are divorce proceedings.

Q Is there anything else Mr O'Donoghue?

Mr. O'Donoghue: I don't think there is anything further we can add other than what Mr Heffernan has just stated.

Now came the "cross examination" by the "informal" Board members. Because of the repetitive nature of what came out of the "cross examination" which covers some 8 or 9 pages, I am just going to give a summary of some of the questions that were asked of me, with a brief account of my answers to them

Counsel for the Board

Q Mr Heffernan I think its common case that you were aware of the Scheme since [no date]----------

A Yes I was aware to some degree as a result of the publicity of some high profile cases, but I did not hear about St Joseph's being mentioned at that stage.

Q So you were aware of the Scheme, and you heard of some of the bigger cases as you say, the high profile cases?

A Yes;

Q And did you take any steps on foot of that information or that knowledge to see whether or not St Joseph's was included in the scheme or whether or not you were entitled to any compensation?

A No not at that stage,

Q I suppose from the point of view of the Board if somebody has been abused in care, and they are aware of the Scheme, the Board wonders why they wouldn't investigate whether or not the

Scheme applies to them when they know something about a scheme for abused children in care?

A I was aware of the Redress Board as a name, but wasn't aware as to what they were doing. It was not till 2009 when I read the Ryan report that I obtained a copy of the actual Redress Act.

Q So, you are saying that during the years 2002 to 2005 you weren't aware of what the Redress Board did?

A No I wasn't fully aware.

Q So you were retired from the Guarda at the time this was going on as well, you retired in 2001?

A Yes I was retired in 2001, also I was busy trying to get myself, and my family sorted out.

Q And I suppose the question would be why didn't you take any steps to find out whether it applied to you or not?

A I didn't take steps as the cases mentioned were high profile cases, as well as high profile institutions, and St Joseph's Institution wasn't one of them.

Q And I suppose from the point of view of the Board, what rank were you in the Guards?

A I was a Detective Sergeant.

Q How long were you in the Guards?

A I was in the Guards for 33 years.

Q So, from that point of view you were somebody that was well capable of investigating the matter yourself or checking it out or taking steps to find ------ you would have known how to go about it?

A Of course I would have. I did afterwards when I became aware of the Ryan report in 2009. I saw where St Joseph's was reported on, and if I had the same information in 2005 I would have done the same thing.

Q Were your sisters in care?

A I had one sister in care;

Q And do you know whether she made an application to the Board?

A No I don't think she did, she's living in London, and she wouldn't make an application.

Q She never discussed it with you?

A No, never discussed it with me.

Q And obviously you didn't meet your brothers in time so you don't know anything about those, they had died by the time you had tracked them down?

A No, the two brothers had died.

Q Sadly, yes. Had you kept up any contact with people that you had met in St Joseph's in Tralee?

A Yes, one or two people, but we never discussed anything.

Q And he never mentioned to you that he had applied or anything like that?

A No, it's one of those things you don't talk about, I haven't spoken to any of my family about this, you are the only people that know about it, and my solicitors.

Q Thank you very much;

Doctor, member of the Board

Q Mr. Heffernan, When did you find out that your two brothers had died?

A Around 2003.

Q Had they been in London?

A Derby, and Nottingham.

Q Now you did mention that you left the house in 2004; is that correct?

A That's right, yes August 2004.

Q Where did you live then?

A I was in addresses in Clondalkin, Kilcock, and then to Co Westmeath

Q So, you were with your partner during those years?

A I was Yes.

Q Now in terms of your health, I think there is a note that you had very minor problems between 2002, and 2005. Just going over that again did you have any particular health problems, now they are the particular years; I know you had something in this year?

A I hadn't had, maybe a hernia operation in 2004 or 2005.

Q Were you on any medication during that time?

A No, shortly after I was on blood pressure tablets.

Q I think this year you had a serious-------?

A It was a ---------

Q Thank you very much.

Chairman

Q Your two brothers have passed on, Mr Heffernan, and your sister in London is still alive?

A Yes I have four sisters still alive.

Q Were any of your four sisters in care?

A The girl that's in London was in care, she is next to me in the family.

Q Are you in touch with her?

A I am by phone, and if I'm in London I would go down to see her.

Q When you were hearing about what you call the something about high profile cases of abuse did you think to mention to your sister about what was being discussed about you were hearing in the newspapers or on the TV?

A I didn't, as I know that she wouldn't have anything to do with it.

Q What about your other three sisters, were they in care?

A No they weren't.

Q And I think you were saying you left the police at the end of 2001?

A Yes.

Q And you were going to take a job with the census?

A Yes, I was actually, but the foot, and mouth came in that year unfortunately.

Q Did you take up other employment after that?

A I did, I started with the company in October 2001, and retired last year.

Q So, you were working throughout the period 2002 to 2005?

A Yes trying to keep the job going as well.

Q And you never thought when you were hearing about the high profile cases to go speak to your own solicitor Mr Bowman or Mr McCabe?

A No I didn't as I thought they were high profile cases. I didn't have enough information on the Redress Board.

Q I know, but you didn't think of going to see if your solicitor would be able to or the citizens advice bureau or your local TD or councillor who would be able to find out some information for you.

A No, not at that time, also there was a lot going on in my private life, leading me to retire when I did.

Q And in terms of the job you were doing, how many hours a day or how many days a week were you working?

A It was a 24/7 job type job,

Q Did you have time off?

A Yes of course.

Q And do you have any children of your own?

A Yes I have six children.

Q What ages are your children?

A The youngest is 21years this year, and the oldest will be nearly 40.;

Q How is your relationship with them?

A Very good, I have a very good relationship with my children.

Q Do they know about your childhood?

A No, I wouldn't have discussed my days in residential institution with anybody.

Q But, I think did you say you disclosed it when you joined the police?

A Well I had to of course, It's on my file yes.

Q Did you tell your wife or your ex-wife? Was she aware?

A She would have been aware to some degree that I went to school in Tralee, but I wouldn't have told her the full facts.

Q But she would be aware that you went to St Joseph's?

A Yes.

Q All right thank you Mr Heffernan is that your case Mr O'Donoghue,

That's our case Mr Chairman, yes;

Chairman; Well we will rise to consider the matter, and will return shortly.

After A Short Pause The Board Resumed As Follows:
Chairman

Now, Mr Heffernan, the doctor, and I have been considering your case, and we want to consider it a little more, but we don't want to keep you here indefinitely while we are doing that. So what we'll do is we'll conclude our deliberations, and we'll issue our decision in writing to your solicitors, and then they'll be in a position to send it on to you. Was there any travel or expenses for today? You came in from Co Westmeath this morning Mr Heffernan.

Okay, thank you for your assistance this morning, and we'll be in touch soon with Bowman McCabe solicitors.

Thank you;

The proceedings then concluded
My Observations

Before I go on any further into the results of my appearance before the Board on the 21/11/2011. I make some observation with regards to the "Hearing" I received from the Board.

Let me first of all ask the question, where in the Residential Institutions Redress Act 2002 does the legislation make any mention of a Late Applications Sub-Division of the Board? Part of the reason I raise this question is that the application sent by my solicitor on my behalf, was on an original application form, which was the same as was being used between 2002, and 2005. It did bear the closing date of December 2005. The form was not shown as a Late Application Form, and it was not shown as a Form for an extension of times either.

I would consider that this was not a Redress hearing as described under the Residential Institutions Redress Act 2002, and I would consider myself as not having appeared before the Redress Board for a Redress hearing.

There was a bit of a contradiction in the chairman's opening remarks when he intimated the they would do their best to be as informal as possible, then goes on to tell me I had to give my evidence of oath, and had to be sworn in. This wasn't an informal hearing it was the same as a court hearing.

The letter from the Christian Brothers confirming my detention at St Joseph's Tralee didn't arrive with the Board until the 28th of November 2011 as I later learned, one week after I had attended for the "Hearing", so the Board weren't in possession of all the supporting facts on the 21/11/2011. Again another indication as to how serious my application was viewed. They did use the information from those documents in their determination, giving me information I was not privy to up to that time.

I had made my preparations for a Redress Board hearing, and had all my necessary papers with me for that purpose. I was prepared to cover my years from 1946 to 1961, which was from the time of the death of my mother to the time I was released from St Joseph's Residential Institution Tralee. At no time during the hearing, was my period of detention at St Joseph's Tralee, discussed.

The whole hearing evolved around the years 2002 to 2005, and why I made a late application. They covered my relationships with my brothers all four of whom had been deceased for a number of years at that time. They didn't indicate if they were aware that I had four brothers. They also wanted to know about, my sisters, my marriage, my current employment, and my previous employment in the police force.

They also wanted to know about my own children, how many I had, and my relationship with them. They never touched on anything about my detention in St Joseph's Tralee, or any of the abuses I suffered. This hearing wasn't supposes to be about me in my 50s, and 60s it was supposed to examine the period of my detention, from the time I was just over 7years of age until I was almost 16years of age, in St Joseph's Institution, Tralee.

I was of course mystified, and totally unprepared as was my solicitor, so much so that after the chairman's introductions, and opening statement, my solicitor had to have an early adjournment to confer with the Boards Counsel as to the procedures for this type of hearing.

Other, matters that arose during the "cross examination", I was asked could I not have investigated some matters myself. I wasn't the investigator in this case the "Board" were there for that purpose. The Board showed a total lack of understanding towards me as an abused person, not taking into consideration the difficulty in coming forward to admit, after all those years that I was abused as a child. They didn't take into consideration the trauma, and the embarrassment that it caused in later life, and to suggest that I should have gone, and spoken to, my local TD, the Citizens Advice Bureau, or my local Councillor, this wasn't a matter for such open discussion with public figures.

Also the counsel for the Board seemed to get confused when asking about my retirement; I retired in December 2000, and was retired in the year 2001. She, and other Board members kept asking about my retirement in 2001, suggesting that I had retired in 2001. The counsel in Q 10 asked why I didn't take any steps to find out if St Joseph's was included in the scheme, when I had already stated in answer to Q 7, that St Joseph's wasn't mentioned in reports that I had heard about.

Again the counsel mentioned that I was retired from the Guards at the time this was going on as well, mentioned again that I retired in 2001. Now, if the counsel was talking about the Redress Board Scheme, as going on at that time, that Scheme did not come into operation until December of 2002. There was no Scheme in operation at the time of my retirement.

It begs the question as to how prepared the Board were themselves with respect to this type of hearing, considering that most of the conversation was about the years between 2002, and 2005.

On reflection now, when I think of the situation that I found myself in November 2011, if it was to occur again, under my current situation, I would certainly have a different approach. When the chairman put it to me that **"we're not concerned today primarily about any abuse that you might have suffered whilst you were in care in Tralee"**, my reaction today would be to stand up, and walk out, as I wasn't there to talk about my life between 2002, and 2005. I was there to talk about my time in St Joseph's Institution between 1952, and

1961. Hindsight of course is a great thing, giving me an insight as to how I could have approached my situation differently. My mindset at the time was different, I was the forever good subordinate, going with the flow, not rocking the boat, and being forever compliant with the system.

CHAPTER THIRTY SIX

Decision of the Board, and their Determination

My solicitor received correspondence from the Registrar to the Late Applications Division of the Board, dated the 2nd February 2012 which included the Formal Order, and Determination of the Board which I summarise as follows;

> The Board had considered the request of the applicant for an extension of the application period in respect of this application.
>
> The Board has considered the request, and decided:
>
> The Board **does not consider** that there are exceptional circumstances within the meaning of the S. 8[2] of the Residential Institutions Act, 2002 [hereinafter "The Act"] such as to allow the Board to exercise its discretion under the Act.
>
> In reaching the decision the Board has considered
>
> [1] The application received from the applicant
>
> [2] All accompanying documentation
>
> [3] All explanations tendered by or on behalf of the applicant together with any submissions made on the applicant's behalf.

The application is therefore **not validly** received within the statutory period provided in the Act, and **will not** be further considered.

The Determination, which consists of four fully typed pages which were also attached, is too repetitive to reproduce in its complete format, but what follows is a general outline of its contents, with comments, and observations by me on some aspects of the Boards Determination, as I go through it.

Applicant: **Maurice Heffernan**
RIRB Ref: **2713L**

Determination

Mr. Heffernan was born on the 10th of September 1945. His application Form was received by the Redress Board on the 18th day of August, 2011. It appears from the papers which the Redress Board received that the Applicant was admitted to St Joseph's Residential Institution, Tralee, in the County of Kerry on the 12th of December 1952, and was discharged on licence on the 5th of August 1961. The Applicant alleges that during his residence in St Joseph's Residential Institution, he was abused within the meaning of the Residential Institution Redress Act 2002.

This was a huge revelation to me as I never knew the date I had been committed to St Joseph's, Tralee, or the date that I had been discharged. I would disagree with the use of the term "admitted" to St Joseph's Residential Institution, Tralee, I didn't seek to go there, I was **sentenced** by a District Justice of the District Court, Tralee, and **committed** to St Joseph's Residential Institution in Tralee. This information, with documents, came late for my hearing from the Christian Brothers, and was totally new to me.

Also the Board states in their determination, that "I alleged I was abused" during my residence in St Joseph's Residential Institution, under the meaning of the Residential Institutions Redress Act 2002. This was not given in my direct evidence at my "Hearing" as I was barred from saying anything about my abuse, during the period I spent at St Joseph's, Tralee. This information would have appeared on my original application, so they decided to comment on that piece from my application even though there was a restriction put on any mention of this at my "Hearing". The use of the term "alleges" would give an indication that I might not be telling the truth.

The Applicants Application for an "extension of time" in which to bring his substantive Application for Redress was initially considered by the "Late Applications Sub-Division" of the Redress Board on the basis of the documents lodged by him. To enable him to give an explanation as why he had not lodged his Application prior to the 15th day of December 2005, an Oral Hearing was held at the Board premises at which the Applicant was represented.

Again the Board is staying with this idea that my application was for an extension of time, and that it was a form of late application, the new closing date in my view was now the 17th of September 2011 as shown in Residential Institutions Redress [Amendment] Act 2011.

> The Board put great emphasise on the fact that I had been a member of An Garda Siochana, and I had been a Detective Sergeant. The fact that I didn't take any steps to investigate the matter, that I would have been capable of investigating matters further regarding the Redress Board, was commented on several times.

The fact that I had been a member of An Garda Siochana certainly played against me with the Redress Board. I think the Board lost the plot with regards to the effects that any abuse would have on people in different walks of life like me. The more you are involved with society, and the public, the less inclined you would be to reveal any type of abuse in your younger years. I think the Board didn't understand the psychological effects of the early years of abuse on any of us former residents. It should not have mattered what role I played in my later life, even if I had achieved a certain amount of success. In my view the Redress Board was using the yardstick for the later years of my life instead of concentrating on my early years in St Joseph's Residential Institution, Tralee.

The Board stated; The above [reference to the evidence provided] constitutes the essential documentary, and oral evidence provided by the Applicant to the Board in relation to which it must decide whether or not to exercise its discretion in favour of granting the Applicant an extension of time in which to bring his substantive Application for redress.

In considering the Application under Section 8[2] of the Residential Institutions Redress Act 2002, the Board must have regard to the provisions of Section 8[1] of the Act which is clear, and unambiguous. Section 8[1] sets out the general rule in relation to the limitation period within which Applications to the Redress Board must be made. This section reads as follows: "An Applicant shall make an Application to the Redress Board within three years of the Establishment Date." By the Residential Institutions Redress Act 2002 [Establishment Day] Order 2002, the 16th of December 2002 was appointed as the Board's Establishment Day. Accordingly, the closing date for receipt of Applications was fixed as the 15th day of December, 2005. However, the Board may under Section 8[2] of the Act "at its discretion, and where it considers there are exceptional circumstances, extend the period referred to in sub section [1]." The Board notes that as of the closing date of 15th December, 2005 the Board had received 14,768 Applications.

There is no definition of "exceptional circumstances" included in the 2002 Act.

The board goes on to quote the Oxford English Dictionary's definition of "exceptional circumstances". They then go on to say that the Board does not consider that it is possible to define in advance what circumstances might be considered exceptional.

However such an approach does not prevent the Board from envisaging or surmising what sort of individual circumstances in a particular case might be considered exceptional, e.g. the effect or impact of mental or physical health problems or conditions on a particular individual; **personal family circumstances, whether in applicant's own life or in the lives of others for whom he cares;** communication problems; or difficulties with legal advice. Any of these types of circumstances, prevailing at a relevant time, could have the effect of preventing or inhibiting an applicant from making an application within the prescribed period, and could be considered exceptional.

I have a number of comments regarding this section of the Boards Determination in which they make comments on sections of the "Act", and also the definition of "exceptional circumstances".

First of all they have concentrated, and quoted the Sections 8[1], and 8[2] of the Act with respect to the time limits for forwarding Applications. They have totally ignored the amendments brought in by the Residential Institutions Redress [Amendment] Act 2011. In that short Act, which has only two sections, 1. And 2; Section 1. of the 2011 Act clearly states; **Section 8 of the Residential Institutions Redress Act 2002 is amended by the inserting the following subsection after subsection [3];** In my view this includes all sub-sections, [1] [2], and [3], which to me allows Applications to be considered up to the 17th of September 2011. From my limited knowledge of interpreting criminal legislation over my service in An Garda Siochana, I would consider that all of Section 8 of the 2002 Act was amended by Section 1 [4] of the 2011 Act.

The board then goes on to discuss what "exceptional circumstances" are, stating that the Board is not prevented from envisaging or surmising what sort of individual circumstances in a particular case might be considered exceptional. They go on to give a number of examples of exceptions, including, **"personal family circumstances, whether in the applicant's own life or in the lives of others whom he or she cares".**

They go on to state that any of the circumstances as they described, prevailing at a relevant time, could have the effect of preventing or inhibiting an applicant from making an application within the prescribed period, and could be considered exceptional. I have to ask the question, should my family circumstances at the relevant time have been considered exceptional? What could be a more "personal family circumstance" than the breakdown of my marriage around that time, and my subsequent divorce some years later?

The Board then commented on their National Advertising Campaign over the course of 2002, and 2005 in various sections of the national media, covering both printed media, and radio, and television media. They stated that the Board was satisfied that the advertising, and information campaign described constituted a more than reasonable effort to make former residents living in the Republic Of Ireland aware of its functions to make awards, particularly when assessed in light of the Boards knowledge of previous, and ongoing departmental initiatives. The Board's conclusion that the efforts made pursuant to Section 5 [1] [b] were reasonable, and that it had complied with its statutory duty under the Subsection it re-enforced when one considers the success of the campaign in Ireland.

Taking what the Board said about their advertising campaign, and their knowledge of previous ongoing departmental initiatives, they failed to take note of a case around that period where the Revenue Department mailed thousands of pensioners in respect of a tax review on pensions, saying at a parliamentary committee of inquiry, "**that they could not rely on advertising campaign**". The Board also made a great play about their compliance with Section 5 [1] [b] of the 2002 Act. That subsection states as follows;

[b] Make all reasonable efforts, through public advertising, "**direct correspondence with persons who were residents of an institution, and otherwise**", to insure that persons who were residents of an institution are made aware of the functions, referred to in "paragraph [a]", of the Board.

Now the Board did its advertising, but it failed to have, **direct correspondence with the residents of institutions.** They had communication with the Christian Brothers Headquarters, and could have received all the information regarding former residents. They had also, as in my own case the name of the company, I was sent to for my first employment, a source, through whom, they could have obtained my Social Welfare number which would have provided them with a current address for contact purposes. It would have been far cheaper than the advertising campaign they were purported to have engaged in. It is my opinion that the Board did not carry out all of its functions, under Section 5 [1] [b] of the Act.

The final comments in the Boards determination were as follows;

The Board has considered in detail the circumstances which existed in the Applicant's life during the period 2002, and 2005, and indeed the case put forward by and on his behalf regarding the difficulties in his life at that time. **The Board notes that during the period in question, the Applicant was able to keep down a full time job,** and was aware of the existence of the Redress Board through media coverage of cases before the Board during 2002-2005. **Mr Heffernan accepted that as a Detective Sergeant in the Gardai, and his membership thereof for a period of thirty three years,** he was capable of ascertaining what the ambit of the Redress Scheme was, had he decided to do so at that time. The Board acknowledges the difficulties which the Applicant experienced, as set out in his oral, and documentary evidence regarding the traumas which occurred in his family life in or around 2002- 2005. However the Board is unable to except that the circumstances of the Applicant in this case come within the definition of "exceptional circumstances" as applied to the Scheme.

Accordingly, taking all relevant factors into account, the Board refuses the Applicant's Application under Section 8 [2] of the 2002 Act, for an extension of time in which to bring his substantive Application for Redress.

Dated this the 31st day of January, 2012

Signed Solicitor
Chairperson
Doctor, board member.

Looking at the final comments from the Board, which made reference to the fact that I had kept down a "full time job" and "had been a Detective Sergeant in the Gardai", I have to raise the question as to what that has to do with my situation when I was seven years, and three months of age when I was "committed" to St Joseph's Institution. I was absolutely disgusted when I read the contents of the "Determination" of the Redress Board, it had all the hallmarks of a "judgement" which had been issued by the courts with respect to my "Hearing" which was supposed to have been an informal affair.

I also felt that the comment with respect to my keeping down a "full time job" was a very demeaning comment, and gave the impression that the Board were very surprised at meeting someone who had done more than just survived the years, after being discharged from an Institution.

I immediately set about, putting down my observation regarding the contents of the document containing the determination of the Board, some aspects of which I have already covered above. I discussed my observations with my solicitor which he forwarded to the Redress Board on my behalf in the form of a response to the Boards Determinations.

With respect to the Board's stated closing date of the 15th of December 2005 for applications, figures given in later years by the Board themselves, indicate that over 20% of applications were received after that closing date.

Some further comments from my own observations which weren't touched on by my solicitor included the following;

As an individual I believe I have done reasonably well under the circumstances, and I have survived many of the pitfalls that can befall a former resident of an Institution. I believe that because I have come through seemingly unscathed has been another factor in the conclusion arrived at by the "Late Applications Subdivision of the Redress Board".

I felt I had been let down again by another "arm of the State" who through their agents at the time of my young life, took me from my family, put me in an institution, fostered me out, put me back into another Institution, during the course of which I was abused, and at times badly treated.

I felt it was a sad state of affairs when one opened up one's soul to a group of total strangers after being asked to do so, on the pretence of delivering Redress for the wrongs done, and then my story to be slapped down as a total fabrication, which amounts to a certain type of abuse in itself.

CHAPTER THIRTY SEVEN

Final Rebuke from the Redress Board

Well the correspondence didn't end with the forwarding of my observations to the Redress Board through my solicitor on the 20th of March 2012, regarding their rejection, and determination of the 31st of January 2012. On the 28th of March 2012 my solicitor received further correspondence with some attachments, dated the 27th of March 2012 from a solicitor to the Board. This was somebody I had never heard about, and who wasn't at my "Hearing".

The attachments included the following, with a covering letter from the "solicitor" to the Board.

Copy of the Transcript of the Hearing of the 21st November 2011, which I had requested.

Copy of the RIRB copy, of the printout from the skills database of the Department of Education which the Board received on the 23rd of August 2011, three months before my Hearing, which I knew nothing about.

Documents from the Archivist for the Christian Brothers with respect to my Detention at St Joseph's Residential Institution, Tralee, containing information I was never privy to, and received by the Board a week after my "Hearing".

The letter [three pages] that arrived with the attachments from the solicitor to the Board is worthy of a full reproduction as it gives a true example of how I, as a survivor of Residential Institution abuse, was treated by the Redress Board. It was on Residential Institution Redress Board, headed paper with references codes, and sent through my solicitor.

Re: Your Client: Maurice Heffernan,
Late Application
27th March 2012

Dear Sirs,

We write in respect of the above, and refer to your letter of the 20th of March, which was received here on the 21st the contents of which we have noted.

Please be advised that when your client filed a Late Application with the Board on the 18th of August 2011 one of the preliminary matters which the Board sets about inquiring is whether or not an Applicant was resident in a Scheduled Institution in accordance with the provisions of Section 7 [1] of the Residential Institutions Redress Act, 2002 a copy of which is enclosed herewith for ease of reference.

The Board has access to a Department of Education, and Skills Database that provides limited information, and in this regard we enclose herewith copy of that Database Printout which the Board took up on the 23rd of August 2011, and placed on your client's file.

In addition to this in order to get a full set of any documents that might exist in relation to your client's residence in a Scheduled Institution the Board writes to the Archivist for the Christian Brothers, and in this regard we enclose a copy of the letter which we forwarded to them on the 2nd of September 2011.

It should be noted that at the time of the Hearing on the 21st of November 2011 the Board had not received a response from the Congregation of Christian Brothers, and the same was only received on the 28th of November 2011, a copy of which is enclosed.

You will see that neither of those documents would have provided the Board with a direct contact address for Mr Heffernan.

With regards to your query as to what the term "discharge on licence" means you will see from the documents furnished that Mr Heffernan was "sentenced" in Tralee District Court on the 12th of December, 1952 to be "detained" in a Scheduled Institution until the 9th of September, 1961 which would have been the eve of his 16th birthday.

Mr Heffernan was in fact "released" from the Scheduled Institution on the 5th day of August 1961 i.e. he was released before his Scheduled discharge date, and it is our understanding that the reference to him being "on licence" refers to the fact that he was let out in advance of his discharge date.

The Board enclosed herewith a full copy of the Transcript of the Hearing which took place at its offices on the 21st of November, 2011.

The Board does not understand how Mr Heffernan would have felt that he was filing an Application as opposed to a Late Application to the Board when he filed an Application on the 16th of September, 2011. [This should have read the 18th August 2011]

You will see from the Form of Application which was completed by Mr Heffernan that it refers to a closing date for Applications being December 2005.

The Scheme established by the Residential Institutions Redress Act, 2002 was for a period of 3 years from the Establishment Date as provided at Section 8 [1] of the Residential Institutions Redress Act, 2002.

The Establishment Date was prescribed by the Minister as the 16th of December 2002 a copy of Ministerial Order is enclosed herewith for your information, and attention.

This means that the board was able to receive ordinary Applications up to, and including midnight on the 15th of December 2005.

However Section 8 [2], and 8 [3] allowed for Applications to be made after that time provided that they met the requirements set out at Section 8 [2], and 8 [3] thereof.

It also became apparent to the Board that in order to complete its work it would be necessary to have amending Legislation enacted that would provide a further closing date for receipt of applications under Section 8 [2], and 8 [3] of the Residential Institutions Redress Act 2002, and this additional closing date was implemented by the Residential Institutions Redress [Amendment] Act, 2011 a copy of which is also enclosed herewith for ease of reference.

The Board is at a loss to understand how it would have made direct contact with Mr Heffernan taking into account of the last details for him appear to be his father's address in Ballylongford, Co Kerry, or the original placement with Weartex Clothing Factory which took place in August 1961.

The Board further notes the comments made by Mr Heffernan in paragraph 7 of his letter of the 20th of March 2012, and have brought these to the attention of the Board who dealt with this Application on that day.

We trust that the above correspondence deals with the matters raised by your client in his correspondence, of course, ultimately it is a matter for yourself, and your client what further action you may take arising from the Formal Order, and Written Determination of the Board which issued in this case on the 31st January 2012.

We trust that this is in order.

All parties are reminded by the Board that confidentiality is of the utmost importance in these matters.

Please be advised that these documents are furnished to you on the strict understanding that you deal with same in accordance with

the provisions of section 28 [6], and [9] of the 2002 Act which states as follows:

"S.28 [6] A person shall not publish any information concerning an application or an award made under the Act that refers to any other person [including an applicant], relevant person or institution by name or which could reasonably lead to the identification of any other person [including an applicant], a relevant person or an institution referred to in an application made under this Act.

S, 28[9] A person who contravenes subsection [1] or subsection [6] shall be guilty of an offence".

Yours faithfully,
Solicitor to the Board
Encls [7]

The above final communication from the solicitor to the Residential Institutions Redress Board, consisting of three pages, broken into twenty paragraphs, was received at my solicitor's office on the 28th of March 2012, which he forwarded to me on the 29th of March 2012. On digesting that communication for some time after, I came to the conclusion that it was a futile exercise entering any further communication with the Residential Institutions Redress Board, as they seemed to be stonewalling their stance with regards to my application.

From time to time I reverted back to the correspondence from the Redress Board, my dealings with them, trying to suppress my anger, my disappointment, my embarrassment, my disgust, at the treatment that was meted out by the Board. I ended up leaving Ireland at a later date resulting partly, from this outrage on my person. I have kept as many documents as I possibly could relating to my "Hearing" by the Board, and now I make some comments, and observations regarding this final communication from a solicitor to the Board.

Comment and Observations
In paragraph 2 the Boards solicitor put great emphasis on the filing of my late application, on the 18th of August 2011, also stating that the

Board had to confirm that I was a resident of a Residential Institution, under the Residential Institutions Redress Act 2002.

Then the solicitor goes on to comment on how I could have felt that I was filing an application, on the 16th of September 2011, typing error or indication of the lack of seriousness in the interest in my case. [This should have read the 18th of August 2011]

Going on to Paragraph 3 of this communication, the solicitor outlined that the Board had access to the Department of Education, and Skills Database, from where they obtained a Database print-out, confirming my detention in St Joseph's Residential Institution, Tralee, which they had possession of on the 23rd of August 2011. The information contained in the Database printout, was confirmed by the documents received from the Christian Brothers on the 28th of November 2011. The information contained in the Database printout is as follows;

RIRB

COPY	Report by School Number, and Pupil Number
School	26
Number	2000
File	Y
Surname	Heffernan
First names	Maurice
Sex	M
DOB	10/09/1945
Court	Tralee DC
Court Date	12/12/1952
Judge	MacEoin
Grounds	Section 58 [1[[b] [y]
Referred by	M O'Regan NSPCC
Admission	12/12/1952
Discharge	09/09/1961
Mother	
Father	John Heffernan, Lislaughtin, Ballylongford, Co Kerry.
Postdischa	Discharged while on licence

Comments   Born at Lislaughtin, Ballylongford, on licence, 05/08/1961, to Mr Grief, Managing Director, Weartex clothing Factory, Aideen Place, Kimmage Road, Dublin. See 26/1818, 27/953-955. Father a widower

Birthplace Kerry

GENREGNO 92874.

23 August 2011.

With respect to the comments made in paragraph 6 about these documents not providing direct contact with "Mr Heffernan" [myself], they had, almost, my full life story up to August 1961 in those documents. There was a huge amount of information contained in both the Department of Education, and Skills Database printout, and the communication forwarded by the Christian Brothers as well as other information in their possession for the period of my detention.

If the Redress Board had, between 2002, and 2005 got all the Database printouts from the Department of Education, and Skills, in respect of all persons who had been residents of Residential Institutions, as well as the information in the possession of the Christian Brothers, they could, with the help of other Government Departments like the Social Welfare Department, have been able to make **direct** contact with most of the residents of Residential Institutions, as with most of us, in our first employment we would have been allocated a Social Welfare number, which today is our PPS Number. They could have as I have previously stated, saved a considerable amount of money on advertising.

Also, you have the mention in paragraph 17, of the "Boards loss of understanding" as to how it would have been able to make direct contact with me a former Resident of an Institution. The Board failed me, and many more former Residents of Institutions miserably in their duties to carry out their functions under Section 5 [1] [b] of the Residential Institutions Redress Act 2002 which states as follows;

Section 5 [1] The Board shall,

[b] make all reasonable efforts, through public advertisement, direct correspondence with persons who were residents of an institution, and otherwise, to ensure that persons who were residents of an institution are made aware of the function, referred to in paragraph [a], of the Board,

There was no direct correspondence with Residents of Institutions by the Redress Board to my knowledge, which is the failing I am referring to.

With respect to my query about being "discharged on licence" I am glad to see that we agree on the terms, "Sentenced" in Tralee, District Court, and "detained" in a Scheduled Institution[St Joseph's Residential Institution]. The Chairman in his final Determination seemed to prefer the use of a milder term "admitted" to St Joseph's Institution.

The reference to being "discharged on licence" would seem to refer to me being "let out" in advance of my discharge date. From reading this part of the communication, it would seem that the authors of this communication are of the opinion that they were dealing with a young juvenile criminal being released from a Scheduled Institution, and not a boy who was detained at seven years, and three months of age, for the "**crime of being a child**".

It seems to me that this was a very misunderstanding Board, as again they didn't understand as to how I would have felt, that I was filing an Application as opposed to a Late Application to the Board. Well it is very simple, I sent in my Application on an "original application form" which my solicitor had downloaded on the instructions from the office of the Redress Board.

As I have previously made reference too, this application form consisted of 9 pages with 14 sections to be completed. Stamped across each page was "closing date for applications was the 15 December 2005". It did not indicate that this was a Late Application Form, nor did it say that this was a "Form for an Extension of Time", terms that have been mentioned on several occasions by the Redress Board. To me this was an application made under the extension granted by the Residential Institutions Redress [Amendment] Act 2011.

In paragraph 16 the author of this communication outlines the reason given for the enacting of further legislation, that would provide a further closing date for receipt of applications under Section 8[2], and 8 [3] of the Residential Institutions Redress Act 2002, and this additional closing date was implemented by the Residential Institutions Redress [Amendment] Act 2011. Now, the author did not go into too much detail about this important piece of legislation, but a copy was enclosed for my information.

Section 1 of the Residential Institutions Redress [Amendment] Act 2011, states, "**Section 8" of the Residential Institutions Act 2002 is amended by inserting the following subsection after subsection [3].**

[4] Notwithstanding the provisions of this Act the Board shall not consider an application under this section that is made on or after 17 September 2011.

Now to my mind anybody reading this piece of legislation with any bit of experience, would see that the amending legislation refers to all of Section 8 of the 2002 Act, it doesn't say that Section 8 [2], and 8 [3] only are amended, it states Section 8 which is comprised of 3 subsections [1] [2], and [3] is amended by the 2011 Act.

Paragraph 18, I take it deals with my reference to the comment made in the determination of the Board where they stated that the "Applicant was able to keep down a full time job" as being a demeaning comment.

The final portion of the three page document refers to "confidentiality being of the utmost importance", which outlined in full, Section 28 of the Act of 2002, to draw my attention to the fact that I would be guilty of a criminal offence if I disclosed any information regarding my "Hearing" or documents received" by me from the Board.

This was the final piece of "informality" surrounding my appearance at my "informal Hearing" on the 21st of November 2011. Yes it was a complete "gagging" order which could be punished by a term of imprisonment. Nice touch by the Redress Board, starting my life in a "Detention Centre", and they want to put me back into "Detention" at the end of my days if I divulge information which effected my whole life. It was my life that was effected so I think I am entitled to tell my story the way I see it.

I suppose that confidentiality clause in the 2002 Act, does not inhibit, the legal profession from using their association with the Redress Board to promote themselves on Google. If you Google the solicitor for the Board, it states: "Experience, I am the sole solicitor for the Irish Redress Board where to date, I have overseen the completion of 16,650 applications, and redress of €953million euros".

Well that about sums up my observations of the workings of the Redress Board, with regards to my own situation. To use a term mentioned in some of the communications from the Redress Board, "I am at a loss" as how a solicitor to the Board, could operate from a London office, were they London based solicitors?, if so their understanding of the Irish situation would be very limited, which is exhibited in the correspondence in my own case. From reading through the correspondence as I have outlined above, it shows a total lack of understanding of my situation with regards to my application to the Redress Board.

CHAPTER THIRTY EIGHT

The fallout from my dealings with the Redress Board, 2011/2012

After the debacle of my Redress Board "Hearing", their issuing of their determination in respect of my case, I wanted to hide myself under the nearest stone. I was still "holding down my job" with the Musgrave Group. My official retirement age with that company was 65yrs, which I had reached the previous September 2010, but I was enticed to stay on for a further period which I did on a contract basis. I set up my own company business name to enable me to stay with the Musgrave Group, which was another enlightening experience for me. I registered my new business under the name "Maurson" in September 2010. I operated under this business name for about three years, which was up to the time I left Ireland.

Then came the Redress Board in 2011. I have already commented on what a year 2011 was for both Sonia, and me with respect to health, and family issues. Well you could extend that extraordinary period to include January to March 2012 when the Redress Boards determination was released through my solicitor. All the courage I had gained in making the decision to present myself before the Redress Board for a "Hearing" vanished after the way I was treated by them, not to re-emerge until 2019 when I picked up courage again to write to the Department of Education, and Skills, after reading that the then Minister for Education, and Skills, Mr McHugh was setting up a Consultation Process for Survivors of Residential Institution Abuse. That report was published in August 2019.

After the rebuke from the Redress Board, whose final communication came to me at the end of March 2012, I discussed the whole matter with Sonia, as at the time she was employed full time in Ireland. I told her I wanted to leave Ireland, and leave this sorry mess behind me. I was in a rage at the time, and I did not want to spend any more time than was necessary in Ireland. None of my family would have been aware of the trauma I was experiencing as I would not have yet enlightened any of them, as to my previous life history. At that time I was also going through my divorce proceedings, and waiting for the date of the hearing to be set.

Sonia being from Malta, and my association with Malta through my sister Joan over the previous twenty years or more was where I decided to fix my sights, as my new destination in which to settle down. I started to do my homework on our exit from Ireland. I got a hearing date set for my divorce in June 2012, which was cancelled, and rescheduled for the 10th of July 2012. My case was heard on that date, and my divorce was granted. Now, we could go into full swing arranging our departure from Ireland which we fixed for September 2013.

In May 2013 we travelled to Malta to arrange to rent a place to stay for our arrival in September. We were successful at our first viewing, a new three bedroom apartment just being completed, unfurnished which suited us fine, as we had planned to bring all our furniture with us. We then also made arrangements for our wedding in Malta, which we wanted to keep a small affair, on a date in September 2013, getting to know what documentation was needed for that purpose.

Working 2001 to 2013

Now going back a bit to the first of October 2001, I had started working with Musgrave Cash, and Carry, Robinhood, Clondalkin, as it was known at that time, as Security Manager. The job specifications at the time included, supervising a number of security personnel, responsibility for overall security of the premises security systems, cash collections, and deliveries, goods going into, and leaving the premises, and security of personnel working in the Cash, and Carry. Over time I was tasked with a number of other responsibilities, Health, and Safety Officer, Fire Safety-holding fire drills, Manual Handling Instructor, Improving energy consumption.

My new boss was Matt Lee, who was the General Manager of Musgrave Robinhood. Strangely enough, I had got to know Matt a number of years previously, as he was also a great friend of Frank Colgan of the Lucan Spa Hotel, where he used to socialise, and where I got to know him well through my dealings with Frank, and through the Lucan Spa Hotel Golf Society. I also had the pleasure of being invited to a number of annual Musgrave customer golf outings prior to my retirement from An Garda Siochana, which continued into my years of employment with Musgrave Robinhood.

I had built up a good relationship with Matt prior to him employing me as his Security Manager at Robinhood. He would have had a good knowledge of my working background at the time.

You would think that when one would go into retirement, and get re-employed in civilian life that your days of "schooling" would be over. That wasn't the case as during the course of my time with Musgrave I assembled quite a few more "Certificates" of qualifications, in a number of other fields related to my new employment, including, Certificates in Health, and Safety, Manual Handling, Fire, and Security, as well as Instructors Certificates in both Manual Handling, and Health, and Safety on behalf of Musgrave. It certainly gave me a good insight as to the strict procedures in the running of a business within the Legislation Governing Large Company's.

Regarding the improvement of energy consumption, the company had employed an outside energy specialist to give advice on energy saving projects. I was the contact person for Musgrave with this energy company. We were successful in introducing some energy saving systems, which resulted in both me, and the energy specialist being presented with an award for our efforts.

I could go on, and on with regards to my time with the Musgrave Group. It was a marvellous experience to be working with a company in civilian life, with the difference in personnel management. Again as with my time in An Garda Siochana, I made many new friends, and comrades while working with the company. As with everything in life there always comes the low period, and the low period for me while with Musgrave was that a few years into my term with Musgrave we were hit with a burglary one night. A large quantity of cigarettes were stolen, which we had no luck in recovering. This put a big damper on my spirits at the time as it happened under my watch.

I had been away a short time before the event, in London visiting one of my sisters. Of course I had my suspicions, that it may have been a repeat performance of an incident of 1993, [a previous burglary], with the same persons involved, as a payback for the term of imprisonment served by the main instigator of that crime at that time. It had also come to my attention some months previous that while I was away, a person had been employed in the delivery section of the warehouse, without having come through my office for vetting. Of course when I heard his name at that time, I nearly exploded as his father was a well-known criminal with all sorts of connections in the criminal world, and would also have been associated with our man from an incident in 1993.

I took the manager of that section to task for signing on this man without checking with me first. His comments to me were that he had signed a contract, and there was nothing he could do at this stage. Not too long after the cigarette burglary this man left Musgrave. It left a lot to speculate on, as to what may have occurred. Well as they say you win some, and you lose some.

During my term with Musgrave I had over those years a number of good security personnel, and we all worked very well as a team. Unfortunately I had the task of ending the contract of one of the security personnel. As it happened he was the employee of a sub-contractor so it was only a matter of having him taken off the roster by his own company as he wasn't a Musgrave employee. Later I arranged for two retired members of An Garda Siochana, Peter, and Tim, who were both very well known to me to be employed with Musgrave on our security team, and they were still with the company when I left in 2013.

The Big Move

Looking back at the year 2013, after we had made our decision to leave Ireland, and relocate to Malta, we had a lot of work to get done over the period of a number of months prior to September 2013. After our return from our visit to Malta in May of 2013, we just had three months to get things done. Mind you when I look back now at the preparations we had to make, it's not something I would want to do too often.

We started to fill our cardboard boxes, making lists as we went along as to what Items each box contained, and numbering all the boxes as we filled them. I had no shortage of cardboard cartons available to me as I was able to save the ones I wanted from the crusher in the Cash, and Carry. This continued over time till our departure date came nearer, when we then had to concentrate on the bulky stuff, like beds, mattresses, box freezer, fridge, and the like which we also added to our list of items, and numbered. We had arranged for a forty foot container to be made available during the first week of September, and to be dropped in front of the house.

During our visit to Malta in May we had made arrangements with a Maltese freight company, Palm Shipping Agency, to look after the transport of the container in conjunction with an Irish freight company. One might ask why get a forty foot container, for the household goods, well we were also going to load Sonia's Z 3 BMW onto the container so we needed the extra space. It's amazing the amount of things that you accumulate over a short few years. We had a huge number of items including the packed cardboard cartons to load on to the container when it arrived.

On the day the container arrived we had plenty of help, my own boys, Mark, Niall, and Ger were there to help as well as some former workmates of Sonia's. When we had everything loaded I'm not sure if we had something to eat or not as most of the kitchen equipment had been loaded onto the container, but I think we kept back some small items as we still had another week to stay in the house so we more than likely had some tea or coffee. All the bedroom furniture was gone so we had to use blowup mattresses for the week. These we had from a previous overland trip we did to Malta in 2008, when we stayed in a few camping sites going through France.

There were also over a dozen items from the garden, the likes of garden furniture, BBQ set, small garden sheds, gardening tools including hedge trimmer, and a lawn mower etc. which we gave to my own boys to take between them. I had told them before they came to bring a trailer with them to carry away these items which they did.

There were some items that we would not put into the container, like of all my crystal glass, and some frames because of safety from breakage including a 19 inch TV. We did have a roof box for our Renault jeep so we had room for whatever we were keeping behind for the week we had left to stay in the house. Some days after the container had been loaded we had to go to the container yard to leave the Z3 BMW for loading. We had been keeping in close contact with the company in Malta through whom we had arranged everything, to discover in late August that the person we had been dealing with, Luke, had left the company. A new person by the name of Claire, had taken over our removal, and from then on we were not happy with the responses we were getting to our inquiries.

The arrangement that we had made with Luke was that we would be loading the container on one of three days, the 4th, 5th or 6th of September 2013, which would be arriving in Malta between the 18th, and 20th of September 2013. That was to be a week before our wedding, as we needed our furniture because we had my sister Lily, and my son Ger coming for the wedding.

Needless to say the container did not arrive on time in Malta, it was going to be a much longer wait than we expected.

Prior to our departure date, which we had arranged for the 10th of September 2013, [my 68th birthday] we still had a lot of finalising to do, matters like organising my medication for my first few months in Malta. I was still taking medication relating to my serious illnesses of

2011, for which I had to get prescriptions to cover my early months in Malta.

I had to give my notification of my finishing up with Musgrave, Robinhood, and Sonia had to arrange her notice of leaving employment with her employers. I have a note in my diary of making a trip to London, at the end of August 2013, which was to see the girls before we departed. Aoife, my youngest daughter, had gone to London on the 27th of June 2013, to stay with her older sister Noeleen. I had also become a grandad again twice before leaving Ireland. Mark, and Yvonne had their second child, a girl, Ella at the end of June. Noeleen, and Andy had their first child, a girl, Zoe in early August.

I also had to visit several Government Departments to arrange my documentation for my upcoming marriage to Sonia, in Malta on the 27th of September 2013. We also had to get our transport into reasonable condition prior to our long overland journey, changing the tyres, and getting good service. I also had to arrange insurance with the AA for a period of thirty days to cover the trip. All this time we kept trying to establish an arrival date for our container in Malta without any success.

Our arrangements for our departure were complete, we loaded up our transport complete with a roof box, and arranged to stay at the Lucan Spa Hotel that night the 9th of September 2013. We had arranged a small send off with a number of colleagues from my old Detective Unit, and from Musgrave's. My three boys were there as well. We had a nice evening at the Lucan Spa Hotel, and of course I was surprised by Matt Lee, who picked up the tab for the evening without me knowing it.

The following morning we headed off towards Rosslare Harbour to catch our ferry to Cherbourg, France. On our way we diverted slightly to meet up with my niece, Jeannie, my sister Kathy's daughter, for a coffee, and a chat. We sailed from Rosslaire at 9.30pm on the 10th of September 2013, and arrived at Cherbourg at around 3.30pm on the following day the 11th of September 2013. There was no turning back;

We travelled through France, Italy, Sicily, and onto Malta, arriving there some time on the 15th of September 2013. We arranged for the key of our new apartment, and moved in over the next couple of days. Again we had a lot of work to do to get the apartment ready for my sister Lily, and my son Ger who were coming for the wedding. We had to do with temporary furniture pieces which we borrowed to put up our guests. There was no sign of our container arriving, and it would not be here before our wedding day.

Of course there were other things to take care of after we had arrived, we had to have our Jeep re-registered with Maltese plates, get covered with local insurance, arrange for my medical attention at our local clinic, and of course trying to keep contacting Palm Shipping Agency with respect to the arrival of our container.

My sister Lily arrived on the 24th of September, and my son Ger arrived on the 25th of September both of whom we collected at the airport on their arrival.

On the afternoon of the 27th of September 2013, our wedding took place at the Mediterranean Centre, in Valletta with a small number of guests as we had arranged. It was a most unusual place for the ceremony with lovely surroundings. The regular office used for marriage ceremonies was in the process of being renovated, so we were one of the lucky few to have had our wedding in this particular venue. Afterwards we all adjourned to the Waterfront, Valletta, where we had a sit down meal in the 516 Restaurant, for about twenty guests including my son Ger, and my two sisters Joan, and Lily, with members of Sonia's family. Ger flew out on the 29th of September, and Lily on the 4th of October 2013.

Now after all the wedding celebrations were over, and our guests had departed for home we got back to concentrating on the whereabouts of our container of household goods. From inquiries with the shipping company Palm Shipping we were informed that our container was on a ship called "Lana", which was arriving at Malta docks on the 14th of October 2013. On that date we went to the docks, and saw that the ship had arrived, and we then made inquiries as to our container. On the following day the 15th of October 2013 we made contact with the people who were responsible for the movement of the container, and it had arrived in their yard.

We spoke with the people at the container yard, and at their suggestion we went to the container yard to have Sonia's Z3 BMW unloaded, as it suited them better to have it unloaded at the yard so as they would not have to bring a low loader with them to our door. Previously Sonia had been in touch with somebody from Palm Shipping who had intimated to her that they would give us a reduction in the cost of the shipping of the container because of the delay on the delivery.

This approach suddenly all changed on the day that the container was to be delivered to our door. We had made the arrangements to have the part of the roadway kept clear for the arrival of the container. This entailed getting the necessary permits from the local council offices which we had done, and had them displayed to have the roadway kept clear of parking. A man appeared at our door, and informed us that he was there to collect the money for the delivery of the container, and there was no discount, we were to pay the full amount due. We looked out, and saw that there was no container in sight. He then said we had to pay the money up front or the container would not be delivered. We were of the opinion that payment was to be made on delivery. After some discussions, and disagreements we eventually paid up the money in cash which was several thousand euros.

Within a few minutes of our paying the cash the container arrived after the man we paid, made a phone call. They had the container parked around on another road nearby waiting for the phone call that payment had been made. This was one of the greatest pieces of blackmail I have personally ever experienced, and in my view, would have amounted to demanding money with menaces. There was nothing we could do at the time, we did visit the offices of Palm Shipping later to make our protest as to the treatment we had received, but it was like talking to a blank wall.

So much for the Maltese welcome, I wasn't a bit impressed by the way we were treated, and for some time after our arrival, I was thinking of taking some form of legal action against Palm Shipping, for the huge delay in the delivery of our container of goods. After making some inquiries regarding taking some action, I put it out of my mind as I learned that anything going through the courts in Malta, with respect to civil actions, could take years.

Settling in to our new life in Malta

Well we put our early disappointments behind us, and went about sorting out our new flat over time as there was no hurry now. We began settling into our new life in Malta, which I always referred to as a most wonderful place that I first fell in love with on my first visit in 1987. I had left the scene of my embarrassment behind me, but it never left my mind.

Sonia started working with one of her former boss's again which was a bit stressful with long late hours, when she didn't get home till well after midnight sometimes. As well as that we were residing in the northern part of the Island, and she had to travel to the south of the Island to her work. Some years previously Sonia had worked for a Government agency, and around 2015 she managed to get re-employed in Government employment, and got a job in the north of the Island nearer home, which was a great relief.

Over time I got my Maltese documentation in order, I got my residence ID card, my Maltese driving licence, and my health entitlements sorted. I began to get to know my way around, doing plenty of walking while Sonia was at work. We were living in St Paul's Bay, which was a sizable area, with one of the largest populations on the Island. It is also a very popular tourist area with lots of tourists coming to the area where there are many hotels, and guesthouses. It is only about a five minute walk to the nearest view of the Mediterranean Sea from where we live. Most of my walking is along the promenade looking out onto the Mediterranean Sea, which covers areas such as , Qawra, Bugibba, Xemxjia, and St Paul's Bay, which could take me an hour or an hour, and a half depending on the route I would take. I take in views of St Paul's Island, not too far away, and during the good weather, which is most of the year; I can see the sister Islands of Comino, and Gozo.

We had arrived at a most opportune time as the weather was beginning to cool down, and the Autumn wind, and rains would be beginning. You learn of course that during the very hot weather which is usually in the months of July, and August, you get out very early for your exercise so as not to be caught in the heat. That's where the siesta for the hot afternoon comes into play. We have our own schedule for different times of the year. In the spring time between April, and early May we pick our crop of capers, which grow wild in the rocks by the sea. When we have about two dozen jars or so picked, we stop as that would be for use for the following year.

We have our two cars of course which we changed over the years to a Dacia Duster, and a Ford Ka, which Sonia uses for work most times, leaving the Dacia Duster for me for whatever appointments I might have to keep. Most times we keep them in a garage which we rent for safety, as well as the shortage of parking in our area. Recently Sonia purchased an electric scooter for work use, as part of her contribution to controlling the carbon emissions.

I'm now able to visit my sister Joan who is now 86 years of age, living in a nursing home not too far from where I live, and keeping up with her family. My own family has all been over at some time or other over the past years with the grandchildren for visits, but have been unable to travel over the past two years [2020/2021] because of the covid-19 restrictions. Hopefully that will change in the next year or so. I had a great surprise for my 70th in 2015 when some of my family arrived without me knowing it. Sonia had organised a little function at one of the local restaurants which was attended by a select few.

Over time since our arrival in Malta, we travelled back to Ireland on a number of occasions including two occasions to attend weddings of two of my family. We also travelled to England a number of times as well, two of those occasions to attend the funerals of two of my sisters in London, and Liverpool. We also travelled for the funeral of one of Sonia's uncles.

We travelled away over two Christmases, once to Dubai, and another time to Vienna, which were wonderful trips. We have also been away on a number of cruises which start, and end in Malta over the past few years, the last one being in 2021 to celebrate my 75th which should have happened the previous year, 2020, but had to be postponed due to covid-19.

Life has been good to us since we arrived, and in 2018 Sonia purchased a nice 19ft. Cruiser which we use for fishing, and travelling between Malta, and her two sister Islands, Gozo, and Comino. Of course because of Insurance restrictions we only use it between May, and September while the weather is favourable. We have had a few of our visitors out for trips in our boat, my nephew Robbie, and his son, my niece Sandra, and her husband Ray, and a good friend, Henry Bauress, and his wife Aida who were over here this year in September 2021.

We have yet to have my family over when our boat is in the water, but hopefully that will change, and we will be able to get the grandchildren onto the boat for a few trips.

A few Christmases ago we stopped going abroad for the festive season, and instead now we book into one of the big hotels in Valletta for the Christmas period, which is most enjoyable, and relaxing, and gives us both a break from home cooking, and chores.

Of course I never stop thinking about the way my life started, which is something that stays with you, never to be forgotten, and it will be with me till the day I die. It is these thoughts at times that make me think of my current situation, the changes in my life, my successes in life, and the successes of my own family, which makes it now for me a "wonderful life". At times when I listen to the radio certain songs come on the air, and bring tears to my eyes, like, the song "Nobody's Child", thinking about the orphanage I was in, "The Working Man" reminds of one of my brothers, Paddy, whom I never met, who worked in the Coal Mines, but then I hear the song "I Did it My Way", which reminds me a little bit of my journey through my later life which I believe I did my way.

August 2019, Report on Consultations with Survivors of Residential Institutional Abuse

In August 2019, which was some years after I began to settle into my new life in Malta, It came to my attention that a report had been published regarding consultations with survivors of Residential Institutional Abuse. I downloaded, and printed off a copy of this report, which had been produced by two facilitators named Barbara Walsh, and Catherine O'Connell on behalf of the Department of Education, and Skills.

I read this report with interest which I thought might be a ray of hope, that the cases of survivors of Residential Institutional Abuse might be reopened, and a renewed effort made for Redress, on behalf of us survivors.

Without going into the full details of the report, which consists of about 30 pages, I am reproducing excerpts from points made in the report, which would relate to my own situation, and I make comments, and observations as I go through each section of the report. In reading the report it reawakened my interest with regards to some form of Redress, after my debacle with the Redress Board in 2011/2012, so much so, that I started to correspond directly with the Department of Education, and Skills in October 2019.

It would seem that this consultation process was suggested sometime in December 2018, so in February 2019 the two facilitators, Ms. Walsh, and Ms. O'Connell were engaged by the Department of

Education, and Skills, to carry out the consultation process with survivors of Residential Institution Abuse.

Summary; page 4 of report

The facilitators in their summary on page four, intimated that in February 2019 the Department of Education, and Skills initiated a scoping study on a consultation process with survivors of Institutional abuse. Survivors were very clear as to what was needed, for all survivors of religious institutions, both those that benefited through the Redress Board, Caranua, and those that did not.

Survivors did not want consultations for consultations sake; they needed urgent action on the known needs which would include, health, housing, social services, and enough income to live with dignity. Survivors also stressed the need for a clear pathway to access medical, housing, financial, and other supports, as well as educational needs of a further generation affected by their time in institutions. Many survivors described their experiences of the Redress process as adversarial, difficult, traumatic, and negative.

Survivors expressed that although they had suffered greatly as a result of being in institutions, throughout their young, and adult lives, they were also resilient, courageous, and forward thinking. They welcomed a survivor led consultation process, focusing on the changing needs of survivors.

A survivor led consultation group has been formed. This is composed of two sub groups, one UK based, and one Ireland based. The group will work with the Government on meeting the needs of survivors over the next year.

From reading their summary, my comments would be that they have ticked many of the boxes with respect to my own views on aspects of the way survivors have been treated. Many of the suggestions put forward are what I would agree with myself, but trying to get them implemented is another matter entirely. Since their initial report was issued in August 2019 there has been no updates from

the survivor led consultation group, to my knowledge. I suspect that the change of Government, along with the problems of the Covid-19 has had a huge impact on the setting up of the consultation group. The comments regarding the Redress process would relate very much to what my own experiences were regarding the Redress Board Process.

Introduction; page 5 of report

Now I suppose any report can have i's "typo" errors. I know it was in December 2018, not in December 2019, as shown, when the Department of Education, and Skills, issued a tender for the scoping, planning, and design of consultation events for survivors of children's residential institutions. The tender specified that the facilitators were to work closely with survivors, and survivor representatives to,

Find out the level of interest,

Find out what issues they wish to consult on, e.g. Experiences of the Redress Board and other government led initiatives.

Find out the most important issues,

Establish a survivor-led working group, for part two of the project.

As facilitators both of them were aware that neither of them were survivors of institutional abuse. They recognize that while they can, and do try to understand survivor experiences, and what the impacts have been on them to the best of their ability, they can never fully comprehend them, because they have never experienced them.

I think that their comments with regards to their non-experience of institutional abuse, and their non-comprehension of the impact on survivors, because they never ever experienced them, says a lot about their understanding of the task in hand. Certainly a very different approach from that used in the process of the Redress Board.

How people were contacted; page 7 of report
Survivor Quote; "Anyone who is going to work with survivors must have empathy"

To make contact, and introduce this phase of the consultation process, the Department of Education, and Skills contacted survivor groups, and survivors on their database, and asked if they would be willing for us to contact them.

They [the facilitators] made contact with people by email, and telephone, who had contacted the Department of Education, and Skills, who were willing to take part in this process.

They had over 30 meetings, and engaged with over 100 people over a six month period from February to July 2019. Prior to, and during the consultation process they read up on several reports written by individuals, and organisations based on their experiences of survivor needs.

Survivor Quote; "What happened before is that they listened, and then did nothing"

It was of great interest to me to note that contact was made with people through the Department of Education, and Skills DataBase, with no mention of an advertising campaign. A far different approach than that made by the Residential Institutions Redress Board, who by the way had access to the Department of Education, and Skills DataBase as well, which they outlined in correspondence to myself, but saying that they had no way of making contact with me. I have already covered in some detail my views, and dealings with the Residential Institutions Redress Board, and their handling of my own case before that Board.

The facilitators outlined how, and whom they met, and spoke with over a period of six months from February to July 2019, that they had over 30 meetings, and engaged with more than 100 people. This would be one of the major faults I would find with this phase one of the consultations as I feel the numbers used for this phase of the process were very small, considering that between 1930, and

1970, over 42,000 boys passed through the institutions in question. Again we can't rule out the possibility that they were given a time limit in which to complete their report.

Again one has to pause, and reflect on how much real interest the Government of the day took, into the plight of survivors of institutional abuse.

Background to this consultation; page 8 of report

The facilitators in this section mention the public apology made by Bertie Ahern while he was Taoiseach, in 1999 to survivors of institutional abuse. They then go on to elaborate on the setting up of the Commission of inquiry into child abuse, the outcome of which was the Ryan Commission Report which was published in 2009. They then go on to state that included in the Ryan Commission recommendations was the setting up of the non-adversarial Residential Institutions Redress Board.

The facilitators give an account of further boards, and agencies that were set up to finance education, and training for former residents of designated institutions, and their relatives. They give an account of the number of people who accessed financial compensation through the Residential Institutions Redress Board, [report of 2016] giving a figure of 16,650. They also mention the body set up in 2013, "Caranua", who were supposed to give financial support to survivors.

There seems to be slight confusion with respect to their facts regarding the Ryan Report of 2009, and the setting up of the Residential Institutions Redress Board. The Residential Institutions Redress Board was established in December 2002, under the Residential Institutions Redress Act, 2002. It had a closing date of the 15th of December 2005, which was four years before the Ryan Commission Report was published. It is easy to understand how confusion can arise as over that period of time, there were several pieces of legislation brought out including the Amendment to the Residential Institutions Redress Act 2002, which came into force in September, 2011.

They quote from the 2016 report of the Residential Institutions Redress Board, where the number of people who accessed financial support up to then was 16,650, which is the same figure quoted by one of the solicitors for the Board on her Google self-promotion account.

The Survivors; Voice, intergenerational trauma; pages 9-10 of the report

The facilitators mentioned that while there is detailed information on the numbers of survivors, who were registered with the Residential Institutions Redress Board, there is no comprehensive information on the population of those survivors, of those institutions generally.

Talking about the submissions by survivors, in the Ryan Commissions Report, the facilitators mentioned that all were detained in Residential Institutions, with little or no control over what happened to them as children, and young adults.

Many survivors recounted how silence covers the shame, the trauma, humiliation, stigma, and judgement, experienced by them in Irish society as a result of having been in the institution they were detained in. This self-imposed secrecy is often a means of self-protection. Survivors spoke at their meetings of never telling anyone, not even their children of what had happened to them.

The planned legislation, which will see records from the Commission to enquire into child abuse, and the Residential Institutions Redress Board, put into the national archives of Ireland, and sealed for over a period of 75years was seen by some as a violation of the rights to their own stories.

Survivors often expressed that although they had suffered greatly as a result of being in institutions, throughout their young, and adult lives, they do not get acknowledgement for "surviving", and managing to live, work, parent their children, and educate them despite their early deprivation, and suffering.

Survivors speak of living with the trauma of the past which is ever present, and which has impacted their lives in ways others cannot understand. Professor Allan Carr [2009] acknowledges this, and states that the prevalence of psychological disorders among abuse survivors is twice that of the general population. He highlights the lifelong impacts of child abuse in institutions. What is now evident is that survivors, their children, and grandchildren are living with the legacy of that abuse.

Some survivors expressed great remorse at being unable to "parent" their children in the way that they would have liked to. For example, several survivors said they were unable to show love even though they loved their children deeply. They showed it by their actions, but yearned to be able to show it physically. Another spoke of their children's lives being "messed up" because they were so messed up themselves as a result of their own experiences. Other survivors spoke of being extra strong as parents to ensure that their children did not experience what they had, and they spoke of focusing all their energies to ensure that their children were educated to the highest level possible.

With reference to what they mentioned regarding the population of survivors of institutions, well there are a number of ways that could be found, to get updated figures, [1] Department of Education, and Skills, which kept all the educational records of residents of institutions, [2] the Christian Brothers Archives, which supplied the necessary information required by the Residential Institutions Redress Board, [3] a programme on RTE1, which was aired on the 2nd, and 3rd of March 2020, which was called "Redress". In that programme there was a figure quoted that more than 42,000 children had passed through Institutions between 1930, and 1970.

This information would seem to compound the failings of the Residential Institutions Redress Board, in their failure to make contact with former residents of Residential Institutions which the legislation directed them to do under section 5 [1] [b] of the Residential Institutions Redress Act, 2002. Now to add further

injury to former residents of institutions, they want to or maybe they already have, buried the records in the national archives for more than 75 years. Not only will they be covering up their inadequacies with respect to their dealings with survivors, but also the cost to the exchequer for their services, or should it be their disservice to the survivors.

I fully concur with the facilitator's paragraph on the voice, shame, secrecy, stigma, and judgement as it totally sums up my own personal journey through my life. I can also relate to Professor Alan Carr's summary with regards to the lifelong legacy of institutional abuse, it never leaves you.

Changing needs of an ageing survivor population;
Survivors living further afield;
What survivors in Ireland, and the UK said? Page 11 of report

80% of survivors are now over the age of 58 years, half of those are over 70 years with 7% over 80 years. [2019] Most of the survivors highlight the urgency of dealing with an ageing population of survivors, where health, housing, social support, and adequate income were vital for a dignified, and secure old age.

The facilitators did not engage with survivors outside the UK, and Ireland.

However many of the experiences, and concerns in both the UK, and Ireland were noted as similar.

I would think that the age profile of survivors would have changed in the recent past [2021] resulting from the effects of the covid-19 virus.

Yes, I am one of those outside of Ireland, and the UK. I would agree with a dedicated survivor web site or other form of communication which would be of interest for information purposes, although I'm of the old school, and not too much of a user of social media.

Survivors concerns in order of priority include; Page 12 of report

An ageing profile, and increased health needs;

Fear of institutionalisation in old age, [hospitals, nursing homes, etc.]

Adequate, and suitable housing,

Poverty - inadequate income,

Fear of isolation, and the need for social supports,

Neglecting the needs of hard to reach survivors,

The restrictions on obtaining counselling services,

Support in managing bureaucracy to access services,

The unequal treatment of survivors who didn't receive redress, and therefor couldn't access services, and funds through Caranua,

Lack of access to information, and files on their own, and their families histories,

Being seen as "helpless victims" rather than "resilient people" who survived despite the lack of support,

Resettlement options for survivors who returned to or wish to return to Ireland.

Priority Issues for Survivors Include; page 13 of report

An enhanced medical card [HAA Medical card] for all survivors regardless of whether they had gone through the Redress Board or not.

Consultation, and support for/with survivors for either home or nursing home care.

Prioritisation of housing needs for survivors.

A contributory pension to be paid to all survivors.

A designated drop-in centre or confidential space for survivors to meet, staffed by personnel that understand the nature, and extent of their needs.

Funeral expenses to be covered.

Free unlimited counselling service for survivors as long as they want it.

Counselling, and psychiatric services for children of survivors.

Education support for the children, and grandchildren of survivors.

Remembering survivors, [Memorials etc.]

Survivors who didn't receive Redress to be included in all services provided.

Tracing services for individuals wishing to find their families, and relatives.

Acknowledgement of the extra burden of racism experienced by some mixed-race survivors.

Records, and files to be made available to survivors.

I note that the two areas mentioned under, Survivor concerns, and Priority issues have many similarities, and duplication of suggestions, although under two different headings; There are many of the issues mentioned which I would have personal experience of myself, which would include the ageing profile. I am now going to be 76 years of age this September 2021.

Also I am no longer living in Ireland due mainly to the humiliation, and embarrassment, resulting from my appearance before the Redress Board on the 21ˢᵗ of November 2011. I'm also afraid that the issue of trying to trace my family members would be too late for me as over the past 40 years, I have succeeded to

some degree in finding most of my family except for two of my older brothers who had passed away by the time I had traced their whereabouts. Also I keep in mind that I only knew my father for about six years as he passed away in 1967, six years after I first met him prior to my leaving St Joseph's Institution, Tralee, in 1961. We never got around to talking about the reasons I had been taken from my home.

While I agree with most of the issues as suggested, that are being prioritised, because of my current situation living away from Ireland, I would more than likely not be able to avail of many of the benefits which might result from the consultation process, if indeed any conclusions were arrived at.

Survivors Experiences of the Redress Board, and Caranua; page 16 of report

Survivors, and their advocates said that there are many survivors living in Ireland, and the UK who did not access any financial compensation through the Redress Board because they chose not to at the time; they felt unable to mentally engage with it at the time; or they were unaware that such a compensation scheme existed in the first place. The date for redress had closed by the time some survivors had heard about it. It was a source of anger in both Ireland, and the UK that survivors who had not received compensation through the Redress Board or the Courts were then excluded from the Residential Institutions Statutory Fund [Caranua] established in March 2013. This was seen as a further injustice, and a sort of "double punishment".

Many whom we spoke to were critical of the Redress Board, and its adversarial approach to determining compensation for what they had suffered at a most vulnerable time in their lives. People spoke of being "on trial", and "going through a court as a guilty person. It was humiliating, and caused distress". According to another survivor, and advocate, "too many very hurt individuals were deeply distressed after their experience with the Board. A complete breakdown of trust followed, and in the end the pain, memories, and hurt linger. Nothing else." The judicial panels were criticised for being in their positions for too long leading them becoming "cold", "hardened", and "indifferent" to survivors which impacted on the decisions they made.

I fully concur with what is expressed in this section of the report, with regards to the experience with the Redress Board. Yes I did for some time feel mentally unable to broach the subject of my detention at St Joseph's Tralee, and the abuse I was subjected to. It was not until 2009 after reading the Ryan report that I picked up the courage to enquire into the Residential Institutions Redress Board, to discover that it had been closed for application since December 2005.

It was not until 2011, when I discovered that the date for applications had been extended to September 2011, that I made an application, got a date for a "Hearing", to be told at that "Hearing" that the Board did not want to hear about my time in St Joseph's from 1952 to 1961, but only wanted to know about what I was doing between 2002, and 2005.

I was asked at my hearing "So, you were working throughout the period 2002 to 2005?"

Again in the Boards determination it stated, "The Board notes that during the period in question, the Applicant was able to keep down a full time job, during 2002 - 2005". It gives some idea, as to the views held by the Board members, regarding survivor applicants. Again, as I may have stated previously, the Board, in my view anyway, were a bit surprised at meeting someone that had some success in the life he had chosen, and was gainfully employed.

The hurt, humiliation, and distress that it caused me, drove me to leaving Ireland in September 2013. I could not face the fact that I had opened my secret life to a bunch of insensitive strangers, and in place of redress I got rebuked.

Priority Needs - Health, Housing, Finance, and Social Supports. Page 18 of report

For Irish, and UK residents, health, end of life care, housing, social support, and finance are paramount. Survivors communicated a huge fear of being forced into an institution at the end of their life, and visits to hospitals were described as traumatic.

Irish residents stressed the need for the HAA medical card which other survivors of institutions have received.

Pension rights are important both in the UK, and Ireland. Wishes for an enhanced pension entitlement that would not impact on welfare benefits, and entitlements are important in the UK. In Ireland survivors wished to obtain a contributory pension to acknowledge the years spent working in Irish Institutions without payment.

I would not be adverse to the granting of the benefits as described above, even though I may not benefit from many of them. I have already forwarded some suggestions to the Department of Education, and Skills, which touch on some of the above suggestions, to be passed on, for the information of the survivor led consultative group, whenever that may convene.

Education; page 20 of report

"We are resilient, courageous, and forward thinking, and not just victims. We didn't get an education, but educated ourselves". [Survivor quote]

Survivors describe the level of education in the institutions they were placed in as very poor, and many survivors spent their lifetime in manual, casual, and other low paid work. They reported that this has had enormous impacts on the educational opportunities for their children, and their grandchildren.

Other survivors spoke of making sacrifices, past, and present, to ensure their children have the education that they were deprived of. Education is seen as a very important pathway to break the intergenerational legacy of institutional abuse.

"I had to struggle hard to get my child through college. My children were too young to benefit from education, and finance grants. I thought that there would be a fund there. That was removed in 2012. We have to break the cycle of abuse, and deprivation. Education is the only way"[survivor quote].

Well I have to totally agree with the sentiments expressed in this section, when you consider I had to put myself through schooling again, throughout my early years in Dublin. I later, put my own six children through their education to third level, had it not been for the good relationship I had built up with my bank, St Raphael's Garda Credit Union at the time, I dread to think what the outcome would have been if I hadn't an understanding with my financial institutions.

Remembering, and Honouring Survivors; page 21 of report

Survivors said that any memorial to survivors of institutional abuse should be in a public centrally- based space in Dublin, which could be seen, and visited easily by the public. Many survivors indicated that it should be a place of learning, and information, and should contain records, photographs, books, films, and documentaries for the families of future generations of survivors, and for society. It should be a place for the study of institutions for all students interested in the issue. It could also be a place where people could document their stories if they wished to do so.

One survivor said that for him, the only memorial should be "A National Day of Atonement" where society takes back the shame that had been wrongly placed on the most vulnerable in our society - children with no power or voice.

Campaigning, and lobbying to provide such a place have recently come to fruition with the recent decision by Dublin City Counsel to designate a former Magdalene Laundry on Sean McDermott Street Dublin as a "Site of Conscience". This has been welcomed by many, and is seen as a way that Irish society can pay homage, and remember those who suffered, and never repeat the harm of the past.

I think that the idea of a memorial to survivors is a welcome one, but I beg the question as to why in Dublin?, I'm not sure what the difference would be, between numbers from Dublin, and the rest of the country with respect to survivors from both areas. I did suggest in my correspondence with the Department, and Skills, in 2020, that any memorial building should be in close proximity to the seat of Government, to remind the current legislators of the input that their predecessors had into the running of the Residential Institutions over the many years that abuse occurred.

I think that the decision to locate a site at Sean McDermott, Street was premature considering that the Survivor Led Consultation Process hadn't yet started. It indicates a lack of co-ordination with respect to dealing with the problems of Survivors, which seems to be an ongoing problem, which is resulting in the inaction by the Government.

Survivor Led Consultation Group

Towards the close of their report the facilitators indicated that a Survivor Led Consultation Group had been formed, by people that expressed an interest in the next phase of the consultation process. The group is made up of survivors from both Ireland, and the UK. The UK based survivors will form a sub group focusing on the specific needs of survivors in the UK. Both groups are gender balanced.

I was delighted to read that the Survivor Led Group was formed, but I must ask the question as to how many more "phases" there must be before we see some concrete action.

I have tried to get an update on what is now happening [July 2021] to the Survivor Led Consultations Group. I googled the Department of Education, and Skills, regarding the Survivor Led Consultations Group, but the last account of it I can come up with was on the 16th January 2020 when they published the above report which I just covered. The silence about the current state of play is deafening. We are all aware of the current limitations regarding meetings etc., because of the pandemic, but at least tell us that that is the problem.

I believe that the publication of the report in August 2019 by both Ms Walshe, and Ms O'Connell was a very welcome step, and raised expectations in the minds of a good number of survivors. But alas, this coming August 2021 will be two years since the publication of the report, and not a word from our legislators. Are we the Survivors of Residential Institutional Abuse going for a big let down once again, I pray not?

CHAPTER FORTY

Direct correspondence with The Department of Education, and Skills

In October 2019, after discovering that a report regarding a series of consultations with survivors of residential institutions abuse had been published by the Department of Education, and Skills, in August 2019, I obtained a copy. After digesting the contents of the report which was issued by two facilitators, Ms Walshe, and Ms O'Connell, I began to correspond with the Department of Education, and Skills, who were responsible for the publishing of the Survivor Consultation Report.

As a result of what I had read, seeing that the then Minister for Education, and Skills of the time was showing some interest in the plight of the residential institutions abuse survivors, it reawakened my long lost courage of 2011, giving me the incentive to start to communicate again regarding my situation.

In the following pages I reproduce copies of the correspondence between The Department of Education, and Skills, and myself, from the 29th of October 2019, up to, and including the 11th of October 2021. One of the most enlightening things that came to my notice was that the office, within the Department of Education, and Skills that replied to my letters was the "Residential Institutions Redress Unit", within the Department of Education, and Skills.

This was totally new information to me, which raised the question again as to what the Residential Institutions Redress Board were doing that they did not get all the information that they required, in order to make contact with former residents of residential institutions, which they were required to do by The Residential Institutions Redress Act of 2002.

I began with my first letter to the Department of Education, and Skills, dated the 29ᵗʰ October 2019 as follows:

> The Office of the Minister
> For Education, and Skills,
>
> 29ᵗʰ October 2019.
>
> Dear Minister,
> If I might intrude on your time, I am writing to you as a "survivor" of Residential Institutional Abuse.
> I noted with interest your publication in August this year 2019, on a series of Consultations with survivors of Residential Institution Abuse.
> I am disappointed that I wasn't included in the Survivors Consultation process which was carried out by Ms. Barbara Walshe, and Ms. Catherine O'Connell ending with their report in July 2019. I may well be at fault myself as I had left Ireland in 2013, after I had attended before the Residential Institutions Redress Board on the 21ˢᵗ November 2011.
> I left Ireland because of the way I was treated with regards to my attendance before the Residential Institutions Board. I felt very embarrassed, and ashamed because I had opened my soul to a group of total strangers on this board. Luckily I had some place to go, and "hide" my embarrassment, and my shame.
> I am not going to go into any details of my story at this time as it would take too long. If I could be put in communication with some person dealing with this matter I would be grateful.

To help verify my situation I am providing a number of points which may be helpful.

[1] My application to the Residential Institutions Redress Board reference code is/was 2713L.

[2] The date of my hearing before the Redress Board was the 21st November 2011.

[3] I was "Detained" at St Joseph's Residential Institution, Tralee, between the 12th December 1952, and 5th of August 1961.

I hope these points will be helpful, I will provide any information required to whichever person will be dealing with this matter.

Maurice Heffernan.

Within the period of two weeks I received the following reply back from the Department of Education, and Skills, acknowledging receipt of my letter.

All of the correspondence came from the Department of Education, and Skills, Cornmaddy, Athlone, Co Westmeath, and addressed to myself at my address in Malta. My correspondence was with the same person in that department over the period till October 2021.

12 November 2019.

Dear Mr. Heffernan,

I refer to your recent correspondence concerning consultative meetings with survivors of residential abuse.

The Department of Education, and Skills, following a request from a number of survivors, published a request for tender in November 2018 to appoint facilitator[s] to plan, and design consultation events for survivors.

This notice was published on the Departments website, [giving the website]

Following this process independent facilitators Ms Barbara Walshe, and Ms Catherine O'Connell were appointed to undertake Phase 1 of the work. The facilitators engaged with over 100 people, and held over 30 meetings in the course of the past six months leading to the publication of the report.

Their report is now published on the Departments website.

I hope this information is of assistance to you.

Yours sincerely;

Residential Institutions Redress Unit

Depart of Education, and Skills.

I replied to that letter on the 20th of November 2019, as follows:

Depart of Education, and Skills,

20th November 2019.

Thank you for your reply in response to my communication dated the 29th of October 2019.

I have read the report that was published by Ms. Barbara Walshe, and Ms. Catherine O'Connell with regards to their consultations with survivors of Residential Institution Abuse.

Is it possible for me to have contact with somebody on the Survivors Consultative Group or whoever?

I want to be assured that my name has been included on the register of Survivors with the Residential Institutions Redress Board, since I did make an application to that Board to be heard without success. I included my reference code, and the date of my hearing in my previous correspondence. Unfortunately I wasn't allowed to go into any details about my time in institutions including St Joseph's, Tralee, as the Board was only interested in why I made a Late application.

I would like to consult with some person with regards to my situation, and give an account of my time in institutions from the time I was about nine months old in 1946 till the time I was released in August 1961 from St Joseph's Institution, Tralee.

At the moment I would like to confine my correspondence to normal posts as I do not want to use social media at present. If some person does make contact with me I will supply a telephone number etc. For contact purposes.

In anticipation,

Yours sincerely.

Maurice Heffernan.

On the 23rd of December 2019 I received a further reply as follows:

Dear Mr. Heffernan,

I refer to your correspondence of the 20th November concerning the consultations of survivors of institutional abuse.

There is no register of survivors as such, the role of the consultative group is to assess, and evaluate the ongoing needs of the survivors of residential institutions.

Currently the tender process is ongoing regarding the appointment of a facilitator for Phase II, of the consultations. To this end a number of proposals have been received, and it is intended to complete this evaluation early in the new year. Once this is in place, and the group agrees on the facilitator, arrangements will be made for the first meeting of Phase II, of the Consultation Process.

Should you wish to contribute to this phase of the process, I will be happy to forward any views you may have to the facilitator once he/she is appointed.

Yours sincerely;

Residential Institutions Redress Unit.

On the 14ᵗʰ January 2020 I forwarded a further letter to the Department as follows:

Department of Education, and Skills;

14ᵗʰ January 2020,

Thank you again for your response on the 23ʳᵈ of December 2019. If I might mention that my post was delayed slightly due to an incomplete address. The street name **"Lampuki"** was omitted from the address, but these things can happen. St Paul's Bay is quite a big place even though we are a small Island. I hope you don't mind me mentioning this.

I am glad to see some progress is being made with respect to the appointment of a facilitator, and I would be grateful to be informed of the appointment of the facilitator.

I would like to take up your offer to forward to you some proposals for consideration in the near future.

I wish to be up front with you at this stage, and state that I would be hoping for some form of financial compensation as a Survivor of Institutional Abuse.

I am going to forward you a copy of a report which I am preparing regarding my time in Residential Institutions between 1946, and 1961 which included the Orphanage in Killarney, with Foster Parents in Cahersiveen, and St Joseph's Residential Institution, Tralee.

As you will see from my report when you receive it, it will show that I was unable to put my case to anybody including the Residential Institution Redress Board who were specifically set up for this purpose.

I would hope that you will pass it on to some person currently responsible for these matters.

Yours sincerely;

Maurice Heffernan.

On the 31st of January 2020, I forwarded a copy of my report I had been working on, as I mentioned in my letter of the 14th of January 2020. I attached a covering letter as well as a number of suggestions for consideration by the facilitator/s when appointed. This report with suggestions is covered in the next chapter [41].

Following on from this I received the following reply dated the 21st February 2020 from the Department of Education, and Skills.

21st February 2020

Dear Mr. Heffernan,

Firstly, apologies regarding the omission of the street name on your address in our last correspondence.

I have received your recent correspondence regarding your suggestions for the Consultative group, your account of your time in St. Joseph's Residential Institution, Tralee, and application to the Redress Board.

In previous correspondence, I outlined the background of the consultative process, and the offer to forward any views you may have to the facilitator/s. I can assure you your suggestions will be forwarded to the facilitator/s as soon as appointments are made.

Regarding your seeking financial compensation, as you may be aware the Redress Board no longer has the power to accept late applications, the following link to the Redress Board's website outlines the relevant legislation on their homepage.....................................

I suggest that you seek independent legal advice regarding any action seeking financial compensation. I am returning your correspondence with the Redress Board as it is not appropriate for the Department to hold or have sight of these records.

Yours sincerely;

Residential Institutions Redress Unit.

Department of Education, and Skills.

On the 13th of March 2020, I forwarded my final letter to the Department, for that period of time as follows, owing to the fact that there was about to be a change of Government, and also the outbreak of the covid-19 pandemic was getting out of control, which caused many restrictions to be brought in on several fronts.

Department of Education, and Skills,

13th March 2020.

Thank you for your reply on the 21st of February 2020.

I would be hoping that my suggestions/proposals which I forwarded to you would come within the ambit of the survivor's consultative group, and the facilitators, for discussion.

I tried to concentrate my suggestions/proposals on some of the areas highlighted in the 2019 report of Barbara Walshe, and Catherine O'Connell regarding the needs of survivors which included, health [medical] needs, finance [income] [pensions], education support for [children] [grandchildren], the national archiving of the residential institutions redress board records, and setting up a proper contact system through use of Depart of Education records.

Regarding my account of my time in institutions [1946 to 1961], I do understand that it will be a matter for somebody other than your office to take up. I wish to state that I would have no objections to the document being passed to the incoming facilitator/s when appointed.

I am aware that the redress board is no longer in existence for compensation purposes. I would be hoping that the survivor-led consultative group would be able to come to some form of agreement with the Government in respect of some long term financial support for all survivors.

I thank you for your suggestion regarding seeking legal advice, regarding any action to seek financial compensation, but that would not be affordable in my situation, unless of course there is some solicitor willing to take such a case in a "no win no fee" situation. I am after all an ageing pensioner, living abroad, paying maintenance to my former wife, and trying to "survive" into my later years.

I was recently informed by my eldest son that R T E were going to screen a programme called "Redress", which was to be aired on the 2nd, and 3rd of March 2020. I tuned in, and watched it over both evenings. It had the effect of re-awakening all the old memories of those past years. The mention of a boy, Joseph Pike who was in St Joseph's, Tralee, with me was very disturbing. He died in unusual circumstances in the late 1950s. I have a photograph of the dance troupe that we both appear in.

I do understand that there may be some slight delay in appointing the promised facilitator/s due to the formation of the new Government, and of course the current outbreak of covid-19.

Thank you for your continued attention.

Yours sincerely;

Maurice Heffernan.

On the 4th of August 2021 I reopened correspondence with the Department of Education and Skills

Department of Education, and Skills;

4th August 2021,

It's been almost 18 months now since my last communication with your office. I would hope all is well with you, and yours in this time of the current health crises. All is well with us here, with our vaccinations received, and our certificates to prove it.

Sorry again to bother you, but I was just hoping for an update on the current situation with regards to the Survivor

Led Consultation Group. I know things have been difficult because of the covid-19 crisis, which was the reason I stopped communicating with your office at that time. Now, that things are easing slightly, and we are learning to live with the situation, I was wondering if there was any movement on the appointment of a facilitator/s to the Survivor Led Consultative Group.

Also I would like to bring you up to date on other communications I have started. As you are aware the new Minister for Education, Norma Foley, is a Tralee woman from Co Kerry, and my old hometown is in her constituency in the County of Kerry. I took the liberty of writing to her at her constituency office in Tralee, and I forwarded her a copy of the report that I had sent to you at the end of January 2020, for her to look at. It was as a result of looking at her profile on Google, where she invited her constituents to get in touch, so I took her up on her offer.

It is in no way a rebuke to you or your office in the handling of my correspondence, indeed I have intimated to her that I have been dealt with very courteously by your office as well as brought up to date at the time, as to the situation regarding the Survivor Led Consultation Group, and I would be communicating with your office again.

I look forward to hearing from you soon.

Yours sincerely;

Maurice Heffernan.

I received the following reply dated the 13ᵗʰ of September 2021

13th September 2021;

Dear Mr Heffernan,

Firstly, apologies for the delay in responding to your letter dated the 4th August regarding the Survivor lead consultative process. I hope all is well with you, and yours in these strange times, and hopefully these vaccinations can provide a source of comfort solace, and expedite us to some sense of normality in the not too distant future.

Just a brief update regarding the consultative process. Both facilitator's were re-appointed, and the Minister met with the forum on 3rd of December last. While it hasn't been possible for the Minister to engage directly with the forum since then, officials from the Department have continued to engage with the Facilitators on all aspects of the process.

A final report [Report on Phase II Consultations] from the Facilitators has also been received, and is currently being considered.

Yours sincerely
Residential Institutions Redress Unit.

On the 11th of October 2021 I forwarded the following reply to the Department of Education, and Skills

11th October 2021;

Department of Education, and Skills;

I received your welcome update regarding "Phase II" of the Survivor Led Consultative process. Just to say I hope you don't mind my addressing you by your first name as I feel it is now appropriate considering the amount of communication I have had with you. There is no need for an apology for any delay, as I am aware that these processes take time, especially under the current circumstances. The situation can only improve with time.

All is well here thanks, with the covid-19 being managed well, so much so that I received my booster shot in the last few weeks.

I am delighted to hear that the two previous facilitators were re-appointed, as they would be up to speed with the current situation regarding the Survivors of Residential Institutions. I am also glad to hear that they have completed their report on "Phase II of the consultations, and I look forward to reading this report when it becomes available.

If I could further impose on your good office, I am currently updating the history of my family, which I have been doing for some time. There were four of my siblings, three sisters, and a brother, who were also put into institutions in 1946, all of whom have now passed away. This was something that we never spoke about as a family while they were alive.

Would it be possible for me to obtain information from the Department of Education, and Skills Data Base, as to what institutions they were committed to? My reason for asking is that I have a copy of information from that Data

Base regarding myself, showing my committal to St Joseph's Residential Institution, Tralee, which I obtained through the Redress Board in 2012.

If that's possible I will forward whatever information I have in my possession, to enable a search to be carried out.

Again thank you for your kind attention.

Yours sincerely;

Maurice Heffernan.

Chapter 41

Department of Education, and Skills,

Following on from my correspondence to you dated the 14th of January 2020; please find enclosed.

1. Copy of my report regarding my time in institutions, foster home, which outline the conditions under which I was detained, and abuses which occurred.
2. A number of proposals for the information of the survivor led consultation group for discussion, and consideration.

It has taken me some time to pick up the courage to formulate this report, but as time passes I am getting less, and less fearful about releasing the facts surrounding my earlier years when I was "detained" in St Joseph's Residential Institution, Tralee.

While I am aware that you may not be dealing with this matter yourself, I would be grateful if you would forward my report to the person or persons currently responsible for this matter.

I apologize for being a burden on you, but you are my only contact at the moment in this matter.

From my reading of the report of the facilitators, Ms. Barbara Walshe, and Ms. Catherine O'Connell, I put forward some proposals for consideration.

Thanking you again for your attention;

Yours sincerely;

Maurice Heffernan.   31st January 2020.

Residential Institutions Redress Unit,   13 Shalom, Flat 3,

Department of Education, and Skills,   Lampuki Street,

Cornamaddy, Athlone,   St Paul's Bay, SPB 3060,

Co Westmeath.   Malta.

Report on my time in Residential Institutions, and with Foster Parents from 1946 to 1961

Date, and place of birth

I was born in Ballylongford, Co Kerry on the 10th of September 1945. I am as I discovered late in life the youngest of a family of ten children, five boys, and five girls. I was born at home with the help of a local midwife, and my information is that my mother remained at home, and was not taken to the local hospital after my birth.

On the 10th of March 1946 my mother died, I was just six months old. From what I have gleaned from my family over the years, I was looked after by my older sisters for a while, the eldest being 12 years old, and going on 13 years at the time.

Killarney Institution as an infant

I understand that I only stayed with my family for a few months after my mother died, and then I was taken away. From information obtained I was brought to an orphanage in Killarney where I remained for some time. As I was so young I have very few recollections of my time at Killarney. I don't ever remember leaving Killarney. Later while trying to do a background on my childhood years I learned that the Killarney Institution was destroyed by fire, and a great many record documents were lost.

Information I have since obtained [2011/2012] from copies of documents in my possession from St Joseph's Residential Institution, Tralee, I learned that I had been fostered out to a family called Coffey's. This information first came to my attention from correspondence with the Redress Board. John Coffey was my foster father, and resided at Ballydarrig, Cahersiveen, Co Kerry with his wife. There were no other children in the house. Looking back I have to say they seemed to be nice people, noting of course that I would have had no experience of any other family life. At that time I would have no knowledge that I had any family, that's something I learned over many years later.

With the Coffey's, Foster Parents, in Cahersiveen

My memories with the Coffey's are of being on a farm, going to school, church, and helping around the farm as much as a child of my age could do. I have a lot of memories of my life there which I don't need to go into at this stage. I don't ever remember arriving at the farm, I was obviously very young, but I have memories of the day I was **taken away**. A big black car arrived at the farm house, and I had been dressed up by Mrs. Coffey, and didn't really take in what was happening. I was put into the car, and I remember Mrs Coffey putting a half crown in my hand before we left. I don't remember having any feelings as we left, I just accepted what was happening. I'm not sure if the driver was on his own or if there was somebody in the car with us.

From documents now in my possession I believe that this was a Mr. M O' Regan, from the NSPCC, as he is the person shown to have brought me to the courts on the 12th December 1952,from where I was committed to St Joseph's Residential Institution, Tralee, on the same date. I will expand further regarding the NSPCC inspectors later in this report.

I know now from my discoveries that we went to Tralee, and we made a stop at the court building. I'll always remember seeing the two big cannons outside the Court building, one on either side. I was 7 years, and three months old at that time. I'm now in possession of documentation outlining what occurred that day in the court house. I was according to one document before a District Justice Johnson, in Tralee District Court, the date being the 12th day of December 1952. The charge was, "having a guardian who does not exercise proper guardianship". My "sentence of detention was 9-9-'61."

After the court appearance I was brought to St Joseph's Residential Institution, Tralee, where I was detained, until the 5th of August 1961, one month before my sixteenth birthday, and a month before my discharge date.

I never heard of or saw my Foster Parents, the Coffey's again. Sometime in around 2012 after discovering the Coffey's address in Cahersiveen, I called to the area, where I met with some relatives of the Coffey's, but discovered the Coffey's had passed away some years previously, I tried to locate where they were buried, but without success.

St Joseph's Residential Institution, Tralee

As already stated above I arrived at St Joseph's Institution, Tralee, on the 12th of December 1952 by commitment order from the District Court Tralee.

I have very little memories of my arrival at the institution. Sometime after I had arrived I met my **"brother"** Jerry. That was the first time I ever known that I had a family. I'm not sure what way I received the news that I had a brother. Although we were both in the institution together we didn't communicate that much. I think that having a brother didn't mean that much to me at the time; I had no understanding of "family".

It wasn't till years later that I learned that I had **four brothers, and five sisters.** My brother Jerry was five or six years older than me so he left the institution years before me. I still had four or five years to "do" before my "release". Apart from meeting my "brother" Jerry at the institution I never met anybody else from my family till later in my life after years of tracing.

When I did locate members of my family around the 1970s they were all in England, but there were still two of my brothers who I never met, still not accounted for, and no other family members knew anything about their whereabouts. Almost thirty years later in the 2000s after a lot of inquiries, and tracing, I discovered that those two older brothers who I never met were dead. I did meet with their families on one occasion, but have had very little contact after that. One had resided in Nottingham, and the other in Derby in England. I later in 2004 did attend my brother's wife's funeral in Derby.

Education

I'm not sure as to what class I started at the school, at the institution, but a note on a document in my possession states I had been in senior infants before arriving there. I attended primary school till I was 12 yrs. or 13 years of age then I went into the technical school which was attached to St Joseph's institution. I did mechanical Drawing, Woodwork, and Irish for which I received a Certificate. [It was a certificate in Manual Training dated 1960.] I still have that Certificate.

Before I went into the technical school I remember being asked by the Superior of the institution if I wanted to go to the secondary school in Tralee town, and of course I said yes. But later he came back to me, and told me that they weren't allowing any more boys to go to the town school because of the misbehavior of some of the boys who had gone previously. In later years I discovered that there were other reasons for this change of mind. I will expand later in this report.

After I finished with technical school I was put into the tailor's shop which was in the same building as the technical school. My Certificate from the technical school is dated 1960 which would indicate that I would have spent just over one year in the tailor's shop before being sent out of St Joseph's institution.

On the 5th of August 1961 I was released on Licence to a Mr. Grief, managing director of "Weartex" clothing factory, which was situated at Kimmage, Dublin 6. I was not yet sixteen years of age. From documentation in my possession, I was discharged from my "detention" on the 9th of September 1961. I was never informed of this discharge, but only discovered this when I obtained documentation in around 2011/2012. In December 1961 according to the documents in my possession there was a follow up report "of conduct after discharge" completed on me.

It read "very satisfactory- attending technical school Parnell Square, three nights per week" this must have been a reference to my attending tailoring classes in the evening after work at the time.

When I left St Joseph's Residential Institution, Tralee on the 5th of August 1961 I never had any contact with anybody from that institution again. Life after that was a whole new world of struggle, and survival for me.

From my calculations I would have spent about eight, and a half years of my life at St Joseph's Residential Institution, Tralee. I didn't know what the norm was in the institution; I accepted the way things were. Looking back now compared to the way children are treated today the regime was very tough. Being beaten, slapped, and generally bullied was the normal routine in the institution. Arriving so young, I would not have known any better, and accepted what happened. Of course who was I, a seven year old child with nobody to turn to?

I must point out some of the positive happenings in the institution. I was trained as an altar boy, I was in the Irish dancing school, I took part in sport and as I got older I became a monitor in the refectory during mealtimes.

Conditions, and Abuses

Conditions at the institution when I arrived first were very bad, especially regarding the food. Sometimes we couldn't eat the food. We were always hungry, and to satisfy our hunger we used to get [steal] turnips from the farm attached to the institution, and in the evenings under darkness we used to break up the turnips against the walls of the ball alley. [There is a reference to this situation in the 2009 CICA report 9.327, and 9.349.] This would have occurred during my earlier years at the Institution.

I'm not sure of the year, but the food did improve after the arrival of a new brother [Brother Laurence] who took charge of the kitchen, and refectory, and ordered the bakery to bake more bread. We had our own bakery in the institution. This brother was very tough, and nobody was spared when he lost his temper. He would fly off the handle, and beat boys around the head with his fists or use his leather strap on the boy's hands. I wasn't spared from his tantrums. No other brothers would come into the kitchen or refectory while he was there, of course the brothers had their own dining room, and kitchen. There was some controversy with this brother because of the death of a boy during my time there. [9.187 to 9.208 of CICA report 2009 refers].

It is only in the year 2020, that I have informed my own children about my early years of my life giving them an edited version, and not including the abuses as outlined below. I kept this from my own family all of those years because of the shame, and stigma associated with being in a residential institution, like St Joseph's Tralee. I suppose you could say I lived a **lie,** for most of my life. The following incidents that I'm describing, I have not shared with my family because of the humiliation in disclosing them. My children are very supportive with respect to the conditions I went through in my earlier years, even going so far as to suggest that I should write my memoirs of my life. I am thinking seriously about following their advice, and may just do that.

I was in my younger years taken advantage of on a number of occasions. This is something I have never disclosed before other than partially to my Solicitors when making the application to the Residential Institutional Redress Board.

I can't give an exact date or time, but it would be in my earlier years while I was still very young, and innocent, and not too long after I had arrived at St Joseph's institution.

As you would be aware from the Ryan report, the school would have been a mixture of older, and younger boys. There was an older boy who was on two crutches as his legs were bad. I was brought upstairs to the toilets attached to the dorms by him. It was on the pretense that he had to take my measurements for new underpants. I was brought into a cubicle, and he sat down on the toilet seat, and took my pants down. He had a tape measure with him. He began to feel my private parts, and he put soap on me, and kept rubbing me. He used the tape measure on me a few times to measure my privates. After a while he stopped, and we left, and went back down to the yard. He did this to me on a number of occasions, and on the last time somebody saw him with me at the toilets, and he never went near me again.

Another incident that occurred was in a classroom in the institution one day. Again I'm not sure of the year, but I was in one of the lower classes, and still wearing short pants. A priest whose name I don't know came to our class to examine us on our religious instruction. Our teacher, who was a brother, left the classroom while the priest was there. The priest asked us questions at the beginning, and then he asked a number of boys including myself to come up to the table he was at to read from the religion book. We had to stand facing the class, and read from the book while standing beside him. I went up when my turn came, and started to read, and then the priest put his arm around me, and pulled me closer to him, and then he put his hand up the leg of my short pants, and started feeling my privates. He continued to do this until I was finished reading, then I went back to my seat. I wasn't the only boy he did this to that day. I would like to point out that this priest was not the priest who was attached to the institution, he was a visiting priest.

These were incidents that have stuck in my memory all these years, and before this I could not relate to anybody what happened to me. I had big reservations about going to the Redress Board at all in 2011, and when I did they refused to hear my case because of my late application. [I will relate to this visit before the Redress Board later in my report] Even now as I write this report I do it with a certain amount of trepidation because of the stigma which is forever imprinted in my mind.

There was a brother at the school [Brother Raphael] who was a peculiar type of man. He seemed elderly, and I think he did some service in China. Looking back now I think he may have been semi-retired. He was responsible for a number of things at the school. They included training, and looking after the altar boys, which I was involved in, looking after the Irish dancing school which I was also attached to, and he was in charge of the Saturday evening showers for the boys. The shower room consisted of about a dozen or more showers along a line, with no cubicles, just open showers where we went in groups to shower totally naked. Sometimes Brother Raphael would strip off, and get into the showers, naked as well. He would ask one of us to scrub his back with a scrub brush. This would have happened very often.

On other occasions during the week evenings he would bring a boy up from the yard to a bathroom in the brother's quarters, and give the boy a full bath. This happened to me on quite a number of occasions. I would strip off, and get into the bath, and he would wash me, and then he would dry me off with a towel, and I would get dressed again, and go back to the yard. I would add that other than the unusual situation of the giving of the bath nothing untoward happened to me.

Today he would be described as having a "fetish" for bathing young boys. It was widely known what he was doing by the community of brothers, but nobody interfered. [CICA report2009 9.262 to 9.291 refers]. Strangely enough I have a memento from Brother Raphael, a small religious picture he gave to me at some stage wishing me "many happy birthdays" which he signed. Mind you I didn't know there was such a thing as birthdays at that time of my life.

I remember on one occasion being called one morning in the dorm by Brother Collins, [pseudonym] with the rest of the boys, there would have been between 40, and 60 boys in the dorm. I was in the junior dorm at the time. I can't remember what actually the reason behind this incident was, but I was chased by Brother Collins, through the dorm, and I ran up a few steps towards the small infirmary , and as I did I hit my head on the corner of a piece of furniture which caught me over my left eye, and I started to bleed. Whatever the reason for the chase was forgotten, and I was looked after, and had my injury seen to. This was the type of happening that occurred often when a brother would "fly off the handle" for some reason. A few days later I met with Brother Collins in the brother's quarters, and he stopped, and asked how I was, and said he was sorry about what happened. I would have to say that Brother Collins was one of the nicer brothers in the school, and was also a very good teacher.

As outlined in the Ryan Report of 2009 there was a climate of fear, and bullying at St Joseph's institution by bigger boys on younger boys. This is something I have to agree with. It was common during my stay there, when I was in my earlier years. I had arrived there as I stated before, when I was just an innocent seven year old boy, and you had boys there who were more than double my age. Some of these boys, as I became aware of later, were sent to this institution for criminal activity. I as well as other younger boys were victims of this bullying, and sexual harassment especially at the toilets attached to the playing yard. They, the bigger boys would follow you into the toilets, and would try to interfere with you while you were at the urinals. I stopped using the urinals, and started using the cubicles instead. Maybe it is the psychological impact of what occurred all those years ago, but today I will not use urinals in toilets anywhere if I can avoid it, I will always look to use a cubicle.

I have highlighted a few, but not all of the incidents relating to myself as they happened during my time at St Joseph's Residential Institution, Tralee between 1952, and 1961. Unfortunately I have not been able to relate these incidents to anybody even the Redress Board who as I describe below did not give me an opportunity to talk about these incidents.

Residential Institutions Redress Board

I was aware from media reports in the earlier years of the 2000s, that there were many cases of very serious abuses in residential institutions in Ireland. These claims of serious abuses were very much in the media at the time, but none of the cases related to St Joseph's institution, Tralee to my knowledge.

It was not until 2009, when I became aware of the Ryan report on Institutional abuse, that I bought a copy of the report which is on disc, and discovered that St Joseph's institution, Tralee had been included in the Commission to Inquire into Child Abuse Report.

I became aware that there had been a Residential Institutions Redress Board set up in respect of former residents of Institutions in Ireland. When I went to enquire I discovered that the closing date for applications to this Board had been in December 2005. This was four years before the Ryan report was released.

In July/August 2011 I was at home recovering from a fairly serious Illness when I read an advertisement in the Irish Times that the Residential Institutions Redress Board had extended the time for applications to the Board until the 16th of September 2011.

On the 16th of August 2011 I forwarded an application to the Residential Institutions Redress Board through my solicitors, which was received by the board on the 18th August 2011. After much correspondence between myself, and the Board through my solicitors I got a hearing date before the board on the 21st of November 2011. My Residential Institutions Redress Board Reference No for the Board is 2713L. I was of the opinion that this was a Redress hearing.

At no time during the hearing before the Redress Board was my abuse or detention at St Joseph's Residential Institution, Tralee discussed. The whole hearing was based around the reasons as to why I had put in my application late. I was mystified, and totally unprepared for this type of hearing as I had made preparation to have my time in St Joseph's Residential Institution discussed. My understanding was that the date for late applications had been extended to the 16th September 2011, and I had applied before the extended date had expired.

On the 2nd of February 2012 the Board gave their Determination. They came to the decision that my application was **not validly** received within the statutory period, and will not be further considered.

I sent a note of my observations of their findings through my solicitors who forwarded the same to the Board. In my submission I brought it to the notice of the Board that as a former resident of an Institution I was not contacted by the Redress Board as they were required to do under section 5 [1] [b] of the Residential Institutions Redress Act, 2002 which states the following.

"make all reasonable efforts, through public advertisement, direct correspondence with persons who were residents of an institution, and otherwise, to ensure that persons who were residents of an institution are made aware of the functions, referred to in paragraph [a], of the Board."

The Boards solicitor stated I could not be contacted because the only addresses available to the board were My Fathers address in Ballylongford, and my job address, Weartex in Dublin, where I was sent on the 5th of August 1961.

When I started work with Weartex I received what is now known as my PPS Number. One phone call to the Welfare Department would have provided a contact address. It would be reasonable to expect that this could have been done without much effort.

The reply I received to my observations from the Boards solicitor, didn't impress me one bit. The tone of the letter would seem to indicate they were dealing with a convicted felon. At the end of the reply a confidentiality clause was quoted to me, after which was stated that anybody contravening these sub-sections of the Redress Act 2002 would be guilty of an offence, which could end in a prison sentence. I refrain from comment in respect of this reply just to say it shows how far removed from the reality of the situation this person seemed. My belief is that I did not receive a hearing by the Redress Board as provided for under the Redress Act 2002.

I did not receive any expenses in respect of the retention of my solicitor.

I have a number of documents covering this situation, which I can make available.

Secondary Education

Earlier in this report I referred to being offered a secondary education opportunity which was withdrawn again for "fictional" reasons as it transpired. From my reading of the 2009 CICA report into St Joseph's Residential Institution, there were considerable concerns regarding the future of St Joseph's Residential institution, Tralee, because of the falling numbers during my time there. [9.11of CICA report]

I have no doubt this situation had a huge impact on decisions as to whether or not to send boys to Tralee, for second level education. Of course I do feel let down by the system of the time, and it has had a profound effect on my further education. Trying to make up for lost time in education was very difficult.

Loss of Family

One of my biggest problems later on in my life was trying to locate my "lost" family as I mentioned earlier. I spent many years at my own expense trying to locate the rest of my brothers, and sisters. Jerry, my youngest brother who was about 5 years older than I, was the only "family" I knew about before leaving the residential institution. The fact that Jerry was my "brother" didn't mean much to me. I also discovered later on in my life that as well as my brother Jerry, and myself being taken to institutions, three of my sisters were also put into an Institution. Over the years after "finding" my family members we never spoke about the fact that we were in institutions. It was a taboo subject. My brother Jerry, and my three sisters I mentioned are all now deceased having passed away over the past number of years, 1986, 1998, 2016, and the last one of those sisters only passing in 2019.

At some stage just before I left the institution, I met my father for the first time in my life. As I understand it, Tralee is no more than about 20 miles from Ballylongford, where I was born, and where my father lived. In all those years at St Joseph's, Tralee [over eight years], there was never any attempt to let me meet up with my father. He passed away in 1967. When my father died I could not afford to go down to the funeral from Dublin, and a person who I became friendly with drove me down in his own car to attend the funeral, and drove me back to Dublin. I will be forever grateful to that person for that kind assistance.

Summary note from the CICA report found that, "separating siblings, and restriction of family contact were profoundly damaging for family relationships – some children lost their sense of identity, and kinship which never was, and could never be recovered."

NSPCC involvement

Some further comments on the NSPCC Inspectors. From my reading of the Ryan report, the section dealing with the NSPCC, it would seem that I would have figured large on their books through a Mr. M O'Regan who would have been an Inspector with that society, and I would go further, and suggest that there are questions to be raised with respect to how I came to be committed to St Joseph's Tralee.

Around the time of my committal to St Joseph's Residential Institution, Tralee, the Ryan report states there were allegations that NSPCC Inspectors were taking bribes as an inducement to send children to residential institutions. This came about as a result of a visitation report in respect of St Joseph's Residential Institution, Tralee around the time of my commitment. The brother superior [resident manager] at the time passed it off as a subscription to the society.

Considering that the NSPCC were making the case at the time that "good" foster homes were a healthier, and happier introduction to life, why then was **I taken** from my foster home in Cahersiveen, and committed to St Joseph's Residential Institution, Tralee? Was I being used for keeping up the numbers at St Joseph's Institution, Tralee? Was there a bribe paid for me?

I note that the fact that I was in Cahersiveen for a number of years, does not appear on the skills database printout which the Redress Board obtained from the Department of Education.

My children

I have six children born between 1972, and 1990, and over their years of attending school, and going to third level colleges it was very difficult financially. Thankfully they have all succeeded in getting true the educational system. I make a point of keeping in constant contact, which can be difficult at times as I have one child in Australia, two in England, three in Ireland, and I'm operating from my residence Malta. I suppose it's something within me, remembering my own young years with no contacts with family members, as I wasn't even aware that I had any family. I also have twelve grandchildren, born between 1995, and 2019.

One of my biggest fears during their young lives was that any one of them, for whatever reason, might end up in an institution like I was in.

If, and when required I will try to supply whatever information I can with respect to Education of my children, tracing of my family members over the years which I'm still working on, and my career, and employment up to my eventual retirement in 2013.

My current situation

I relocated to Malta in September 2013 where I was married to Sonia, my present wife. She had been working in Ireland for nine years before I decided I had to leave Ireland. I was also working for a company on contract at that time.

I had made the decision to leave Ireland in early 2012 after receiving the Residential Redress Board communication of rejection with regards to my attendance before that Board on the 21st November 2011. I felt very much ashamed, and let down by the way I was treated by the Board, and the fact that they had excluded me from the hearing of my complaint.

I had to await the outcome of my divorce hearing in the courts in July 2012 before I could make arrangements to depart Ireland.

The outcome of my divorce left me in a very poor financial situation. I lost my house which I was paying for. I had substantial outstanding loans which had accumulated as a result of re-mortgaging my house, to further the education of my children over the years, which I continued to pay, two years after my divorce. I finished paying for these loans in October 2014.

I am also paying maintenance each month into my former spouse's bank account, which is by order of the court.

To sum up

I think I have covered as best I can, my situation regarding my being in the Orphanage in Killarney, being fostered out to family in Cahersiveen, and my eventual "Detention" in St Joseph's Residential Institution, Tralee between December 1952, and August 1961.

I would be hoping for some form of compensation for my years of abuse, and neglect at St Joseph's Residential Institution, and the reason for my detention there at all, considering I was taken from a safe place in a foster home, and committed to St Joseph's Institution, Tralee. Also I totally lost my family, and had no contact with my father who only lived some twenty miles from St Joseph's, until just before I was sent out of the institution, to Dublin.

Considering the "route" I had taken in my life, I feel I came out reasonably successful. I know that a great many of the boys who went through the same system were not so lucky.

I would hope that because I had a certain amount of success in my chosen career I would not be excluded from whatever compensation is eventually agreed to. We are after all dealing with my years in Residential Institutions between 1946, and 1961. It has haunted me over all those years of keeping these happenings to myself, and I no longer want to live this **"lie"**.

Yours Sincerely

Maurice Heffernan.

A number of suggestions for consideration by the consultative group of survivors of Institutional abuse.

[1] Special Survivors Pension

There should be a special Pension system introduced for all of us survivors of Residential Institutions, it should be in addition to any other pension or entitlement we are currently in receipt of, it should be tax free, and should not be means tested.

It would be a much fairer system rather than survivors going "cap in hand" each time they require something.

It should include all survivors whether or not we were dealt with by the Residential Institutions Redress Board or Caranua.

Considering the age profile of the remaining survivors, it would not be an excessive draw on the exchequer, and would be on a reducing outlay each year as the numbers of survivors decrease over time.

There is a precedent for the introduction of a Special Pension. In 1924 the then Irish Free State Government passed legislation to award pensions to veterans of the Irish Revolution, and Civil War, and it included all service personnel not just those with disabilities as a result of the conflict.

[2] Survivors Register & Identification card system

I agree with the appointment of a Survivor Led Consultative Group as members of such a group would have a better understanding of what was experienced by all survivors of Residential Institutions.

Indeed this is borne out by the facilitators, Ms Barbara Walshe, and Ms Catherine O'Connell in their report of July 2019, dealing with the understanding of survivor experiences.

A necessary part of their work should be the setting up of a register of survivors of residential institutions, which can then be used to communicate the progress of the survivor's consultative group, and get feedback.

Also a special survivor's Identification card system should be introduced to enable all of us to be able to access the services, and entitlements agreed between the consultative group, and the Government.

Contact with survivors seemed to have been very haphazard as most of us discovered, and have experienced with the likes of the Residential Institutions Redress Board.

[3] Education support

I would suggest that all children of survivors, whether they were successful in life careers or not should be allowed a tax break or some form of grant for the education of their children, **[our grandchildren]** as many of the children of the survivors would be out of the education system by now, and would not benefit from such a scheme themselves.

This would in some way compensate for the difficult financial situation that we, their surviving parents, found ourselves in during our earlier years as a result of being residents of residential institutions.

To expand on my own situation, out of a family of ten siblings, five of us were in residential institutions, one brother, and three sisters.

Of the five of us four have passed away, and I'm the last family member "standing" as a survivor of residential institutions.

My four siblings had families,[nine children between them], and experienced hardship throughout their lives. I would think they would be worthy of inclusion in whatever proposals are agreed by the residential survivors group.

I'm sure there are other survivors with similar family situations.

Taking my previous suggestion, [1. above] as outlined, the education support could be taken into consideration when setting a figure on a special pension system thus avoiding duplication of payments systems.

[4] Remembering Survivors with Honour

I would not be totally against some form of memorial building to be used to archive all the historical records of Residential Institutions, but would make the following proposals.

It should be placed somewhere close to Government Buildings to remind future political inhabitants of that establishment, of the involvement of the government of the time, that they were in some way responsible, for the way survivors were treated in residential institutions.

I would be totally against the planned legislation to have the records of the Residential Institutions Redress Board put into the National Archives, and sealed for 75 years. They should be placed in the proposed memorial building Archives for all generations to see, to show the workings of the Residential Institutions Redress Board in its treatment of some of the survivors.

[5] Health Cover

Not being resident in Ireland any longer, I would not benefit from the suggested enhanced Irish medical card or other benefits. Yes for those living in Ireland it would be beneficial if indeed that was put in place.

In the light of that I would like to put forward, that some form of additional allowance or support be put in place for survivors who for one reason or another no longer reside in Ireland.

In my own case I am contributing a sum annually towards my medical insurance for my medical expenses, which of course become more important for me with every passing year, given my age profile. There may be many other survivors in the same situation, and in some way some form of assistance should be given.

Again this could be taken into consideration if a special pension system was agreed to by the survivor-led consultative group in discussion with the Government of the day.

Conclusion

Well this could become a never ending life story, if I don't draw a line somewhere. What better time now than today, the 21st of November 2021, just ten years after the date of my "Hearing", before the Residential Institutions Redress Board. Also it's coming close to Christmas 2021.

Aside from my memoirs, I intend to continue with my communications with the Department of Education, and Skills with regards to the Survivor Led Consultative Process, as to where it is going from here, and what it may lead to, as well as following information on some other family matters.

As has been communicated to me in the latest correspondence from the Department of Education, and Skills on the 13th of September 2021, the Phase II report has been completed, and has been submitted to the Department. It is currently being considered by the powers that be, as to where to go next, maybe another Phase of consultations?. Reports would suggest that the Residential Institutions Survivor members of the Consultative Group are not too happy with the slow progress of their final report to the Government, considering that the Survivor Group have put so much faith in this current process.

With regards to my last communication with the Department of Education, and Skills in October 2021, in connection with the obtaining of information about my brother, and three sisters, who like myself were put into institutions, because of the untimely death of our mother in March 1946, I received communication from the freedom of information section of the Department, as to how to go about making an application, to obtain that information.

I have acknowledged this communication, and I have started the ball rolling by making contact with the families of my brother, and three sisters to obtain documentation required for attaching to the applications.

I feel with regards to my memoirs, I have told my story as best I could, given all the circumstances that prevailed. I have tried to put into writing, my journey through, what I believe to have been an extraordinary, but interesting life. There are many reasons why somebody like me wishes to tell his life story, and as I finish, I reflect on what some of those reasons would be.

Reflections

There is the support of my own family members, to put my full life story down in writing after I had given all of them, a short edited version of the early years of my life as a child, which they would not have been aware of until my revelations to them.

What I thought was the most unusual start to my life, with me now asking, for what reason did I end up being incarcerated by the courts, in St Joseph's Residential Institution, Tralee, just twenty miles from my home, never to see my father until I was almost sixteen years of age.

To show the failure of the Government of the day, during that time, to ensure proper supervision of all institutions, which was their responsibility, as these institutions came under their Department of Education.

The thoughts also of the reaction of some of the residents of the town of Tralee, to the information that came into the public domain, through the publication of the Ryan Report in 2009. In that report there is a reference, that during the 1940s, and 1950s , some of the ancestors of the current population, where able to live cheaply from the cheap produces they obtained from the farm at St Joseph's Residential Institution, Tralee, while we the boy's in that institution were starving because of the lack of food.

How my life evolved from being a desolate, and bereft child, to becoming a member of An Garda Siochana, rising to the rank of Detective Sergeant, and being qualified for the rank of Inspector. In this regard I have expanded on some of the various types of individuals that I crossed paths with during the course of my almost 33 years of service, within the force, which was likened to an institution in itself. It has been a marvelous journey, and experience, to have served in An Garda Siochana, with the comradeship, and friendships that I developed with many members of the force over my years of service.

My mistreatment at the hands of the Residential Institutions Redress Board, at my "Hearing" on the 21st November 2011. This Redress Board was set up to assist survivors of residential institutions, not as a source of rebuke, and embarrassment to survivors, which resulted in my decision to leave Ireland in disgust, and live abroad.

I am also mindful that there are many survivors of residential institutions who were not as lucky as I was, to have come through the system, and have at least some success in life. Those survivors are still waiting for some recognition by the state.

My concern is also the thought of how many more survivors will have passed away, before any decisive action is taken by the Government, the longer they drag their feet the smaller our numbers get. I hope we will never again see a repeat of the abuse, and lack of care for the vulnerable children of Ireland.

This exercise has brought me out of my fear of revealing the truths, the fear of exposure, gave me the courage to face the remainder of my life without having to live a "lie". As a result I have been able to open up communications with various bodies, without holding back on my past. Of course it is something that will never vanish from my mind till the day I die.

I also reflect on my discoveries during the course of my inquiries into my "lost family" history that as well as myself, there were four other members of my family, Ann, Lily, Jerry, and Kathy, taken in 1946, and put into institutions, all four of whom, are now deceased. It was something we never spoke about when we did eventually meet up in later life.

The loss of my identity, becoming an unknown in my own hometown, where I was born. An outsider looking in at what should have been my own community. My sister Joan who was ten years older than myself, during many of my visits to her, talked about how she loved her time in "Bally" [Ballylongford], and all the families, and people she knew. This created a huge void in my life, not having family or community contacts.

I look back at some of the extreme hardships, and circumstances, in getting my three boys, and my three girls educated. I succeeded in managing to get them all through third level education, with great determination from the children themselves, with very little help from the state.

My hope is that in some way, I have revealed some of the truths surrounding the residential institution that I had been detained in for a period of more than eight years of my young life. That I have enlightened you to some of the hardships, traumas, fears, and mistreatment resulting from being incarcerated in St Joseph's Residential Institution, Tralee. I would hope that I have shown that given all the circumstances, one can do more than just survive, by going forward, and having a reasonably successful career in society, as I was blessed to have had.

In my earlier years I met with many people along my way, who were more than understanding as to my situation, and put me on the right track through my earlier life. I also came across people in later life, who lacked any understanding of the situation regarding Institutionalization, here of course, the Residential Institutions Redress Board, stands out on their own in this group of misguided people.

I hope this has been an informative read for you.

Please Review

Dear reader,
Thank you for taking the time to read this book. I would really appreciate if you could spread the word about it and if you purchased it online, if you would leave a review.

Thank You,

Maurice

Printed in Great Britain
by Amazon

40290110R00268